THE

CLASSIC 1000
RECIPES

Everyday Eating made more exciting
 foulsham

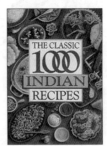

			QUANTITY	AMOUNT
Classic 1000 Recipes	0-572-01671-9	£4.99		
Classic 1000 Chinese	0-572-01783-9	£4.99		
Classic 1000 Indian	0-572-01863-0	£4.99		
Classic 1000 Italian	0-572-01940-8	£4.99		
Classic 1000 Cocktails	0-572-02161-5	£4.99		
Classic 1000 Pasta & Rice	0-572-02300-6	£4.99		

*Please allow 75p per book for post & packing in UK
Overseas customers £1 per book.*

* POST & PACKING

TOTAL

Foulsham books are available from local bookshops. Should you have any difficulty obtaining supplies please send Cheque/Eurocheque/Postal Order (£ sterling only) made out to BSBP or debit my credit card:

[ ] ACCESS [ ] VISA [ ] MASTER CARD

[ ][ ][ ][ ][ ][ ][ ][ ][ ][ ][ ][ ][ ][ ][ ][ ][ ][ ][ ]

EXPIRY DATE   SIGNATURE

ALL ORDERS TO:
Foulsham Books, PO Box 29, Douglas, Isle of Man IM99 1BQ
Telephone 01624 675137, Fax 01624 670923, Internet http://www.bookpost.co.uk.

NAME

ADDRESS

Please allow 28 days for delivery.
Please tick box if you do not wish to receive any additional information [ ]
Prices and availability subject to change without notice.

THE
CLASSIC 1000
RECIPES

COMPILED BY
WENDY HOBSON

foulsham
LONDON · NEW YORK · TORONTO · SYDNEY

foulsham

The Publishing House, Bennetts Close,
Cippenham, Berkshire, SL1 5AP, England

ISBN 0-572-01671-9

Typeset by Typesetting Solutions, Slough, Berks.
Printed in Great Britain by St Edmundsbury Press Ltd.,
Bury St Edmunds, Suffolk

Contents

Introduction

However many cookery books you have on your shelf, everyone has one favourite — the one which contains all their everyday recipes as well as special occasion dishes. With 1,000 super recipes in this book, it is guaranteed to become a favourite. It contains everything from simple soups to exotic main courses, from family puddings and snacks to desserts for the best dinner parties. Simply arranged so that you can find everything you need quickly and easily, and convenient for browsing when you are looking for something new. Dip into this tremendous range of recipes and you'll be sure to find everything you need!

Notes on the Recipes

1. Do not mix metric and Imperial measures. Follow one set only.
2. Spoon measurements are level.
3. Eggs are size 3. If you use a different size, adjust the amount of liquid added to obtain the right consistency.
4. Always wash fresh foods before preparing them.
5. Peel or scrub ingredients as appropriate to the recipe. For example, onions are always peeled, so it is not listed in the recipe. Carrots can be washed, scrubbed or peeled depending on whether they are young or old.
6. Seasoning and the use of strongly-flavoured ingredients, such as onions and garlic, are very much a matter of personal taste. Taste the food as you cook and adjust seasoning to suit your own taste.
7. Use freshly ground black pepper, if possible. Many people no longer use salt in cooking; they may wish to add additional herbs to some dishes instead.
8. You can use fresh or dried herbs in most recipes. Herbs which are commonly available in the garden or local shops, such as parsley, chives and mint are best used fresh and are listed as 'chopped parsley' and so on. Other herbs, such as oregano, are assumed to be dried. Fresh herbs are, however, becoming more widely available and if you prefer to use them chop them finely and use twice the quantity specified for dried herbs. Always use fresh herbs for garnishing or sprinkling on cooked dishes.
9. Use your own discretion in substituting ingredients and personalising the recipes. Make notes of particular successes as you go along.
10. Use whichever type of butter or margarine you prefer. Some margarines state on the packet that they are most suitable for particular uses.
11. Use whichever kitchen gadgets you like to speed up the preparation and cooking times: mixers for whisking, food processors for grating, slicing, mixing or kneading, blenders for liquidising.
12. Everyone has their favourite saucepans and dishes for particular types of recipes. You can use whatever is most suitable for that particular meal.
13. All ovens vary, so cooking times have to be approximate. Especially if you have a fan oven, adjust cooking times to suit your own appliance.

8

Hors D'Oeuvres

Hors d'oeuvres can vary from a simply prepared prawn salad to a lavish and expensive dish. What they have in common is that they whet the appetite for the main course and the flavours complement the food to follow. It is therefore a good idea when planning a meal to choose the main course first, then go back and find a suitable starter to introduce the style and tastes to come.

Sweet Rollmops

Serves 4

8 Rollmop herrings, drained and sliced

1 Onion, sliced

2 Apples, cored and sliced

15 ml/1 tbsp Lemon juice

150 ml/¼ pt Soured cream

2 Gherkins, finely chopped

Pinch of cayenne pepper

Salt and pepper

Arrange the herrings on a serving plate and place the onions on top. Toss the apples in the lemon juice, then arrange them over and around the onions. Mix the soured cream with the gherkins and cayenne pepper and season to taste with salt and pepper. Spoon over the herrings and chill before serving.

Toasted Herring Roes

Serves 4

25 g/1 oz Butter or margarine

225 g/8 oz Herring roes

Pepper

Few drops of anchovy essence

4 Slices of buttered toast

Melt the butter or margarine, add the roes, season to taste with pepper and anchovy essence and fry gently for 6 to 8 minutes. Prepare the buttered toast, divide the roes between the slices, sprinkle with pepper and serve immediately.

Prawn Fritters

Serves 4

225 g/8 oz Plain flour

Salt

100 g/4 oz Butter or margarine

2 Egg yolks

45 ml/3 tbsp Single cream

225 g/8 oz Prawns

30 ml/2 tbsp Lemon juice

Oil for deep frying

1 Lemon, cut into wedges

Mix the flour and salt and rub in the butter or margarine until the mixture resembles fine breadcrumbs. Stir in the egg yolks and cream and work to a smooth pastry. Chill for 30 minutes. Sprinkle the prawns with the lemon juice and leave to stand. Roll the dough into long sausage shapes and slice off 2 cm/1 in pieces. Press a prawn into each one and work the dough into little balls. Fry in deep hot oil until golden brown, then drain well and serve with the lemon wedges.

Scallops with Dill

Serves 4

12 Scallops

300 ml/½ pt Milk

Salt and pepper

25 g/1 oz Flour

25 g/1 oz Butter or margarine

6 Dill sprigs

Remove the scallops from the shells, cut away the black parts and wash them thoroughly. Put them in a greased ovenproof dish and pour over the milk. Season to taste with salt and pepper and bake in a preheated oven at 190°C/375°F/gas mark 5 for 45 minutes.

Mix the flour and butter to a paste in a small saucepan, adding a little milk if necessary. Transfer the scallops to a warmed serving dish and keep them warm. Mix the liquor from the dish into the saucepan, bring to the boil and simmer for 4 minutes, stirring continuously, until the sauce is smooth. Chop most of the dill and stir it into the sauce. Season to taste with salt and pepper, pour over the scallops and garnish with the remaining dill.

Mackerel Pâté

Serves 4

225 g/8 oz Smoked mackerel,
   skinned

Juice of ½ lemon

50 g/2 oz Butter or margarine,
   melted

45 ml/3 tbsp Soured cream

Pepper

Break the mackerel into small pieces and purée in a food processor or blender with the lemon juice, melted butter and soured cream. Season to taste with pepper, then turn into a serving dish and chill before serving.

Smoked Haddock Mousse

Serves 4

450 g/1 lb Smoked haddock fillet,
  cut into pieces

1 Small onion, sliced

250 ml/8 fl oz Milk

1 Bay leaf

25 g/1 oz Unsalted butter

15 g/½ oz Plain flour

2.5 ml/½ tsp Cayenne pepper

Salt and pepper

15 g/½ oz Gelatine

30 ml/2 tbsp Water

Juice and grated rind of 1 lemon

150 ml/¼ pt Double cream,
  whipped

½ Cucumber, sliced.

Put the haddock, onion, milk and bay leaf in a saucepan, bring to the boil, cover and simmer for 10 minutes. Strain the fish and reserve the cooking liquor. Remove the skin and bones and flake the fish finely. Melt the butter, stir in the flour and cook for 2 minutes until the mixture is light brown. Whisk in the milk and cook, stirring, for 3 minutes. Season to taste with cayenne pepper, salt and pepper, then remove from the heat, cover and leave to cool. Mix the gelatine with the water and lemon juice, then dissolve over a pan of hot water. Blend the fish and gelatine into the sauce with the lemon rind and cream. Pour into a soufflé dish and leave until set. Garnish with the cucumber and serve with thin brown bread and butter.

Salmon Mousse

Serves 4

15 g/½ oz Gelatine

150 ml/¼ pt Water

225 g/8 oz Canned red salmon,
  drained

Juice of ½ lemon

150 ml/¼ pt Soured cream

Salt and pepper

150 ml/¼ pt Double cream,
  whipped

175 g/6 oz Cucumber, peeled and
  diced

Dissolve the gelatine in 45 ml/3 tbsp water then purée it in a food processor or blender with the remaining water, salmon and lemon juice, soured cream and salt and pepper to taste. Turn into a bowl and fold in the cream and cucumber when just beginning to set. Turn into a greased 900 ml/1½ pt mould and chill until set. Serve with thinly sliced wholemeal bread.

Avocado and Tuna Mousse

Serves 4

1 Avocado pear, peeled and halved
185 g/6½ oz Canned tuna fish,
   drained
30 ml/2 tbsp Natural yoghurt
5 ml/1 tsp Tabasco sauce
5 ml/1 tsp Lemon juice
Pepper

Purée the avocado pear in a food processor or blender, then add the remaining ingredients and process until smooth. Season to taste with freshly ground black pepper and add extra tabasco if liked. Pile into a dish and chill before serving with crisp toast.

Taramasalata

Serves 4

12 White bread slices without crusts
300 ml/½ pt Milk
175 g/6 oz Smoked cod's roe,
   skinned
¼ Onion, chopped
Juice of 2 lemons
250 ml/8 fl oz Oil

Soak the bread in the milk until soft, then squeeze it dry. Purée in a food processor or blender with the roe, onion and lemon juice. Still blending, pour in the oil gradually until the mixture becomes smooth and creamy. Chill well and serve with hot pitta bread.

Chicken and Mushroom Pâté

Serves 4

60 g/2½ oz Butter or margarine
1 Onion, chopped
225 g/8 oz Chicken livers
15 ml/1 tbsp Dry sherry
30 ml/2 tbsp Double cream
100 g/4 oz Cooked chicken, finely
   chopped
100 g/4 oz Mushrooms, sliced

Melt 25 g/1 oz butter or margarine in a frying pan and fry the onion until soft but not browned. Add the chicken livers and fry for 10 minutes until just cooked. Stir in the sherry, then add the cream and 25 g/1 oz butter and purée the mixture with the chicken in a food processor or blender until smooth. Spread the remaining butter on the base of a small loaf tin and arrange half the mushrooms on the base. Spread half of the pâté on top, then arrange the remaining mushrooms on top, followed by the remaining pâté. Cover with foil and place in a baking dish half full of water. Bake in a preheated oven at 180°C/350°F/gas mark 4 for 30 minutes. Leave to cool in the tin, then weigh down with tins and chill overnight. Turn out, cut into slices and serve well chilled.

Country Pâté

Serves 4

| 1 Onion, finely chopped |
| 1 Garlic clove, crushed |
| 100 g/4 oz Streaky bacon, rinded and finely chopped |
| 225 g/8 oz Lambs' liver, chopped |
| 225 g/8 oz Lean pork, finely chopped |
| 25 g/1 oz Butter or margarine |
| 2.5 ml/½ tsp Ground mace |
| 30 ml/2 tbsp Single cream |
| Salt and pepper |

Mix together all the ingredients and season to taste with salt and pepper. You can vary how finely you chop the ingredients depending on whether you like a smooth or coarse pâté. For a really smooth pâté, use a food processor or blender to mix all the ingredients. Spoon the mixture into a 1.2 litre/2 pt dish, cover and stand in a baking dish filled with water to come half way up the sides of the dish. Bake in a preheated oven at 180°C/350°F/gas mark 4 for 1½ hours. Leave to cool, then chill overnight with weights on top of the dish. Serve cold, sliced, with granary bread.

Hummus

Serves 4

| 100 g/4 oz Chick peas, soaked overnight and drained |
| 1 Onion, chopped |
| 1 Garlic clove, chopped |
| 150 ml/¼ pt Natural yoghurt |
| 10 ml/2 tsp Lemon juice |
| 15 ml/1 tbsp Oil |
| 2.5 ml/½ tsp Ground cumin |
| Salt |

Place the chick peas in a saucepan and just cover with water. Add the onion and garlic, bring to the boil and simmer for at least 1 hour until tender. Drain, then purée in a food processor or blender. Add the yoghurt, lemon juice, oil and cumin and season to taste with salt. Process again to mix everything together. Chill overnight before serving with pitta bread or French bread.

Tzatziki

Serves 4

| ½ Cucumber, skinned and diced |
| Salt and pepper |
| 150 ml/¼ pt Natural firm-set yoghurt |
| 1 Garlic clove, crushed |
| 15 ml/1 tbsp Chopped mint |

Place the cucumber in a colander, sprinkle with salt and leave to stand for 30 minutes. Rinse, drain well and pat dry. Place in a serving bowl and mix with the remaining ingredients. Cover and chill in the fridge before serving with warmed pitta bread.

13

Crudités with Mint Yoghurt Dip

Serves 4

150 ml/¼ pt Natural yoghurt
150 ml/¼ pt Soured cream
30 ml/2 tbsp Mint Sauce (page 229)
5 ml/1 tsp Lime or lemon juice
30 ml/2 tbsp Ground almonds
2.5 cm/1 in Cucumber, peeled and
    chopped
Salt and pepper
Pinch of paprika
12 Small corn cobs
1 Red pepper, sliced
1 Red-skinned apple, cored and
    sliced
2 Celery stalks, cut into strips
2 Carrots, cut into strips

Mix the yoghurt, soured cream, mint sauce, lime or lemon juice, ground almonds and cucumber and season to taste with salt and pepper. Spoon into a serving bowl and sprinkle with paprika. Arrange the crudités on a serving plate and serve with the dip.

Garlic Bread

Serves 4

1 French baguette
100 g/4 oz Garlic butter (page 233)

Slice the baguette diagonally into thick slices without cutting right through the loaf. Spread all the cut sides with garlic butter and wrap the loaf in foil. Bake in a preheated oven at 180°C/350°F/gas mark 4 for 20 minutes. Serve alone, with dips or with a main course.

Spicy Salami Dip

Serves 4

75 g/3 oz Salami, chopped
175 g/6 oz Cream cheese
30 ml/2 tbsp Mayonnaise (page 250)
15 ml/1 tbsp Tomato ketchup
30 ml/2 tbsp Olive oil
15 ml/1 tbsp Worcestershire sauce
5 ml/1 tsp Mustard powder
Salt and pepper

Purée all the ingredients in a food processor or blender, then chill. Serve with savoury biscuits.

Stuffed Eggs

Serves 4

6 Hard-boiled eggs, halved
3 Parsley sprigs
185 g/6½ oz Canned tuna, drained
100 g/4 oz Cream cheese
50 g/2 oz Butter or margarine,
    melted
Pepper
1 Bunch of watercress
2 Tomatoes, sliced
1 Lemon, sliced

Place the egg whites in a bowl of water to keep them soft. Purée the egg yolks, parsley, tuna, cream cheese and butter in a food processor or blender. Season to taste with freshly ground black pepper. Pile or pipe the mixture into the drained and dry egg whites. Arrange the watercress on a serving plate, lay the eggs on top, and garnish with the tomato and lemon slices.

Blue Cheese Tartlets

Serves 4

50 g/2 oz Butter or margarine
25 g/1 oz Lard
175 g/6 oz Plain flour
75 g/3 oz Blue cheese, crumbled
45 ml/3 tbsp Water
8 Spring onions, chopped
300 ml/½ pt Single cream
2 Eggs, beaten
Salt and pepper

Rub the butter or margarine and lard into the flour until the mixture resembles breadcrumbs. Mix in one-third of the cheese and add enough water to bind the mixture to a pastry. Roll out on a floured surface and use to line 4 greased 10 cm/4 in flan tins. Sprinkle the onions in the flans. Beat the cream and eggs together, then season to taste with salt and pepper. Stir in the remaining blue cheese and pour the mixture into the pastry cases. Bake in a preheated oven at 200°C/ 400°F/gas mark 6 for 20 minutes until golden brown. Serve hot or warm.

Cheese Courgettes

Serves 4

2 Large courgettes, halved
50 g/2 oz Cheese, grated
1 Hard-boiled egg, chopped
50 g/2 oz Cooked ham, chopped
5 ml/1 tsp Chopped parsley
Salt and pepper

Scoop out the centres of the courgettes and arrange the shells in a shallow ovenproof dish. Mix the courgette flesh with half the cheese, the egg, ham and parsley and season to taste. Spoon into the courgette shells and sprinkle with the cheese. Bake in a preheated oven at 190°C/ 375°F/gas mark 5 for 30 minutes until golden brown.

Ham Gougère

Serves 4

15 ml/1 tbsp Oil
1 Onion, chopped
100 g/4 oz Mushrooms, chopped
175 g/6 oz Cooked ham, chopped
Salt and pepper
75 g/3 oz Butter or margarine
200 ml/7 fl oz Water
100 g/4 oz Plain flour
3 Eggs, beaten
50 g/2 oz Breadcrumbs
100 g/4 oz Cheese, grated

Heat the oil and fry the onions and mushrooms until soft but not browned. Add the ham and season to taste with salt and pepper. Put to one side. Heat the butter and water in a saucepan, bring to the boil, then tip in the flour all at once and beat until the pastry comes away cleanly from the sides of the pan. Leave to cool slightly, then gradually beat in the eggs. Spread half the pastry on the base of a greased pie dish and pile the rest round the edge. Spoon the ham mixture into the centre and sprinkle with the breadcrumbs and cheese. Bake in a preheated oven at 200°C/400°F/gas mark 6 for 30 minutes until golden brown.

Courgette and Egg Bake

Serves 4

350 g/12 oz Courgettes, sliced
15 ml/1 tbsp Chopped mint
2 Eggs, beaten
75 ml/5 tbsp Single cream
Salt and pepper
50 g/2 oz Parmesan cheese, grated
30 ml/2 tbsp French Dressing (page 249)
2 Tomatoes, sliced
½ Box of cress

Cook the courgettes in boiling salted water for 5 minutes. Drain and purée in a food processor or blender. Stir in the eggs and cream and season to taste with salt and pepper. Pour into greased individual ovenproof dishes, sprinkle with cheese and bake in a preheated oven at 180°C/350°F/gas mark 4 for 30 minutes until set. Leave to cool, then chill. Turn out on to individual plates and spoon over the French dressing. Serve with tomatoes and cress.

Nut and Cream Eggs

Serves 4

½ Lettuce, shredded
4 Hard-boiled eggs, sliced
300 ml/½ pt Soured cream
25 g/1 oz Mixed nuts, chopped
15 ml/1 tbsp Chopped parsley
Salt and pepper

Arrange the lettuce leaves on individual plates with the eggs on top. Mix the cream with the nuts and parsley and season to taste with salt and pepper. Spoon the sauce over the eggs and serve with wholemeal bread slices.

Cheese and Walnut Sables

Serves 4

75 g/3 oz Plain flour
Salt
75 g/3 oz Butter or margarine
75 g/3 oz Cheese, grated
25 g/1 oz Walnuts, chopped
1 Egg, beaten

Mix the flour and salt and rub in the butter or margarine until the mixture resembles breadcrumbs. Stir in the cheese and walnuts and press into a firm dough. Roll out on a floured surface to a rectangle about 18 x 10 cm/7 x 4 in. Beat a pinch of salt into the egg and brush it over the pastry. Cut it into 5 cm/2 in strips and cut each strip into triangles. Place them on a greased baking sheet and bake in a preheated oven at 190°C/375°F/gas mark 5 for 10 minutes. Sprinkle with salt while still hot and leave on the tray until just warm before serving.

Bacon and Cheese Palmiers

Serves 4

225 g/8 oz Puff Pastry (page 146)

1 Egg, beaten

100 g/4 oz Gruyère cheese, grated

100 g/4 oz Bacon, rinded and finely chopped

5 ml/1 tsp Cayenne pepper

Salt and pepper

Roll out the pastry into a rectangle and brush with the beaten egg. Sprinkle the cheese and bacon over the pastry, sprinkle with cayenne pepper and season to taste with salt and pepper. Roll up the pastry from opposite edges so that the rolls meet in the centre. Slice through the roll, and lay the slices on a damp baking sheet. Brush again with egg and bake in a preheated oven at 200°C/400°F/gas mark 6 for 15 minutes until browned, then lift off the sheet and leave to cool.

Blue Cheese Bites

Makes 30

75 g/3 oz Unsalted butter, softened

75 g/3 oz 81% extraction flour

75 g/3 oz Blue cheese, crumbled

30 ml/2 tbsp Egg, beaten

Pepper

45 ml/3 tbsp Natural yoghurt

30 ml/2 tbsp Celery seeds

Rub the butter into the flour, then mix in the cheese. Beat in the egg and season with pepper. Chill the dough for 1 hour.

Roll out the dough to 3 mm/⅛ in thick, cut into rounds and place them on ungreased baking sheets. Brush with yoghurt and sprinkle with celery seeds. Bake in a preheated oven at 180°C/350°F/gas mark 4 for 12 minutes until crisp and browned. Cool on a wire rack then store in an airtight container.

Vegetable and Cheese Bakes

Serves 4

1 Carrot, grated

2 Spring onions, sliced

100 g/4 oz Courgettes, sliced

75 ml/5 tbsp Vegetable Stock (page 24)

15 g/½ oz Garlic sausage, chopped

50 g/2 oz Ricotta cheese, grated

225 g/8 oz Canned tomatoes, chopped

Pepper

Sprinkle half the carrot, the spring onions and courgettes in 4 individual soufflé dishes, followed by the stock, garlic sausage and cheese and the remaining vegetables. Season the tomatoes well with pepper then divide between the dishes. Cover with foil and bake in a preheated oven at 180°C/350°F/gas mark 4 for 45 minutes.

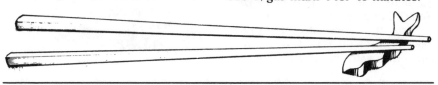

Mushrooms in Batter with Herb Sauce

Serves 4

15 g/½ oz Butter or margarine
1 Onion, chopped
120 g/4½ oz Plain flour
5 ml/1 tsp Tomato purée
225 g/8 oz Canned tomatoes, chopped
150 ml/¼ pt Chicken Stock (page 24)
5 ml/1 tsp White wine vinegar
Pinch of paprika
Salt and pepper
30 ml/2 tbsp Chopped parsley
30 ml/2 tbsp Chopped chervil
30 ml/2 tbsp Chopped watercress
300 ml/½ pt Milk
1 Egg, separated
5 ml/1 tsp Oil
225 g/8 oz Button mushrooms
Oil for frying

Melt the butter or margarine and fry the onion until soft but not browned. Stir in 15g/½ oz flour and the tomato purée, then add the tomatoes, stock, wine vinegar and paprika. Season to taste with a little salt and plenty of pepper. Add the herbs and watercress, bring to the boil and simmer for 10 minutes.

Beat together the milk, egg yolk, remaining flour and oil until smooth. Whisk the egg white until stiff, then fold it into the batter. Dip the mushrooms in the batter then fry in hot oil for 5 minutes until golden brown. Remove and drain.

Purée the sauce into a food processor or blender and serve in a small dish with the mushrooms.

Mushroom Turnovers

Serves 4

25 g/1 oz Butter or margarine
1 Onion, chopped
350 g/12 oz Mushrooms, sliced
15 ml/1 tbsp Chopped chives
15 ml/1 tbsp Chopped parsley
1 Bunch of watercress, chopped
3 Eggs, beaten
Pinch of nutmeg
Salt and pepper
450 g/1 lb Puff Pastry (page 146)
1 Egg yolk
50 g/2 oz Parmesan cheese, grated

Melt the butter or margarine and fry the onion until soft but not browned. Add the mushrooms and fry for 2 minutes. Stir in the herbs. Season the eggs with nutmeg, salt and pepper to taste, then pour over the mushroom mixture and cook, stirring, until set. Leave to cool.

Roll out the pastry and cut into 10 cm/4 in squares. Divide the mixture between the pastry squares, fold over and seal the edges together. Place on a damp baking sheet and bake in a preheated oven at 200°C/400°F/gas mark 6 for 15 minutes. Remove them from the oven, brush with egg yolk and sprinkle with the Parmesan cheese, then return them to the oven for a further 5 minutes until golden brown. Serve hot or cold.

Mushrooms in Wine

Serves 4-6

60 ml/4 tbsp Oil
1 Onion, finely chopped
1 Garlic clove, crushed
200 ml/7 fl oz Dry white wine
1 Bay leaf
5 ml/1 tsp Thyme
2.5 ml/½ tsp Rosemary
30 ml/2 tbsp Chopped parsley
4 Peppercorns
5 ml/1 tsp Coriander seeds
450 g/1 lb Button mushrooms
Salt and pepper

Heat the oil and fry the garlic and onion until soft but not browned. Stir in the wine, bay leaf, thyme, rosemary and half the parsley, bring to the boil, then simmer for 2 minutes. Add the peppercorns, coriander and mushrooms and season to taste with salt and pepper. Stir until the mixture is well combined. Transfer to a serving dish and chill for 4 hours, stirring occasionally. Sprinkle with the remaining parsley and serve with granary rolls.

Melon with Spicy Mushrooms

Serves 4

225 g/8 oz Button mushrooms
300 ml/½ pt Ginger wine
20 ml/1½ tbsp Soft brown sugar
1 Small honeydew melon
Mint leaves to garnish

Put the mushrooms, wine and sugar in a saucepan, bring slowly to the boil, then cover and simmer gently for 10 minutes until the wine has reduced and become syrupy. Pour into a warm jar, put the lid on loosely and leave to cool. When cold, screw the lid down tightly and keep in a cool place until required. The mushrooms will keep for several days.

Cut the melon flesh into small balls, toss the melon with the spiced mushrooms and serve garnished with a few mint leaves.

Mushrooms with Yoghurt and Onion

Serves 4

450 g/1 lb Button mushrooms
300 ml/½ pt Vegetable Stock
  (page 24)
60 ml/4 tbsp Water
60 ml/4 tbsp White wine vinegar
1 Garlic clove, finely chopped
5 ml/1 tsp Finely chopped mint
45 ml/3 tbsp Low fat natural
  yoghurt
1 Small onion, finely sliced
Pepper
15 ml/1 tbsp Finely chopped chives

Place the mushrooms in a saucepan, just cover with stock and simmer gently for 10 minutes. Place the water, wine vinegar, garlic and mint in another saucepan, bring to the boil, then simmer for 3 minutes. Add the drained mushrooms and simmer for a further 10 minutes, then remove from the heat and leave to cool. Drain the mushrooms and mix with the yoghurt and onion. Season and serve sprinkled with chives.

Tomato Angelo

Serves 4

4 Large tomatoes

Salt and pepper

150 g/5 oz Cream cheese

30 ml/2 tbsp Crème fraîche

1 Garlic clove, crushed

2.5 ml/½ tsp Salt

30 ml/2 tbsp Chopped chives

30 ml/2 tbsp Chopped parsley

30 ml/2 tbsp Chopped cress

Juice of ½ lemon

Few drops of Worcestershire sauce

1 Radicchio, shredded

1 Chicory, sliced

Few drops of raspberry vinegar

5 ml/1 tsp Olive oil

Cut the lids off the tomatoes and remove the seeds. Place upside down on a rack to drain, then sprinkle with salt and pepper. Mix the cream cheese, crème fraîche, garlic, salt, herbs, cress, lemon juice and Worcestershire sauce. Season to taste with salt and pepper. Fill the tomatoes with this mixture. Arrange the radicchio and chicory on a serving plate and sprinkle with raspberry vinegar and oil. Stand the tomatoes on top and serve.

Peperonata

Serves 4

15 ml/1 tbsp Olive oil

1 Onion, sliced

1 Red pepper, sliced

1 Green pepper, sliced

1 Yellow pepper, sliced

1 Garlic clove, crushed

225 g/8 oz Canned tomatoes, chopped

Salt and pepper

Heat the oil and fry the onion until soft but not browned. Add the peppers and garlic and simmer for 15 minutes until the peppers are tender. Stir in the tomatoes and season to taste with salt and pepper. Turn into a serving dish and leave to cool.

Spiced Tofu Nibbles

Serves 4

275 g/10 oz Block of firm tofu, cubed

60 ml/4 tbsp Corn oil

150 ml/¼ pt Soy sauce

30 ml/2 tbsp Red wine vinegar

30 ml/2 tbsp Soft brown sugar

Pinch of mustard powder

15 ml/1 tbsp Grated root ginger

1 Garlic clove, crushed

Drain the tofu well. Mix the remaining ingredients and pour over the tofu. Refrigerate for 24 hours, turning several times, and serve as cocktail nibbles.

Vine-Leaf Fruit Parcels

Serves 4

225 g/8 oz Canned vine leaves, drained

175 g/6 oz Cooked long-grain rice

1 Onion, finely chopped

100 g/4 oz Dried apricots, finely chopped

50 g/2 oz Sultanas

Pinch of cinnamon

Pinch of allspice

15 ml/1 tbsp Chopped mint

15 ml/1 tbsp Lemon juice

300 ml/½ pt Orange juice

150 ml/¼ pt Water

Rinse the vine leaves and pat dry. Arrange a few leaves on the base of a deep casserole dish. Mix the rice, onion, apricots, sultanas, spices, mint and lemon juice. Place spoonfuls of the mixture on individual vine leaves and fold up into parcels. Make a layer of parcels in the casserole, cover with a few more vine leaves, then a second layer of parcels, covered with leaves. Pour in the orange juice and water and bake in a preheated oven at 160°C/325°F/gas mark 3 for 1½ hours, then serve immediately.

Variation
You can leave the parcels to cool, then arrange on uncooked leaves on a serving dish and chill before serving.

Tropical Fruit Cocktail

Serves 4

1 Avocado, peeled, stoned and sliced

15 ml/1 tbsp Lemon juice

1 Pawpaw, sliced

2 Kiwi fruit, sliced

1 Bunch of spring onions, sliced

225 g/8 oz Gouda cheese, diced

100 g/4 oz Cherries, stoned

45 ml/3 tbsp Cider vinegar

5 ml/1 tsp Honey

30 ml/2 tbsp Walnut oil

Salt and pepper

15 ml/1 tbsp Sparkling wine

Dash of angostura bitters

Toss the avocado in the lemon juice, then carefully mix together all the cocktail ingredients. Mix the cider vinegar, honey and oil and season to taste with salt and pepper. Pour over the salad, toss carefully and leave to chill for 30 minutes. Arrange the salad in cocktail glasses, add a dash of sparkling wine and sprinkle with a little angostura before serving.

Prawn and Dill Avocados

Serves 4

60 ml/4 tbsp Cream cheese
60 ml/4 tbsp Crème fraîche
30 ml/2 tbsp Horseradish sauce
15 ml/1 tbsp Chopped dill
Salt and pepper
100 g/4 oz Cooked shelled prawns
30 ml/2 tbsp Lemon juice
2 Avocados
4 Dill sprigs

Mix together the cream cheese, crème fraîche, horseradish and dill and season to taste with salt and pepper. Fold in the prawns and half the lemon juice. Halve the avocados, remove the stones and brush with the remaining lemon juice. Pile the mixture into the avocados and serve garnished with dill sprigs.

Cream Cheese Nectarines

Serves 4

½ Iceberg lettuce, shredded
4 Nectarines, halved and stoned
225 g/8 oz Full fat soft cheese
30 ml/2 tbsp Single cream
100 g/4 oz Mixed nuts, chopped
Salt and pepper
50 g/2 oz Lumpfish roe

Arrange the lettuce on individual plates and place the nectarine halves on top. Beat the cheese with the cream and nuts and season to taste with salt and pepper. Spoon the mixture on the top of the nectarines and garnish with the lumpfish roe.

Strawberry and Melon Salad

Serves 4

1 Iceberg lettuce, shredded
1 Melon, skinned, seeded and cubed
100 g/4 oz Strawberries, sliced
¼ Cucumber, sliced
60 ml/4 tbsp French Dressing (page 249)
30 ml/2 tbsp Chopped mint
Salt and pepper
50 g/2 oz Flaked almonds

Arrange the lettuce on a serving plate and arrange the melon, strawberries and cucumber attractively on top. Mix the dressing with the mint and season to taste with salt and pepper. Pour over the salad just before serving and sprinkle with almonds.

Gingered Melon and Parma Ham

Serves 4

1 Honeydew melon
100 g/4 oz Parma ham, thinly sliced and cut into strips
25 g/1 oz Stem ginger, chopped
30 ml/2 tbsp Stem ginger syrup
5 ml/1 tsp Lemon juice
45 ml/3 tbsp Oil
Pepper

Quarter the melon lengthways and remove the seeds and skin. Cut into long slices and wind the ham round the melon slices. Arrange on a serving plate. Whisk the remaining ingredients together well and pour over the melon. Cover and chill for 1 hour before serving.

Stocks and Soups

Nothing need go to waste in the kitchen, and if you use meat or poultry bones or carcasses to make stocks, they can form the basis of delicious and simple home-made soups, or you can use them for gravies and sauces.

Because it takes a little time to make a stock, it is a good idea to make fairly large quantities, boil them down to reduce the quantity and freeze them in smaller containers. Then you can take out exactly the quantity you need for a particular recipe. Never leave stocks standing around in the kitchen, or store them for too long in the fridge as they will go off.

If you do not make your own stocks, you can substitute a stock cube in the recipes, although they do tend to be salty, so take care when you are seasoning.

To skim stock, simply slide a shallow spoon across the top.

Fat will solidify on the top of cold stock and can be removed with the blade of a large knife.

To remove fat from hot stock, dip a clean cloth in cold water and strain the hot liquid through it. The hot fat will solidify when it touches the cold cloth and the fat-free stock will strain through into the bowl.

While stock is cooking, float a few pieces of kitchen paper on the top until they absorb the fat.

Beef or Chicken Stock

Makes 1 litre/1¾ pts

1 kg/2 lb Cooked or raw bones of
   meat or poultry and cooked or
   raw meat trimmings

5 ml/1 tsp Salt

450g/1 lb Vegetables (carrot, celery,
   leek, onion, etc.), roughly
   chopped

1 Bay leaf

8 Black peppercorns

Place the meat in a large saucepan
and cover with cold water. Bring to
the boil and add the remaining
ingredients. Bring back to the boil
and simmer very gently, uncovered,
for about 3 hours, topping up with
water as necessary. Strain and skim
off any fat before using.

Notes

If you are going to freeze the stock or
if you need a concentrated stock,
boil it until it has reduced to half
quantity.

Brown Stock is made with beef.
Leave the onion skins on to give a
good colour.

Giblet Stock

Makes about 1 litre/1¾ pts

Giblets of a turkey or goose

1 Onion, sliced

1 Carrot, sliced

1 Bunch of mixed herbs

1 litre/1¾ pts Water

Place all the ingredients in a large
saucepan with just enough water to
cover. Bring to the boil, cover and
simmer gently for 3 to 4 hours. Strain
and skim off any fat. If you want to
freeze the stock or need a concentrated stock, boil to reduce by half.

Fish Stock

Makes 1 litre/1¾ pts

1 kg/2 lb Bones, skins and heads
   from filleted fish or other white
   fish trimmings

1 litre/1¾ pts Water

5 ml/1 tsp Salt

1 Onion, chopped

1 Celery stalk, chopped

6 White peppercorns

1 Bouquet garni

Wash the fish and discard the eyes.
Place all the ingredients in a large
saucepan, bring to the boil, cover
and simmer gently for 40 minutes.
Strain.

Vegetable Stock

Makes 1 litre/1¾ pts

2 Carrots, sliced

1 Onion, sliced

2 Celery stalks, sliced

1 Medium turnip, chopped

1 litre/1¾ pts Water

6 Peppercorns

1 Bay leaf

Place all the ingredients in a large
saucepan, bring to the boil, cover and
simmer gently for 2 hours. Strain.

Scotch Broth

Serves 4-6

675 g/1½ lb Scrag end neck, mutton or lamb

1.75 litres/3 pts Chicken Stock (page 24)

100 g/4 oz Pearl barley, blanched

50 g/2 oz Peas

1 Large carrot, diced

1 Large onion, diced

1 Medium turnip, diced

2 Celery stalks, diced

Salt and pepper

5 ml/1 tsp Chopped parsley

Put the meat, stock and barley in a large saucepan, bring to the boil and simmer for 1 hour, skimming as necessary. Add the vegetables, season to taste with salt and pepper, cover and simmer for a further 1 hour, stirring occasionally. Remove from the heat, take out the bones and skim off the fat. Add the parsley, adjust the seasoning if necessary and reheat.

Blanching Pearl Barley
To blanch barley or rice, place the well-washed grain in a saucepan, cover with cold water and bring to the boil. Strain and rinse in cold water.

Curried Apple Soup

Serves 4

25 g/1 oz Butter or margarine

1 Onion, chopped

40 g/1½ oz Plain flour

15 ml/1 tbsp Curry powder

900 ml/1½ pts Chicken Stock (page 24)

750 g/1½ lb Cooking apples, peeled, cored and sliced

15 ml/1 tbsp Lemon juice

Salt and pepper

90 ml/6 tbsp Natural yoghurt

Melt the butter or margarine and fry the onion until soft but not browned. Stir in the flour and curry powder and cook for 1 minute, stirring. Add the stock, apples and lemon juice and bring to the boil, stirring continuously. Season to taste with salt and pepper. Simmer for 10 minutes until the apples are soft, then purée in a food processor or blender. Return to the pan to reheat, then serve in warmed soup bowls with a swirl of yoghurt in each one.

Green Bean Soup

Serves 4

25 g/1 oz Butter or margarine
450 g/1 lb Runner beans,
  chopped
3 Onions, chopped
1 Carrot, chopped
900 ml/1½ pts Vegetable Stock
  (page 24)
Salt and pepper

Melt the butter or margarine and fry the beans, onions and carrot until soft but not browned. Add the stock, bring to the boil, cover and simmer gently for about 30 minutes until the vegetables are tender. Purée in a food processor or blender, then return the soup to the pan, season to taste with salt and pepper and reheat.

Apple and Wine Soup

Serves 4

75 g/3 oz Sugar
Pinch of salt
600 ml/1 pt Water
1.5 kg/3 lb Cooking apples, peeled,
  cored and chopped
50 g/2 oz Breadcrumbs
1 Cinnamon stick
Thinly pared rind of 1 lemon
Juice of 2 lemons
450 ml/¾ pt Dry red wine
45 ml/3 tbsp Redcurrant jelly
60 ml/4 tbsp Natural yoghurt

Put the sugar, salt and water in a saucepan, bring to the boil and add the apples, breadcrumbs, cinnamon and lemon rind. Simmer, stirring, for 10 minutes until the apples are soft. Remove the cinnamon and lemon rind and purée the apple mixture in a food processor or blender. Return the mixture to the pan, add the lemon juice, wine and redcurrant jelly and simmer gently, stirring, until the jelly dissolves and the soup is warmed through. Pour the soup into warmed soup bowls and swirl a spoonful of yoghurt into each one.

Bacon and Pea Soup

Serves 4

25 g/1 oz Butter or margarine
100 g/4 oz Streaky bacon, finely
  chopped
1 Garlic clove, chopped
225 g/8 oz Dried peas, soaked
  overnight
1 litre/1¾ pts Vegetable Stock
  (page 24)
5 ml/1 tsp Mint
Pepper

Melt the butter or margarine and fry the bacon until crisp, then remove the bacon and keep it warm. Add the garlic to the pan and fry until just browned. Add the drained peas, stock and mint and season to taste with pepper. Bring to the boil, then simmer gently for 1 hour until tender. Purée in a food processor or blender, then return the soup to the pan and reheat gently. Serve sprinkled with the bacon pieces.

Beetroot Soup

Serves 4

25 g/1 oz Butter or margarine
1 Onion, chopped
1 Celery stalk, chopped
4 Beetroots
225 g/8 oz Tomatoes, skinned
600 ml/1 pt Vegetable Stock
  (page 24)
Salt and pepper
30 ml/2 tbsp Soured cream

Melt the butter or margarine and fry the onion and celery until soft but not browned. Add the beetroots, tomatoes and stock, bring to the boil, cover and simmer gently for about 1 hour until the beetroots are tender. Purée in a food processor or blender, then pass through a sieve. Return the soup to the saucepan, season to taste with salt and pepper and reheat. Swirl in the soured cream before serving.

Smooth Carrot Soup

Serves 4

15 ml/1 tbsp Oil
1 Onion, chopped
1 Garlic clove, chopped
450 g/1 lb Carrots, chopped
600 ml/1 pt Chicken Stock
  (page 24)
Pinch of sugar
Salt and pepper
150 ml/¼ pt Single cream
Fried bread croûtons (page 28)

Heat the oil and fry the onion and garlic until soft but not browned. Stir in the carrots, then add the stock and sugar and season to taste with salt and pepper. Simmer for 15 minutes until the carrots are soft. Purée in a food processor or blender, then return the soup to the pan and stir in the cream. Heat through gently and serve hot with croûtons.

Celery Soup

Serves 4-6

25 g/1 oz Butter or margarine
1 Celery head, chopped
4 Onions, chopped
100 g/4 oz Potatoes, peeled and
  chopped
600 ml/1 pt Chicken Stock
  (page 24)
300 ml/½ pt Milk
150 ml/¼ pt Single cream
Salt and pepper

Melt the butter or margarine and fry the celery, onions and potatoes until soft but not browned. Add the stock, bring to the boil, cover and simmer gently for about 25 minutes until the vegetables are tender. Purée in a food processor or blender, then return the soup to the pan, add the milk and cream, season to taste with salt and pepper and reheat.

27

Curried Chicken and Lentil Soup

Serves 4

150 ml/¼ pt Oil
1 Onion, chopped
10 ml/2 tsp Curry powder
15 ml/1 tbsp Dry sherry
1.2 litres/2 pts Chicken Stock (page 24)
4 Carrots, cut into sticks
225 g/8 oz Cooked chicken, chopped
100 g/4 oz Lentils
Salt and pepper
100 g/4 oz Wholemeal bread, cut into 1 cm/½ in cubes

Heat 15 ml/1 tbsp oil in a large saucepan and fry the onion until soft but not browned. Add the curry powder and fry gently for 1 minute. Stir in the sherry, then add the stock, carrots, chicken and lentils. Bring to the boil and simmer for 15 minutes until the vegetables are tender. Season to taste.

Croûtons
To make croûtons, heat the remaining oil and fry the bread until crisp, drain and serve with the soup.

Irish Milk Soup

Serves 4

25 g/1 oz Butter or margarine
1 Onion, chopped
4 Potatoes, diced
2 Celery stalks, chopped
600 ml/1 pt Water
Salt and pepper
600 ml/1 pt Milk

Melt the butter or margarine and fry the onion, potatoes and celery until soft but not browned. Add the water and salt, bring to the boil, cover and simmer for 20 minutes until the vegetables are tender. Purée in a food processor or blender, then return the soup to the pan with the milk. Season to taste with salt and pepper and bring just to the boil before serving.

Lentil Soup

Serves 4

25 g/1 oz Butter or margarine
1 Onion, chopped
1 Carrot, chopped
2 Celery stalks, chopped
225 g/8 oz Lentils, soaked overnight then drained
1.75 litres/3 pts Water
300 ml/½ pt Milk
Salt and pepper
15 ml/1 tbsp Plain flour (optional)
15 ml/1 tbsp Butter (optional)

Melt the butter or margarine and fry the onion, carrot and celery until soft but not browned. Add the lentils and water, bring to the boil and simmer for about 1 hour until the lentils are soft. Purée in a food processor or blender, then return the soup to the pan. Add the milk, season to taste with salt and pepper and bring back to the boil. If the sauce is not thick enough, mix the additional flour and butter to a paste and stir this into the soup.

Bouillabaisse

Serves 4

| 450 g/1 lb Fish bones and trimmings |
| 900 ml/1½ pts Water |
| 1 Onion, finely chopped |
| 30 ml/2 tbsp Chopped parsley |
| 1 Bouquet garni |
| 600 ml/1 pt Milk |
| Salt and pepper |
| 1 Egg yolk, beaten |

Place the fish, water, onion, parsley and bouquet garni in a large saucepan, bring to the boil, cover and simmer gently for 1 hour. Strain and return the liquor to the pan. Add the milk, season to taste with salt and pepper and stir in the egg yolk, but do not allow the soup to boil.

Leek and Pasta Soup

Serves 4

| 25 g/1 oz Butter or margarine |
| 6 Leeks, thinly sliced |
| 1.2 litres/2 pts Chicken or Vegetable Stock (page 24) |
| 50 g/2 oz Vermicelli |
| Salt and pepper |
| 150 ml/¼ pt Single cream |

Melt the butter or margarine and fry the leeks until soft but not browned. Add the stock, bring to the boil, cover and simmer for 30 minutes, stirring frequently. Add the vermicelli and cook for a further 15 minutes. Season to taste with salt and pepper, stir in the cream and reheat.

Mulligatawny Soup

Serves 4

| 25 g/1 oz Butter or margarine |
| 25 g/1 oz Bacon |
| 2 Onions, chopped |
| 2 Dessert apples, peeled, cored and chopped |
| 1 Carrot, chopped |
| 1 Turnip, chopped |
| 1 Bunch of parsley or other herbs, chopped |
| 15 ml/1 tbsp Curry powder |
| 50 g/2 oz Plain flour |
| 10 ml/2 tsp Curry paste |
| 1.2 litres/2 pts Vegetable Stock (page 24) |
| 30 ml/2 tbsp Tomato purée |
| Cayenne pepper |
| Salt |
| 1½ Lemons |
| 225 g/8 oz Long-grain rice |
| 600 ml/1 pt Water |

Melt the butter or margarine and fry the bacon until soft. Remove from the pan, then fry the onions, apples, carrot, turnip and herbs until soft. Blend the curry powder, flour and curry paste and stir into the vegetables. Add the stock and tomato purée, season to taste with cayenne pepper and salt and bring to the boil. Squeeze the juice from half a lemon and quarter the remainder. Add the lemon juice to the soup.

Meanwhile, cook the rice in the boiling salted water until tender. Drain and serve with the soup and lemon quarters.

Ham and Sweetcorn Chowder

Serves 4

25 g/1 oz Butter or margarine
1 Onion, finely chopped
45 ml/3 tbsp Plain flour
75 g/3 oz Full fat soft cheese
300 ml/½ pt Chicken Stock
  (page 24)
150 ml/¼ pt Milk
450 g/1 lb Canned sweetcorn,
  drained
Salt and pepper
150 ml/¼ pt Double cream
100 g/4 oz Ham, finely chopped

Melt the butter in a large saucepan and fry the onion until soft but not browned. Stir in the flour and cook for 1 minute. Stir in the cheese, then whisk in the stock and milk. Add the sweetcorn, season to taste with salt and pepper and simmer for 10 minutes. Stir in the cream and heat through. Sprinkle with the ham and serve with hot crusty bread.

Potage Julienne

Serves 4

25 g/1 oz Butter or margarine
1 Onion, sliced
3 Carrots, sliced
3 Celery stalks, sliced
1 Turnip, chopped
1.75 litres/3 pts Chicken Stock
  (page 24)
Salt and pepper
15 g/1 tbsp Sugar
15 ml/1 tbsp Single cream

Melt the butter or margarine and fry the vegetables until golden brown. Add the stock, bring to the boil, cover and simmer for 1 hour. Purée in a food processor or blender, then return the soup to the pan, season to taste with salt, pepper and sugar, stir in the cream and reheat.

Kidney Soup

Serves 4

225 g/8 oz Kidney, skinned and
  cored
25 g/1 oz Butter or margarine
1 Onion, chopped
5 ml/1 tsp Tomato purée
1 Carrot, chopped
1 Potato, chopped
900 ml/1½ pts Beef Stock
  (page 24)
1 Bay leaf
Salt and pepper
3 drops of Worcestershire
  sauce

Soak the kidneys in water for 1 hour, then drain and dice. Melt the butter or margarine and fry the onion until browned. Stir in the tomato purée and add the carrot, potato, stock, kidney slices and bay leaf. Bring to the boil, cover and simmer for about 1 hour until tender. Season to taste with salt, pepper and Worcestershire sauce. Purée in a food processor or blender, then return the soup to the pan to reheat.

Mushroom Soup

Serves 4

225 g/8 oz Mushrooms, diced

1 Celery stalk

1.2 litres/2 pts Vegetable Stock
(page 24)

600 ml/1 pt Milk

Salt and pepper

15 ml/1 tbsp Plain flour

Place the mushrooms, celery and stock in a large saucepan, bring to the boil and simmer for 15 minutes until the vegetables are tender. Remove the celery. Reserve 15 ml/ 1 tbsp milk, stir the rest into the soup and season to taste with salt and pepper. Bring back to the boil. Mix the flour and the reserved milk to a paste, stir into the soup and simmer for 3 minutes before serving.

French Onion Soup

Serves 4

50 g/2 oz Butter or margarine

3 Large onions, sliced

100 g/4 oz Bacon, rinded and
chopped

2 Potatoes, chopped

1.2 litres/2 pts Beef Stock
(page 24)

Salt and pepper

50 g/2 oz Cheese, grated

2.5 ml/½ tsp French mustard

2.5 ml/½ tsp Mixed herbs

½ loaf French bread, sliced

Melt the butter or margarine and fry the onions until golden brown. Add the bacon, potatoes and stock, bring to the boil, cover and simmer for 15 minutes. Season to taste with salt and pepper.

Meanwhile, mix together the cheese, mustard and herbs and season to taste with salt and pepper. Spread the mixture on the bread slices and toast under the grill until golden brown. Float the bread on top of the soup to serve.

Oxtail Soup

Serves 4

50 g/2 oz Lard

1 Oxtail, jointed

1 Onion, chopped

1 Carrot, chopped

1.2 litres/2 pts Beef Stock
(page 24)

6 Peppercorns

Salt and pepper

5 ml/1 tsp Lemon juice

15 ml/1 tbsp Plain flour
(optional)

Melt the lard and brown the oxtail. Remove the joints to a large saucepan and fry the onion and carrot until browned. Add to the saucepan with the stock and peppercorns, bring to the boil, cover and simmer gently for 5 hours. Strain the soup and skim off all the fat. Return to the pan, season to taste with salt, pepper and lemon juice and reheat. If necessary, mix the flour with a little water, then stir it into the soup and simmer for 2 minutes to thicken it.

Creamy Pea Soup

Serves 4

25 g/1 oz Butter or margarine
4 Spring onions, chopped
100 g/4 oz Bacon, chopped
450 g/1 lb Peas
1.2 litres/2 pts Vegetable Stock
  (page 24)
25 g/1 oz Parsley, chopped
6 Mint leaves, chopped
Salt and freshly ground black
  pepper
Mint leaves to garnish

Melt the butter or margarine and fry the onions and bacon until soft but not browned. Add the peas, stock, parsley and mint, bring to the boil, cover and simmer gently for about 30 minutes. Purée in a food processor or blender, then return the soup to the pan, season to taste with salt and pepper and reheat. Serve garnished with mint leaves.

Split Pea Soup

Serves 4

675 g/1½ lb Split peas, soaked
  overnight then drained
2 Onions, chopped
1 Carrot, chopped
½ Turnip, chopped
1 Celery stalk, chopped
2 Sprigs parsley, chopped
2.25 litres/4 pts Vegetable Stock
  (page 24)
Salt and pepper
150 ml/¼ pt Single cream

Place the peas in a large saucepan with the onions, carrot, turnip, celery, parsley and stock. Bring to the boil, cover and simmer for about 30 minutes until the vegetables are soft. Purée in a food processor or blender, then return the soup to the pan. Season to taste with salt and pepper, stir in the cream and reheat.

Pumpkin Soup

Serves 4

675 g/1½ lb Pumpkin, diced
600 ml/1 pt Water
600 ml/1 pt Milk
25 g/1 oz Butter or margarine
Salt and pepper
15 g/1 tbsp Sugar
15 ml/1 tbsp Chopped parsley
Fried bread croûtons (page 28)

Place the pumpkin and water in a saucepan, bring to the boil, cover and simmer for about 20 minutes until tender. Strain off the water and purée the pumpkin, then return it to the pan with the milk and butter or margarine and season to taste with salt and pepper. Bring back to the boil and simmer for a few minutes. Stir in the sugar and sprinkle with parsley just before serving with the croûtons.

Creamy Rice and Celery Soup

Serves 4

50 g/2 oz Butter or margarine
2 Spanish onions, thinly sliced
3 Celery stalks, chopped
30 ml/2 tbsp Long-grain rice
600 ml/1 pt Water
900 ml/1½ pts Milk, boiling
30 ml/2 tbsp Chopped parsley
Salt and pepper

Melt half the butter or margarine and fry the onions and celery until soft but not browned. Stir in the rice and water, bring to the boil, cover and simmer for 1 hour, stirring frequently. When the rice is quite tender, add the boiling milk and parsley and season to taste with salt and pepper. Bring back to the boil and simmer for a further 5 minutes, then stir in the remaining butter.

Tomato Soup

Serves 4

25 g/1 oz Butter or margarine
2 Onions, chopped
1 Celery stalk, chopped
1 kg/2 lb Tomatoes, skinned and chopped
2 Carrots, chopped
1.75 litres/3 pts Vegetable Stock (page 24)
Salt and pepper
15 ml/1 tbsp Plain flour (optional)
Fried bread croûtons (page 28)

Melt the butter or margarine and fry the onions and celery until just soft. Add the remaining vegetables and stock, bring to the boil, cover and simmer for about 30 minutes until all the vegetables are tender. Purée in a food processor or blender, then return the soup to the pan. Season to taste with salt and pepper and reheat. If the soup is not thick enough, mix the flour with a little water and stir it into the soup. Serve with croûtons.

Tomato and Barley Soup

Serves 4

25 g/1 oz Butter or margarine
1 Onion, chopped
1 Carrot, chopped
1 Celery stalk, chopped
450 g/1 lb Tomatoes, skinned and quartered
25 g/2 tbsp Crushed barley
900 ml/1½ pts Chicken Stock (page 24)
1 Bouquet garni
Salt and pepper
30 ml/2 tbsp Cream

Melt the butter or margarine and fry the onion, carrot and celery until transparent. Add the tomatoes, barley, stock and bouquet garni, cover and simmer for 45 minutes. Remove the bouquet garni and season to taste with salt and pepper. Purée in a food processor or blender, then pass the soup through a sieve. Return it to the pan to reheat and swirl in the cream before serving.

33

Tomato and Orange Soup

Serves 4

450 g/1 lb Tomatoes, halved
1 Potato, chopped
1 Carrot, chopped
Sprig of basil
900 ml/1½ pts Chicken Stock
  (page 24)
Salt and pepper
Juice of ½ orange
150 ml/¼ pt Single cream

Put the tomatoes, potato, carrot, herbs and stock in a saucepan and season to taste with salt and pepper. Bring to the boil, then simmer for 20 minutes. Purée in a food processor or blender, then return the soup to the pan and reheat, stirring in the orange juice and adjusting the seasoning if necessary. Serve hot, pouring a little cream into each dish.

Winter Vegetable Soup

Serves 4

15 ml/1 tbsp Oil
1 Onion, chopped
1 Garlic clove, chopped
1 Potato, chopped
1 Carrot, chopped
1 Leek, chopped
1 Celery stalk, chopped
45 ml/3 tbsp Sherry
900 ml/1½ pts Chicken Stock
  (page 24)
5 ml/1 tsp Mixed herbs
Salt and pepper

Heat the oil in a large saucepan and fry the onion and garlic until soft but not browned. Stir in the potato, carrot, leek and celery. Stir in the sherry and stock, season to taste with herbs, salt and pepper, bring to the boil and simmer gently for 20 minutes. Serve hot with grated cheese or croûtons.

Potage Crécy

Serves 4

50 g/2 oz Butter or margarine
1 Onion, sliced
5 Carrots, sliced
1 Turnip, diced
1 Celery stalk, sliced
1.2 litres/2 pts Vegetable Stock
  (page 24)
15 ml/1 tbsp Chopped parsley
Salt and pepper

Melt the butter or margarine and fry the onion until soft but not browned. Add the carrots, turnip and celery and fry for 5 minutes, then stir in the stock and parsley and season to taste with salt and pepper. Bring to the boil, then cover and simmer gently for 1½ hours. Adjust the seasoning if necessary and serve with crusty bread.

Watercress Soup

Serves 4

450 g/1 lb Potatoes

1.2 litres/2 pts Water

5 ml/1 tsp Salt

25 g/1 oz Butter or margarine

25 g/1 oz Plain flour

2 Bunches of watercress, leaves picked and finely chopped

Salt and pepper

Fried bread croûtons (page 28)

Place the potatoes, water and salt in a large saucepan, bring to the boil and simmer for about 15 minutes until tender. Drain and reserve the liquid, then purée the potatoes. Melt the butter or margarine and stir in the flour until smooth. Add the potato water and purée, bring to the boil, cover and simmer for about 30 minutes. Add the watercress, season to taste with salt and pepper and simmer for a further 5 minutes. Serve with fried bread croûtons.

Iced Cucumber Soup

Serves 4

15 g/½ oz Butter or margarine

1 Onion, chopped

1 Cucumber, peeled and sliced

450 ml/¾ pt Chicken Stock (page 24)

1 Egg yolk, beaten

45 ml/3 tbsp Natural yoghurt

10 ml/2 tsp Cornflour

Few mint leaves, chopped

Melt the butter or margarine and fry the onion until soft but not browned. Add the cucumber and stock, bring to the boil and simmer for 20 minutes. Beat the egg yolk, 15 ml/1 tbsp yoghurt and the cornflour until smooth. Add the hot soup and purée in a food processor or blender until smooth and creamy. Allow to cool. Pour into individual dishes and garnish with the remaining yoghurt and the chopped mint.

Jajik

Serves 4

1 Cucumber, peeled and halved

Salt and pepper

1 Garlic clove, crushed

15 ml/1 tbsp Chopped mint

2.5 ml/½ tsp Chopped fennel

5 ml/1 tsp White wine vinegar

5 ml/1 tsp Olive oil

450 ml/¾ pt Natural yoghurt

300 ml/½ pt Water

Ice cubes to garnish

Scoop the seeds out of the cucumber, chop the flesh and sprinkle with salt. Leave to stand for 1 hour, then rinse and drain well.

Mix the garlic, 5 ml/1 tsp mint, the fennel, wine vinegar, oil and yoghurt. Add just enough water to make a thin cream and fold in the cucumber. Season to taste with salt and pepper. Chill for 2 hours before serving in chilled soup bowls, sprinkled with the remaining mint and with a few ice cubes in each bowl.

Fish and Shellfish

The number of delicious fish dishes is endless, from simple grilled dishes to those baked in tasty sauces. You can experiment with your favourite types of fish.

Steaming is an ideal method for cooking fish as the fish stays whole and retains its delicious flavour. If you do not have a fish steamer, place the fish on a suitable plate with about 30 ml/2 tbsp milk and a knob of butter and cover with another plate. Rest the plates on top of a saucepan of boiling water and steam for about 15 minutes. You can use the liquor in your sauce for the fish.

Boiling fish can cause the fish to break up and lose its flavour, so you must take care if using this method. Rub the fish with lemon before cooking and add a little salt and vinegar to the water. Use a slotted spoon to remove any scum which rises to the surface and only simmer very gently otherwise the outside of the fish will break up before the inside is cooked.

Oil is best for frying fish, but should be hot before adding the fish otherwise the fish will become sodden and greasy. Do not add too much fish at a time or the temperature of the oil will drop and the fish will not be crisp.

Baking is a simple way to cook fish and is particularly suitable for whole fish. Sprinkle the fish with flour and season to taste with salt and pepper. Dot with butter and baste frequently while baking.

Prawn and Beansprout Stir-Fry

Serves 4

30 ml/2 tbsp Oil
1 Leek, sliced
50 g/2 oz Mushrooms, sliced
½ Red pepper, sliced
100 g/4 oz Shelled prawns
225 g/8 oz Beansprouts
30 ml/2 tbsp Dry sherry
Few drops of soy sauce

Heat the oil and fry the leek u
then add the mushrooms
until just browned. Add the
and fry for 2 minutes, then a
prawns and fry until browne
the beansprouts and fry
minutes, stirring well. Mix the
and soy sauce and pour into th
Stir well for 1 minute, then
immediately.

Prawns in Beer Batter

Serves 4

150 ml/¼ pt Beer
1 Egg, beaten
15 ml/1 tbsp Oil
75 g/3 oz Plain flour
Salt
Cayenne pepper
450 g/1 lb Shelled prawns
Oil for deep frying
1 Lemon, cut into wedges

Mix the beer, egg, oil and flour
together to make a smooth batter.

Season with salt and cayenne pepper.
Add a few drops of milk or some
more flour if the batter is too thick
or too thin. Leave it to stand for
5 minutes. Dip the prawns in the
batter and fry a few at a time in deep
hot oil for a few minutes until crispy
and golden brown. Drain on kitchen
paper and keep them

wn, Egg and Tomato Bake

erves 4

225 g/8 oz Shelled prawns
2 Hard-boiled eggs, sliced
4 Tomatoes, skinned and sliced
50 g/2 oz Butter or margarine
40 g/1½ oz Plain flour
00 ml/½ pt Milk, warmed
g/2 oz Cheese, grated
and pepper
/1 tbsp Single cream

rs of prawns, eggs a

. Whisk in the milk and
cook, stirring, until the sauce thickens. Remove from the heat and stir in
the cheese. Season to taste with salt
and pepper and stir in the cream.
Pour the sauce over the dish and
bake in a preheated oven at 180°C/
350°F/gas mark 4 for 15 minutes
until heated through and golden
brown on top.

37

Creole Prawns

Serves 4

45 ml/3 tbsp Oil
1 Onion, chopped
1 Green pepper, chopped
2 Celery stalks, chopped
1 Garlic clove, chopped
25 g/1 oz Plain flour
45 ml/3 tbsp Tomato purée
5 ml/1 tsp Lemon juice
2.5ml/½ tsp Worcestershire sauce
Few drops of tabasco sauce
1 Bay leaf
300 ml/½ pt Water
Salt and pepper
450 g/1 lb Shelled prawns

Heat the oil and fry the onion, pepper, celery and garlic until soft but not browned. Stir in the flour and cook for 2 minutes. Add the tomato purée, lemon juice, Worcestershire sauce, tabasco sauce, bay leaf and water. Season to taste with salt and pepper, bring to the boil and simmer for 3 minutes. Add the prawns and stir well. Simmer for about 10 minutes until cooked through. Remove the bay leaf. Serve with rice or pasta.

Variation
You can substitute the prawns with any cooked and flaked white fish.

Shrimp Jambalaya

Serves 4

4 Bacon rashers, rinded and chopped
1 Onion, sliced
½ Green pepper, diced
1 Garlic clove, crushed
75 g/3 oz Long-grain rice
300 ml/½ pt Chicken Stock (page 24)
225 g/8 oz Canned tomatoes, chopped
2.5 ml/½ tsp Chilli powder
1 Bay leaf
Salt and pepper
225 g/8 oz Shelled prawns
8 Green olives, stoned and sliced
15 ml/1 tbsp Chopped basil

Fry the bacon until crisp, then drain and set aside. Add the onion, garlic and pepper and fry gently until soft. Return the bacon to the pan with the rice and stir until the rice is coated in fat. Stir in the stock, tomatoes, chilli powder and bay leaf and season to taste with salt and pepper. Bring to the boil, cover and simmer for 20 minutes until the rice is just tender. Stir in the prawns and olives and reheat, then remove the bay leaf and serve sprinkled with basil.

Shrimp Toasts

Serves 4

5 Bread slices
100 g/4 oz Shelled shrimps
50 g/2 oz Butter or margarine
2.5 ml/½ tsp Curry paste
Pinch of coriander
3 Parsley sprigs

Break one slice of bread into bread-crumbs, flatten the others with a rolling pin then cut them into rounds and toast them lightly. Reserve a few shrimps for garnish. Chop the remainder, blend in the butter or margarine, then stir in the curry paste, breadcrumbs and coriander. Divide the mixture between the toast rounds and grill under a hot grill for 5 minutes until golden. Garnish with the reserved shrimps and the parsley.

Coquilles St Jacques

Serves 4

50 g/2 oz Breadcrumbs
12 Scallops
50 g/2 oz Butter or margarine
2 Shallots, chopped
15 ml/1 tbsp Plain flour
150 ml/¼ pt Dry white wine
150 ml/¼ pt Double cream
5 ml/1 tsp Cayenne pepper
Salt and pepper

Spread half the breadcrumbs on the base of a greased ovenproof dish. Melt half the butter or margarine and fry the scallops gently, then lay them in the dish. Fry the shallots until soft, then transfer them to the dish. Stir the flour into the pan and cook, stirring, for 1 minute. Stir in the wine and cream, bring to the boil and season to taste with cayenne pepper, salt and pepper. Cook until the sauce thickens, then pour it over the scallops and top with the remaining breadcrumbs. Dot with the remaining butter and bake in a preheated oven at 190°C/375°F/gas mark 5 for 20 minutes.

Moules Marinière

Serves 4

1.75 kg/4 lb Mussels
Pepper
1 Parsley sprig
1 Thyme sprig
2 Shallots, chopped
150 ml/¼ pt Dry white wine
15 ml/1 tbsp Chopped parsley
100 g/4 oz Butter or margarine
1 Garlic clove, crushed

Scrape and beard the mussels and wash them in several changes of water. Put them in a large saucepan with pepper to taste, the parsley, thyme and shallots. Add the wine, bring to the boil, stir well, cover and heat until the mussels open. Discard any that do not open. Transfer the mussels to a warmed serving dish and keep them warm. Boil the liquor until reduced by half, then stir in the parsley, butter or margarine and garlic. When the butter has melted, pour over the mussels and serve hot.

Angels on Horseback

Serves 4

24 Oysters
24 Bacon rashers
15 g/½ oz Plain flour
Salt
1 Egg, separated
15 g/½ oz Butter or margarine,
  melted
Oil for deep frying
4 Sprigs of parsley
2 Lemons, cut into wedges

Open the oysters and free them from the shells, then roll each one in a rasher of bacon. Mix the flour and salt, add the egg yolk and butter or margarine, beat well and leave to stand for 30 minutes. Just before it is needed, beat the egg white stiffly and fold it into the batter. Pick up each oyster on a skewer, dip into the batter and fry in deep hot oil for a few minutes until golden brown. Drain well and garnish with parsley and lemon wedges.

Note
You can use frozen or canned oysters for this recipe.

Oyster Patties

Serves 4

225 g/8 oz Puff Pastry (page 146)
12 Oysters
15 g/½ oz Plain flour
Salt and pepper
25 g/1 oz Butter or margarine
120 ml/ 4 fl oz Single cream
5 ml/1 tsp Lemon juice

Roll out the pastry and make into 12 small pastry cases. Fill with grease-proof paper and baking beans and bake in a preheated oven at 220°C/425°F/gas mark 7 for 10 minutes.
  Meanwhile, open the oysters and free them from their shells. Beard them, cut the oysters into small pieces and drain the liquor into a saucepan. Add the flour and season to taste with salt and pepper. Add the butter or margarine, bring to the boil and simmer for 3 minutes. Remove from the heat and stir in the cream, lemon juice and oysters. Return to the heat and heat gently for 5 minutes but do not boil. Pour the mixture into the hot pastry cases and serve.

Note
You can use frozen or canned oysters for this recipe.

Dressed Crab

Serves 4

1 Crab

10 ml/2 tsp Vinegar

50 g/2 oz Breadcrumbs

Pinch of nutmeg

25 g/1 oz Butter or margarine, cut into pieces

Salt and pepper

Remove the meat from the shell, clean the shell well and mix the meat with the other ingredients, seasoning to taste with the salt and pepper. Return the mixture to the shell and bake in a preheated oven at 190°C/375°F/gas mark 5 for about 15 minutes.

Variation

For a cold dish, omit the bread-crumbs and add 15 ml/1 tbsp oil and a little white pepper.

Janson's Temptation

Serves 4

50 g/2 oz Butter or margarine

1 Spanish onion, chopped

4 Potatoes, cut into strips

150 ml/¼ pt Single cream

150 ml/¼ pt Milk

Salt and pepper

50 g/2 oz Canned anchovy fillets, drained

50 g/2 oz Breadcrumbs

Heat the butter or margarine and fry the onion until soft but not browned. Add the potatoes and fry for 3 minutes,

stirring well. Stir in the cream and milk and season to taste with a very little salt and some pepper. Simmer gently for 5 minutes until the potatoes begin to soften. Transfer half the mixture to a shallow oven-proof dish, arrange the anchovy fillets over the top, cover with the remaining potato mixture and sprinkle on the breadcrumbs. Bake in a preheated oven at 200°C/400°F/gas mark 6 for 20 minutes until well cooked through and crispy on top.

Fish Cakes

Serves 4

225 g/8 oz Cooked white fish, flaked

225 g/8 oz Mashed potatoes

15 ml/1 tbsp Finely chopped parsley

Few drops of lemon juice

Few drops of anchovy essence

Salt and pepper

1 Egg, beaten

Plain flour

100 g/4 oz Breadcrumbs

Oil for frying

Mix the fish with the potatoes and parsley and season to taste with lemon juice, anchovy essence, salt and pepper. Bind with a little beaten egg. Turn on to a floured board and form into flat patties. Coat with egg and breadcrumbs and fry in hot oil until golden brown on both sides.

Cod in Golden Sauce

Serves 4

25 g/1 oz Butter or margarine
15 g/½ oz Plain flour
300 ml/½ pt Milk
15 ml/1 tbsp French mustard
15 ml/1 tbsp Vinegar
10 ml/2 tsp Sugar
Salt and pepper
450 g/1 lb Cooked cod fillets, flaked
4 Cooked potatoes, cubed
45 ml/3 tbsp Oil
4 Bread slices, cubed

Melt the butter or margarine, stir in the flour and cook for 1 minute. Whisk in the milk and cook, stirring, until the sauce thickens. Remove from the heat and stir in the mustard, vinegar and sugar and season to taste with salt and pepper. Stir in the cod and potatoes, return to the heat and gently heat through. Heat the oil and fry the bread until crispy and golden. Pour the cod mixture on to a warmed serving plate and garnish with the croûtons.

Family Fish Pie

Serves 4

750 g/1½ lb Potatoes, cubed
300 ml/½ pt Milk
50 g/2 oz Butter or margarine
2.5 ml/½ tsp Nutmeg
350 g/12 oz White fish
25 g/1 oz Plain flour
15 ml/1 tbsp Chopped parsley
Salt and pepper
50 g/2 oz Shelled prawns or shrimps
1 Hard-boiled egg, chopped
25 g/1 oz Cheese, grated

Cook the potatoes in boiling salted water until tender, then drain and mash with 30 ml/2 tbsp milk, half the butter and the nutmeg. Poach the fish in 150 ml/¼ pt milk for 8 minutes then remove the fish, take off the skin and flake the flesh. Melt the remaining butter in a saucepan, stir in the flour and cook for 1 minute. Whisk in the milk in which the fish was cooked with the remaining milk and cook, stirring, until the sauce thickens. Add the parsley and season to taste with salt and pepper. Spread half the potatoes on the base of an ovenproof dish and cover with the prawns or shrimps and hard-boiled egg. Pour on the fish and sauce, sprinkle with grated cheese and pipe the remaining potato around the edge of the dish. Bake in a preheated oven at 200°C/400°F/gas mark 6 for 30 minutes until hot and lightly browned.

Cod with Mushrooms

Serves 4

| 450 g/1 lb Cod fillets, skinned |
| 275 g/10 oz Canned concentrated cream of mushroom soup |
| 15 ml/1 tbsp Milk |
| 15 ml/1 tbsp Dry sherry |
| 2.5 ml/½ tsp Cayenne pepper |
| 2.5 ml/½ tsp Mustard powder |
| Salt and pepper |

Put the fish into a greased ovenproof dish. Heat the soup, stirring in the milk, sherry, cayenne pepper and mustard and seasoning to taste with salt and pepper. Pour over the fish. Cover and bake in a preheated oven at 190°C/375°F/gas mark 5 for 25 minutes.

Variations

You can use this recipe with any white fish. Instead of the soup, you can stir 100 g/4 oz chopped mushrooms into a white sauce (page 223).

Anguilles à la Tartare

Serves 4

| 450 g/1 lb Eels, skinned and cut into 7 cm/3 in pieces |
| Water |
| Salt |
| 2 Eggs, beaten |
| 45 ml/3 tbsp Milk |
| 100 g/4 oz Breadcrumbs |
| Oil for deep frying |
| 4 Parsley sprigs |
| 150 ml/¼ pt Tartare Sauce (page 229) |

Put the eels in a saucepan and just cover with salted water. Bring to the boil and simmer for 15 minutes then leave to cool in the water. Drain and pat dry on kitchen paper. Mix the beaten eggs and milk and dip the eels in, roll in breadcrumbs and fry in deep hot oil. Drain well, garnish with parsley and serve with tartare sauce.

Creole Fishcakes

Serves 4

| 450 g/1 lb Cooked haddock, flaked |
| 15 g/½ oz Butter or margarine, melted |
| 225 g/8 oz Breadcrumbs |
| 1 Large onion, chopped |
| 1 Garlic clove, crushed |
| 15 ml/1 tbsp Chopped parsley |
| 5 ml/½ tsp Thyme |
| 1 Egg, beaten |
| 45 ml/3 tbsp Oil |
| 4 Watercress sprigs |

Mix the haddock, butter or margarine, 125 g/5 oz breadcrumbs, onion, garlic, parsley and thyme. Add a little milk if the mixture does not bind together. Shape into small round flat cakes and coat with egg, then breadcrumbs. Heat the oil and fry the cakes until cooked through and crispy on both sides. Serve garnished with watercress.

Seafood Soufflé

Serves 4

225 g/8 oz Haddock
150 ml/¼ pt Milk
15 g/½ oz Butter or margarine
15 g/½ oz Plain flour
Salt and pepper
3 Eggs, separated
100 g/4 oz Shelled prawns
15 g/½ oz Breadcrumbs
25 g/1 oz Cheese, grated

Poach the haddock in the milk for 8 minutes, remove the fish, take off the skin and flake the flesh. Melt the butter or margarine in a saucepan, stir in the flour and cook for 1 minute. Whisk in the milk in which the fish was cooked, season to taste with salt and pepper and cook, stirring, until the sauce thickens. Remove from the heat and beat in the egg yolks, then add the haddock and prawns. Whisk the egg whites until stiff, fold them into the sauce, then pour it into a greased 18 cm/7 in soufflé dish. Sprinkle with breadcrumbs and cheese and bake in a preheated oven at 200°C/400°F/gas mark 6 for 30 minutes until well risen and golden brown. Serve immediately.

Note
You can use any variety of white or smoked white fish for this recipe.

Tomato Fish Bake

Serves 4

450 g/1 lb Haddock fillet, skinned
50 g/2 oz Breadcrumbs
50 g/2 oz Cheese, grated
1 Onion, chopped
2.5 ml/½ tsp Mixed herbs
Salt and pepper
350 ml/12 fl oz Milk
25 g/1 oz Butter or margarine
50 g/2 oz Mushrooms, sliced
25 g/1 oz Plain flour
30 ml/2 tbsp Tomato purée
5 ml/1 tsp Lemon juice
Pinch of sugar
450 g/1 lb Potatoes, peeled and
    chopped
15 ml/1 tbsp Chopped parsley

Flake half the fish over the base of a greased shallow ovenproof dish. Mix the breadcrumbs, cheese, onion and herbs and season to taste with salt and pepper. Bind with 45 ml/3 tbsp milk, spread over the fish and cover with the remaining fish. Melt the butter or margarine and fry the mushrooms until soft. Add the flour, remaining milk, tomato purée, lemon juice and sugar and season to taste with salt and pepper. Bring to the boil, stirring, and simmer until the sauce thickens. Pour over the fish and bake in a preheated oven at 190°C/375°F/gas mark 5 for 20 minutes.

Meanwhile, cook the potatoes in boiling, salted water until tender. Drain and mash. Pipe a border of mashed potato around the dish and return it to the oven or place under the grill to brown. Serve garnished with parsley.

St Peter's Pie

Serves 4

450 ml/¾ pt Milk
1 Bay leaf
2.5 ml/½ tsp Nutmeg
2.5 ml/½ tsp Ground mace
225 g/8 oz Cod fillet
225 g/8 oz Smoked haddock fillet
50 g/2 oz Butter or margarine
15 g/½ tbsp Plain flour
Salt and pepper
15 ml/1 tbsp Olive oil
30 ml/2 tbsp Double cream
1 Garlic clove, crushed
2 Hard-boiled eggs, sliced
25 g/1 oz Parmesan cheese, grated
25 g/1 oz Gruyère cheese, grated

Bring the milk to the boil with the bay leaf, a pinch of nutmeg and the mace. Place the fish in a casserole and pour over the milk. Cover and cook in a preheated oven at 180°C/350°F/gas mark 4 for 30 minutes. Strain and reserve the cooking liquor. Remove the bones and skin from the fish and flake the flesh. Melt half the butter or margarine, stir in the flour and cook for 1 minute. Whisk in 300 ml/½ pt of the milk and cook, stirring, until the sauce thickens. Add a pinch of nutmeg and season to taste. Leave the sauce to keep warm, stirring occasionally. Stir the remaining butter and the oil into the fish, followed by the cream, garlic and 45ml/3 tbsp of the milk. Season to taste with salt and pepper, transfer the mixture to a pie dish and cover with the hard-boiled eggs. Fold the cheese into the sauce, pour it over the fish and bake in a preheated oven at 220°C/425°F/gas mark 7 for 5 minutes until the top is golden brown.

Orange Halibut

Serves 4

4 Halibut Steaks
600 ml/1 pt Fish Stock (page 24)
15 g/½ oz Butter or margarine
15 ml/1 tbsp Oil
1 Onion, chopped
150 ml/¼ pt Frozen concentrated orange juice
5 ml/1 tsp Tarragon
15 ml/1 tbsp Chopped parsley
Salt and pepper
10 ml/2 tsp Cornflour
15 ml/1 tbsp Water
150 ml/¼ pt Soured cream
1 Orange, peeled and sliced

Place the halibut in a greased flame-proof dish, pour over the fish stock, bring to the boil and poach for 10 minutes. Transfer the fish to a warmed serving dish, remove the skin and bones and keep it warm. Reserve 150 ml/¼ pt of the cooking liquor. Heat the butter or margarine and oil and fry the onion until soft, then stir in the orange juice, fish liquor and herbs and season to taste with salt and pepper. Bring to the boil and simmer for 4 minutes. Mix the cornflour with the water, stir it into the sauce and cook, stirring, until the sauce thickens. Remove from the heat and stir in the soured cream, then pour the sauce over the halibut and serve garnished with the orange slices.

Soused Herrings

Serves 4

6 Herrings
Salt and pepper
1 Bay leaf
2 Cloves
10 Peppercorns
150 ml/¼ pt Water
150 ml/¼ pt Vinegar

Bone the herrings, sprinkle with salt and pepper and roll up, skin side outwards. Place the herrings in an ovenproof dish just large enough to hold them. Sprinkle over the bay leaf, cloves and peppercorns and add enough water and vinegar to cover. Cover and bake in a preheated oven at 160°C/325°F/gas mark 3 for 30 minutes.

Variation
You can also use mackerel for this dish.

Mackerel with Gooseberry Sauce

Serves 4

50 g/2 oz Breadcrumbs
15 ml/1 tbsp Chopped parsley
Grated rind of 1 lemon
1 Egg, beaten
Pinch of nutmeg
Salt and pepper
4 Mackerel, boned
50 g/2 oz Butter or margarine, melted
225 g/8 oz Gooseberries
45 ml/3 tbsp Water
50 g/2 oz Sugar

Mix the breadcrumbs, parsley, lemon rind, egg and nutmeg and season to taste with salt and pepper. Stuff the mackerel with the stuffing, roll them up and secure with cocktail sticks. Place the fish in a greased ovenproof dish, brush with half the butter, cover and bake in a preheated oven at 190°C/375°F/gas mark 5 for 30 minutes. Cook the gooseberries with the water, sugar and remaining butter until they pop open. Purée and rub through a sieve, then return to the pan to heat through. Transfer the fish on to a warmed serving dish and pour on the sauce.

Baked Mackerel in Mustard

Serves 4

4 Mackerel
15 g/½ oz Plain flour
25 g/1 oz Butter or margarine
10 ml/2 tsp Prepared mustard
30 ml/2 tbsp White wine vinegar
30 ml/2 tbsp Water
Salt and pepper

Clean the fish and lay them side by side in a greased ovenproof dish. Mix the mustard, wine vinegar and water and pour them over the fish. Season to taste with salt and pepper and dot with the remaining butter. Cover and bake in a preheated oven at 190°C/375°F/gas mark 5 for about 30 minutes, basting occasionally.

Variation
You can also use herring for this recipe, but reduce the cooking time by about 10 minutes.

Plaice and Cucumber Sauce

Serves 4

50 g/2 oz Butter or margarine
30 ml/2 tbsp Anchovy paste
750 g/1½ lb Plaice fillets
1 Small cucumber, diced
5 ml/1 tsp Chopped dill
275 g/10 oz Condensed mushroom
  soup
60 ml/4 tbsp Natural yoghurt
1 Tomato, skinned, seeded and
  chopped
Salt and pepper

Melt the butter or margarine, add the anchovy paste and plaice and fry until the fish is golden brown. Combine the remaining ingredients, season to taste with salt and pepper and spoon the mixture over the fish. Cover and cook gently for 5 minutes. Transfer the plaice to a warmed serving dish and pour over the sauce.

Plaice with Cream and Mushrooms

Serves 4

4 Plaice fillets
225 g/8 oz Mushrooms, sliced
10 ml/2 tsp Lemon juice
Salt and pepper
25 g/1 oz Butter
150 ml/¼ pt Single cream

Arrange the plaice in a greased flameproof dish. Place the mushrooms on top, pour over the lemon juice and season to taste with salt and pepper. Dot with butter and bake in a preheated oven at 180°C/ 350°F/gas mark 4 for 30 minutes, basting frequently. When ready to serve, pour the cream over the top and brown under a hot grill.

Goujons of Plaice with Sauce Tartare

Serves 4

120 g/4½ oz Plain flour
1 Egg, separated
15 ml/1 tbsp Oil
Salt and pepper
300 ml/½ pt Milk
450 g/1 lb Plaice, skinned and cut
  into strips
Oil for deep-frying
150 ml/¼ pt Tartare Sauce
  (page 229)

Reserve 15 g/½ oz flour and whisk the remainder with the egg yolk, oil, a pinch of salt and the milk to a batter. Whisk the egg white until frothy and fold it into the batter. Season the reserved flour with salt and pepper and roll the strips of plaice in it. Dip the fish in the batter and fry in deep hot oil for 5 minutes until crisp. Drain well on kitchen paper and serve with the tartare sauce.

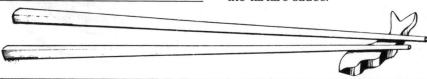

47

Salmon Cheesecake

Serves 4-6

150 g/5 oz Wholemeal biscuits, crushed	
25 g/1 oz Rolled oats, toasted	
75 g/3 oz Butter or margarine, melted	
100 g/4 oz Low fat curd cheese	
100 g/4 oz Tofu	
60 ml/4 tbsp Oil	
15 ml/1 tbsp Lemon juice	
150 ml/¼ pt Natural yoghurt	
3 Eggs, separated	
200 g/7 oz Canned pink salmon, drained	
15 g/½ oz Gelatine	
15 ml/1 tbsp Water	
Salt and pepper	
½ Lemon, sliced	
¼ Cucumber, sliced	

Mix the biscuits and oats and stir in the butter or margarine. Press into a 23 cm/9 in loose-bottomed flan ring. Beat together the cheese, tofu, oil, lemon juice, yoghurt, egg yolks and salmon. Dissolve the gelatine in the water over a pan of hot water, then stir it into the salmon mixture. Whisk the egg whites until stiff, then fold them into the mixture. Season to taste with salt and pepper, pour into the flan case and chill until firm. When set, remove from the flan ring and decorate with the cucumber and lemon slices.

Salmon Mould with White Butter Sauce

Serves 4

225 g/8 oz Cooked salmon, flaked	
2 Eggs, beaten	
25 g/1 oz Butter or margarine, melted	
15 g/½ oz Breadcrumbs	
1 Shallot, finely chopped	
30 ml/2 tbsp Vinegar	
100 g/4 oz Butter or margarine, cut into pieces	

Mix the fish with the eggs, butter or margarine and breadcrumbs and turn into a greased fish mould. Cover with greased greaseproof paper and steam slowly for about 1 hour until the mixture is quite firm.

Meanwhile, mix the shallot and vinegar and simmer gently until most of the liquid has evaporated. Add the butter or margarine, a piece at a time, stirring continuously until the sauce thickens. Carefully turn out the salmon mould on to a warmed serving plate, pour over the sauce and serve immediately.

Cheesy Salmon Bake

Serves 4

225 g/8 oz Cooked salmon, flaked

Salt and pepper

50 g/2 oz Butter or margarine

300 ml/½ pt Béchamel Sauce
  (page 225)

50 g/2 oz Breadcrumbs

100 g/4 oz Cheese, grated

Season the salmon to taste with salt and pepper and place the fish in a well greased ovenproof dish, then cover with the béchamel sauce. Mix together the breadcrumbs and cheese and sprinkle over the top. Dot with the remaining butter and bake in a preheated oven at 190°C/375°F/gas mark 5 for 20 minutes until heated through and browned on top.

Salmon Croquettes

Serves 4

450 g/1 lb Canned salmon, finely
  flaked

300 ml/½ pt White Sauce
  (page 223)

5 ml/1 tsp Worcestershire sauce

Salt and pepper

1 Egg, beaten

100 g/4 oz Breadcrumbs

Oil for deep-frying

Mix the salmon with just enough sauce to make a thick mixture and season to taste with Worcestershire sauce, salt and pepper. Shape into croquettes. Dip in egg, then breadcrumbs and fry in deep hot oil for about 4 minutes until crispy and golden brown.

Baked Sole Layer

Serves 4

75 g/3 oz Butter, melted

100 g/4 oz Mushrooms, chopped

15 ml/1 tbsp Chopped parsley

Salt and pepper

4 Sole fillets

120 ml/4 fl oz Fish Stock (page 24)

2.5 ml/½ tsp Lemon juice

50 g/2 oz Breadcrumbs

1 Lemon, sliced

Melt 50 g/2 oz butter and pour it into an ovenproof dish. Sprinkle with half the mushrooms and parsley and season to taste with salt and pepper. Lay the sole on top and cover with the remaining mushrooms and parsley. Season again. Pour over the stock, add the lemon juice and sprinkle with breadcrumbs. Dot with the remaining butter and bake in a preheated oven at 180°C/350°F/gas mark 4 for about 30 minutes until well browned. Serve garnished with slices of lemon.

Sole with Grated Cheese

Serves 4

75 g/3 oz Butter or margarine
15 ml/1 tbsp Chopped parsley
Few drops of anchovy essence
1 Onion, chopped
1 Large sole
2 Tomatoes, sliced
50 g/2 oz Breadcrumbs
100 g/4 oz Cheese, grated

Mix 50 g/2 oz butter with the parsley, anchovy essence and half the onion. Cut the sole down the centre and separate the flesh from the backbone. Stuff with the butter mixture and lay the fish in a greased ovenproof dish. Scatter over the remaining onion and cover with sliced tomatoes. Mix the breadcrumbs and cheese and sprinkle them over the top. Dot with the remaining butter and bake in a preheated oven at 180°C/350°F/gas mark 4 for about 20 minutes until cooked through and golden brown on top.

Sole with White Grapes

Serves 4

4 Sole fillets
Salt and pepper
16 Seedless white grapes
25 g/1 oz Butter or margarine
15 g/½ oz Plain flour
150 ml/¼ pt Milk
150 ml/¼ pt Single cream
50 g/2 oz Cheese, grated

Season the sole with salt and pepper, lay the grapes along the top, roll up as tightly as possible and secure with cocktail sticks. Place the sole in a greased ovenproof dish. Melt the butter or margarine in a saucepan, stir in the flour and cook for 1 minute. Whisk in the milk and cream and cook, stirring, until the sauce thickens, then remove from the heat and stir in the cheese. Pour the sauce over the sole and bake in a preheated oven at 180°C/350°F/gas mark 4 for 30 minutes.

Sole Provençale

Serves 4

4 Sole fillets
Salt and pepper
Pinch of nutmeg
30 ml/2 tbsp Chopped parsley
50 g/2 oz Butter or margarine
15 ml/1 tbsp Oil
150 ml/¼ pt Dry white wine
4 Onions, sliced
5 ml/1 tsp Lemon juice

Season the sole with salt and pepper, nutmeg and half the parsley. Place in an ovenproof dish, dot with half the butter or margarine and pour over the wine. Cover and bake in a preheated oven at 180°C/350°F/gas mark 4 for 30 minutes.

Meanwhile, heat the remaining butter and oil and fry the onions until golden brown. Drain well on kitchen paper. Arrange the onions round the fish and serve sprinkled with the remaining parsley and the lemon juice.

Polish Sole

Serves 4

4 Sole fillets
150 ml/¼ pt Dry white wine
150 ml/¼ pt Fish Stock (page 24)
450 g/1 litre Potatoes, sliced
2 Egg Yolks
50 g/2 oz Butter or margarine
15 g/½ oz Plain flour
150 ml/¼ pt Milk
4 Lobster meat slices
50 g/2 oz Parmesan cheese, grated
4 Truffle slices

Place the sole in a saucepan. Mix the wine and stock and pour just enough into the pan to cover the fish. Bring to the boil, cover and simmer gently for 15 minutes until the fish is cooked, then drain the fish and keep it warm, reserving the liquor.

Meanwhile, cook the potatoes in boiling salted water until tender then drain and mash them with the egg yolks and half the butter or margarine. Melt the remaining butter or margarine, stir in the flour and cook for 1 minute. Whisk in the milk and 150 ml/¼ pt cooking liquor and cook, stirring, until the sauce thickens. Pipe the potato in swirls round the edge of an oval flameproof serving dish and spoon a little of the sauce into the centre. Lay the fish on top and place a slice of lobster meat on top of each. Pour over the remaining sauce, sprinkle with cheese and brown under a hot grill. Serve with a truffle slice on each piece of lobster.

Skate with Egg and Lemon Sauce

Serves 4

For the Court Bouillon:
2 Carrots, chopped
1 Onion, chopped
2 Celery stalks, chopped
2 Shallots, chopped
1 Bay leaf
3 Parsley sprigs
2 Thyme sprigs
30 ml/2 tbsp Lemon juice
300 ml/½ pt Dry white wine
750 ml/1¼ pts Water
Salt and pepper

450 g/1 lb Skate
2 Egg yolks
Juice of one lemon

Place all the court bouillon ingredients in a large saucepan, bring to the boil, cover and simmer for 15 minutes, then leave to cool slightly. Strain enough over the skate in a clean saucepan to almost cover the fish, bring back to the boil and simmer gently for 10 minutes until the fish is cooked.

Meanwhile, reheat the remaining strained court bouillon. Beat the egg yolks and lemon juice and pour on a little of the court bouillon, beating all the time. Stir the egg mixture into 30 ml/½ pt court bouillon and heat, stirring, until it thickens, but do not let the mixture boil. Arrange the fish on a warmed serving dish and pour over the sauce.

Skate in Wine

Serves 4

450 g/1 lb Skate wings
2 Shallots, chopped
1 Onion, sliced
Salt and pepper
50 g/2 oz Mushrooms, sliced
30 ml/2 tbsp Chopped parsley
150 ml/¼ pt Dry white wine
15 g/½ oz Butter or margarine
15 ml/1 tbsp Plain flour
50 g/2 oz Breadcrumbs

Skin the skate and cut it into pieces. Put it in a greased flameproof dish, sprinkle with the shallots and onion and season to taste with salt and pepper. Mix the mushrooms and half the parsley with the wine and add it to the dish. Cover and bake in a preheated oven at 180°C/350°F/gas mark 4 for 45 minutes. Transfer the fish to a warmed serving dish and keep it warm. Mix the butter or margarine and flour together and stir it into the sauce, heating gently until the sauce thickens. Pour the sauce over the fish and sprinkle with the breadcrumbs. Brown under a hot grill and serve sprinkled with the remaining parsley.

Trout with Almonds

Serves 4

4 Trout
50 g/2 oz Butter or margarine
50 g/2 oz Flaked almonds
60 ml/4 tbsp Lemon juice
Pepper
4 Watercress sprigs

Make 3 slits in the skin of the trout on each side, dot with butter or margarine and grill for about 10 minutes, turning once. Transfer the fish to a warmed serving dish and keep them warm.

Pour the butter from the grill into a frying pan. Add the almonds and a little extra butter if needed. Fry gently until the almonds begin to brown. Add the lemon juice and pepper and pour over the fish. Serve garnished with watercress.

Tuna Parcels

Serves 4

225 g/8 oz Plain flour
Pinch of salt
50 g/2 oz Butter or margarine
50 g/2 oz Lard
45 ml/3 tbsp Water
100 g/4 oz Canned tuna fish, drained
15 ml/1 tbsp Tomato purée
15 ml/1 tbsp Worcestershire sauce
Salt and pepper

Mix the flour and salt, then rub in the fats until the mixture resembles fine breadcrumbs. Stir in just enough water to mix to a smooth pastry. Chill. Mix the remaining ingredients together well and season to taste with salt and pepper. Roll out the pastry and cut into small squares. Place spoonfuls of the mixture on to each square, damp the edges and seal into triangles. Place the triangles on a greased baking sheet and bake in a preheated oven at 200°C/400°F/gas mark 6 for 20 minutes until golden brown.

Tuna Fish Curry

Serves 4

4 Tuna steaks
Salt and pepper
15 ml/1 tbsp Olive oil
50 g/2 oz Canned anchovy fillets, drained
50 g/2 oz Butter or margarine
2 Bananas, sliced
15 ml/1 tbsp Plain flour
15 ml/1 tbsp Curry powder
300 ml/½ pt Fish Stock (page 24)
15 ml/1 tbsp Chopped parsley

Lay the tuna in a greased shallow flameproof dish, season with salt and pepper and pour over the oil. Arrange the anchovies on top, cover and bake in a preheated oven at 190°C/375°F/gas mark 5 for 25 minutes.

Meanwhile, melt the butter or margarine and fry the bananas until soft. Arrange the cooked fish on a warmed serving plate, place the bananas round the edge and keep them warm. Stir the flour and curry powder into the pan and cook, stirring, for 2 minutes, then stir in the stock, bring to the boil and cook, stirring, until the sauce thickens. Pour the sauce over the fish and serve sprinkled with parsley.

Tuna and Cashew Casserole

Serves 4

50 g/2 oz Butter or margarine
2 Spring onions, chopped
6 Celery stalks, chopped
200 g/7 oz Canned tuna, drained and flaked
275 g/10 oz Canned mushroom soup
250 ml/8 fl oz Natural yoghurt
225 g/8 oz Chinese noodles
100 g/4 oz Cashew nuts, chopped

Melt the butter or margarine and fry the onions and celery until soft but not browned. Stir in the tuna, soup and yoghurt and transfer to an ovenproof casserole. Cover and cook in a preheated oven at 180°C/350°F/gas mark 4 for 30 minutes.

Meanwhile, cook the noodles in plenty of boiling salted water for 5 minutes until half cooked. Drain well. Spread the noodles over the fish mixture and sprinkle with the cashews. Reduce the heat to 160°C/325°F/gas mark 3 and cook for a further 15 minutes.

Sweet and Sour Fish Kebabs

Serves 4

60 ml/4 tbsp Clear honey
30 ml/2 tbsp Lemon juice
15 ml/1 tbsp Soy sauce
Pinch of chilli powder
750 g/1½ lb Whiting or red mullet fillets
2 Onions, sliced
4 Courgettes, sliced
1 Lemon, sliced

Warm the honey, lemon juice, soy sauce and chilli powder in a saucepan. Cut the fish into 4 cm/1½ in slices, then thread the fish, onions, courgettes and lemon alternately on 4 skewers. Lay them in a shallow dish and pour the marinade over them. Leave for 30 minutes, turning occasionally.

Remove the skewers from the marinade and grill under a medium grill for 15 minutes, basting with the marinade and turning frequently.

Creamy Whiting

Serves 4

4 Small whiting
15 g/½ oz Plain flour
50 g/2 oz Butter or margarine
2 Spring onions, chopped
15 ml/1 tbsp Chopped parsley
150 ml/¼ pt Milk
30 ml/2 tbsp Double cream
Salt and pepper
1 Lemon, cut into wedges

Dust the fish with flour. Melt the butter or margarine and fry the fish for 10 minutes, turning once. Mix the onion, parsley, milk and cream and season to taste with salt and pepper. Pour the sauce over the fish, bring to the boil and cook for 5 minutes, stirring gently to avoid breaking up the fish. Transfer the fish to a warmed serving dish and pour over the sauce. Serve garnished with lemon wedges.

Beef

Many cuts of beef are expensive, and as most of us are trying to cut down on red meats, it makes sense to make the best of beef when you do eat it by preparing and cooking it carefully. Choose a good quality beef for any quick-cook recipes; recipes which demand a long slow cooking time will benefit from the cheaper cuts. Trim the meat well before cooking to avoid excess fat. When choosing minced beef, select those with a lower fat content, or buy from a quality butcher where you can see the meat he puts into his mince.

Stilton Steaks

Serves 4

100 g/4 oz Stilton cheese, crumbled
25 g/1 oz Butter or margarine, softened
50 g/2 oz Walnuts, finely chopped
Salt and pepper
4 Sirloin steaks

Mix the cheese, butter or margarine and walnuts and season to taste with salt and pepper. Season the steaks with pepper and grill them under a hot grill for 4 minutes each side, or until just done to your liking. Remove from the grill and press the cheese mixture over the steaks, then return to the grill for a further 1 minute until browned. Serve with new or mashed potatoes.

Mustard Steaks

Serves 4

50 g/2 oz Wholegrain mustard
15 g/½ oz Plain flour
4 Sirloin steaks
30 ml/2 tbsp Chopped parsley
30 ml/2 tbsp Chopped thyme
Salt and pepper

Mix the mustard and flour, spread on top of the steaks, and sprinkle with the herbs and season to taste with salt and pepper. Grill them under a hot grill for 10 minutes, or until done just to your liking.

Brandy Peppered Steaks

Serves 4

900 g/1½ lb Fillet steak, cut into
  4 slices
60 ml/4 tbsp Green peppercorns,
  crushed
50 g/2 oz Butter or margarine
25 g/1 oz Plain flour
250 ml/8 fl oz Beef Stock (page 24)
30 ml/2 tbsp Brandy
30 ml/2 tbsp Single cream
Salt and pepper

Press the peppercorns into the steaks. Melt the butter or margarine and fry the steaks for 4 minutes until browned on both sides and cooked to your liking. Transfer them to a warmed serving plate and keep them warm. Stir the flour into the pan and cook for 1 minute, then stir in the stock, bring to the boil and simmer for 5 minutes, stirring until the sauce thickens. Stir in the brandy and cream, season to taste with salt and pepper and cook until heated through. Pour over the steak and serve.

Peppercorn Steaks with Lemon Cream

Serves 4

4 Sirloin steaks
30 ml/2 tbsp Green peppercorns,
  crushed
50 g/2 oz Butter or margarine
Grated rind and juice of 1 lemon
15 ml/1 tbsp Chopped chives
30 ml/2 tbsp Double cream

Press the peppercorns into both sides of the steaks. Melt the butter or margarine and fry the steaks for 4 minutes on each side for medium steaks, slightly less or more if you prefer them rare or well done. Remove the steaks to a warmed serving plate and keep them warm. Add the lemon rind to the pan with 15 ml/1 tbsp lemon juice and the chives and cook until reduced slightly. Remove from the heat and stir in the cream. Pour over the steaks and serve with new potatoes.

Mushroom-Stuffed Steak

Serves 4

25 g/1 oz Butter or margarine
1 Onion, chopped
100 g/4 oz Mushrooms, finely
  chopped
50 g/2 oz Bacon, rinded and chopped
25 g/1 oz Breadcrumbs
10 ml/2 tsp Chopped parsley
5 ml/1 tsp Thyme
Salt and pepper
900 g/2 lb Rump steak

Melt the butter or margarine and fry the onion until soft but not browned. Stir in the mushrooms and bacon and cook for 3 minutes, then remove from the heat and stir in the breadcrumbs, parsley and thyme and season to taste with salt and pepper. Leave to cool.

Slit the steak in half lengthways and fill with the stuffing, then tie round with 'string. Roast in a preheated oven at 200°C/400°F/gas mark 6 for 30 minutes.

Pâté Steaks

Serves 4

4 Bread slices
40 g/2½ oz Unsalted butter
15 ml/1 tbsp Oil
4 Tournedos steaks
60 ml/4 tbsp Medium sherry
100 ml/4 fl oz Beef Stock (page 24)
60 ml/4 tbsp Brown sauce
Salt and pepper
100 g/4 oz Liver pâté, sliced into 4

Cut the bread into circles a little larger than the steaks. Heat 15 g/½ oz butter with the oil and fry the bread until crisp, then transfer to a warmed serving dish and keep them warm. Trim the steaks into neat rounds and seal them quickly on both sides then put them on top of the fried bread. Stir in the sherry, stock and sauce, bring to the boil and simmer for 4 minutes until slightly thickened, then pour into a sauce boat.

Meanwhile, melt the remaining butter in a pan and fry the liver pâté slices until browned but not melted. Place them on top of the steaks and serve with the sauce.

Flemish Steak

Serves 4

500 g/1¼ lb Frying steak, sliced
45 ml/3 tbsp Olive oil
25 g/1 oz Plain flour
Salt and pepper
2 Onions, chopped
100 g/4 oz Button mushrooms, chopped
275 g/10 oz Canned condensed onion soup
15 g/½ oz Soft brown sugar

Marinate the steak in the oil for 8 hours, then drain. Season the flour with salt and pepper and toss the steaks in the flour. Heat the oil and fry the steaks until golden brown on both sides, then transfer them to an ovenproof dish. Fry the onions until just browned, then transfer to the casserole and spread the mushrooms on top. Put the soup and sugar in the frying pan, bring to the boil and simmer for 2 minutes, stirring well to stir in all the meat juices from the pan. Pour over the steaks, cover and bake in a preheated oven at 180°C/350°F/gas mark 4 for 1 hour.

Beef Olives with Bacon Stuffing

Serves 4

50 g/2 oz Bacon, rinded and chopped

50 g/2 oz Shredded suet

100 g/4 oz Breadcrumbs

30 ml/2 tbsp Chopped parsley

2.5 ml/½ tsp Mixed herbs

Pinch of grated lemon rind

Salt and pepper

1 Egg, beaten

500 g/1¼ lb Rump steak, cut into 4 thin slices

25 g/1 oz Plain flour

25 g/1 oz Lard

1 Onion, sliced

600 ml/1 pt Beef Stock (page 24)

15 ml/1 tbsp Tomato ketchup

1 Carrot, sliced

Mix the bacon, suet, breadcrumbs, parsley, herbs and lemon rind and season to taste with salt and pepper. Bind together to a stuffing with egg. Beat the steak slices flat and leave to stand for 30 minutes. Divide the stuffing equally between them, roll up the slices round the stuffing and tie with string. Season the flour with salt and pepper and dust the rolls with the flour. Heat the lard in a flameproof casserole and fry the beef olives until browned on all sides. Remove them from the casserole and keep them warm. Fry the onion until browned, then add to the olives. Stir the remaining flour into the casserole and brown for 1 minute, stirring well to scrape up the meat juices. Stir in the stock and tomato ketchup and return the olives and onions to the casserole. Add the carrot and season to taste with salt and pepper. Cover and cook in a preheated oven at 160°C/325°F/gas mark 3 for 2 hours. Serve with mashed potato.

Beef in Red Wine

Serves 4

50 g/2 oz Butter or margarine

2 Onions, finely chopped

150 ml/¼ pt Red wine

60 ml/4 tbsp Water

5 ml/1 tsp Thyme

2 Bay leaves

4 Sirloin steaks

60 ml/4 tbsp Brandy

Salt and pepper

150 ml/¼ pt Single cream

30 ml/2 tbsp Chopped parsley

Melt half the butter or margarine and fry the onions until soft. Stir in the wine, water, thyme and bay leaves and simmer until the liquid is reduced by half. Melt the remaining butter in a separate pan and fry the steaks until browned on both sides. Add the brandy and cook for 2 minutes until you can no longer smell the alcohol. Transfer the steaks to a warmed serving plate and season to taste with salt and pepper. Pour the wine sauce into the pan, stirring well to mix in the' meat juices. Stir in the cream and heat through, then pour over the steaks and serve sprinkled with parsley.

Stir-Fry Beef with Ginger

Serves 4

15 ml/1 tbsp Oil
450 g/1 lb Steak, cut into strips
25 g/1 oz Root ginger, peeled and grated
1 Garlic clove, crushed
100 g/4 oz Small corn cobs
50 g/2 oz Mangetout
1 Red pepper, cut into strips
200 g/7 oz Canned water chestnuts, drained
50 g/2 oz Cashew nuts
30 ml/2 tbsp Soy sauce
5 ml/1 tsp Chinese five-spice powder
5 ml/1 tsp Sesame seeds

Heat the oil and fry the beef, ginger and garlic until browned. Stir in the corn, mangetout, pepper, water chestnuts and nuts and stir-fry for 3 minutes. Add the remaining ingredients and cook for 1 minute then serve immediately with fried rice.

Quick and Tasty Beef

Serves 4

15 ml/1 tbsp Olive oil
25 g/1 oz Butter or margarine
4 Lean beef slices
250 ml/8 fl oz Soured cream
½ Red pepper, chopped
½ Green pepper, chopped
½ Yellow pepper, chopped
5 ml/1 tsp Wholegrain mustard
10 Green peppercorns
Salt and pepper

Heat the oil, then add the butter or margarine. When it has melted, add the beef and brown on both sides then cook for 4 minutes. Stir in the soured cream and peppers and cook for 3 minutes. Then stir in the remaining ingredients and season to taste with salt and pepper. Heat through gently and serve with rice or pasta.

Beef and Vegetable Stir-Fry

Serves 4

45 ml/3 tbsp Olive oil
350 g/12 oz Steak, cut into strips
6 Spring onions, sliced
1 Garlic clove, chopped
½ Red pepper. cut into strips
½ Yellow pepper, cut into strips
175 g/6 oz Carrots, cut into strips
275 g/10 oz Canned small corn cobs, drained
5 ml/1 tsp Cornflour
75 ml/5 tbsp Dry cider
30 ml/2 tbsp Soy sauce
150 ml/¼ pt Beef Stock (page 24)
100 g/4 oz Beansprouts
Salt and Pepper

Heat the oil and fry the steak until browned. Remove from the pan and keep it warm. Fry the onions, garlic, peppers, carrots and corn cobs for 3 minutes. Mix the cornflour with the cider and soy sauce, add it to the pan and bring to the boil, stirring until the sauce thickens. Stir in the stock, beansprouts and beef, season to taste with salt and pepper and heat through. Serve with boiled rice.

Beef Stroganoff

Serves 4

50 g/2 oz Butter or margarine
2 Onions, chopped
100 g/4 oz Mushrooms, sliced
15 g/½ oz Plain flour
Salt and pepper
750 g/1½ lb Fillet steak, cut into strips
300 ml/½ pt Beef Stock (page 24)
5 ml/1 tsp Mixed herbs
15 ml/1 tbsp Tomato purée
10 ml/2 tsp French mustard
150 ml/¼ pt Soured cream
15 ml/1 tbsp Chopped parsley

Melt half the butter or margarine and fry the onions until just browned. Add the mushrooms and fry for 2 minutes, then remove them from the pan and keep them warm. Season the flour with salt and pepper and toss the steak in the flour. Melt the remaining butter and fry the steak quickly until browned, then transfer it to the dish with the mushrooms and onions. Stir the stock, herbs, tomato purée and mustard into the pan and bring to the boil, stirring well to scrape up any pan juices. Return the meat and vegetables to the pan, stir in the soured cream and heat through but do not allow to boil. Serve sprinkled with parsley.

Beef and Pepper Strips

Serves 4

500 g/1¼ lb Rump steak, cut into strips
10 ml/2 tsp Cornflour
60 ml/4 tbsp Soy sauce
45 ml/3 tbsp Oil
2 Red peppers, cut into thin strips
10 ml/2 tsp Chilli powder
1 Onion, sliced
1 Garlic clove, crushed
25 g/1 oz Root ginger, peeled and grated
5 ml/1 tsp Sugar
30 ml/2 tbsp Dry sherry

Sprinkle the meat with the cornflour and soy sauce and leave to stand for 15 minutes. Heat 15 ml/1 tbsp oil and fry the peppers, chilli powder, onion, garlic and ginger for 3 minutes. Remove from the pan and set aside. Heat the remaining oil and fry the meat for 3 minutes. Return the pepper mixture to the pan with the remaining soy sauce, the sugar and sherry and stir-fry for 1 minute to heat through. Serve with rice.

Beef Puchero

Serves 4

100 g/4 oz Haricot beans, soaked overnight and drained
1 Carrot, diced
½ Turnip, diced
2 Onions, diced
2 Tomatoes, skinned and diced
225 g/8 oz Bacon, diced
900 ml/1½ pts Beef Stock (page 24)
1 Bouquet garni
900 g/1½ lb Stewing beef, cut into 4 cm/1½ in pieces
Salt and pepper
15 g/½ oz Plain flour (optional)
15 g/½ oz Butter or margarine (optional)

Place the beans, vegetables, bacon, stock and bouquet garni in a large saucepan. Bring to the boil, cover and simmer gently for about 2 hours. Add the meat, season to taste with salt and pepper and simmer for a further 1 hour. Remove the bouquet garni and adjust the seasoning if necessary. Mix the flour and butter or margarine to a paste and stir this into the puchero to thicken the gravy, if necessary. Serve with mashed potatoes.

Beef Pot Roast

Serves 4

1.75 kg/4 lb Brisket of beef, boned and rolled
Salt and pepper
25 g/1 oz Lard
1 Onion stuck with 4 cloves
300 ml/½ pt Water
4 Carrots, halved lengthways
4 Small onions, halved
150 ml/¼ pt Beef Stock (page 24)

Tie the meat securely, pat dry with kitchen paper and season with salt and pepper. Heat the lard in a flameproof casserole and fry the meat until browned on all sides. Add the onion and water, cover and cook in a preheated oven at 150°C/300°F/ gas mark 2 for 2 hours, basting occasionally. Remove from the oven, lift out the meat and add the carrots and onions. Place the meat on top, cover and return to the oven for a further 1 hour.

Remove the meat and vegetables from the casserole and keep them warm. Skim off excess fat, stir in the stock well to scrape up all the meat juices, bring to the boil and strain the gravy into a gravy boat.

Beef with Green Noodles

Serves 4

175 g/6 oz Green tagliatelle
15 ml/1 tbsp Oil
1 Onion, chopped
1 Garlic clove, crushed
750 g/1½ lb Minced beef
100 g/4 oz Mushrooms, sliced
25 g/1 oz Plain flour
150 ml/¼ pt Beef Stock (page 24)
400 g/14 oz Canned tomatoes,
    chopped
15 ml/1 tbsp Worcestershire sauce
15 ml/1 tbsp Soy sauce
15 ml/1 tbsp Tomato purée
5 ml/1 tsp Oregano
Salt and pepper
25 g/1 oz Butter or margarine
300 ml/½ pt Milk
75 g/3 oz Cheddar cheese, grated
50 g/2 oz Breadcrumbs

Cook the tagliatelle in boiling salted water for 4 minutes until partly cooked. Drain and rinse in hot water, then place half the noodles in a casserole dish. Heat the oil and fry the onion and garlic until soft, then add the beef and fry until browned. Add the mushrooms, stir in half the flour and cook for 1 minute. Stir in the stock, tomatoes, Worcestershire sauce, soy sauce, tomato purée and oregano and season to taste with salt and pepper. Bring to the boil, then pour over the noodles and cover with the remaining noodles. Melt the butter or margarine, stir in the remaining flour and cook for 1 minute. Stir in the milk, bring to the boil, stirring, and simmer for 2 minutes then pour over the casserole. Mix the cheese and breadcrumbs and sprinkle over the casserole. Cook in a preheated oven at 200°C/400°F/gas mark 6 for 30 minutes until browned and crispy on top.

Beef Hot Pot

Serves 4

450 g/1 lb Shin of beef, boned and
    cubed
30 ml/2 tbsp Vinegar
15 g/½ oz Plain flour
Salt and pepper
225 g/8 oz Pork sausages, cut into
    pieces
450 g/1 lb Potatoes, sliced
1 Apple, peeled, cored and sliced
225 g/8 oz Tomatoes, skinned and
    sliced
1 Onion, sliced
300 ml/½ pt Beef Stock (page 24)

Put the beef and vinegar in a bowl and leave to stand for 1 hour, stirring occasionally. Drain and pat dry. Season the flour with salt and pepper, then toss the meat and sausages in the flour. Place a layer of potatoes, apples and tomatoes in the bottom of a casserole, then add a layer of meat and continue layering until all the ingredients are used up, finishing with a layer of potatoes. Add enough stock to come one-third of the way up the casserole. Cover and cook in a preheated oven at 160°C/325°F/gas mark 3 for 2½ hours or until the meat is tender. Remove the lid and turn the heat up to 200°C/400°F/gas mark 6 for 10 minutes to crisp the top.

Rich Beef and Mushroom Cobbler

Serves 4

30 ml/2 tbsp Oil
1 Onion, chopped
1 Garlic clove, chopped
450 g/1 lb Chuck steak, chopped
100 g/4 oz Mushrooms, sliced
15 ml/1 tbsp Plain flour
450 ml/¾ pt Beef Stock (page 24)
15 ml/1 tbsp Tomato purée
5 ml/1 tsp Worcestershire sauce
4 Juniper berries, crushed
Salt and pepper
225 g/8 oz Self-raising flour
5 ml/1 tsp Baking powder
50 g/2 oz Soft margarine
10 ml/2 tsp Mixed herbs
150 ml/¼ pt Milk

Heat the oil in a large saucepan and fry the onion and garlic until soft. Add the steak and fry until browned. Add the mushrooms and fry for 1 minute. Stir in the flour and cook for 1 minute, then stir in the stock, tomato purée, Worcestershire sauce and juniper berries. Season to taste with salt and pepper. Bring to the boil and simmer, stirring occasionally, for 15 minutes. Pour into a casserole dish.

Mix the flour and baking powder, then rub in the margarine until the mixture resembles fine breadcrumbs. Stir in the herbs, then gradually add the milk until the mixture forms a soft dough. Roll into small balls and arrange around the edge of the casserole. Bake in a preheated oven at 220°C/425°F/gas mark 7 for 20 minutes.

Oxtail Provençale

Serves 4

1 Large oxtail, cut up
Seasoned flour
30 ml/2 tbsp Oil
2 Onions, sliced
1–2 Garlic cloves, crushed
2 Carrots, sliced
2 Celery sticks (stalks), sliced
400 g/14 oz can Red tomatoes
15 ml/1 tbsp tomato purée (paste)
600 ml/1 pint/2½ cups Stock
10 ml/2 tsp Oregano
Salt and freshly ground black pepper
12 Black olives

Trim the oxtail of excess fat and coat the pieces in seasoned flour. Fry in the oil until evenly browned all over. Transfer to a large ovenproof casserole.

Fry the onions and garlic in the same oil until lightly coloured then add to the casserole with the carrots, celery, tomatoes, tomato purée, stock, oregano and plenty of seasoning. Cover tightly and cook in a preheated oven at 160°C/325°F/gas mark 3 for 3 hours.

If possible, cool and chill overnight in order to remove the layer of fat easily. If not, spoon off all the fat from the surface before continuing. Add the olives, taste and adjust the seasoning and return the casserole to the oven for another hour before serving.

Casserole Provençale

Serves 4

900 g/2 lb Stewing beef, cubed

100 g/4 oz Belly of pork, rinded and
cubed

1 Onion, chopped

5 ml/1 tsp Mixed herbs

Salt and pepper

250 ml/8 fl oz Red wine

25 g/1 oz Plain flour

30 ml/2 tbsp Olive oil

2 Garlic cloves, chopped

½ Green pepper, chopped

60 ml/4 tbsp Water

225 g/8 oz Canned tomatoes,
chopped

5 ml/1 tsp Paprika

1 Bouquet garni

6 Black olives, stoned

Put the beef, pork, onion and herbs in
a dish, season to taste with salt and
pepper and cover with red wine.
Leave to marinate overnight.

Remove the meat, pat it dry and
toss it in the flour. Heat the oil in a
flameproof casserole and fry the
meat until browned, then add the
garlic and pepper and fry for
2 minutes. Stir in all the remaining
ingredients except the olives and
bring to the boil. Transfer the casserole to a preheated oven and cook at
140°C/275°F/gas mark 1 for 4 hours.
Remove the bouquet garni, leave to
cool and skim off any fat. When ready
to serve, bring the casserole back to
the simmering point and add the
olives.

Hungarian Beef

Serves 8

1.5 kg/3 lb Joint of beef

6 Smoked bacon rashers, rinded
and halved

100 g/4 oz Smoked sausage, sliced

1 Onion, chopped

Salt and pepper

30 ml/2 tbsp Oil

Cut some holes in the beef joint. Roll
the bacon and sausage pieces and
press them into the holes. Sprinkle
the meat with onion, season well
with salt and pepper and leave to
stand for 1½ hours, then shake off
the onion.

Heat the oil and fry the meat on all
sides to seal the joint. Put the meat
in a roasting tin, cover and roast in
a preheated oven at 180°C/350°F/
gas mark 4 for 1½ hours, basting
occasionally.

Danish Beef Casserole

Serves 4

10 Shallots

30 ml/2 tbsp Oil

750 g/1½ lb Braising steak

15 g/½ oz Plain flour

300 ml/½ pt Beef Stock (page 24)

60 ml/4 tbsp Tomato purée

30 ml/2 tbsp Port

Pinch of ground cumin

5 ml/1 tsp Cinnamon

100 g/4 oz Danish blue cheese,
crumbled

Cook the shallots in boiling water for 3 minutes, then drain and transfer to a casserole dish. Heat the oil and fry the steak until browned, then transfer it to the casserole. Add the flour to the pan and cook for 1 minute, stirring well to scrape up the meat juices. Stir in the stock, tomato purée, port, cumin and cinnamon, bring to the boil and pour into the casserole. Cook in a preheated oven at 180°C/350°F/gas mark 4 for 1½ hours. Top the casserole with the cheese and leave to stand for 5 minutes before serving.

Hungarian Goulash

Serves 4

25 g/1 oz Plain flour
Salt and pepper
450 g/1 lb Braising steak
30 ml/2 tbsp Oil
3 Onions, chopped
1 Garlic clove, crushed
1 Green pepper, sliced
30 ml/2 tbsp Paprika
300 ml/½ pt Beef Stock (page 24)
225 g/8 oz Canned tomatoes,
  chopped
15 ml/1 tbsp Tomato purée
1 Bouquet garni
Salt and pepper
150 ml/¼ pt Soured cream

Season the flour with salt and pepper and toss the beef in the flour. Heat the oil and fry the steak until browned, then transfer it to a casserole dish. Fry the onions until soft, then add the garlic and pepper and fry for 1 minute.

Stir in the paprika and fry for 1 minute, then stir in the stock, tomatoes, tomato purée and bouquet garni, bring to the boil and season to taste with salt and pepper. Pour into the casserole dish and cook in a preheated oven at 160°C/325°F/gas mark 3 for 2 hours until the meat is tender. Remove the bouquet garni and swirl in the soured cream before serving.

Pepperpot Beef

Serves 4-6

25 g/1 oz Plain flour
5 ml/1 tsp Ground ginger
30 ml/2 tbsp Salt and pepper
900 g/2 lb Stewing steak, cubed
30 ml/2 tbsp Oil
400 g/14 oz Canned tomatoes,
  chopped
100 g/4 oz Button mushrooms,
  sliced
5 ml/1 tsp Chilli sauce
15 ml/1 tbsp Worcestershire sauce
25 g/1 oz Soft brown sugar
30 ml/2 tbsp Red wine vinegar
2 Garlic cloves, crushed
1 Bay leaf
30 ml/1 tbsp Chopped parsley

Mix the flour and ginger and season with salt and pepper. Toss the steak in the flour. Heat the oil and fry the steak until browned, then transfer to an ovenproof casserole. Stir in the remaining ingredients and cook in a preheated oven at 160°C/325°F/gas mark 3 for 3 hours. Remove the bay leaf and serve sprinkled with parsley.

Spiced Beef and Beans

Serves 4

50 g/2 oz Plain flour
5 ml/1 tsp Ground ginger
Salt and pepper
750 g/1½ lb Braising steak, cubed
30 ml/2 tbsp Oil
2 Onions, chopped
1 Garlic clove, crushed
15 g/½ oz Root ginger, grated
300 ml/½ pt Beef Stock (page 24)
400 g/14 oz Canned tomatoes, chopped
30 ml/2 tbsp Red wine vinegar
15 ml/1 tbsp Honey
15 ml/1 tbsp Worcestershire sauce
300 g/11 oz Canned red kidney beans, rinsed and drained

Mix the flour and ginger and season with salt and pepper. Toss the steak in the flour. Heat the oil and fry the steak until browned, then transfer it to a casserole dish. Fry the onions, garlic and root ginger until just browned, then stir in the remaining flour and cook for 1 minute. Stir in the stock, tomatoes, wine vinegar, honey and Worcestershire sauce and season to taste with salt and pepper. Bring to the boil, then pour into the casserole. Cook in a pre-heated oven at 160°C/325°F/gas mark 3 for 1½ hours, then add the kidney beans and return to the oven for a further 40 minutes.

Beef in Beer

Serves 4

30 ml/2 tbsp Oil
750 g/1½ lb Chuck steak, cubed
100 g/4 oz Gammon steak, rinded and cubed
2 Onions, sliced
1 Garlic clove, crushed
300 ml/½ pt Light ale
150 ml/¼ pt Brown ale
5 ml/1 tsp Dark brown sugar
5 ml/1 tsp Ground nutmeg
1 Bouquet garni
Salt and pepper
5 ml/1 tsp Red wine vinegar
15 ml/1 tbsp Chopped parsley

Heat the oil and fry the steak and gammon until browned, then transfer them to a casserole. Fry the onions and garlic until just browned, then add them to the casserole. Add the beer, sugar and nutmeg to the pan and bring to the boil, stirring well to mix in the meat juices, then pour it into the casserole, add the bouquet garni and season to taste with salt and pepper. Cover and cook in a pre-heated oven at 140°C/275°F/gas mark 1 for 3 hours. Stir in the wine vinegar, remove the bouquet garni and serve sprinkled with parsley.

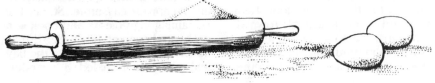

Boeuf en Croute

Serves 6

225 g/8 oz Plain flour

Pinch of salt

120 g/5 oz Butter or margarine

30 ml/2 tbsp Water

1.5 kg/3 lb Fillet of beef

50 g/2 oz Smooth liver pâté

5 ml/1 tsp Thyme

1 Egg

15 ml/1 tbsp Oil

Mix the flour and salt, then rub in 50 g/2 oz butter or margarine until the mixture resembles fine breadcrumbs. Add just enough water to mix to a soft pastry, then chill. Grate 50 g/2 oz butter. Roll out the pastry to a large rectangle and sprinkle with the butter. Fold the pastry into thirds, enclosing the butter, then roll out and fold again. Wrap the pastry and chill for 15 minutes, then repeat the rolling and folding 3 more times. Chill.

Spread the remaining butter over the top of the beef and seal in a preheated oven at 220°C/425°F/gas mark 7 for 15 minutes then leave to cool.

Roll out the pastry to a rectangle large enough to enclose the meat. Spread the pâté on top of the meat and place it, pâté side down, in the centre of the pastry. Sprinkle with thyme. Fold the pastry round the meat, sealing the edges well. Turn the parcel over and decorate with pastry trimmings. Chill. Beat the egg and oil together and brush over the pastry. Stand the pastry on a damp baking tray and bake in a preheated oven at 220°C/425°F/gas mark 7 for 35 minutes until golden brown.

Note

The meat will be rare. If you prefer your beef well done, cook the joint for a little longer before wrapping in pastry.

Boeuf à l'Orange

Serves 4

30 ml/2 tbsp Oil

750 g/1½ lb Braising steak, cubed

225 g/8 oz Shallots, sliced

1 Garlic clove, crushed

100 g/4 oz Button mushrooms, halved

15 g/½ oz Plain flour

300 ml/½ pt Beef Stock (page 24)

2 Oranges

15 ml/1 tbsp Tomato purée

45 ml/3 tbsp Brandy

15 ml/1 tbsp Black treacle or molasses

Salt and pepper

15 ml/1 tbsp Chopped parsley

Heat the oil and fry the steak until browned, then transfer to a casserole dish. Fry the onions and garlic until browned, then transfer to the casserole with the uncooked mushrooms. Stir the flour into the frying pan and cook for 1 minute, then stir in the stock and bring to the boil. Peel the rind from 1 orange, cut into thin strips and add it to the pan. Stir in the juice from both oranges, the tomato purée, brandy, and treacle or molasses. Season to taste with salt and pepper and pour into the casserole. Cover and cook in a preheated oven at 160°C/325°F/gas mark 3 for 2½ hours. Serve sprinkled with parsley.

Perfect Roast Beef

Serves 8

1.75 kg/4 lb Roasting joint of beef
  (fillet, ribs, sirloin or topside)

50 g/2 oz Dripping or fat

Clean and dry the joint and place it on a trivet in a roasting tin just large enough to take it comfortably with the fattiest side uppermost and largest cut surface exposed. Brush the meat with fat or oil and put 2 knobs of dripping on top. Roast in a preheated oven at 220°C/425°F/gas mark 7 for 10 minutes to seal the meat, then turn down the oven to 180°C/350°F/gas mark 4 for 20 minutes per 450 g/1 lb plus 20 minutes extra for rare meat and 40 minutes extra for well done. Baste the joint frequently. Allow the meat to rest for 30 minutes before carving.

Cooking times will vary depending on whether the joint is boned, rolled or stuffed and depending on its shape and your own taste. Test the meat when you think it is ready by inserting a skewer into the thickest part or by using a meat thermometer.

Aberdeen Roll

Serves 4

225 g/8 oz Bacon, rinded and
  minced

450 g/1 lb Minced beef

225 g/8 oz Breadcrumbs

10 ml/2 tsp Mixed herbs

Salt and pepper

2 Eggs, beaten

Mix the bacon, beef, 175 g/6 oz breadcrumbs and herbs and season to taste with salt and pepper. Bind the mixture together with the eggs, tie firmly in a floured cloth and boil for 3 hours. Toast the remaining breadcrumbs under the grill until browned. When the roll is almost cold, unwrap and roll it in the breadcrumbs. Serve cold, cut into slices.

Beefburger Buns

Serves 4

450 g/1 lb Minced beef

100 g/4 oz Breadcrumbs

1 Onion, finely chopped

10 ml/2 tsp Mixed herbs

Salt and pepper

1 Egg, beaten

30 ml/2 tbsp Oil

4 Baps

4 Lettuce leaves

60 ml/4 tbsp Cucumber relish

4 Gherkins, sliced

Mix together the beef, breadcrumbs, onion and herbs and season to taste with salt and pepper. Bind with the egg and shape into burgers. Heat the oil and fry the burgers until cooked through and browned on both sides. Split the rolls and put the lettuce leaves on the bottom half. Place the burgers on top and cover with the cucumber relish and gherkins, or other pickles of your choice. Top with the other half of the roll and serve with chips.

Nutty Beef Roll

Serves 4

200 g/7 oz Self-raising flour
10 ml/2 tsp Baking powder
Pinch of salt
100 g/4 oz Shredded suet
Pinch of caraway seeds
30 ml/2 tbsp Cold water
15 ml/1 tbsp Oil
450 g/1 lb Minced beef
1 Onion, chopped
45 ml/3 tbsp Mango chutney
50 g/2 oz Walnuts, chopped
25 g/1 oz Breadcrumbs

Mix the flour, baking powder, salt, suet and caraway seeds. Add enough cold water to mix to a soft dough. Roll out on a floured surface to about 28 x 33 cm (11 x 13 in). Heat the oil and fry the mince and onion for 5 minutes. Stir in the remaining ingredients and spread over the pastry to within 1 cm/ ½ in of the edges. Damp the edges and roll up the pastry from one short side, finishing with the seam underneath. Pinch the ends to seal, cover in greased kitchen foil, place on a baking sheet and bake in a preheated oven at 160°C/325°F/gas mark 3 for 1 hour. Remove the foil and turn up to 190°C/375°F/gas mark 5 for a further 10 minutes to brown the pastry. Serve sliced with gravy.

Mexican Meatballs with Chilli Tomato Sauce

Serves 4-6

750 g/1½ lb Minced beef
25 g/1 oz Breadcrumbs
2 Onions, finely chopped
10 ml/2 tsp Oregano
1 Egg, beaten
Salt and pepper
30 ml/2 tbsp Plain flour
40 ml/2½ tbsp Oil
1 Garlic clove, crushed
2 Chilli peppers, chopped
2.5 ml/½ tsp Sugar
400 g/14 oz Canned tomatoes
30 ml/2 tbsp Tomato ketchup
300 ml/½ pt Beef Stock (page 24)
3 Spring onions, chopped

Mix the mince, breadcrumbs, 1 onion, oregano and egg and season to taste with salt and pepper. Divide the mixture into 16 pieces and shape into balls using floured hands. Heat 30 ml/ 2 tbsp oil and fry the meatballs until browned and cooked through. Drain on kitchen paper and place in a warmed ovenproof dish.

To make the sauce, heat the remaining oil and fry the remaining onion with the garlic and chilli peppers until soft. Add the sugar, tomatoes, ketchup and stock and season to taste with salt and pepper. Simmer, uncovered, for 15 minutes until the sauce has reduced and thickened slightly. Mix in the spring onions, pour the sauce over the meatballs and bake in a preheated oven at 180°C/350°F/gas mark 4 for 15 minutes. Serve with brown rice and tortilla chips.

Crispy-Topped Mince Pie

Serves 4

100 g/4 oz Butter or margarine
1 Onion, chopped
1 Garlic clove, chopped
450 g/1 lb Minced beef
100 g/4 oz Plain flour
300 ml/½ pt Beef Stock (page 24)
2.5 ml/½ tsp Thyme
2.5 mi/½ tsp Rosemary
2.5 ml/½ tsp Nutmeg
Salt and pepper
100 g/4 oz Cheddar cheese, grated

Melt 25 g/1 oz butter and fry the onion and garlic until soft, then add the meat and fry until browned. Stir in 15 ml/1 tbsp flour and cook for 1 minute, then stir in the stock, thyme, rosemary and nutmeg and season to taste with salt and pepper. Simmer for 5 minutes, then transfer to an ovenproof dish. Rub 50 g/2 oz butter or margarine into the remaining flour, then stir in the cheese. Spread the mixture on top of the mince and dot with the remaining butter. Bake in a preheated oven at 180°C/350°F/gas mark 4 for 45 minutes until golden brown and crispy.

Beef and Ham Roll

Serves 4

450 g/1 lb Minced beef
225 g/8 oz Minced ham
175 g/6 oz Fresh breadcrumbs
15 ml/1 tbsp Worcestershire sauce
Salt and pepper
400 g/14 oz Canned tomatoes, chopped

Mix together all the ingredients except the tomatoes and season to taste with salt and pepper. Form into a roll and place in a greased loaf tin. Bake at 180°C/350°F/gas mark 4 for 40 minutes, then pour over the tomatoes and bake for a further 15 minutes. Serve with potatoes and a green vegetable.

Meatballs in Tomato Sauce

Serves 4

4 Juniper berries, crushed
100 g/4 oz Wholemeal breadcrumbs
30 ml/2 tbsp Chopped parsley
4 Dried prunes, soaked, drained and chopped
450 g/1 lb Minced beef
2.5 ml/½ tsp Nutmeg
1 Egg, beaten
Salt and pepper
30 ml/2 tbsp Oil
400 g/14 oz Canned tomatoes, chopped
3 Basil sprigs, chopped
5 ml/1 tsp Worcestershire sauce
15 ml/1 tbsp Sherry
15 g/½ oz Plain flour
50 g/2 oz Parmesan cheese, grated

Mix the berries, breadcrumbs, parsley, prunes, beef and nutmeg, bind together with the egg and season to taste with salt and pepper. Make into 16 balls and place them in an ovenproof dish. Mix the oil, tomatoes, basil, Worcestershire sauce, sherry and flour until smooth, by hand or in a blender. Pour the mixture over the meatballs and bake in a preheated oven at 200°C/400°F/gas mark 6 for 30 minutes. Sprinkle with Parmesan cheese and serve with pasta.

Swedish Meatballs

Serves 4

50 g/2 oz Breadcrumbs
10 ml/2 tsp Cornflour
1 Onion, chopped
250 ml/8 fl oz Single cream
250 ml/8 fl oz Milk
Salt and pepper
450 g/1 lb Minced beef
30 ml/2 tbsp Oil

Mix the breadcrumbs, cornflour, onion, cream and milk and season to taste with salt and pepper. Cook gently over a low heat for 10 minutes, stirring well, then add the meat and stir until browned. Remove from the heat and roll the meat into small balls. Heat the oil and fry the meat-balls for about 8 minutes until browned.

Chilli Con Carne

Serves 4

30 ml/2 tbsp Oil
2 Onions, chopped
1 Garlic clove, crushed
550 g/1¼ lb Minced beef
5 ml/1 tsp Cayenne pepper
5 ml/1 tsp Chilli powder
10 ml/2 tsp Oregano
300 ml/½ pt Beef Stock (page 24)
400 g/14 oz Canned tomatoes, chopped
225 g/8 oz Canned red kidney beans, drained and rinsed
30 ml/2 tbsp Tomato purée
Few drops of Worcestershire sauce
Salt and pepper
4 Pitta breads

Heat the oil and fry the onions and garlic until soft, then stir in the meat and fry until browned. Stir in the cayenne pepper, chilli powder and oregano and cook for 1 minute. Stir in the stock, tomatoes, kidney beans, tomato purée and Worcestershire sauce, bring to the boil and simmer for 10 minutes. Season to taste with salt and pepper. Partly cover the pan and simmer for 1 hour, stirring occasionally and adding a little extra stock if necessary. Serve with warmed pitta breads.

Monday Pie

Serves 4

350 g/12 oz Cold roast beef, chopped
2 Onions, chopped
225 g/8 oz Canned tomatoes, chopped
225 g/8 oz Canned baked beans
5 ml/1 tsp Plain flour
5 ml/1 tsp Gravy powder
Salt and pepper
450 g/1 lb Potatoes, sliced
100 g/4 oz Cheddar cheese, grated

Mix the beef, onions, tomatoes, beans, flour and gravy powder and season to taste with salt and pepper. Spoon the mixture into a 1.2 litre/2 pt pie dish and arrange the potato slices on top of the meat. Bake in a pre-heated oven at 190°C/375°F/gas mark 5 for 30 minutes, then sprinkle with the cheese and bake for a further 10 minutes.

Veal

Veal is an extremely easy meat to prepare, and as it is lean, there is little waste. It has a subtle flavour which lends itself well to all kinds of recipes, from the classic Wiener Schnitzel to vealburgers.

Veal with Tomatoes

Serves 4

30 ml/2 tbsp Oil
2 Garlic cloves, chopped
4 Veal escalopes, flattened
250 ml/8 fl oz Dry white wine
400 g/14 oz Canned tomatoes, chopped
30 ml/2 tbsp Tomato purée
2.5 ml/½ tsp Worcestershire sauce
5 ml/1 tsp Oregano
5 ml/1 tsp Marjoram
Salt and pepper

Heat the oil and fry the garlic for 1 minute. Add the veal and fry until browned on both sides. Pour off any remaining oil and stir in the wine and tomatoes, bring to the boil and simmer for 8 minutes. Stir in the tomato purée, Worcestershire sauce, oregano and marjoram and season to taste with salt and pepper. Simmer for 10 minutes before serving.

Mozzarella Veal with Anchovies

Serves 4

4 Veal escalopes, flattened
Salt and pepper
25 g/1 oz Plain flour
15 g/½ oz Butter or margarine
15 ml/1 tbsp Oil
25 g/1 oz Anchovies, mashed
3 Tomatoes, skinned and sliced
10 ml/2 tsp Oregano
100 g/4 oz Mozzarella cheese, sliced
4 Black olives, stoned
15 ml/1 tbsp Chopped basil

Season the veal with salt and pepper and toss in the flour. Melt the butter or margarine with the oil and fry the veal until golden brown on both sides. Spread the veal thinly with the anchovies, cover with tomato slices, sprinkle with oregano and top with cheese. Place an olive on top and heat under a hot grill until the cheese softens. Sprinkle with basil and serve immediately.

Veal in Madeira

Serves 4

| 4 Veal escalopes, flattened |
| Salt and pepper |
| 60 ml/4 tbsp Madeira |
| 100 g/4 oz Unsalted butter |
| 1 Shallot, finely chopped |
| 100 g/4 oz Mushrooms, finely chopped |
| 4 Tomatoes, skinned, seeded and chopped |
| 300 ml/½ pt Double cream |
| 5 ml/1 tsp Paprika |

Season the veal lightly with salt and pepper. Lay it in a flat dish and spoon over the Madeira. Leave to marinate for 2 hours.

Remove the meat and pat it dry. Melt the butter and fry the veal for about 4 minutes, turning once. Transfer the veal to a warmed serving dish and keep it warm. Pour off a little butter from the pan, add the shallot and fry until soft, then add the mushrooms and cook for 5 minutes. Add the tomatoes and cook them to a pulp. Pour in the marinade, bring to the boil and simmer until the sauce is reduced and thickened slightly. Stir in the cream and paprika and season to taste with salt and pepper. When the sauce is creamy, remove it from the heat and stir in the chilled butter, shaking the pan till the sauce is glossy. Pour over the escalopes and serve immediately.

Veal Camembert

Serves 4

| 40 g/1½ oz Butter or margarine |
| 15 ml/1 tbsp Oil |
| 4 Veal escalopes, flattened |
| 1 Onion, chopped |
| 15 ml/1 tbsp Plain flour |
| 300 ml/½ pt Chicken Stock (page 24) |
| 30 ml/2 tbsp Red wine |
| 5 ml/1 tsp Mixed herbs |
| 1 Bay leaf |
| Salt and pepper |
| 1 Garlic clove, crushed |
| 225 g/8 oz Tomatoes, skinned, seeded and chopped |
| 225 g/8 oz Camembert cheese, sliced |

Melt 25 g/1 oz butter or margarine with the oil and fry the veal until browned on both sides. Remove the veal from the pan and keep it warm. Fry the onion until soft, then add the flour and cook for 1 minute. Stir in the stock, wine, herbs and bay leaf and bring to the boil, stirring to scrape up the meat juices. Season to taste with salt and pepper and simmer for 8 minutes until the veal is tender.

Melt the remaining butter or margarine in a clean saucepan, add the garlic and tomatoes and simmer for 5 minutes. Transfer the veal to a warmed flameproof serving dish, remove the bay leaf and pour over the tomato sauce. Top with the cheese and place under a hot grill for 5 minutes until the cheese bubbles. Serve the sauce with the escalopes.

Wiener Schnitzel

Serves 4

4 Veal escalopes, flattened
1 Egg, beaten
30 ml/2 tbsp Oil
100 g/4 oz Breadcrumbs
Salt and pepper
75 g/3 oz Butter or margarine
8 Anchovy fillets, drained
4 Lemon slices
15 ml/1 tbsp Chopped parsley
150 ml/¼ pt Chicken Stock
  (page 24)

Pat the veal dry on kitchen paper. Beat the egg with a few drops of oil and dip the veal into the egg. Season the breadcrumbs with salt and pepper and dip the veal into the breadcrumbs, pressing them down firmly. Melt 50 g/2 oz butter or margarine with the remaining oil and fry the veal for about 6 minutes each side, turning once. When cooked, transfer to a warmed serving plate and arrange 2 crossed anchovy fillets on top of each escalope and top with a lemon slice. Stir the parsley, stock and remaining butter into the pan and bring to the boil, stirring to scrape up the meat juices. Serve as a sauce with the escalopes.

Danish Veal

Serves 4

50 g/2 oz Butter or margarine
4 Veal escalopes, flattened
100 g/4 oz Button mushrooms
4 Pineapple rings
300 ml/½ pt Double cream

Melt the butter or margarine and fry the veal until golden brown on both sides. Add the mushrooms and cook for a further 5 minutes. Remove the meat from the pan and arrange on a warmed serving dish. Remove the mushrooms from the pan and keep them warm. Heat the pineapple rings in the pan for 2 minutes, then put 1 on each fillet and top with the mushrooms. Pour the cream into the pan and bring to the boil, stirring to scrape up all the meat juices. Pour over the meat and serve at once.

Veal Stroganoff

Serves 4

50 g/2 oz Butter or margarine
1 Onion, sliced
100 g/4 oz Button mushrooms, sliced
30 ml/2 tbsp Tomato purée
15 ml/1 tbsp Plain flour
4 Veal escalopes, flattened and cut into strips
150 ml/¼ pt Soured cream
30 ml/2 tbsp Lemon juice
Salt and pepper

Melt half the butter and fry the onion and mushrooms until soft but not browned. Stir in the tomato purée and flour and cook, stirring, for 1 minute. Remove from the heat. Melt the remaining butter in a clean pan and fry the veal until golden brown on both sides. Return the sauce to the heat, add the veal and stir in the cream and lemon juice. Season to taste with salt and pepper, heat through and serve immediately.

Continental Veal Rolls

Serves 4

4 Ham slices
4 Veal escalopes, flattened
15 ml/1 tbsp Olive oil
1 Garlic clove, chopped
25 g/1 oz Pine nuts
25 g/1 oz Raisins
25 g/1 oz Parmesan cheese, grated
30 ml/2 tbsp Chopped parsley
Salt and pepper
100 g/4 oz Emmenthal cheese, sliced
300 ml/½ pt Dry white wine
2 Tomatoes, skinned, seeded and chopped

Lay a slice of ham on each escalope and brush with olive oil. Mix the garlic, nuts, raisins, cheese and half the parsley and sprinkle over the meat. Season to taste with salt and pepper. Top with a slice of Emmenthal, roll up and secure the meat with cocktail sticks. Heat the remaining oil and fry the veal until browned on all sides. Add the wine, bring to the boil, cover and simmer for 30 minutes until tender. Transfer the veal to a warmed serving dish and keep them warm. Boil the liquid until reduced by half, then stir in the tomatoes and the remaining parsley, season to taste with salt and pepper and spoon over the veal. Serve with rice.

Veal in Cream and Mushroom Sauce

Serves 4

350 g/12 oz Button mushrooms
Juice of ½ lemon
25 g/1 oz Butter or margarine
450 g/1 lb Veal escalopes, cubed
1 Onion, chopped
15 ml/1 tbsp Plain flour
150 ml/¼ pt Chicken Stock (page 24)
150 ml/¼ pt Dry white wine
300 ml/½ pt Single cream
5 ml/1 tsp Paprika
Salt and pepper

Cook the mushrooms in the lemon juice for 2 minutes. Remove the mushrooms from the pan and keep them warm. Reserve the cooking liquid. Melt the butter or margarine and fry the veal and onion until lightly browned, then remove them from the pan and keep them warm. Stir in the flour and cook for 1 minute, then stir in the stock, wine and mushroom juice and cook for 3 minutes. Stir in the cream, mushrooms and veal and heat through gently. Add the paprika and season with salt and pepper to taste. Serve with noodles and a green salad.

Veal and Leek Casserole

Serves 4

50 g/2 oz Butter or margarine
45 ml/3 tbsp Oil
750 g/1½ lb Veal steaks, cubed
450 g/1 lb Leeks, sliced
15 ml/1 tbsp flour
90 ml/6 tbsp Dry white wine
150 ml/¼ pt Milk
1 Bouquet garni
Salt and pepper
50 g/2 oz Sultanas
15 ml/1 tbsp Lemon juice

Melt the butter or margarine with the oil and fry the veal until browned. Add the leeks and fry gently until soft. Stir in the flour and cook for 1 minute, then stir in the wine and milk and cook, stirring, until the sauce thickens. Add the bouquet garni and season to taste with salt and pepper. Simmer gently for 30 minutes, then remove the bouquet garni and stir in the sultanas and lemon juice before serving.

Tarragon Veal

Serves 4

4 Veal escalopes, flattened
Salt and pepper
100 g/4 oz Butter or margarine
30 ml/2 tbsp Chopped tarragon
225 g/8 oz Mushrooms, sliced
300 ml/½ pt Single cream
2 Tarragon sprigs

Season the veal with salt and pepper. Melt the butter or margarine and fry the veal until browned on both sides.

Transfer to a warmed serving dish and keep it warm. Mix the tarragon with the mushrooms and fry for 5 minutes until soft. Transfer the mushrooms to the serving plate. Stir the cream into the pan and bring to the boil, stirring, to scrape up any meat juices. Pour the sauce over the meat and serve garnished with tarragon.

Zealand Veal

Serves 4

450 g/1 lb Cheddar cheese, grated
1 Onion, finely chopped
15 ml/1 tbsp Chopped parsley
4 Veal escalopes, flattened
4 Streaky bacon rashers, rinded
50 g/2 oz Butter or margarine
25 g/1 oz Plain flour
300 ml/½ pt Milk
Salt and pepper

Mix together 275 g/10 oz cheese, the onion and parsley and press the mixture into the centre of each veal slice. Roll up the slices, wrap a bacon rasher round each one and secure with cocktail sticks. Melt half the butter or margarine and fry the meat until golden brown. Place it in a shallow casserole. Add the remaining butter to the pan, stir in the flour and cook, stirring, for 1 minute. Whisk in the milk and cook, stirring, until the sauce thickens. Remove from the heat and stir in the remaining cheese, then pour the sauce over the veal. Cover and bake in a preheated oven at 180°C/350°F/gas mark 4 for 40 minutes, then remove the lid and cook for a further 10 minutes to brown the top.

Fruity Veal Olives

Serves 4

4 Veal escalopes, flattened

Juice of 1 lemon

Pepper

25 g/1 oz Breadcrumbs

1 Apple, peeled, cored and chopped

350 g/12 oz Onion, chopped

5 ml/1 tsp Sage

1 Egg, beaten

1 Orange, peeled and sliced

25 g/1 oz Curd cheese

30 ml/2 tbsp Oil

100 g/4 oz Canned tomatoes, chopped

150 ml/¼ pt Beef Stock (page 24)

15 ml/1 tbsp Chopped parsley

Coat the veal slices in lemon juice and sprinkle with freshly ground black pepper. Mix together the breadcrumbs, apple, onion, sage and egg. Chop all but 2 of the orange slices and mix them into the stuffing. Spread the veal slices with the curd cheese, then cover with the stuffing mixture, roll up and secure the rolls with cocktail sticks. Gently fry the olives on all sides in the oil until browned, then transfer them to a covered ovenproof dish, cover with the chopped tomatoes and stock and bake in a preheated oven at 180°C/ 350°F/gas mark 4 for 30 minutes. Serve garnished with orange twists and chopped parsley.

Veal Chops Monarque

Serves 4

75 g/3 oz Butter or margarine

4 Veal chops

100 g/4 oz Mushrooms, chopped

50 g/2 oz Gruyère cheese, grated

Salt and pepper

150 ml/¼ pt Port

225 g/8 oz Pasta shells

50 g/2 oz Ham, cut into strips

Melt 25 g/1 oz butter or margarine and fry the chops on one side, then remove them from the frying pan. Add the mushrooms and cook for 2 minutes, then stir in the cheese until it melts and season to taste with salt and pepper. Spread this mixture on the cooked side of the chops. Melt 25 g/1 oz butter and cook the other side of the chops for 5 minutes. Place the chops in an ovenproof dish and bake in a preheated oven at 200°C/ 400°F/gas mark 6 for 10 minutes to glaze. Add the port to the pan, stirring to scrape up all the meat juices, then pour over the chops.

Meanwhile, cook the pasta in boiling salted water until just tender, then drain and rinse in hot water. Return to the saucepan with the remaining butter and the ham and season with black pepper. Heat until the butter has melted and the mixture is thoroughly warmed through. Serve the chops surrounded by pasta shells.

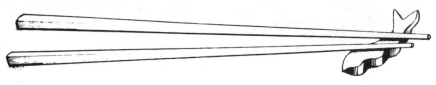

Saltinbocca alla Romana

Serves 6-8

8 Veal escalopes, flattened

Salt and pepper

15 ml/1 tbsp Plain flour

50 g/2 oz Butter or margarine

225 g/8 oz Mozzarella cheese, sliced

8 Parma ham slices

150 ml/¼ pt Dry white wine

75 ml/5 tbsp V8 juice

275 g/10 oz Canned condensed
  chicken soup

10 ml/2 tsp Lemon juice

Sprinkle the veal with salt and pepper and dust with flour. Melt the butter and fry the veal until browned on both sides. Remove from the pan and place in a greased casserole dish. Place 1 slice of cheese and 1 slice of ham on each cutlet and bake in a preheated oven at 190°C/375°F/gas mark 5 for 10 minutes. Meanwhile, add the flour to the pan and cook for 1 minute, then stir in the wine, juice, soup and lemon juice and cook, stirring, until the sauce thickens. Place the cutlets on a warmed serving plate and spoon the sauce over the top.

Veal in Sorrel Sauce

Serves 4

50 g/2 oz Butter or margarine

750 g/1½ lb Pie veal, cubed

1 Onion, chopped

1 Garlic clove, crushed

1 Carrot, sliced

450 ml/¾ pt Chicken Stock
  (page 24)

10 ml/2 tsp Thyme

10 ml/2 tsp Marjoram

1 Bay leaf

Salt and pepper

50 g/2 oz Chopped sorrel

15 ml/1 tbsp Plain flour

150 ml/¼ pt Single cream

15 ml/1 tbsp Lemon juice

Melt half the butter or margarine and fry the veal, onion, garlic and carrot until just browned, stirring continuously. Stir in 300 ml/½ pt stock and the herbs and season to taste with salt and pepper. Bring to the boil, cover and simmer for 1½ hours until tender.

Simmer the sorrel in the remaining stock for 5 minutes. Leave to cool slightly, then purée in a food processor or blender. Melt the remaining butter, stir in the flour and cook, stirring, for 1 minute. Stir in the sorrel purée. When the veal is cooked, stir the purée into the casserole. Stir in the cream and lemon juice and season to taste with salt and pepper. Remove the bay leaf and serve with boiled potatoes and carrots.

Veal in Herbs

Serves 4

50 g/2 oz Butter or margarine
1 Onion, chopped
2 Carrots, chopped
1.25 kg/2½ lb Veal joint, boned and
  rolled
150 ml/¼ pt Dry white wine
150 ml/¼ pt Chicken Stock
  (page 24)
3 Parsley sprigs
3 Dill sprigs
Salt and pepper
150 ml/¼ pt Mayonnaise
  (page 250)
5 ml/1 tsp Dijon mustard
60 ml/4 tbsp Natural yoghurt
15 ml/1 tbsp Chopped dill
15 ml/1 tbsp Chopped parsley
15 ml/1 tbsp Chopped chives

Melt half the butter or margarine and fry the onion and carrots until soft but not browned, then transfer them to a casserole dish just large enough to hold the meat. Melt the remaining butter and fry the veal joint until browned and sealed on all sides, then transfer it to the casserole dish. Stir the wine and stock into the pan, bring to the boil, add the parsley and dill sprigs and season to taste with salt and pepper. Simmer for 2 minutes, then pour over the veal. Cover and cook in a preheated oven at 180°C/350°F/gas mark 4 for 1½ hours until tender. Lift out the meat and leave it to cool. Strain and reserve the cooking liquor.

Make the mayonnaise, then beat in the mustard, yoghurt and chopped herbs with 45 ml/3 tbsp of the reserved cooking liquor. Serve the veal sliced with the sauce poured over.

Veal in Orange Sauce

Serves 4

900 g/2 lb Veal joint
1 Onion, sliced
1 Garlic clove, crushed
Juice of 1 lemon
Juice of 2 oranges
15 ml/1 tbsp Basil
1 Bouquet garni
15 ml/1 tbsp Oil
Salt and pepper
25 g/1 oz Caster sugar
60 ml/4 tbsp White wine vinegar
1 Orange, peeled and sliced

Place the veal in a bowl. Mix the onion, garlic, lemon and orange juice, basil and bouquet garni, pour over the veal and marinate for 12 hours.

Lift the veal from the marinade and pat dry on kitchen paper. Heat the oil and fry the veal until browned on all sides, then transfer it to a casserole dish. Stir the marinade into the pan, bring to the boil and simmer for 4 minutes, stirring to scrape up all the meat juices. Season to taste with salt and pepper, then pour over the veal, cover and cook in a preheated oven at 150°C/300°F/gas mark 2 for 1 hour.

Transfer the veal to a warmed serving plate and keep it warm. Dissolve the sugar in the wine vinegar and whisk it into the stock. Remove the bouquet garni, add the orange slices and simmer for 3 minutes, then spoon over the veal and serve.

Osso Buco

Serves 4

900 g/2 lb Shin of veal, cut into
   5 cm/2 in pieces

Salt and pepper

50 g/2 oz Butter or margarine

1 Onion, sliced

1 Celery stalk, sliced

1 Carrot, sliced

1 Leek, sliced

150 ml/¼ pt Dry white wine

400 g/14 oz Canned tomatoes

150 ml/¼ pt Chicken Stock
   (page 24)

15 ml/1 tbsp Tomato purée

5 ml/1 tsp Oregano

15 ml/1 tbsp Chopped parsley

1 Garlic clove, finely chopped

Grated rind of 1 lemon

Season the veal with salt and pepper. Melt the butter or margarine and fry the veal until just browned, then add the onion, celery, carrot and leek and fry until just browned. Stir in the wine, bring to the boil, then stir in the tomatoes, stock, tomato purée and oregano. Bring back to the boil, cover and simmer for 1½ hours. Transfer to a warmed serving dish. Mix together the parsley, garlic and lemon rind and sprinkle over the dish.

Fricassée of Veal

Serves 4

450 g/1 lb Fillet of veal, cubed

1 Onion, sliced

1 Parsley sprig

6 Peppercorns

1 Strip of lemon rind

2.5 ml/½ tsp Salt

300 ml/½ pt Boiling water

8 Streaky bacon rashers, rinded

25 g/1 oz Butter or margarine

25 g/1 oz Plain flour

150 ml/¼ pt Milk

1 Lemon, cut into wedges

Put the veal and onion in a casserole dish. Tie the parsley, peppercorns and lemon rind in a piece of muslin and add it to the casserole with salt and boiling water. Cover and cook in a pre-heated oven at 160°C/325°F/gas mark 3 for 2 hours. Stretch the bacon rashers with a knife, then roll them onto metal skewers and roast for the last 15 minutes of cooking time.

Melt the butter or margarine, stir in the flour and cook for 1 minute. Stir in the milk and 150 ml/¼ pt of the cooking liquor and bring to the boil, stirring until the sauce thickens. Transfer the meat to a warmed serving dish, pour the sauce over and arrange the bacon rolls and lemon wedges around the edge.

Blanquette de Veau

Serves 4

450 g/1 lb Fillet of veal
25 g/1 oz Plain flour
50 g/2 oz Butter or margarine
150 ml/¼ pt Chicken Stock
  or Vegetable Stock (page 24)
2 Cloves
1 Bay leaf
Salt and pepper
8 Small potatoes
15 g/½ oz Plain flour (optional)
15 g/½ oz Butter or margarine
  (optional)

Coat the veal with the flour. Melt the butter or margarine in a large saucepan and fry the veal until well browned on both sides. Add the stock, cloves and bay leaf and season to taste with salt and pepper. Bring to the boil, cover and simmer for 1 hour. Add the potatoes and simmer for a further 30 minutes.

Remove the meat, slice it thinly and arrange it on a serving dish with the potatoes. Either add a little water to the pan or thicken the remaining gravy with the flour mixed to a paste with the butter or margarine. Stir well and strain over the meat.

Lemon Veal

Serves 4

2 Onions
6 Cloves
50 g/2 oz Butter or margarine
15 ml/1 tbsp Oil
3 Carrots, diced
1 Garlic clove, crushed
750 g/1½ lb Pie veal, cubed
25 g/1 oz Plain flour
150 ml/¼ pt Dry white wine
150 ml/¼ pt Chicken Stock (page 24)
150 ml/¼ pt Water
Juice of 3 lemons
3 Tomatoes, skinned, seeded and
  chopped
1 Bouquet garni
Salt and pepper
15 ml/1 tbsp Chopped parsley

Chop 1 onion and stick the cloves into the other one. Melt the butter or margarine with the oil and fry the onions, carrots and garlic until just beginning to brown. Transfer them to a casserole dish. Fry the veal until browned on all sides, then transfer it to the casserole. Stir the flour into the pan and cook for 1 minute. Stir in the wine, stock and water and bring to the boil, stirring to scrape up the meat juices. Add the lemon juice, tomatoes and bouquet garni and season to taste with salt and pepper. Bring back to the boil, then pour over the veal, cover and cook in a preheated oven at 180°C/350°F/gas mark 4 for 1 hour until tender. Remove the bouquet garni and clove-studded onion and serve sprinkled with parsley.

Vealburgers

Serves 4

1 Garlic clove

150 ml/¼ pt Canned ratatouille

Salt and pepper

2.5 ml/½ tsp Basil or thyme

50 g/2 oz Cooked white rice

450 g/1 lb Lean veal, minced

50 g/2 oz Boiled ham, minced

30 ml/2 tbsp Chopped parsley

1 Egg, beaten

Plain flour

25 g/1 oz Butter or margarine

15 ml/1 tbsp Oil

Squeeze the garlic over the ratatouille in a saucepan, season with salt and pepper and add the basil or thyme. Bring to the boil and simmer for 5 minutes or until any free liquid with the ratatouille has almost evaporated. Mince the rice and both meats and stir into the ratatouille with the parsley. Season to taste with salt and pepper. Mix in enough egg to bind the ingredients. With floured hands, shape into 8 burgers and refrigerate until needed. Just before cooking, sprinkle the burgers with flour and brush with butter or margarine and oil. Grill under a medium grill for 20 minutes, turning once and basting occasionally with butter and oil.

Lamb

Lamb is a versatile meat, delicious in slowly-cooked stews, and ideal for quick evening meals made with chops or cutlets. It can be a little fatty, but if well trimmed cooks quickly and simply in all sorts of dishes.

Lemon and Mint Lamb

Serves 4

4 Lamb chops
15 g/½ oz Plain flour
30 ml/2 tbsp Oil
1 Onion, sliced
Grated rind and juice of 1 lemon
30 ml/2 tbsp Chopped mint
15 ml/1 tbsp Demerara sugar
300 ml/½ pt Chicken Stock (page 24)
Salt and pepper

Toss the chops in the flour, then heat the oil and fry the chops until browned on both sides. Transfer them to a casserole dish. Add the onions to the pan and fry until soft but not browned. Stir in the lemon rind and juice, mint, sugar and stock and season to taste with salt and pepper. Bring to the boil, then pour over the chops and bake in a pre-heated oven at 180°C/350°F/gas mark 4 for 1¼ hours until tender.

Piquant Chops

Serves 4

225 g/8 oz Butter or margarine
15 ml/1 tbsp Capers, drained and
  chopped
10 ml/2 tsp Soft brown sugar
8 Lamb chops
Salt and pepper
30 ml/2 tbsp Honey
30 ml/2 tbsp White wine vinegar

Soften half the butter and mix in the capers and sugar. Shape into a roll and chill. Season the chops with salt and pepper. Heat the remaining butter or margarine with the honey and vinegar until the butter melts. Brush both sides of the chops with the glaze and grill them under a medium grill for about 20 minutes, brushing frequently with the glaze. Transfer the chops to a warmed serving plate and top with the chilled piquant butter.

Noisettes of Lamb with Fennel

Serves 4

4 Noisettes of lamb
Salt and pepper
10 ml/2 tsp Coriander
15 ml/1 tbsp Oil
1 Onion, sliced
2 Fennel bulbs, chopped
300 ml/½ pt Beef Stock (page 24)
15 ml/1 tbsp Cornflour
15 ml/1 tbsp Water
50 g/2 oz Breadcrumbs
50 g/2 oz Strong cheese, grated
2 Fennel sprigs

Season the noisettes to taste with salt and pepper and sprinkle with coriander. Heat the oil and fry the noisettes until browned on both sides, then transfer them to a casserole dish. Fry the onion until soft and lightly browned, then turn the fennel with the onion and spoon into the casserole dish. Stir the stock into the pan and bring to the boil, then pour over the meat, cover and cook in a preheated oven at 180°C/350°F/gas mark 4 for 1 hour until the meat is tender. Transfer the meat and vegetables to a warmed flameproof serving dish and keep them warm. Transfer the pan juices to a saucepan. Mix the cornflour and water and stir them into the juices, bring to the boil and simmer, stirring well, until thickened, then pour over the meat. Sprinkle with the breadcrumbs and cheese and brown under a hot grill. Serve garnished with the fennel sprigs.

Lamb in Cider

Serves 4

15 ml/1 tbsp Oil
8 Lamb chops
Salt and pepper
1 Onion, sliced
1 Garlic clove, chopped
1 Red pepper, sliced
100 g/4 oz Plain flour
300 ml/½ pt Dry cider
150 ml/¼ pt Chicken Stock (page 24)
30 ml/2 tbsp Chopped parsley
5 ml/1 tsp Baking powder
50 g/2 oz Shredded suet
30 ml/2 tbsp Water

Heat the oil. Season the lamb chops with salt and pepper and fry in the oil until browned on both sides, then transfer to a casserole dish. Add the onion and garlic to the pan and fry until soft but not browned. Add the pepper and cook for 2 minutes, then stir in 15 ml/1 tbsp flour and cook for 1 minute. Stir in the cider and stock, bring to the boil, then stir in half the parsley, season to taste with salt and pepper and pour over the lamb. Cover and cook in a preheated oven at 180°C/350°F/gas mark 4 for 1 hour.

Meanwhile, mix the remaining flour with the baking powder, suet and the remaining parsley. Stir in enough water to mix to a firm dough, then roll into 8 dumplings. Skim any fat off the top of the casserole, add the dumplings, cover and cook for a further 30 minutes until the meat is tender and the dumplings are cooked through.

Braised Lamb with Vegetables

Serves 4

| 4 Lamb chops |
| 30 ml/2 tbsp Oil |
| 100 g/4 oz Back bacon, rinded and halved |
| 15 g/½ oz Butter or margarine |
| 100 g/4 oz Carrots, sliced |
| 225 g/8 oz Onions, sliced |
| 1 Turnip, cut into wedges |
| 2 Celery stalks, sliced |
| 1 Bouquet garni |
| Salt and pepper |
| 300 ml/½ pt Beef Stock (page 24) |
| 15 ml/1 tbsp Cornflour |
| 15 ml/1 tbsp Water |

Trim the chops, heat the oil and fry the chops until lightly browned on both sides. Remove from the pan and cover each one with a piece of bacon. Melt the butter or margarine and fry the vegetables until golden brown, stirring continuously. Add the bouquet garni and season to taste with salt and pepper. Pour in enough stock almost to cover the vegetables, lay the chops on top, bring to the boil, cover and simmer for 40 minutes until the chops are tender. Transfer the chops to a baking tin and bake in a preheated oven at 220°C/425°F/gas mark 7 for 10 minutes until the bacon is crisp.

Meanwhile, transfer the vegetables to a warmed serving dish and keep them warm. Make up the cooking liquid to 300 ml/½ pt with any reserved stock and discard the bouquet garni. Mix the cornflour to a smooth paste with the water, then stir it into the stock and bring to the boil, stirring until the sauce thickens. Arrange the baked chops on top of the vegetables and serve the gravy separately.

Lamb Cutlets with Soubise Sauce

Serves 4

| 8 Lamb cutlets |
| 1 Egg, beaten |
| 100 g/4 oz Breadcrumbs |
| 45 ml/3 tbsp Oil |
| 225 g/8 oz Onions, chopped |
| 150 ml/¼ pt Water |
| 25 g/1 oz Butter or margarine |
| 25 g/1 oz Plain flour |
| 450 ml/¾ pt Milk |
| 15 ml/1 tbsp Single cream |
| Salt and pepper |
| 2 Parsley sprigs |

Dip the lamb cutlets in egg and breadcrumbs. Heat the oil and fry the lamb until cooked through and golden brown, turning once. Transfer to a warmed serving dish and keep them warm.

Meanwhile, put the onions and water in a saucepan, bring to the boil and simmer for 10 minutes, then purée in a food processor or blender. Melt the butter or margarine, stir in the flour and cook for 1 minute. Whisk in the milk and cook, stirring, until the mixture thickens. Remove from the heat and stir in the onion purée and cream and season to taste with salt and pepper. Pour the sauce over the cutlets and serve garnished with parsley sprigs.

Paprika Lamb Chops

Serves 4

25 g/1 oz Unsalted butter
8 Lamb chops
2 Onions, sliced
2 Garlic cloves, crushed
30 ml/2 tbsp Paprika
30 ml/2 tbsp Tomato purée
Salt and pepper
300 ml/½ pt Chicken Stock
  (page 24)
150 ml/¼ pt Dry white wine
1 Bay leaf
15 g/½ oz Plain flour
400 g/14 oz Canned tomatoes,
  chopped
150 ml/¼ pt Natural yoghurt
30 ml/2 tbsp Chopped parsley

Melt half the butter and fry the chops until browned, then add the onions and cook until soft. Remove from the heat and stir in the garlic, paprika and tomato purée and season to taste with salt and pepper. Stir in the stock, wine and bay leaf, bring to the boil, cover and simmer for 50 minutes until the meat is tender, stirring occasionally, Mix the flour to a paste with the remaining butter and stir it into the stew until the sauce thickens. Simmer for a few minutes, then stir in the tomatoes and heat through. Transfer to a warmed serving dish, remove the bay leaf, stir in the yoghurt and serve sprinkled with parsley.

Minted Lamb Steaks with Sharp Fruits

Serves 4

50 g/2 oz Butter or margarine,
  melted
30 ml/2 tbsp Chopped mint
4 Lamb leg steaks
Salt and pepper
1 Apple, cored and thinly sliced
15 ml/1 tbsp Lemon juice
2 Peaches, peeled and sliced
2 Kiwi fruits, peeled and sliced
½ White cabbage, shredded
150 ml/½ pt Mayonnaise
  (page 250)

Mix the butter or margarine with the mint and brush it over the steaks. Season to taste with salt and pepper and cook the steaks under a medium grill until cooked through to your liking and browned on both sides.

Meanwhile, toss the apple slices in the lemon juice, then mix with the remaining salad ingredients and toss lightly in the mayonnaise. Chill before serving with the hot steaks.

Lamb with Redcurrant Sauce

Serves 4

150 ml/¼ pt Soured cream
1 Garlic clove, crushed
10 ml/2 tsp Wholegrain mustard
Salt and pepper
450 g/1 lb Lamb fillet
75 ml/5 tbsp Red wine
45 ml/3 tbsp Redcurrant jelly

Mix 60 ml/4 tbsp cream with the garlic and mustard and season to taste with salt and pepper. Spread over the lamb, and place it in a roasting tin. Cook in a preheated oven at 180°C/350°F/gas mark 4 for 50 minutes until tender. Slice the lamb thickly and arrange on a warmed serving dish. Add the wine and redcurrant jelly to the tin and bring to the boil, stirring to scrape up all the meat juices, then stir in the remaining soured cream and simmer until slightly thickened. Pour over the lamb and serve with potatoes and a green vegetable.

Sweet and Sour Lamb

Serves 4

25 g/1 oz Butter or margarine
8 Lamb cutlets
1 Onion, chopped
25 g/1 oz Cornflour
30 ml/2 tbsp White wine vinegar
5 ml/1 tsp Soy sauce
400 g/14 oz Canned pineapple rings
150 ml/¼ pt Chicken Stock (page 24)
15 ml/1 tbsp Chopped parsley
Salt and pepper
4 Glacé cherries

Melt the butter or margarine and fry the lamb cutlets for 10 minutes each side until crisp and brown. Place on a warmed serving dish and keep them warm. Fry the onion until soft but not browned, then drain off any excess fat. Mix the cornflour, wine vinegar and soy sauce and add it to the pan

with the juice from the pineapple and the stock. Bring to the boil, stirring, and boil for a few minutes until the sauce thickens. Add the cutlets and parsley, season to taste with salt and pepper and simmer for 15 minutes. Serve garnished with pineapple rings and glacé cherries.

Lamb and Mushrooms

Serves 4

15 ml/1 tbsp Oil
4 Lamb leg steaks
1 Onion, chopped
1 Garlic clove, crushed
100 g/4 oz Mushrooms, sliced
400 g/14 oz Canned tomatoes, chopped
15 ml/1 tbsp Chopped parsley
2.5 ml/½ tsp Rosemary
2.5 ml/½ tsp Basil
2.5 ml/½ tsp Sugar
60 ml/4 tbsp Chicken Stock (page 24)

Heat the oil and fry the steaks until browned on both sides, then reduce the heat and fry gently until cooked through. Transfer them to a warmed serving dish and keep them warm. Add the onion and garlic to the pan and fry until soft but not browned, then stir in all the remaining ingredients, bring to the boil and simmer, stirring occasionally, for 10 minutes until thick and well combined. Spoon over the steaks and serve with new potatoes.

Lamb in Sherry

Serves 4

50 g/2 oz Butter or margarine
1 Onion, chopped
1 Celery stalk, finely chopped
75 g/3 oz Breadcrumbs
75 g/3 oz Mixed nuts, chopped
Grated rind and juice of 1 lemon
Salt and pepper
1 Egg, beaten
4 Lamb fillets
25 g/1 oz Plain flour
300 ml/½ pt Beef Stock
   (page 24)
75 ml/5 tbsp Sweet sherry

Melt half the butter or margarine and fry the onions and celery until soft but not browned. Stir in the breadcrumbs, half the nuts and the lemon rind, season to taste with salt and pepper and bind with the egg. Remove from the pan. Melt the remaining butter and fry the lamb until browned on both sides, then place 2 of the fillets in a casserole dish just large enough to hold them. Spread the stuffing mixture on top and top with remaining fillets. Stir the flour into the pan and cook for 1 minute, then stir in the stock and sherry, bring to the boil and add the lemon juice. Season to taste with salt and pepper and pour over the lamb. Cover and cook in a preheated oven at 180°C/350°F/gas mark 4 for 1½ hours until the meat is tender. Slice the meat on to a warmed serving dish and sprinkle with the remaining nuts. Strain the sauce into a sauce boat and serve separately.

Lamb with Cumin and Sesame Seed

Serves 4

30 ml/2 tbsp Olive oil
Juice of 1 lemon
45 ml/3 tbsp Sesame seeds, crushed
15 ml/1 tbsp Cumin seeds, crushed
1 Garlic clove, crushed
2.5 ml/½ tsp Cayenne pepper
Salt and pepper
4 Lamb fillets
45 ml/3 tbsp Chopped mint
150 ml/¼ pt Natural yoghurt

Mix together all the ingredients except the mint and yoghurt and spread the mixture over the lamb fillets. Leave to marinate overnight, then bake in a preheated oven at 230°C/450°F/gas mark 8 for 15 minutes, then reduce the heat to 180°C/350°F/gas mark 4 for a further 15 minutes until cooked through. Cut the fillets into thin slices, season to taste with salt and pepper and pour over the meat juices. Stir the mint into the yoghurt and serve with the lamb.

Malaysian Lamb Curry

Serves 4

50 g/2 oz Desiccated coconut
2 Dried red chilli peppers
15 ml/1 tbsp Cumin seeds, toasted
15 ml/1 tbsp Coriander seeds, toasted
6 Green peppercorns
25 g/1 oz Root ginger, grated
2 Garlic cloves, chopped
5 ml/1 tsp Turmeric
30 ml/2 tbsp Lemon juice
30 ml/2 tbsp Oil
3 Onions, chopped
450 g/1 lb Lamb, cubed
225 g/8 oz Canned tomatoes, chopped
Salt and pepper

Purée the coconut, chilli peppers, cumin, coriander, peppercorns, ginger, garlic, turmeric and lemon juice in a food processor or blender. Heat the oil and fry the onions until soft but not browned, then stir in the paste and fry for 4 minutes. Stir in the lamb and cook for 5 minutes, then add the tomatoes and season to taste with salt and pepper. Bring to the boil, cover and simmer for 1 hour until tender. Serve with boiled rice.

Lamb Ragout

Serves 4

50 g/2 oz Butter or margarine
900 g/2 lb Leg of lamb, boned and cubed
3 Onions, sliced
1 Garlic clove, crushed
15 ml/1 tbsp Paprika
15 ml/1 tbsp Plain flour
15 ml/1 tbsp Tomato purée
150 ml/¼ pt Dry white wine
300 ml/½ pt Chicken Stock (page 24)
1 Bouquet garni
Salt and pepper

Heat the butter or margarine in a saucepan and fry the lamb until browned on all sides, then remove from the pan. Add the onions and garlic and fry until soft, then stir in the paprika and flour and cook for 1 minute. Stir in the tomato purée, wine and stock, add the bouquet garni and season to taste with salt and pepper. Bring to the boil, cover and simmer for 1 hour until the meat is tender, stirring occasionally. Remove the bouquet garni and serve with fried rice.

Sasaties

Serves 6

1.5 kg/3 lb Leg of lamb
1 Garlic clove
4 Onions, quartered
30 ml/2 tbsp Soft brown sugar
300 ml/½ pt Milk
15 ml/1 tbsp Lamb dripping
15 ml/1 tbsp Lime juice cordial (undiluted)
15 ml/1 tbsp Curry powder
2.5 ml/½ tsp Cloves
2.5 ml/½ tsp Whole allspice
120 ml/4 fl oz White wine vinegar
Salt and pepper
Oil for brushing
15 ml/1 tbsp Plain flour
15 ml/1 tbsp Butter or margarine, chilled and cut into pieces

Cut the lamb into 5 cm/2 in cubes. Rub the inside of a large earthenware bowl with the cut side of the garlic clove. Lay the meat in the bowl. Add 2 onions, the sugar and milk. Heat the dripping in a frying pan and fry the remaining onions until lightly browned. Add the lime juice, spices and wine vinegar and season to taste with salt and pepper. Pour over the meat and leave overnight.

Remove the meat and onions with a slotted spoon and thread on to 6 skewers, alternating meat and onions. Pat dry and brush with oil. Turn the marinade into a saucepan, sprinkle on the flour and stir in the butter or margarine, bring to the boil and simmer, stirring constantly, until slightly thickened. Place the kebabs under a medium grill and cook for about 20 minutes until cooked through, turning frequently. Serve with rice and salad and serve the sauce in a jug.

Chelow Kabab with Rice Nests

Serves 6-8

750 g/1½ lb Leg or shoulder mutton or lamb, boned
Salt and pepper
175 ml/6 fl oz Natural yoghurt
4 Tomatoes, halved
Oil for cooking
Potato crisps
340 g/12 oz Long-grain rice
4 Egg yolks
50 g/2 oz Butter or margarine

Cut the mutton or lamb into strips about 18 x 5 cm/7 x 2 in and rub with salt and pepper. Marinate them in yoghurt for 3 hours. Season the tomatoes with salt and pepper and brush with oil.

Weave the meat strips lengthways on to long skewers and beat them flat with a mallet. Oil lightly, then grill under a medium grill for 25 minutes, turning frequently. Add the tomatoes to the grill for the last 5 minutes of cooking. Warm the crisps in the oven for 10 minutes.

Meanwhile, cook the rice in plenty of boiling salted water for 15 minutes until just tender, drain and serve in individual bowls with an egg yolk and a knob of butter or margarine in the centre of each bowl. The egg and butter are mashed into the hot rice and eaten with the meat, crisps and tomatoes.

Lancashire Hot Pot

Serves 4

900 g/2 lb Potatoes, thickly sliced

50 g/2 oz Lard

750 g/1½ lb Middle neck of lamb, cut into pieces

2 Sheep's kidneys, skinned, cored and sliced

2 Onions, sliced

Salt and pepper

300 ml/½ pt Chicken Stock (page 24), hot

Put a thick layer of potato slices in the bottom of a greased casserole dish. Add the meat, kidneys and onions and season to taste with salt and pepper. Pour over the hot stock and cover with the remaining potatoes in an overlapping layer. Brush well with the remaining fat. Cover and cook in a preheated oven at 180°C/350°F/gas mark 4 for 2 hours until the meat and potatoes are tender. Remove the lid and cook at 220°C/425°F/gas mark 7 for a further 20 minutes until lightly browned.

Apricot and Chestnut Lamb

Serves 6

1 Onion, finely chopped

150 g/6 oz Breadcrumbs

100 g/4 oz Dried apricots, chopped

100 g/4 oz Chestnuts, chopped

1 Egg, beaten

Salt and pepper

1.5 kg/3 lb Shoulder of lamb, boned

Mix together the onion, breadcrumbs

apricots, chestnuts and egg and season to taste with salt and pepper. Lay the lamb joint flat and cover with the stuffing. Tie round with string and cook in a preheated oven at 190°C/375°F/gas mark 5 for 2 hours, basting occasionally.

Bordeaux-Braised Lamb

Serves 6-8

1.5 kg/3 lb Leg of lamb, boned

300 ml/½ pt Red wine

30 ml/2 tbsp Oil

100 g/4 oz Button mushrooms

1 Onion, chopped

1 Garlic clove, chopped

2 Carrots, sliced

15 g/½ oz Plain flour

150 ml/¼ pt Chicken Stock (page 24)

1 Bouquet garni

Salt and pepper

Marinate the lamb in the wine overnight. Remove the meat from the marinade, drain and pat dry with kitchen paper. Heat the oil and fry the meat until browned, then transfer it to a casserole dish and cover with the uncooked mushrooms. Fry the onion, garlic and carrots until just browned, then add the flour and cook for 1 minute. Stir in the stock and 150 ml/¼ pt of the wine marinade, bring to the boil, then pour into the casserole, add the bouquet garni and season to taste with salt and pepper. Cover and cook in a preheated oven at 150°C/300°F/gas mark 2 for 2½ hours. Remove the bouquet garni before serving.

Butterflied Lamb

Serves 6-8

60 ml/4 tbsp Lemon juice
150 ml/¼ pt Dry white wine
30 ml/2 tbsp Worcestershire sauce
30 ml/2 tbsp Oil
2 Garlic cloves, chopped
5 ml/1 tsp Basil
5 ml/1 tsp Marjoram
5 ml/1 tsp Rosemary
Salt and pepper
1.25 kg/2½ lb Leg of lamb, boned

Mix all the ingredients except the lamb in a plastic bag. Open out the lamb into the shape of a butterfly, lay it in the marinade, close the bag securely and leave the meat to marinate for 24 hours, turning occasionally.

Bake the lamb in a preheated oven at 200°C/400°F/gas mark 6 for about 1 hour, basting occasionally with a little marinade, until cooked to your liking. Let the meat rest for 10 minutes before slicing it.

Roast Lamb French Style

Serves 6

1.75 kg/4 lb Leg of lamb
3 Garlic cloves, sliced
Pinch of rosemary
Pinch of sage
Pinch of thyme
5 ml/1 tsp Cayenne pepper
15 ml/1 tbsp Oil
300 ml/½ pt Chicken Stock (page 24)
120 ml/4 fl oz Red wine
2 Tomatoes, skinned, seeded and chopped
15 ml/1 tbsp Worcestershire sauce
15 ml/1 tbsp Tomato purée
5 ml/1 tsp Mint

Pat the meat dry on kitchen paper and cut tiny slits in the surface of the meat. Push the garlic into the cuts and rub the meat with herbs and cayenne pepper. Roast in a preheated oven at 220°C/425°F/gas mark 7 for 15 minutes, then reduce the temperature to 180°C/350°F/gas mark 4 and roast for a further 30 minutes. Bring the stock and wine to the boil and pour it over the meat, then continue roasting for a further 30 minutes, basting frequently. When the meat is cooked to your liking, transfer it to a warmed serving plate and keep it warm. Add the tomatoes, Worcestershire sauce, tomato purée and mint to the liquid in the tin, bring to the boil and simmer, stirring well, until the liquid is reduced by one-third. Strain the sauce, then return it to the pan to reheat. Carve the lamb and serve with the sauce spooned over the meat.

Guard of Honour

Serves 6

900 g/2 lb Best end of neck of lamb cut into 2 pieces, each having about 6 chops

50 g/2 oz Breadcrumbs

225 g/8 oz Pork sausagemeat

50 g/2 oz Mushrooms, finely chopped

10 ml/2 tsp Lemon juice

2.5 ml/½ tsp Prepared mustard

Salt and pepper

4 Medium tomatoes

15 ml/1 tbsp Chopped rosemary leaves

50 g/2 oz Butter or margarine

5 ml/1 tsp French mustard

1 Garlic clove, crushed

Ask the butcher to remove the chine bone from the meat then cut off the top 2.5 cm/1 in at the thin end, leaving the bones exposed. Discard the fat. Trim the meat between the bones and scrape each bone to clean it. Chop the meat finely, then mix it with the breadcrumbs, sausagemeat, mushrooms, half the lemon juice and the mustard and season to taste with salt and pepper. Cut the tomatoes in half and scoop out the seeds. Stir these into the stuffing. Use half the stuffing to fill the tomato shells. Stand the lamb so that the exposed bones interlock. Form the remaining stuffing into a thick sausage and place in the middle of the two pieces of lamb. Place in a shallow ovenproof dish. Mix the rosemary, butter or margarine, 5 ml/1 tsp lemon juice, French mustard and garlic. Score lines on the fatty side of the meat with a sharp knife and spread the butter over the outside. Bake in a preheated oven at 190°C/375°F/gas mark 5 for 30 minutes, covering the bones with pieces of foil if they appear to be burning.

Roast Lamb with Mint

Serves 8

1.75 kg/4 lb Boned leg of lamb

Salt and pepper

3 Garlic cloves, crushed

1 Bunch of mint, chopped

45 ml/3 tbsp Olive oil

Juice of 1 lemon

1 Celery stalk, finely chopped

1 Carrot, finely chopped

1 Onion, finely chopped

300 ml/½ pt Water

Open out the lamb, season to taste with salt and pepper and sprinkle with the garlic and half the mint. Roll up and tie securely. Season the outside of the joint and place it on a rack in a roasting tin, fat side up. Pour over the oil and lemon juice, surround with the vegetables and roast in a preheated oven at 230°C/450°F/gas mark 8 for 20 minutes, then reduce the heat to 180°C/350°F/gas mark 4, add the water to the roasting tin and roast for a further 1¼ hours until the meat is tender and crisp on the outside. Transfer the lamb to a warmed serving dish. Skim any excess fat off the pan juices, stir in the remaining mint and bring to the boil, then pour into a sauce boat and serve with the lamb.

Lamb Meatloaf with Taco Topping

Serves 4

| 2 Onions, chopped |
| 1 Garlic clove, chopped |
| 450 g/1 lb Minced lamb |
| 5 ml/1 tsp Chilli pepper |
| 50 g/2 oz Breadcrumbs |
| 5 ml/1 tsp Tabasco sauce |
| Salt and pepper |
| 100 g/4 oz Strong cheese, grated |
| 150 ml/¼ pt Taco sauce |
| 25 g/1 oz Corn chips, broken |

Mix the onions, garlic, lamb, chilli pepper, breadcrumbs and tabasco sauce and season to taste with salt and pepper. Press half the mixture into a greased 900 g/2 lb loaf tin, sprinkle in half the cheese and top with the remaining mince. Cover and bake in a preheated oven at 180°C/350°F/gas mark 4 for 45 minutes, then leave to stand for 10 minutes. Turn the loaf out on to an ovenproof plate and brush with the taco sauce. Sprinkle with the remaining cheese and the corn chips. Return to the oven at 200°C/400°F/gas mark 6 for 10 minutes until the cheese has melted. Serve in slices, hot or cold.

Grilled Kofta

Serves 4

| 3 Bread slices, crusts removed |
| 45 ml/3 tbsp Dry white wine |
| 450 g/1 lb Minced lamb |
| 1 Onion, chopped |
| 1 Egg, beaten |

| 4 Parsley sprigs, chopped |
| Salt and pepper |
| 30 ml/2 tbsp Olive oil |
| 4 Pitta bread |
| 150 ml/¼ pt Sharp Yoghurt Dressing (page 251) |

Moisten the bread with the wine and a little water if needed. Squeeze it dry and put it with all the other ingredients except the oil, pitta bread and dressing in a food processor or blender and process until smooth and pasty. Shape into rissoles the size of small eggs with floured hands, leave to stand for 30 minutes, then thread carefully on to shish kebab skewers and brush with olive oil. Grill under a hot grill for 20 minutes, turning frequently, until well browned on all sides. Serve with warm pitta bread and yoghurt dressing.

Crispy Topped Lamb and Watercress

Serves 4

| 450 g/1 lb Minced lamb |
| 2 Onions, chopped |
| 2 Bunches of watercress, chopped |
| 5 ml/1 tsp Oregano |
| 40 g/1½ oz Plain flour |
| 300 ml/½ pt Chicken Stock (page 24) |
| 60 ml/4 tbsp Dry white wine |
| Salt and pepper |
| 50 g/2 oz Butter or margarine |
| 600 ml/1 pt Milk |
| 225 g/8 oz Cheshire cheese, crumbled |
| 225 g/8 oz Lasagne slices |

Fry the lamb in a saucepan until browned on both sides, then add the onions and fry until soft. Add the watercress, oregano and 30 ml/2 tbsp flour and cook for 1 minute, then stir in the stock and wine and season to taste with salt and pepper. Bring to the boil, then simmer for 40 minutes, stirring occasionally. Meanwhile, melt the butter or margarine, stir in the remaining flour and cook for 1 minute. Whisk in the milk and cook, stirring, until the sauce thickens. Remove from the heat and stir in half the cheese. Cook the lasagne in boiling salted water until just tender, then drain, or use the ready-to-use variety. Layer the mince, lasagne and half the cheese sauce in a shallow greased ovenproof dish, finishing with a layer of lasagne. Pour over the remaining cheese sauce, sprinkle with the remaining cheese and bake in a preheated oven at 190°C/375°F/gas mark 4 for 40 minutes until cooked through and well browned.

Samosas

Serves 4

175 g/6 oz Self-raising flour	
75 g/3 oz Shredded suet	
Pinch of salt	
30 ml/2 tbsp Water	
1 Onion, chopped	
5 ml/1 tsp Curry powder	
15 ml/1 tbsp Oil	
175 g/6 oz Cooked lamb, finely chopped	
Salt and pepper	
15 ml/1 tbsp Sweet chutney	
Oil for deep frying	

Mix the flour, suet and salt, then bind to a firm dough with the water. Roll out and cut into 8 rounds. Mix the onion and curry powder. Heat the oil and fry the onion until soft, then add the lamb and cook for 5 minutes. Season to taste with salt and pepper and stir in the chutney. Leave to cool. Put a spoonful of the mixture in the centre of each pastry round, bring up the edges and pinch together to make a pasty shape. Fry in hot oil for about 5 minutes until golden brown.

Pytt i Panna

Serves 4

50 g/2 oz Unsalted butter	
15 ml/1 tbsp Olive oil	
450 g/1 lb Boiled potatoes, chopped	
450 g/1 lb Cooked lamb, diced	
225 g/8 oz Streaky bacon, diced	
1 Onion, chopped	
Salt and pepper	
15 ml/1 tbsp Chopped parsley	
5 ml/1 tsp Worcestershire sauce	
4 Eggs	

Melt the butter with the oil and fry the potatoes until golden brown. Remove them from the pan, drain well and keep them warm. Fry the meat, bacon and onion until the onion is soft but not browned, then stir the potatoes back into the pan and season to taste with salt and pepper. Cook for 5 minutes, shaking the pan gently, then stir in the parsley and Worcestershire sauce. Meanwhile, fry the eggs lightly. Turn the lamb mixture into a warmed serving dish and serve topped with the fried eggs.

Moussaka

Serves 4

2 Aubergines, sliced
Salt and pepper
15 ml/1 tbsp Oil
1 Onion, chopped
1 Garlic clove, chopped
350 g/12 oz Cooked lamb, minced
10 ml/2 tsp Tomato purée
5 ml/1 tsp Cornflour
45 ml/3 tbsp Dry white wine
150 ml/¼ pt Chicken Stock
(page 24)
5 ml/1 tsp Oregano
25 g/1 oz Butter or margarine
25 g/1 oz Plain flour
450 ml/¾ pt Milk
75 g/3 oz Cheese, grated

Lay the sliced aubergines in a dish, sprinkle with salt and leave to stand. Heat the oil and fry the onion and garlic until soft but not browned. Stir in the lamb, tomato purée, cornflour, wine and stock and cook until thickened. Sprinkle with oregano. Turn the mixture into an ovenproof dish. Drain, rinse and pat dry the aubergines and layer them on top of the meat. Melt the butter in a clean saucepan, stir in the flour and cook for 1 minute. Whisk in the milk, bring to the boil and simmer until thickened, stirring continuously. Remove from the heat and stir in half the cheese, then pour the sauce over the aubergines. Sprinkle with the remaining cheese and bake in a pre-heated oven at 200°C/400°F/gas mark 6 for 30 minutes until golden brown.

Lamb in Rich Spicy Sauce

Serves 4

15 ml/1 tbsp Oil
1 Garlic clove, chopped
1 Onion, chopped
15 ml/1 tbsp Curry powder
400 g/14 oz Canned tomatoes
15 ml/1 tbsp Tomato purée
15 ml/1 tbsp Lemon juice
15 ml/1 tbsp Mango chutney
10 ml/2 tsp Garam masala
50 ml/2 fl oz Natural yoghurt
450 g/1 lb Cooked lamb, diced

Heat the oil and fry the garlic and half the onion until browned. Add the curry powder and cook for 1 minute, then add the tomatoes, tomato purée, lemon juice and chutney and cook for 20 minutes. Blend in the garam masala then pour the mixture into a food processor or blender and process until smooth. Add the yoghurt and process again until mixed. Return the mixture to the pan, add the lamb and remaining onion, bring to the boil and simmer gently for 15 minutes. Serve with rice and extra mango chutney.

Pork

Pork lends itself particularly well to recipes with a sweet and sour flavour and is delicious cooked with fruits or in a little well chosen alcohol! Pork should always be thoroughly cooked, so take care to check that the meat is completely cooked through before serving.

Pork in Whisky

Serves 4

25 g/1 oz Butter or margarine
15 ml/1 tbsp Oil
4 Pork chops
Salt and pepper
150 ml/¼ pt Whisky
150 ml/¼ pt Beef Stock (page 24)
25 g/1 oz Soft brown sugar
15 ml/1 tbsp French mustard
5 ml/1 tsp Cornflour
15 ml/1 tbsp Water

Melt the butter with the oil and fry the chops until browned on both sides, then season to taste with salt and pepper. Stir in the whisky and simmer until the aroma subsides, then stir in the stock, sugar and mustard, bring to the boil, cover and simmer for 15 minutes until the chops are cooked. Mix the cornflour and water and stir it into the sauce, cooking until the sauce thickens.

Pork Chops Avesnoise

Serves 4

15 g/½ oz Butter or margarine
15 ml/1 tbsp Olive oil
4 Pork chops
Salt and pepper
100 g/4 oz Gruyère cheese, grated
10 ml/2 tsp Dijon mustard
150 ml/¼ pt Single cream
1 Garlic clove, crushed

Melt the butter or margarine with the oil and fry the chops until browned on both sides. Season to taste with salt and pepper, transfer to a shallow casserole and bake in a preheated oven at 180°C/350°F/gas mark 4 for 45 minutes until tender. Mix the cheese, mustard, cream and garlic and spread it over the top of the chops. Return the chops to the oven for a further 10 minutes until the topping is golden. Serve with a crisp green salad.

Devilled Pork Chops

Serves 4

15 ml/1 tbsp Oil
4 Pork chops
1 Onion, chopped
½ Green pepper, chopped
15 g/½ oz Plain flour
Salt and pepper
400 g/14 oz Canned tomatoes, chopped
10 ml/2 tsp Made mustard
15 ml/1 tbsp Worcestershire sauce
2.5 ml/½ tsp Soft brown sugar
Salt and pepper

Heat the oil in a large frying pan and brown the chops on both sides. Transfer to an ovenproof dish. Fry the onion and pepper in the oil until soft but not browned, stir in the flour and cook for 1 minute, then add the remaining ingredients and season to taste with salt and pepper. Bring to the boil, stirring constantly, until the sauce is thick and smooth. Pour over the chops, cover and bake in a preheated oven at 180°C/350°F/gas mark 4 for 30 minutes.

Foil Pork Parcels

Serves 4

25 g/1 oz Butter or margarine
4 Pork chops
1 Onion, chopped
225 g/8 oz Mushrooms, sliced
75 ml/5 tbsp Dry cider
30 ml/2 tbsp Lemon juice
150 ml/¼ pt Soured cream
Salt and pepper

Melt the butter or margarine and fry the chops until browned on both sides, then transfer them to 4 squares of kitchen foil. Add the onion and mushrooms to the pan and fry until soft but not browned. Stir in the cider and lemon juice, bring to the boil and boil until reduced by half, then remove from the heat, stir in the cream and season to taste with salt and pepper. Spoon over the chops, then fold up the foil and seal the edges into parcels. Place the parcels in an ovenproof dish and bake in a preheated oven at 180°C/350°F/gas mark 4 for 1 hour. Serve the pork in the foil and let everyone open their own parcel.

Pork in Cider

Serves 4

50 g/2 oz Butter or margarine
4 Pork chops
1 Onion, sliced
350 g/12 oz Cooking apples, peeled, cored and sliced
450 ml/¾ pt Dry cider
Salt and pepper

Melt the butter or margarine and fry the chops until browned, then transfer them to a casserole dish. Fry the onion and apples until lightly browned, then spoon them into the casserole. Pour the cider into the pan and season to taste with salt and pepper, bring to the boil, then pour over the meat. Cover and bake in a preheated oven at 180°C/350°F/gas mark 4 for 50 minutes until the meat is tender. Serve with boiled rice.

Pork with Apple Rings

Serves 4

4 Pork chops
Salt and pepper
50 g/2 oz Butter or margarine
1 Onion, chopped
25 g/1 oz Plain flour
150 ml/¼ pt Chicken Stock (page 24)
150 ml/¼ pt Milk
2 Cooking apples, peeled and cored
15 ml/1 tbsp Chopped parsley

Season the chops with salt and pepper and fry in half the butter until lightly browned and cooked through. Transfer to a warmed serving dish and keep them warm. Gently fry the onion until soft but not browned. Add the flour and cook for 1 minute. Whisk in the stock and milk and bring to the boil, stirring continuously. Return the chops to the pan. Chop one apple and stir it into the pan. Simmer for 15 minutes.

Meanwhile slice the second apple into rings and fry lightly in the remaining butter. Serve the pork with the apple slices and garnish with the parsley.

Honeyed Pork Steaks

Serves 4

150 ml/¼ pt Tomato ketchup
30 ml/2 tbsp Clear honey
30 ml/2 tbsp Lemon juice
30 ml/2 tbsp Corn oil
15 ml/1 tbsp Worcestershire sauce
4 Pork steaks
4 Tomatoes

Mix the ketchup, honey, lemon juice, oil and Worcestershire sauce in a saucepan over a low heat and warm through. Pour over the steaks in a shallow dish and leave to marinate for 30 minutes, turning once. Cook under a medium grill for about 30 minutes, basting frequently with the marinade while cooking. Cut a cross in the tomatoes and add them to the grill for the final 5 minutes of cooking.

Sweet and Sour Pork Steaks

Serves 4

15 ml/1 tbsp Oil
1 Onion, chopped
100 g/4 oz Mushrooms, sliced
30 ml/2 tbsp Tomato purée
30 ml/2 tbsp Demerara sugar
30 ml/2 tbsp Lemon juice
30 ml/2 tbsp Cider vinegar
30 ml/2 tbsp Worcestershire sauce
400 g/14 oz Canned tomatoes, chopped
Salt
4 Pork steaks

Heat half the oil in a frying pan and fry the onion and mushrooms until soft but not browned. Stir in all the remaining ingredients except the remaining oil and the steaks, bring to the boil, cover and simmer for 20 minutes. Brush the steaks with the remaining oil and grill under a medium heat for 7 minutes each side. Pour the sauce over the steaks and serve with green noodles.

South Sea Spare Ribs

Serves 4

90 ml/6 tbsp Soy sauce

60 ml/4 tbsp Red wine

90 ml/6 tbsp Tomato ketchup

75 ml/5 tbsp Pineapple juice

15 ml/1 tbsp Basil

5 ml/1 tsp Sage

225 ml/8 fl oz Oil

Pepper

1.5 kg/3 lb Pork spare ribs

Mix together all the ingredients except the pork and season to taste with pepper. Marinate the pork in the mixture overnight, then drain and dry well. Put the pork in a greased baking tin and bake in a preheated oven at 180°C/350°F/gas mark 4 for 20 minutes, then turn the chops and bake for a further 20 minutes, basting frequently with the marinade. Drain the pork and finish off under the grill for 5 minutes until glazed.

Pork and Peppers

Serves 4

15 ml/1 tbsp Oil

15 g/1 oz Butter or margarine

1 Onion, chopped

25 g/1 oz Root ginger, grated

1 Garlic clove, crushed

4 Pork steaks

1 Red pepper, sliced

1 Green pepper, sliced

1 Yellow pepper, sliced

60 ml/4 tbsp Dry sherry

30 ml/2 tbsp Soy sauce

150 ml/¼ pt Pineapple juice

Salt and pepper

Heat the oil and butter and fry the onion, ginger and garlic until soft but not browned, then remove them from the pan. Add the steaks and fry until browned on both sides, then add the peppers, sherry, soy sauce and pineapple juice and return the onion mixture to the pan. Mix thoroughly and season to taste with salt and pepper, bring to the boil, cover and simmer for 15 minutes until the steaks are cooked through. Transfer the steaks to a warmed serving dish and keep them warm. Bring the sauce to the boil and boil to reduce and thicken the sauce, then pour it over the steaks and serve with rice.

Lemon Pork

Serves 6

15 ml/1 tbsp Oil

900 g/2 lb Pork fillet, cubed

300 ml/½ pt Dry white wine

30 ml/2 tbsp Cumin

2 Garlic cloves, crushed

Salt and pepper

1 Lemon, sliced

10 ml/2 tsp Coriander

Heat the oil and fry the pork until browned on all sides, stirring well. Stir in half the wine and the cumin and garlic. Season to taste with salt and pepper. Bring to the boil, cover and simmer for 30 minutes until tender. Remove the lid and add the remaining wine, lemon slices and coriander and simmer until the sauce has reduced and thickened slightly. Transfer to a warmed serving dish and serve with boiled rice.

Mississippi Grill

Serves 6

2 Eating apples, sliced
60 ml/4 tbsp Oil
450 g/1 lb Pork fillet, cubed
2 Green peppers, cubed
100 g/4 oz Button mushrooms
6 Small tomatoes
Salt and pepper

Brush the eating apples with the oil as soon as you have sliced them. Thread the pork, apple, peppers, mushrooms and tomatoes on 6 skewers. Brush generously with the remaining oil. Grill under a medium grill for 25 minutes until the pork is well cooked through.

Pork with Pâté

Serves 4

2 Pork tenderloins, cut through
  horizontally
125 g/4 oz Smooth pâté
Salt and pepper
25 g/1 oz Butter or margarine
1 Garlic clove, crushed
100 g/4 oz Mushrooms, sliced
150 ml/¼ pt Dry sherry
150 ml/¼ pt Dry white wine
5 ml/1 tsp Dijon mustard
2.5 ml/½ tsp Worcestershire sauce
5 ml/1 tsp Chopped parsley
45 ml/3 tbsp Double cream

Flatten out the pork and spread with the pâté, then fold over and sew the edges, enclosing the pâté. Melt the butter or margarine and fry the pork until browned on all sides, then remove it from the pan. Add the garlic to the pan and fry until lightly browned. Add the mushrooms and cook for 2 minutes, then stir in the sherry, wine, mustard, Worcestershire sauce and parsley, bring to the boil, return the pork to the pan, cover and simmer for 40 minutes. Remove the pork from the pan, slice it and arrange it on a warmed serving dish and keep it warm. Boil the sauce until thickened, then stir in the cream and heat through for 3 minutes before pouring the sauce over the meat to serve.

Pork Spare Ribs in Wine

Serves 4

15 ml/1 tbsp Chopped parsley
1 Garlic clove, chopped
3 Juniper berries, crushed
8 Pork spare ribs
Salt and pepper
30 ml/2 tbsp Oil
150 ml/¼ pt Dry white wine
300 ml/½ pt Chicken Stock
  (page 24)
Juice of 2 oranges

Mix the parsley, garlic and juniper berries and rub them into the spare ribs, then season to taste with salt and pepper. Heat the oil and fry the spare ribs until browned on all sides, then stir in the wine and bring to the boil. Stir in the stock and orange juice, bring back to the boil and simmer, uncovered, for 30 minutes until the meat is tender and the sauce has thickened.

Stuffed Pork Fillet

Serves 4

9 Prunes, chopped

25 g/1 oz Breadcrumbs

100 g/4 oz Butter or margarine, softened

5 ml/1 tsp Mixed herbs

Salt and pepper

750 g/1½ lb Pork fillet

8 Streaky bacon rashers, rinded

Mix the prunes, breadcrumbs and 75 g/3 oz butter or margarine together well, then stir in the mixed herbs and season to taste with salt and pepper. Slice the fillets almost in half, fill the centre with the stuffing, then fold the meat over again. Stretch the bacon rashers with a knife on a board, then wrap them around the meat. Lay the rolls in an ovenproof dish and dot with the remaining butter. Bake in a preheated oven at 200°C/400°F/gas mark 6 for 30 minutes until cooked through and crispy. Serve with rice or pasta.

Pork Fillet with Orange Sauce

Serves 4

50 g/2 oz Butter or margarine

450 g/1 lb Pork fillet, thinly sliced

1 Onion, chopped

15 g/½ oz Plain flour

Grated rind and juice of 1 orange

30 ml/2 tbsp Redcurrant jelly

300 ml/½ pt Chicken Stock (page 24)

Salt and pepper

Melt the butter or margarine and fry the pork until browned on both sides, then remove from the pan. Add the onion and fry until soft but not browned, then stir in the flour and cook for 1 minute. Stir in the orange rind and juice, the redcurrant jelly and stock and season to taste with salt and pepper. Bring to the boil, return the pork to the pan, cover and simmer gently for 15 minutes until the meat is cooked through. Serve with carrots and new potatoes.

Caribbean Pork

Serves 4

30 ml/2 tbsp Oil

30 ml/2 tbsp Sugar

750 g/1½ lb Pork fillet, cubed

5 ml/1 tsp Allspice

5 ml/1 tsp Thyme

1 Onion, chopped

2 Garlic cloves, chopped

15 ml/1 tbsp Wine vinegar

50 g/2 oz Creamed coconut

300 ml/½ pt Water

100 g/4 oz Mushrooms, sliced

1 Green pepper, sliced

Juice of ½ lime

Heat the oil in a large frying pan, add the sugar and heat until caramelised. Add the pork and fry until browned. Add the allspice and thyme, cover and simmer for 10 minutes. Stir in the onion, garlic, wine vinegar, coconut and water, cover and simmer for 20 minutes. Add the mushrooms and pepper, cover and simmer for 10 minutes. Stir in the lime juice before serving.

Paprika Pork

Serves 4

50 g/2 oz Butter or margarine
15 ml/1 tbsp Oil
450 g/1 lb Pork fillet, cubed
3 Onions, sliced
15 ml/1 tbsp Paprika
25 g/1 oz Plain flour
300 ml/½ pt Chicken Stock (page 24)
15 ml/1 tbsp Lemon juice
15 ml/1 tbsp Tomato purée
400 g/14 oz Canned tomatoes, chopped
50 g/2 oz Raisins
Salt and pepper
60 ml/4 tbsp Soured cream

Melt the butter or margarine with the oil and fry the pork until browned on all sides, then transfer it to a casserole dish. Add the onions to the pan and fry until lightly browned, then stir in the paprika and flour and cook for 1 minute. Stir in the stock, tomato purée, lemon juice, tomatoes and raisins, season to taste with salt and pepper and bring to the boil. Pour the mixture into the casserole and bake in a preheated oven at 180°C/350°F/gas mark 4 for 1½ hours until the meat is tender. Swirl the soured cream into the casserole just before serving.

Exotic Pork Curry

Serves 4

750 g/1½ lb Pork fillet, cubed
25 g/1 oz Plain flour
30 ml/2 tbsp Oil
2 Onions, sliced
1 Red pepper, sliced
1 Green pepper, sliced
5 ml/1 tsp Turmeric
15 ml/1 tbsp Curry powder
5 ml/1 tsp Cumin
5 ml/1 tsp Ground ginger
2.5 ml/½ tsp Chilli powder
400 g/14 oz Canned tomatoes, drained and chopped
15 ml/1 tbsp Tomato purée
300 ml/½ pt Chicken Stock (page 24)
450 g/1 lb Small new potatoes, scrubbed
425 g/15 oz Canned mango slices, drained

Coat the pork in the flour. Heat the oil and fry the pork until just browned. Add the onion and peppers and cook for 2 minutes. Add the spices and cook for 1 minute, stirring continuously. Stir in the tomatoes, tomato purée, stock and potatoes, bring to the boil, cover and cook for 20 minutes. Add the mango and cook for a further 5 minutes until the meat and vegetables are cooked through. Serve with rice and mango chutney.

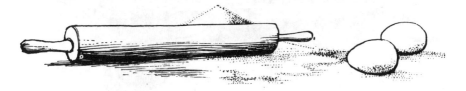

Pork in Calvados

Serves 4

750 g/1½ lb Pork fillet, cubed
Salt and pepper
50 g/2 oz Butter or margarine
225 g/8 oz Mushrooms, sliced
60 ml/4 tbsp Calvados
150 ml/¼ pt Chicken Stock (page 24)
150 ml/¼ pt Single cream
10 ml/2 tsp Cornflour
50 g/2 oz Mixed nuts, chopped
15 ml/1 tbsp Chopped parsley

Season the pork with salt and pepper. Melt half the butter or margarine and fry the meat until lightly browned, then transfer it to a casserole dish. Melt the remaining butter or margarine and fry the mushrooms for 2 minutes, then stir in the Calvados and stock, season to taste with salt and pepper, bring to the boil and simmer for 3 minutes. Pour the sauce into the casserole, cover and bake in a preheated oven at 180°C/350°F/gas mark 4 for 45 minutes until the meat is tender. Mix the cream and cornflour and stir them into the sauce, then return the casserole to the oven for 10 minutes. Mix the nuts and parsley and sprinkle over the casserole to serve.

Navarin of Pork

Serves 4

15 g/½ oz Plain flour
Pinch of nutmeg
Salt and pepper
750 g/1½ lb Pork fillet, cubed
30 ml/2 tbsp Oil
2 Large parsnips, diced
½ Turnip, diced
2 Carrots, diced
1 Onion, chopped
300 ml/½ pt Chicken Stock (page 24)
5 ml/1 tsp Worcestershire sauce
1 Bay leaf

Season the flour with the nutmeg and salt and pepper and toss the meat in the flour. Heat the oil and fry the meat until browned on all sides, then transfer it to a casserole dish. Add the vegetables to the pan and fry until lightly browned, then add them to the casserole dish. Pour the stock into the pan, add the Worcestershire sauce and season to taste with salt and pepper. Bring it to the boil, then pour it into the casserole dish and add the bay leaf. Cover and cook in a preheated oven at 160°C/325°F/gas mark 3 for 1¼ hours until tender. Discard the bay leaf before serving.

Boston Baked Beans

Serves 4

350 g/12 oz Haricot beans, soaked overnight

450 g/1 lb Belly of pork, rinded and cubed

2 Onions, sliced

10 ml/2 tsp Salt

10 ml/2 tsp Mustard powder

Pepper

30 ml/2 tbsp Black treacle or molasses

30 ml/2 tbsp White wine vinegar

6 Whole cloves

15 ml/1 tbsp Tomato purée

15 ml/1 tbsp Chopped parsley

Drain the beans well, then mix with all the other ingredients except the parsley in a casserole dish. Add just enough water barely to cover the ingredients, cover tightly and bake in a preheated oven at 150°C/300°F/gas mark 2 for 6 hours. Stir well, add a little boiling water if the casserole is too dry, cover again and bake for a further 1 hour. Discard the cloves and serve sprinkled with parsley.

Roast Pork with Apple and Nut Stuffing

Serves 6

1.5 kg/3 lb Shoulder of pork, boned

25 g/1 oz Butter or margarine

1 Onion, chopped

50 g/2 oz Cashew nuts, chopped

50 g/2 oz Bread, cubed

1 Cooking apple, peeled, cored and chopped

1 Celery stalk, chopped

15 ml/1 tbsp Chopped parsley

2.5 ml/½ tsp Savory

2.5 ml/½ tsp Lemon juice

Salt and pepper

30 ml/2 tbsp Oil

150 ml/¼ pt Dry cider

Melt the butter or margarine and fry the onion and nuts until just browned, then stir in the bread, apple and celery and fry until soft. Stir in the parsley, savory and lemon juice and season to taste with salt and pepper. Flatten the joint and spread the stuffing over the meat, then roll it up and tie it securely with string. Place in a roasting tin, brush well with oil and sprinkle with salt, then bake in a preheated oven at 200°C/400°F/gas mark 6 for 20 minutes, then reduce the heat to 180°C/350°F/gas mark 4 and cook for a further 1½ hours until the meat is well cooked through. Transfer the meat to a warmed serving dish and keep it warm. Pour the cider into the tin and bring to the boil, stirring to scrape up all the meat juices. Simmer until reduced and thickened slightly, then pour it into a sauce boat and serve with the pork.

Oriental Pork

Serves 4

30 ml/2 tbsp Oil
450 g/1 lb Belly of pork, rinded and cubed
1 Onion, chopped
15 ml/1 tbsp Plain flour
225 g/8 oz Canned pineapple chunks
15 ml/1 tbsp Vinegar
1 Green pepper, sliced
150 ml/¼ pt Chicken Stock (page 24)
5 ml/1 tsp Soy sauce
Salt and pepper

Heat the oil and fry the pork and onion until browned on all sides. Stir in the flour and cook for 1 minute, then stir in the remaining ingredients and season to taste with salt and pepper. Bring to the boil, stirring, then cover and simmer for 35 minutes until tender. Serve with boiled rice.

Pork and Prune Casserole

Serves 4

100 g/4 oz Prunes
Grated rind and juice of 1 lemon
15 g/½ oz Plain flour
Salt and pepper
750 g/1½ lb Pork fillet, cubed
30 ml/2 tbsp Oil
5 ml/1 tsp Plain flour (optional)
5 ml/1 tsp Soft margarine (optional)

Put the prunes and lemon rind in a saucepan, just cover with water, bring to the boil and simmer until the prunes are tender. Season the flour with salt and pepper and toss the meat in the flour. Heat the oil and fry the pork until browned on all sides, then transfer it to a casserole dish. Add the prunes, lemon juice and 300 ml/½ pt of the prune cooking liquid. Season to taste with salt and pepper and bake in a preheated oven at 180°C/350°F/gas mark 4 for 1 hour until the meat is tender. Thicken the sauce, if necessary, by mixing together the extra flour and margarine and stirring it into the sauce.

Spicy Pork Curry

Serves 4

30 ml/2 tbsp Oil
450 g/1 lb Pork fillet, cubed
1 Onion, sliced
2 Garlic cloves, crushed
5 ml/1 tsp Chilli powder
10 ml/2 tsp Cumin
5 ml/1 tsp Cinnamon
10 ml/2 tsp Coriander
300 ml/½ pt Water
Salt and pepper
150 ml/¼ pt Natural yoghurt

Heat the oil and fry the meat until browned on all sides, then remove from the pan. Add the onion and garlic and fry until lightly browned, then stir in the spices and cook for 1 minute. Stir in the water, season to taste with salt and pepper and bring to the boil, then simmer for 1 hour until the pork is cooked. Stir in the yoghurt and reheat, then serve with rice.

Mustard Roast

Serves 6

| 1.5 kg/3 lb Pork joint, boned and rolled |
| Oil |
| Salt |
| 30 ml/2 tbsp Made English mustard |
| 15 ml/1 tbsp Honey |
| 5 ml/1 tsp Coriander |

Brush the pork with oil and sprinkle with salt. Place in a preheated oven at 200°C/400°F/gas mark 6 for 10 minutes, then turn the heat down to 180°C/350°F/gas mark 4 and continue cooking for 35 minutes per 450g/1 lb. Mix together the remaining ingredients, pour them over the pork and return it to the oven for a final 30 minutes cooking.

Fried Pork with Sweet and Sour Sauce

Serves 4

| 450 g/1 lb Minced pork |
| 50 g/2 oz Breadcrumbs |
| 1 Onion, finely chopped |
| 2.5 ml/½ tsp Sage |
| 1 Egg, beaten |
| Salt and pepper |
| 45 ml/3 tbsp Oil |
| 400 g/14 oz Canned apricots in syrup |
| 15 ml/2 tbsp Cornflour |
| 45 ml/3 tbsp Soy sauce |
| 45 ml/3 tbsp Tomato purée |
| 150 ml/¼ pt Chicken Stock (page 24) |
| 2 Red peppers, chopped |
| 15 g/½ oz Root ginger, grated |

Mix the pork, breadcrumbs, onion, sage and egg and season to taste with salt and pepper. Shape into small balls. Heat the oil and fry the balls until golden brown on all sides and cooked through. Drain well and keep them warm.

Meanwhile, drain the apricot syrup into a saucepan and mix in the cornflour, soy sauce, tomato purée and stock. Bring to the boil, stirring, then add the peppers and ginger and simmer for 5 minutes. Add the pork balls, stirring gently, and simmer for a further 5 minutes. Slice the apricots and add them to the sauce, heat through gently and serve with a crisp salad.

Pork with Beer Sauce

Serves 4

750 g/1½ lb Loin of pork
Salt and pepper
1 Garlic clove, crushed
30 ml/2 tbsp Oil
3 Onions, sliced
450 ml/¾ pt Guinness or brown ale
150 ml/¼ pt Single cream
15 ml/1 tbsp Cornflour

Season the meat with salt and pepper and rub it with the garlic. Heat the oil in a flameproof casserole and fry the meat until browned on all sides. Add the onions and fry until lightly browned. Stir in the Guinness or brown ale, cover and simmer gently for 1½ hours, basting occasionally. When the meat is thoroughly cooked, transfer it to a warmed serving dish and slice it thickly, then keep it warm. Blend the cream and cornflour together and stir into the beer. Bring to the boil and simmer, stirring, until the sauce thickens. Season to taste with salt and pepper and strain into a sauce boat.

Minced Pork and Potato Pie

Serves 4

450 g/1 lb Minced pork
1 Onion, chopped
400 g/14 oz Canned baked beans
5 ml/1 tsp Mixed herbs
450 g/1 lb Boiled potatoes
50 g/2 oz Butter or margarine
30 ml/2 tbsp Milk
Salt and pepper

Heat the mince gently in a saucepan until the fat begins to run, then increase the heat and fry until browned. Drain off excess fat, add the onion and fry until soft. Stir in the beans and herbs and place in a shallow ovenproof dish. Mash the potatoes with half the butter or margarine and milk and season to taste with salt and pepper. Top the pork mixture with the potato, fluff up with a fork and dot with the remaining butter or margarine. Bake in a preheated oven at 180°C/350°F/gas mark 4 for 45 minutes until golden brown and crispy on top.

Bacon, Ham and Sausages

A meal with bacon or ham makes a pleasant change from other meats as it has a distinctive flavour. As it is a salty meat, take care to adjust seasoning as you cook, and team the meat with suitable vegetables to complement the strong flavours. There are now a variety of sausages available, although the most popular are still the pork sausages. Try spiced sausages for a change as there is a range of tastes in most supermarkets.

Bacon Roly Poly

Serves 4

350 g/12 oz Self-raising flour
125 g/5 oz Suet
Salt
75 ml/5 tbsp Water
3 Large onions, chopped
225 g/8 oz Bacon rashers, rinded
  and chopped
Pinch of sage

Mix the flour, suet and salt and gradually add enough water to make a light dough. Roll out the dough to a rectangle 1 cm/½ in thick and sprinkle with the bacon, onion and sage. Roll up and coil into a greased basin. Cover the basin, place it in a saucepan of boiling water and boil for 2½ hours, topping up with boiling water as necessary.

Bacon and Kidney Rolls

Serves 4

½ Onion, finely chopped
25 g/1 oz Breadcrumbs
100 g/4 oz Kidneys, cored and
  chopped
2.5 ml/½ tsp Mixed herbs
3 drops Tabasco sauce
2.5 ml/½ tsp Tomato purée
12 Streaky bacon rashers, rinded
  and stretched

Mix together all the ingredients except the bacon. Place a teaspoon of the mixture on the end of each piece of bacon and roll up. Grill under a hot grill for 10 minutes, turning once. Serve hot with rice and a green salad.

Bacon Stuffed Cabbage Leaves

Serves 4

50 g/2 oz Long-grain rice

8-10 Large cabbage leaves

15 ml/1 tbsp Oil

1 Onion, chopped

25 g/1 oz Mushrooms, sliced

225 g/8 oz Bacon, rinded and chopped

185 g/6½ oz Canned pimentos, drained

50 g/2 oz Breadcrumbs

50 g/2 oz Cashew nuts, chopped

Salt and pepper

400 g/14 oz Canned tomatoes

Cook the rice in plenty of boiling salted water for about 10 minutes, then drain and rinse in cold water. Pour boiling water over the cabbage leaves and leave to stand for 5 minutes to soften. Heat the oil and fry the onion until browned. Add the mushrooms and bacon and fry lightly, then remove from the heat. Chop half the pimentos and add them to the pan with the breadcrumbs and nuts and season to taste with salt and pepper. Drain the cabbage leaves and lay them on a work surface. Divide the mixture between them, roll them up and lay, rolled side down, in a shallow ovenproof dish. Purée the remaining pimentos with the tomatoes in a food processor or blender. Pour the mixture over the cabbage leaves, cover and bake in a preheated oven at 180°C/350°F/gas mark 4 for 45 minutes.

Cold Bacon with Angostura Bitters

Serves 6-8

1.75 kg/4 lb Joint of bacon, soaked

30 ml/2 tbsp Angostura bitters

4 Bay leaves

Place the joint on a large piece of foil and sprinkle with angostura bitters. Place the bay leaves on top and wrap up tightly. Bake in a preheated oven at 180°C/350°F/gas mark 4 for 1¼ hours. Leave to cool in the foil, then remove the rind before serving.

Bacon Steaks with Orange and Peppercorn Sauce

Serves 4

4 Bacon steaks

Grated rind and juice of 1 orange

150 ml/¼ pt Chicken Stock (page 24)

15 ml/1 tbsp Soft brown sugar

Green peppercorns

45 ml/3 tbsp Orange marmalade

1 Bunch of watercress

Grill the steaks until tender. Meanwhile, mix the orange rind and juice, stock, sugar, peppercorns and marmalade. Bring to the boil and simmer for 8 minutes until the sauce thickens. Transfer the cooked steaks on to a warmed serving dish, pour over some of the sauce and garnish with watercress. Serve the remaining sauce in a sauce boat.

Bacon and Bean Casserole

Serves 4

30 ml/2 tbsp Oil

450 g/1 lb Bacon, chopped

3 Onions, sliced

2 Garlic cloves, chopped

1 Red pepper, sliced

300 g/11 oz Canned kidney beans, drained

400 g/14 oz Canned tomatoes, chopped

15 ml/1 tbsp Oregano

450 ml/¾ pt Chicken Stock (page 24)

Salt and pepper

30 ml/2 tbsp Chopped parsley

Heat the oil and fry the bacon until cooked through, then transfer it to a casserole dish. Fry the onions, garlic and pepper until soft, then transfer to the casserole with the kidney beans, tomatoes, oregano and chicken stock. Season to taste with salt and pepper and bake in a preheated oven at 200°C/400°F/gas mark 6 for 20 minutes, then reduce the heat to 150°C/300°F/gas mark 2 for a further 2 hours. Serve sprinkled with parsley.

Honey Glazed Bacon

Serves 6

1.5 kg/3 lb Bacon joint, boned and rolled

1 Bay leaf

1 Blade of mace

4 Peppercorns

4 Whole cloves

45 ml/3 tbsp Honey

Juice of 1 orange

15 ml/1 tbsp Cornflour

Salt and pepper

Place the bacon in a large saucepan with the bay leaf, mace, peppercorns and cloves. Cover with water, bring to the boil and simmer for 50 minutes. Drain, reserving 300 ml/½ pt stock for the gravy.

Place the joint in a roasting tin and score the rind into a diamond pattern. Mix together the honey and orange juice and slowly spoon over the bacon so that the glaze soaks into the incisions in the rind. Roast in a preheated oven at 180°C/350°F/gas mark 4 for 1 hour until tender. Remove the bacon to a warmed serving plate. Blend the cornflour with a little of the reserved stock, then pour the stock into the pan, bring to the boil, stirring, and cook until thickened. Taste and season if necessary with salt and pepper, but do not overseason or the stock will be salty.

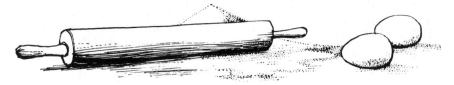

Bacon Chops in Ale

Serves 4

4 Bacon chops
300 ml/½ pt Beer
Pepper
1 Bay leaf
3 Onions, sliced
60 ml/4 tbsp Black treacle or
  molasses
Juice of ½ lemon
15 ml/1 tbsp Oil

Put the bacon chops in a shallow dish with the beer, pepper, bay leaf and onions, cover and refrigerate overnight.

Strain off the beer marinade into a saucepan, bring to the boil and simmer until reduced by half then add the molasses and lemon juice. Meanwhile, start the chops cooking under a medium grill. Brush the marinade over the chops and grill for about 15 minutes. Turn the chops, baste with the remaining marinade and continue cooking for about 10 minutes until tender and glazed.

Meanwhile, remove the bay leaf from the onions, heat the oil in a frying pan and fry the onions until soft and browned. Cover the chops with the onion and serve.

Pineapple Grill

Serves 4

4 Gammon steaks
300 g/11 oz Canned pineapple
  chunks, drained
15 ml/1 tbsp Honey
100 g/4 oz Breadcrumbs
Salt and pepper

Grill the gammon steaks for 5 minutes, then turn them over. Chop two-thirds of the pineapple finely and mix with the honey and breadcrumbs. Pile the mixture on top of the steaks and season to taste with salt and pepper. Grill for 10 minutes until crispy, then top with the remaining pineapple and serve hot.

Ham and Cheese Fingers

Serves 4

100 g/4 oz Butter or margarine
225 g/8 oz Plain flour
30 ml/2 tbsp Cold water
100 g/4 oz Ham, finely shredded
50 g/2 oz Soft white breadcrumbs
5 ml/1 tsp Tomato purée
Pinch of mustard powder
100 g/4 oz Cheese, grated
1 Egg, beaten

Rub the butter or margarine into the flour until the mixture resembles fine breadcrumbs. Add the water and mix to a pastry, knead lightly, then roll out on a floured surface into a 30 cm/12 in square. Cut in half and chill for 15 minutes.

Place one rectangle on a damp baking sheet. Mix the ham, breadcrumbs, tomato purée and mustard and spread the mixture on the pastry, leaving 1 cm/½ in gap around the edge. Scatter the cheese on top. Brush the edges of the pastry with egg and seal on the second pastry sheet. Mark a criss-cross pattern on the top with a knife and brush with egg, then bake in a preheated oven at 220°C/425°F/gas mark 7 for 25 minutes. Cool, then cut into fingers.

Spiced Island Steaks

Serves 4

150 ml/¼ pt Pineapple juice
45 ml/3 tbsp Soy sauce
2 Garlic cloves, crushed
75 ml/5 tbsp Honey
15 ml/1 tbsp Dry sherry
2.5 ml/½ tsp Paprika
1 Small onion, chopped
4 Whole cloves
1 Bay leaf
5 ml/1 tsp Lemon juice
Pinch of grated ginger
4 Gammon steaks
1 Kiwi fruit, sliced

Mix together all the sauce ingredients, bring to the boil and simmer for 15 minutes until thickened slightly. Meanwhile, grill the gammon steaks until cooked through, then place them on a warmed serving dish and arrange the kiwi fruit around them. Pour over a little of the sauce and serve the remaining sauce in a sauce boat.

Ham and Pineapple Layer

Serves 4

4 Round ham steaks
4 Crumpets
100 g/4 oz Cheddar cheese, grated
2.5 ml/½ tsp Mustard powder
45 ml/3 tbsp Milk
4 Pineapple rings
4 Watercress sprigs

Grill the ham steaks for 8 minutes each side and toast the crumpets. Mix the cheese, mustard and milk to a paste, spread it over the crumpets and toast until golden brown and bubbling. Place the grilled ham on top and top with the pineapple rings. Grill for 3 minutes to heat through and serve garnished with watercress.

Ham Cornets

Serves 4

6 Black peppercorns
1 Bay leaf
1 Onion, chopped
200 ml/7 fl oz Milk
50 g/2 oz Butter or margarine
25 g/1 oz Plain flour
Salt and pepper
75 g/3 oz Pâté
2.5 ml/½ tsp French mustard
60 ml/4 tbsp Double cream
8 slices Ham

Place the peppercorns, bay leaf and onion in the milk in a saucepan, bring to the boil, remove from the heat and leave to infuse for 30 minutes. Melt 50 g/2 oz butter or margarine, stir in the flour and cook, stirring, for 1 minute. Strain the flavoured milk into the pan, season to taste with salt and pepper and bring to the boil, stirring until the sauce thickens. Pour into a food processor or blender, add the pâté, mustard and the remaining butter, cut into pieces, and blend until smooth. Allow to cool slightly, turn into a bowl and fold in the cream. Use the ham to line cornet moulds and support them upright, or roll the ham into the cornet shapes. Pipe the mixture into the cornets and chill for 2 hours before serving.

Sweet and Sour Ham Steaks

Serves 4

4 Gammon steaks
50 g/2 oz Demerara sugar
10 ml/2 tsp Mustard powder
10 ml/2 tsp Water
1 Lemon, cut into wedges
15 ml/1 tbsp Chopped parsley

Grill one side of the gammon under a hot grill for 5 minutes. Mix the sugar, mustard and water to a smooth paste. Turn over the gammon and spread the mixture on the gammon. Grill for 3 minutes until golden brown. Serve immediately with lemon wedges dipped in parsley, and creamed potatoes and mangetout.

Sausage Pickle

Serves 4

15 ml/1 tbsp Oil
450 g/1 lb Pork sausages
4 Onions, sliced
15 ml/1 tbsp Tomato purée
45 ml/3 tbsp Water
3 Tomatoes, skinned and chopped
100 g/4 oz Sweet pickle
Salt and pepper

Heat the oil and fry the sausages gently for 10 minutes. Add the onion and fry for a further 10 minutes until the sausages are cooked. Remove the sausages. Add the tomato purée and water, bring to the boil, then add the tomatoes and pickle and season to taste with salt and pepper. Heat through, then serve with hot sausages.

Country Sausage Flan

Serves 4

225 g/8 oz Shortcrust pastry
  (page 145)
15 ml/1 tbsp Oil
1 Onion, chopped
2 Leeks, chopped
3 Bacon rashers, chopped
100 g/4 oz Mushrooms, sliced
450 g/1 lb Pork sausagemeat
5 ml/1 tsp Made mustard
15 ml/1 tbsp Chopped parsley
Salt and pepper
2 Eggs, beaten

Roll out the pastry and use to line a greased 20 cm/8 in pie dish. Heat the oil and fry the onion, leeks and bacon until the onion is soft. Add the mushrooms and sausagemeat and fry for 15 minutes, then stir in the mustard and parsley and season to taste with salt and pepper. Turn the mixture into the pastry case and pour the eggs over the top. Bake in a preheated oven at 190°C/375°F/gas mark 5 for 45 minutes.

Cidered Sausage Skuets

Serves 4

90 ml/6 tbsp Medium dry cider
90 ml/6 tbsp Clear honey
45 ml/3 tbsp Tomato purée
Juice of 1 lemon
900 g/2 lb Large pork sausages
12 Streaky bacon rashers, rinded
225 g/8 oz Button mushrooms
Oil
Salt and pepper

Mix the cider, honey, tomato purée and lemon juice over a low heat until well blended. Pinch the sausages in the middle, twist them into 2 short links then separate them. Wrap each in a bacon rasher and thread the stubby sausages on to kebab skewers alternately with the button mushrooms. Brush with oil and season lightly with salt and pepper. Grill under a medium grill, turning frequently and brushing with the baste, for about 20 minutes until cooked through.

Barbecued Bangers

Serves 4

2 Onions
225 g/8 oz Canned tomatoes, chopped
75 ml/5 tbsp Dry cider
45 ml/3 tbsp Tomato ketchup
15 ml/1 tbsp Worcestershire sauce
1 Bay leaf
1 Garlic clove, chopped
3 Celery stalks, finely chopped
5 ml/1 tsp Lemon juice
30 ml/2 tbsp Muscovado sugar
300 ml/½ pt Water
450 g/1 lb Pork sausages

Chop 1 onion and cut the other into wedges. Mix the chopped onion and all the remaining ingredients except the sausages, bring to the boil, cover and simmer for 30 minutes, then remove the bay leaf. Grill the sausages and onion wedges under a hot grill until cooked through and golden brown, turning frequently. Serve with the hot sauce.

Sausagemeat Moussaka

Serves 4

50 g/2 oz Butter or margarine
1 Onion, sliced
450 g/1 lb Sausagemeat
5 ml/1 tsp Sage
1 Garlic clove, crushed
400 g/14 oz Canned tomatoes, chopped
Salt and pepper
450 g/1 lb Potatoes, sliced
225 g/8 oz Cooking apples, peeled, cored and sliced
25 g/1 oz Plain flour
300 ml/½ pt Milk
100 g/4 oz Strong cheese, grated

Melt the butter or margarine and fry the onion until soft. Stir in the sausagemeat and fry gently for 10 minutes, stirring. Remove from the heat, drain off excess fat, stir in the sage, garlic and tomatoes and season to taste with salt and pepper. Parboil the potatoes for 10 minutes, then drain. Layer half the potatoes on the base of a greased casserole dish and spread half the meat mixture on top. Spread with the apple slices, then a layer of meat and finally potatoes. Melt the butter in a saucepan, stir in the flour and cook for 1 minute. Whisk in the milk and cook, stirring, until the sauce thickens. Season to taste with salt and pepper, remove from the heat and stir in most of the cheese. Pour the cheese sauce over the casserole and sprinkle on the remaining cheese. Bake in a preheated oven at 190°C/375°F/gas mark 5 for 30 minutes until browned and crispy on top.

Soudzoukakia

Serves 4

50 g/2 oz Breadcrumbs
75 ml/5 tbsp Milk
450 g/1 lb Pork sausagemeat
2 Onions, chopped
1 Garlic clove, chopped
Salt and pepper
25 g/1 oz Plain flour
30 ml/2 tbsp Olive oil
400 g/14 oz Canned tomatoes,
  chopped
5 ml/1 tsp Sugar
1 Bay leaf
Pinch of cumin

Moisten the breadcrumbs with the milk and squeeze dry. Mix with the sausagemeat, 1 onion and the garlic and season to taste with salt and pepper. Shape into little fat sausages and roll in the flour. Heat the oil and fry the sausages until browned on all sides and cooked through, then drain well.

Meanwhile, put all the remaining ingredients into a saucepan and simmer for 45 minutes. Remove the bay leaf and purée the sauce in a food processor or blender, then add the sausages and return to the pan to reheat.

Toad in the Hole

Serves 4

450 g/1 lb Pork sausages
300 ml/½ pt Milk
2 Eggs
225 g/8 oz Plain flour
Pinch of salt

Put the sausages in a greased baking tin and bake in a preheated oven at 200°C/400°F/gas mark 6 for 30 minutes. Beat the milk, eggs, flour and salt together well to a thick batter and pour into the pan. Raise the heat to 230°C/450°F/gas mark 8 and bake for 15 minutes until well risen and golden brown.

Sausage-Stuffed Potatoes

Serves 4

4 Large baking potatoes
8 Pork sausages
225 g/8 oz Cheddar cheese, grated
30 ml/2 tbsp Milk
Butter or margarine
1 Egg, beaten
15 ml/1 tbsp Soured cream
Salt and pepper

Prick the potatoes with a fork and bake in a preheated oven at 190°C/375°F/gas mark 5 for 1¼ hours until soft. Place the sausages in a roasting tin and bake with the potatoes for the last 45 minutes of cooking time. Slice the potatoes in half lengthways and scoop out the insides. Mix with the cheese, milk, butter or margarine, egg and cream and season to taste with salt and pepper. Pile half the mixture back into the potato skins, place a sausage on each, and pile on the remaining mixture. Return to the oven for 10 minutes until browned and crispy on top.

Variation
You can use crisply grilled chopped bacon rashers instead of the sausages if you prefer.

Offal

Although many people do not often cook liver, kidneys or other types of offal, there is a great variety to choose from, and there are plenty of tasty recipes to bring out the best flavours. Most types of offal are available frozen from supermarkets, and as these are ready prepared, they can save both time and wastage for the busy cook.

Old-Fashioned Liver and Bacon

Serves 4

15 ml/1 tbsp Oil
4 Onions, sliced
450 g/1 lb Lambs' liver, sliced
15 g/½ oz Plain flour
300 ml/½ pt Beef Stock (page 24)
Salt and pepper
8 Streaky bacon rashers

Heat the oil and fry the onions until just beginning to brown. Add the liver and fry gently until browned on both sides. Stir in the flour and cook for 1 minute, then stir in the stock and bring to the boil, stirring, until the sauce thickens. Cover and simmer for 10 minutes until the liver is tender.

Meanwhile, grill the bacon rashers until crisp and browned. Transfer the liver and onions to a deep warmed serving dish, surround with the bacon and serve immediately with potatoes and a green vegetable.

Liver and Bacon with Lemon Sauce

Serves 4

25 g/1 oz Butter or margarine
6 Back bacon rashers, rinded and halved
450 g/1 lb Lambs' liver, sliced
15 g/½ oz Plain flour
Salt and pepper
60 ml/4 tbsp Red wine
15 ml/1 tbsp Chopped parsley
1 Lemon, cut into wedges

Melt the butter and fry the bacon until crisp, then remove from the pan. Coat the liver in the flour and season to taste with salt and pepper. Add to the pan and fry until browned on both sides. Stir in the wine, stock, lemon juice and bacon, cover and simmer for 15 minutes until tender. Serve garnished with parsley and lemon wedges.

Spicy Liver with Pasta

Serves 4

50 g/2 oz Plain flour
2.5 ml/½ tsp Cinnamon
5 ml/1 tsp Mixed spice
Salt and pepper
350 g/12 oz Lambs' liver, cut into
  strips
50 g/2 oz Butter or margarine
2 Onions, sliced
100 g/4 oz Mushrooms
150 ml/¼ pt Beef Stock
  (page 24)
150 ml/¼ pt Milk
15 ml/1 tbsp Tomato ketchup
15 ml/1 tbsp Worcestershire sauce
375 g/12 oz Pasta spirals

Mix half the flour, the cinnamon and spice and season with salt and pepper. Coat the liver in the seasoned flour. Melt the butter or margarine and fry the onions until soft but not browned. Add the liver and mushrooms and fry for 10 minutes. Stir in the remaining flour and cook for 1 minute, then stir in the stock, milk, tomato ketchup and Worcestershire sauce, bring to the boil, stirring, and cook until the sauce thickens.

Meanwhile, cook the pasta in boiling salted water for about 15 minutes until just tender. Drain and rinse in hot water, then serve with the liver.

Chicken Livers en Brochette

Serves 4

100 g/4 oz Chicken livers, quartered
3 Bacon rashers, cut into squares
8 Small mushrooms
4 Small tomatoes, halved
Salt and pepper
45 ml/3 tbsp Oil
1 Bunch of watercress

Thread the chicken livers, bacon, mushrooms and tomatoes on 4 skewers. Season to taste with salt and pepper and brush with oil. Bake in a preheated oven at 190°C/375°F/gas mark 5 for 15 minutes, turning several times, until cooked through. Serve garnished with watercress.

Liver with Yoghurt and Sherry

Serves 4-6

25 g/1 oz Plain flour
Salt and pepper
750 g/1½ lb Calves' liver, diced
50 g/2 oz Butter or margarine
300 ml/½ pt Plain yoghurt
30 ml/2 tbsp Sherry

Season the flour with salt and pepper, then coat the liver in the flour. Melt the butter or margarine in a frying pan and fry the liver for 2 minutes on each side. Stir in the yoghurt and sherry and season to taste with salt and pepper. Cook gently, without boiling, until the liver is tender, stirring continuously.

Stuffed Baked Liver

Serves 4

450 g/1 lb Calves' liver, sliced

15 g/½ oz Butter or margarine

75 g/3 oz Breadcrumbs

5 ml/1 tsp Chopped parsley

2.5 ml/½ tsp Mixed herbs

1 Small onion, grated

Salt and pepper

30 ml/2 tbsp Tomato ketchup

6 Back bacon rashers, rinded

150 ml/¼ pt Beef Stock
(page 24)

Overlap the liver in a greased pie dish. Mix the breadcrumbs, parsley, herbs and onion and season to taste with salt and pepper. Stir in the tomato ketchup. Spread the stuffing over the liver and arrange the bacon in an overlapping layer on top. Pour the stock down the side of the dish, cover and bake in a preheated oven at 180°C/350°F/gas mark 4 for 45 minutes, then remove the lid and bake for a further 15 minutes to allow the top to crisp.

Calves' Liver Casserole

Serves 4

25 g/1 oz Butter or margarine

25 g/1 oz Salt pork, diced

750 g/1½ lb Calves' liver

2 Carrots, sliced

2 Onions, sliced

2 Tomatoes, skinned and chopped

1 Celery stalk, sliced

30 ml/2 tbsp Sherry

90 ml/6 tbsp Dry white wine

150 ml/¼ pt Beef Stock
(page 24)

1 Bouquet garni

Salt and pepper

Melt half the butter and fry the pork until browned. Add the remaining butter, the liver and vegetables and fry until the meat starts to colour. Add the sherry and wine and bring to the boil, then add the stock and herbs and season to taste with salt and pepper. Transfer to a casserole dish, cover and bake in a preheated oven at 150°C/300°F/gas mark 2 for 2 hours.

Just before serving, transfer the meat and vegetables to a warmed serving dish and discard the bouquet garni. If the gravy is too thin, boil it down to reduce it a little before pouring it over the meat. Serve with new potatoes.

Liver with Garden Herbs

Serves 4

50 g/2 oz Butter or margarine
1 Onion, finely chopped
450 g/1 lb Calves' liver sliced
45 ml/3 tbsp Chopped Sage
30 ml/2 tbsp Chopped parsley
Salt and pepper
30 ml/2 tbsp Dry sherry
45 ml/3 tbsp Oil
450 g/1 lb Potatoes, diced

Melt the butter or margarine and fry the onion until soft but not browned. Add the liver, sage and half the parsley, season to taste with salt and pepper and fry until browned and tender, then transfer the liver to a warmed serving dish and keep it warm. Add the sherry to the pan, bring to the boil, stirring, and simmer for 1 minute, then pour over the liver.

Meanwhile, heat the oil and fry the potatoes until golden and tender. Drain well, arrange on the serving plate and serve sprinkled with parsley.

Parslied Hearts

Serves 4

4 Large lambs' hearts
Salt and pepper
45 ml/3 tbsp Chopped parsley
50 g/2 oz Butter or margarine
150 ml/¼ pt Beef Stock
  (page 24)
5 ml/1 tsp Worcestershire sauce
8 Small new potatoes

Cut the excess fat off the hearts and snip out any tubes and membranes. Season with salt and pepper and half-fill each one with parsley and a knob of butter. Close the tops with cocktail sticks. Melt the remaining butter and fry the hearts until browned on all sides. Add the stock and Worcester-shire sauce, bring to the boil, then transfer to a shallow casserole, add the potatoes, cover and bake in a preheated oven at 180°C/350°F/gas mark 4 for 1 hour.

Tripe and Onions

Serves 4

450 g/1 lb Dressed tripe, cubed
225 g/8 oz Onions, chopped
Salt
4 Peppercorns
4 Parsley sprigs
450 ml/¾ pt Milk, boiling
20 g/¾ oz Butter or margarine
20 g/¾ oz Plain flour
4 Parsley sprigs

Put the tripe and onions in a casserole and season to taste with salt. Tie the peppercorns and parsley sprigs in muslin and add to the casserole. Pour in the milk, cover and bake in a preheated oven at 160°C/325°F/gas mark 3 for the time recommended by the butcher, as butchers parboil tripe for a variable time before sale. Transfer the tripe to a warmed serving dish and keep it warm.

Melt the butter in a pan, stir in the flour and cook for 1 minute. Whisk in the cooking liquor and cook, stirring, until the sauce thickens. Pour over the tripe and garnish with parsley.

Kidneys Turbigo

Serves 4

12 Pickling onions
50 g/2 oz Butter or margarine
5 Lambs' kidneys, halved and cored
100 g/4 oz Chipolata sausages
100 g/4 oz Button mushrooms, quartered
10 ml/2 tsp Plain flour
5 ml/1 tsp Tomato purée
15 ml/1 tbsp Sherry
150 ml/¼ pt Beef Stock (page 24)
1 Bay leaf
Salt and pepper
45 ml/3 tbsp Oil
Fried bread croûtons
15 ml/1 tbsp Chopped parsley

Blanch the onions in boiling salted water for 1 minute, then drain. Heat the butter or margarine and fry the kidneys until lightly browned. Remove them from the pan and add the sausages and fry until browned on all sides, then remove them from the pan. Add the onions and mushrooms and fry for 3 minutes. Remove the pan from the heat, stir in the flour, tomato purée, sherry and stock and bring to the boil. Add the bay leaf and season to taste with salt and pepper. Slice the kidneys and sausages and add them to the pan, cover and simmer gently for 20 minutes until tender.

Meanwhile, heat the oil and fry the bread until crisp and golden brown. Transfer the kidneys to a warmed serving plate, discard the bay leaf, surround with the croûtons and serve sprinkled with parsley.

Sweet and Sour Kidneys

Serves 4

30 ml/2 tbsp Honey
45 ml/3 tbsp Dry sherry
60 ml/4 tbsp Soy sauce
30 ml/½ pt Beef consommé
1 Garlic clove, crushed
Pinch of five-spice powder
450 g/1 lb Lambs' kidneys, halved and cored
25 g/1 oz Plain flour
Salt and pepper
50 g/2 oz Butter or margarine
15 ml/1 tbsp Cornflour
15 ml/1 tbsp Water
2 Spring onions, sliced

Mix the honey, sherry, soy sauce, consommé, garlic and five-spice powder. Add the kidneys and marinate for 1 hour. Remove the kidneys and pat dry. Season the flour with salt and pepper and coat the kidneys in the flour. Melt the butter or margarine and fry the kidneys until just browned, then remove from the pan. Add the marinade to the pan and bring to the boil. Mix the cornflour and water, stir it into the pan and cook until the sauce thickens. Return the kidneys to the pan and season to taste with salt and pepper. Cook for 2 minutes until heated through and serve garnished with spring onions.

Kidney and Onion Dumplings

Serves 4

225 g/8 oz Self-raising flour
100 g/4 oz Shredded suet
Pinch of salt
30 ml/2 tbsp Water
4 Large onions
Salt and pepper
4 Lambs' kidneys

Mix the flour, suet and salt, then add the water and mix to a firm dough. Roll out and cut into 4 squares. Scoop out the centres of the onions, season inside and put a kidney in each one. Place an onion in each pastry square and seal round to enclose the onions completely. Turn upside down on a baking sheet so that the joins come underneath. Bake in a preheated oven at 180°C/350°F/gas mark 4 for 1¼ hours. Remove from the sheet carefully and serve with gravy.

Turkish-Style Kidneys

Serves 4

15 g/½ oz Butter or margarine
1 Onion, chopped
8 Lambs' kidneys, skinned, cored and halved
15 ml/1 tbsp Plain flour
600 ml/1 pt Beef Stock (page 24)
15 ml/1 tbsp Dry sherry
Salt and pepper
120 ml/4 fl oz Natural yoghurt
15 ml/1 tbsp Chopped parsley

Melt the butter or margarine and fry the onion until soft but not browned. Add the kidneys and cook on both sides for 2 minutes. Place the mixture in an ovenproof casserole. Stir the flour into the pan and cook for 1 minute, then stir in the stock and sherry and bring to the boil, stirring continuously. Season to taste with salt and pepper and simmer until thick and smooth. Pour the gravy into the casserole, cover and cook in a preheated oven at 140°C/275°F/gas mark 1 for 2½ hours. Stir in the yoghurt, sprinkle with parsley and serve with boiled rice.

Kidney and Bacon Pasties

Serves 4

450 g/1 lb Shortcrust Pastry (page 145)
175 g/6 oz Lambs' kidneys, chopped
100 g/4 oz Streaky bacon, chopped
225 g/8 oz Minced beef
2 Onions, chopped
5 ml/1 tsp Worcestershire sauce
Salt and pepper
1 Egg, beaten

Roll out the pastry and cut into 6 rounds. Mix the remaining ingredients except the egg and season to taste with salt and pepper. Put spoonfuls of the mixture on to the pastry rounds and seal into pasties with the beaten egg. Place on a greased baking sheet, brush with egg and bake in a preheated oven at 220°C/425°F/gas mark 7 for 15 minutes, then reduce the heat to 180°C/350°F/gas mark 4 for a further 45 minutes.

Kidney and Mushroom Lasagne

Serves 4

| 1 Onion, chopped |
| 15 ml/1 tbsp Oil |
| 100 g/4 oz Mushrooms, sliced |
| 30 ml/2 tbsp Sherry |
| 15 ml/1 tbsp Tomato purée |
| 50 g/2 oz Plain flour |
| 450 ml/¾ pt Vegetable Stock (page 24) |
| Salt and pepper |
| 450 g/1 lb Calves' or pigs' kidneys, sliced |
| 40 g/1½ oz Butter or margarine |
| 600 ml/1 pt Milk |
| 2.5 ml/½ tsp Nutmeg |
| 6 slices Lasagne |
| 25 g/1 oz Parmesan cheese, grated |

Fry the onion in half the oil until soft but not browned, then add half the mushrooms and fry gently. Add the sherry, tomato purée, 15 g/½ oz flour and the stock and season to taste with salt and pepper. Bring to the boil and simmer for 10 minutes. Allow to cool slightly, then purée in a food processor or blender. Fry the kidney in the remaining oil, add the reserved mushrooms, then pour the sauce round them and simmer for 5 minutes.

Melt the butter or margarine in a separate saucepan, then stir in the remaining flour and cook for 1 minute. Whisk in the milk, and keep whisking until the sauce thickens. Add the nutmeg and season to taste with salt and pepper.

Cook the lasagne according to the directions on the packet.

Layer the kidney mixture and the lasagne in a shallow ovenproof dish, pour over the white sauce and sprinkle with Parmesan cheese. Bake in a preheated oven at 200°C/400°F/gas mark 6 for 30 minutes.

Kidney Flan

Serves 4

| 350 g/12 oz Shortcrust Pastry (page 145) |
| 25 g/1 oz Butter or margarine |
| 1 Onion, chopped |
| 1 Green pepper, chopped |
| 6 Lambs' kidneys, chopped |
| 3 Eggs, beaten |
| 45 ml/3 tbsp Milk |
| Salt and pepper |

Roll out the pastry and use to line a greased 20 cm/8 in flan ring. Bake blind in a preheated oven at 200°C/400°F/gas mark 6 for 10 minutes, then reduce the heat to 180°C/350°F/gas mark 4. Melt the butter or margarine and fry the onion until soft but not browned. Add the pepper and kidneys and fry for 4 minutes, stirring continuously. Spread the mixture over the base of the flan. Beat the eggs with the milk and season to taste with the salt and pepper, then pour over the flan. Bake for 40 minutes until set.

Kidneys in Cream

Serves 4

25 g/1 oz Butter or margarine
8 Lambs' kidneys, skinned, cored
  and halved
1 Onion, chopped
1 Garlic clove, crushed
15 g/½ oz Plain flour
150 ml/¼ pt Beef Stock
  (page 24)
150 ml/¼ pt Double cream
Salt and pepper

Melt the butter or margarine and fry the kidneys, onion and garlic for 4 minutes until browned. Stir in the flour and cook for 2 minutes, then stir in the stock and cream and heat gently without boiling. Season to taste with salt and pepper and serve with boiled rice.

Kidney Pudding

Serves 4

4 Lambs' kidneys, chopped
5 ml/1 tsp Shredded suet
75 g/3 oz Breadcrumbs
10 ml/2 tsp Chopped parsley
5 ml/1 tsp Mixed herbs
Pinch of nutmeg
Salt and pepper
1 Egg, beaten
75 ml/5 tbsp Milk

Mix the kidneys, suet, breadcrumbs, parsley, herbs and nutmeg and season to taste with salt and pepper. Mix the egg and milk and stir into the breadcrumb mixture. Spoon into a greased pudding basin, cover and steam for 1½ hours, topping up with boiling water as necessary. Serve with rich gravy.

Veal Kidney in Mustard Sauce

Serves 4

50 g/2 oz Butter or margarine
1 Veal kidney, sliced
100 g/4 oz Mushrooms, sliced
2 Spring onions, cut into slivers
Few drops of lemon juice
1 Garlic clove, crushed
Salt and pepper
4 Bread slices, halved
5 ml/1 tsp Dijon mustard
150 ml/¼ pt Single cream

Melt half the butter and fry the kidney until browned. Add the mushrooms, onions, lemon juice and garlic and season to taste with salt and pepper. Cook for 5 minutes. Melt the remaining butter and fry the bread until crisp. Stir the mustard into the cream in a separate saucepan, bring the mixture to the boil, then pour it over the kidneys. Stir the juices together in the pan and serve immediately with the fried bread.

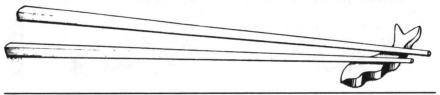

Poultry and Game

As a healthier alternative, chicken and other types of poultry are becoming increasingly popular. Not only healthy, of course, they are reasonably priced and very versatile, lending themselves to all kinds of recipes. Free-range and corn-fed chickens are now readily available in most supermarkets and are well worth trying, although, of course, they will cost a little more. Various cuts of turkey meat are also widely available now, so it is no longer just at Christmas that you can enjoy turkey meat. Duck and game birds are usually bought frozen, a convenient way to enjoy a little luxury now and again.

Chicken Catalan

Serves 4

60 ml/4 tbsp Oil

4 Chicken breasts, skinned and boned

2 Onions, sliced

1 Garlic clove, crushed

350 g/12 oz Long-grain rice

15 ml/1 tbsp Tomato purée

2.5 ml/½ tsp Turmeric

600 ml/1 pt Chicken Stock (page 24)

2.5 ml/½ tsp Paprika

Salt and pepper

100 g/4 oz Garlic sausage, cubed

1 Green pepper, sliced

1 Red pepper, sliced

50 g/2 oz Stuffed green olives

15 ml/1 tbsp Chopped parsley

Heat half the oil in a flameproof casserole and fry the chicken until browned on both sides. Remove from the pan and keep it warm. Add the onions and garlic and fry until soft. Add the remaining oil and the rice and cook to a golden colour, then stir in the tomato purée, turmeric, stock and paprika and season to taste with salt and pepper. Bring to the boil, then add the chicken, garlic sausage and peppers. Simmer over a low heat for 30 minutes or until the rice is just tender, stirring occasionally. Add a little more hot stock if necessary. Add the olives and heat through, then serve sprinkled with parsley.

Chicken Rossini

Serves 4

4 Chicken breasts, skinned
Salt and pepper
100 g/4 oz Firm pâté
75 g/3 oz Butter or margarine
175 g/6 oz Button mushrooms, sliced
45 ml/3 tbsp Brandy
90 ml/6 tbsp Chicken Stock (page 24)
60 ml/4 tbsp Double cream
30 ml/2 tbsp Oil
4 Bread slices, diced

Flatten the chicken and season with salt and pepper. Slice the pâté into 4, wrap in pieces of chicken and secure with cocktail sticks. Melt 50 g/2 oz butter or margarine and fry the chicken until lightly browned, then transfer it to a flameproof casserole dish. Fry the mushrooms for 1 minute, then add the brandy and stock and bring to the boil. Season to taste with salt and pepper and pour over the chicken. Cover and cook in a preheated oven at 180°C/350°F/ gas mark 4 for 40 minutes until cooked through. Heat the oil and fry the bread until crispy and golden, then drain and place on a warmed serving dish. Lift out the chicken from the casserole, remove the cocktail sticks and place on top of the croûtons. Stir the cream into the sauce and season to taste with salt and pepper. Bring back to the boil, then spoon over the chicken.

Orange Chicken Supreme

Serves 4

4 Chicken breasts, skinned
200 ml/7 fl oz Water
2 Dill fronds
Salt and pepper
Finely pared rind and juice of 1 orange
50 g/2 oz Butter or margarine
60 ml/4 tbsp Double cream
4 Watercress sprigs

Place the chicken, water and dill in a saucepan and season with salt and pepper. Bring to the boil, then simmer gently for 15 minutes. Remove from the heat and leave to stand for 10 minutes, then transfer the chicken to a serving plate and keep it warm. Place the orange rind and juice in a saucepan with the butter or margarine and simmer gently for 5 minutes until the mixture thickens slightly, then stir in the cream and simmer for a further 5 minutes. Season to taste and pour over the chicken. Serve garnished with watercress.

Stir-Fried Chicken

Serves 4

45 ml/3 tbsp Oil
350 g/12 oz Chicken breast, cut into strips
1 Green pepper, cut into strips
100 g/4 oz Carrots, finely sliced
175 g/6 oz Cabbage, finely shredded
225 g/8 oz Canned pineapple chunks in natural juice
10 ml/2 tsp Soy sauce
15 ml/1 tbsp White wine vinegar

Heat 30 ml/2 tbsp oil in a frying pan and fry the chicken until white all over. Remove the chicken from the pan. Add the remaining oil to the pan with the pepper and carrots and stir-fry for 2 minutes. Add the cabbage and stir-fry for 1 minute. Replace the chicken and stir in the pineapple and juice, soy sauce and wine vinegar. Simmer gently for 3 minutes and serve hot with noodles.

Chicken Escalopes with Cream and Wine Sauce

Serves 4

100 g/4 oz Breadcrumbs
30 ml/2 tbsp Chopped parsley
4 Chicken breasts
1 Egg, beaten
15 ml/1 tbsp Milk
Salt and pepper
45 ml/3 tbsp Oil
50 g/2 oz Butter
60 ml/4 tbsp Dry white wine
10 ml/2 tsp Lemon juice
60 ml/4 tbsp Single cream

Mix the breadcrumbs and parsley and flatten the chicken breasts with a rolling pin. Mix the egg and milk and season to taste with salt and pepper. Dip the chicken in the egg then press it into the breadcrumbs. Fry the chicken in the hot oil for 8 minutes each side until cooked through. Lift out on to a warmed serving dish. Melt the butter in the pan, add the wine and lemon juice and stir well. Add the cream, stir and heat through and pour over the chicken breasts. Serve immediately.

Sweet and Sour Chicken

Serves 4

15 g/¼ oz Fresh yeast
150 ml/¼ pt Warm water
15 ml/1 tbsp Oil
100 g/4 oz Plain flour
1 Egg, separated
2 Carrots, grated
150 g/5 oz Canned pineapple
10 ml/2 tsp Soft brown sugar
15 ml/1 tbsp White wine vinegar
15 ml/1 tbsp Soy sauce
300 ml/½ pt Cold water
15 ml/1 tbsp Cornflour
2 Boned chicken breasts, cubed
Oil for frying

Blend the yeast, warm water, oil, flour and egg yolk. Leave to stand for 20 minutes. Whisk the egg white until stiff.

Place the carrots, pineapple and juice, sugar, wine vinegar, soy sauce and cold water in a food processor or blender and process until smooth. Pour into a saucepan, bring to the boil and simmer for 10 minutes. Mix the cornflour with a little water, then stir it into the sauce and simmer, stirring, until it thickens.

Fold the egg white into the yeast mixture, dip the chicken into the batter and fry in hot oil for 5 minutes until light, fluffy and golden brown. You may need to do this in batches. Serve with the sweet and sour sauce and rice, noodles or beansprouts.

Pink Pineapple Chicken

Serves 4

100 g/4 oz Butter or margarine, softened

15 g/½ oz Plain flour

30 ml/2 tbsp Tomato purée

10 ml/2 tsp Mustard powder

2.5 ml/½ tsp Salt

Pepper

5 ml/1 tsp Worcestershire sauce

15 ml/1 tbsp Vinegar

400 g/14 oz Canned pineapple chunks in natural juice, chopped

4 Chicken breasts

15 ml/1 tbsp Cornflour

15 ml/1 tbsp Water

Mix together the butter or margarine, flour, tomato purée, mustard, salt, pepper, Worcestershire sauce and vinegar. Stir in a little chopped pineapple. Place the chicken breasts in a flameproof casserole and spread the mixture over the top. Pour the remaining pineapple and juice over and bake in a preheated oven at 180°C/350°F/gas mark 4 for 1 hour. Transfer the chicken to a serving dish and keep it warm. Mix the cornflour and water, stir it into the sauce, bring to the boil and boil, stirring, until the sauce thickens. Pour it over the chicken and serve with rice or potatoes.

Chicken Saffron

Serves 4

4 Chicken portions

15 ml/1 tbsp Oil

1 Onion, sliced

1 Thyme sprig

1 Bay leaf

300 ml/½ pt Low fat natural yoghurt

Pinch of saffron powder

5 ml/1 tsp Lemon juice

Salt and pepper

Lemon wedges to garnish

Fry the chicken joints in the oil until just browned, then fill the pan half full with water, add the onion, thyme and bay leaf and simmer for about 20 minutes until the chicken is cooked. Remove the chicken to a serving dish and keep it warm. Mix the yoghurt, saffron and lemon juice with 250 ml/8 fl oz of the strained cooking liquor and season to taste with freshly ground black pepper. Heat the sauce gently but do not allow it to boil or the yoghurt will separate. Pour the sauce over the chicken and garnish with lemon wedges.

Quick Barbecue Chicken

Serves 4

120 ml/4 fl oz Tomato ketchup

100 g/4 oz Chutney, chopped

45 ml/3 tbsp Soft dark brown sugar

4 Chicken portions

Mix the tomato ketchup, chutney and sugar, brush it over the chicken and leave it to stand for 1 hour. Brush again with any remaining mixture and place the chicken in a roasting tin. Bake in a preheated oven at 190°C/375°F/gas mark 5 for 40 minutes until cooked through, turning occasionally and basting with more sauce if necessary.

Braised Lemon Chicken

Serves 4

| 1 Celery stalk, chopped |
| 1 Onion, chopped |
| 1 Cooking apple, peeled, cored and sliced |
| 50 g/2 oz Butter or margarine, softened |
| 5 ml/1 tsp French mustard |
| 5 ml/1 tsp Mixed herbs |
| Grated rind and juice of ½ lemon |
| Salt and pepper |
| 4 Chicken portions |
| 300 ml/½ pt Chicken Stock (page 24) |

Place the celery, onion and apple in the bottom of an ovenproof dish. Mix the butter or margarine with the mustard, herbs, lemon rind and juice and season to taste with salt and pepper. Make 2 slits across the top of each chicken portion and spread liberally with the lemon butter. Place the portions on top of the vegetables, add the stock and cover. Bake in a preheated oven at 200°C/400°F/gas mark 6 for 35 minutes then remove the lid and return the dish to the oven for a further 10 minutes to brown.

Chicken Paprika

Serves 4

| 30 ml/2 tbsp Oil |
| 4 Chicken portions |
| 2 Onions, sliced |
| 50 g/2 oz Mushrooms, sliced |
| 4 Tomatoes, skinned and sliced |
| 1 Garlic clove, crushed |
| 15 ml/1 tbsp Paprika |
| 450 ml/¾ pt Chicken Stock (page 24) |
| Salt and pepper |
| 15 ml/1 tbsp Cornflour |
| 15 ml/1 tbsp Water |
| 30 ml/2 tbsp Chopped parsley |

Heat the oil and fry the chicken portions until lightly browned on all sides, then remove them from the pan. Add the onions and fry until browned, then add the mushrooms and tomatoes and cook for 2 minutes. Stir in the garlic and paprika, return the chicken portions, pour over the stock and season to taste with salt and pepper. Bring to the boil, cover and simmer for 45 minutes until the chicken is cooked through. Transfer the chicken to a warmed serving dish and keep it warm. Mix the cornflour and water, stir it into the sauce, bring to the boil and boil, stirring, until the sauce thickens. Pour the sauce over the chicken, sprinkle with parsley and serve with mashed potatoes and a green vegetable.

Sesame Drumsticks

Serves 4

8 Chicken drumsticks
1 Egg, beaten
100 g/4 oz Sesame seeds
2.5 ml/½ tsp Chilli powder
Salt and pepper

Brush the chicken with beaten egg.
Mix the sesame seeds and chilli
powder and season to taste with salt
and pepper. Roll the chicken in the
seeds. Place the chicken in a roasting
tin and bake in a preheated oven
at 180°C/350°F/gas mark 4 for
35 minutes until golden brown and
cooked through.

Crunchy Coated Chicken Drumsticks

Serves 4

75 g/3 oz Breadcrumbs
100 g/4 oz Cashew nuts or peanuts,
    chopped
Pepper
5 ml/1 tsp Coriander
8 Chicken drumsticks
1 Egg, beaten

Mix together the breadcrumbs, nuts,
pepper and coriander. Dip the
chicken drumsticks in the egg, then
in the breadcrumb mixture and bake
in a preheated oven at 190°C/375°F/
gas mark 5 for 30 minutes.

Coconut Drumsticks

Serves 4

100 g/4 oz Apricot jam
60 ml/4 tbsp Orange juice
8 Chicken drumsticks
100 g/4 oz Desiccated coconut

Warm the apricot jam and mix in the
orange juice. Brush liberally over the
drumsticks and coat them in the
coconut. Place in a roasting tin and
bake in a preheated oven at 190°C/
375°F/gas mark 5 for 30 minutes,
turning once or twice, until golden
brown and cooked through.

Chicken Satay

Serves 4

120 ml/4 fl oz Coconut cream
Salt and pepper
1 kg/2 lb Chicken, cut into
    4 cm/1½ in cubes
60 ml/4 tbsp Smooth peanut
    butter
2.5 ml/½ tsp Chilli powder
5 ml/1 tsp Grated lemon rind
10 ml/2 tsp Soft brown sugar
225 ml/8 fl oz Water
Juice of ½ lime

Mix the coconut cream with salt and
pepper to taste and marinate the
chicken pieces for 2 hours. Drain,
reserving the marinade. Thread the
meat on to skewers and grill under a
medium grill for 20 minutes, turning
frequently and basting with the
marinade until cooked through.

Meanwhile, mix the peanut butter, chilli powder, lemon rind, sugar and water in a saucepan, bring to the boil and simmer for 20 minutes. Stir in the lime juice and serve with the satay sticks.

Gardener's Chicken

Serves 4

| 100 g/4 oz Butter or margarine |
| 50 g/2 oz Streaky bacon, rinded and chopped |
| 2 Onions, sliced |
| 3 Celery stalks, sliced |
| 100 g/4 oz Mushrooms, sliced |
| 1 Chicken, jointed |
| 450 g/1 lb Small new potatoes |
| 225 g/½ lb Turnips, sliced |
| 400 g/14 oz Canned tomatoes |
| 1 Bouquet garni |
| Salt and pepper |
| 15 ml/1 tbsp Chopped parsley |

Melt half the butter or margarine and fry the bacon, onions, celery and mushrooms until soft but not browned. Transfer to a casserole dish. Add the remaining butter or margarine and fry the chicken portions until lightly browned, then transfer them to the casserole and add the potatoes, turnips, tomatoes and bouquet garni. Season to taste with salt and pepper. Cover tightly and cook in a preheated oven at 160°C/325°F/gas mark 3 for 2 hours until tender. Discard the bouquet garni and serve sprinkled with parsley.

Chicken Maryland

Serves 4

| 175 g/6 oz Plain flour |
| Salt and pepper |
| 1.5 kg/3 lb Chicken, jointed |
| 2 Eggs, beaten |
| 100 g/4 oz Breadcrumbs |
| 50 g/2 oz Butter or margarine |
| 30 ml/2 tbsp Oil |
| 4 Bacon rashers |
| 4 Bananas |
| 150 ml/¼ pt Milk |
| 300 g/11 oz Canned creamed sweetcorn |
| Salt and pepper |

Season 50 g/2 oz flour with salt and pepper and coat the chicken joints in the flour. Dip them in the eggs, then the breadcrumbs. Heat the butter and oil and fry the chicken pieces until lightly browned all over, reduce the heat and continue frying gently for 20 minutes or until cooked through. Drain on kitchen paper, place on a serving dish and keep them warm.

Stretch the bacon rashers and cut in half. Roll the pieces round a skewer and grill until crisp, then place on the serving dish.

Cut the bananas in half lengthways and fry in hot butter for 3 minutes, turning once. Place on the serving dish. Whisk the remaining flour with the milk and sweetcorn and season to taste with salt and pepper. Fry spoonfuls of the batter in hot butter until browned, turning once. Place on the serving dish, and serve the chicken with the fritters, bacon rolls and bananas.

Chicken with Parsley Dumplings

Serves 4

30 ml/2 tbsp Oil
1 Chicken, jointed
2 Onions, sliced
1 Garlic clove, crushed
25 g/1 oz Plain flour
600 ml/1 pt Chicken Stock (page 24)
1 Bay leaf
10 ml/2 tsp Mixed herbs
Salt and pepper
100 g/4 oz Self-raising flour
50 g/2 oz Shredded suet
30 ml/2 tbsp Chopped parsley
1 Egg, beaten

Heat the oil and fry the chicken pieces until browned on all sides, then transfer them to a casserole dish. Fry the onions and garlic until soft but not browned, then transfer them to the casserole. Stir the flour into the pan and cook for 1 minute, stirring. Stir in the stock, bring to the boil and cook, stirring, until the sauce thickens. Add the bay leaf and herbs and season to taste with salt and pepper. Pour over the chicken, cover and cook in a preheated oven at 180°C/350°F/gas mark 4 for 1 hour.

Mix the flour, suet and parsley and bind together with the egg. Roll into small dumplings and add to the casserole. Cook, uncovered, for a further 30 minutes. Discard the bay leaf before serving.

Chicken in Milk

Serves 4

1.2 litres/2 pts Milk
3 Onions
3 Cloves
1 Bay leaf
6 Peppercorns
2.5 ml/½ tsp Salt
50 g/2 oz Butter or margarine
100 g/4 oz Bacon, diced
1 Chicken, jointed
100 g/4 oz Mushrooms, sliced
1 Bouquet garni

Place the milk in a saucepan. Stud 1 onion with cloves and add it to the pan with the bay leaf, peppercorns and salt, bring to the boil, then leave to infuse for 45 minutes.

Chop the remaining onions. Melt the butter and fry the onions until soft, add the bacon and fry until just browned, then transfer them to a casserole dish. Brown the chicken joints in the butter, then transfer them to the dish. Fry the mushrooms lightly, then tip them over the chicken with the remaining butter and add the bouquet garni. Bring the milk back to the boil again, then strain it over the chicken and bake in a preheated oven at 150°C/300°F/ gas mark 2 for 2½ hours until the chicken is tender.

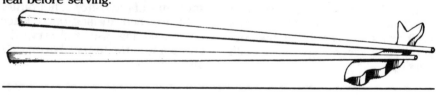

Sweet Curried Chicken

Serves 4

60 ml/4 tbsp Honey
10 ml/2 tsp Curry powder
1 Chicken, jointed
Salt and pepper
50 g/2 oz Butter or margarine
15 g/½ oz Plain flour
300 ml/½ pt Chicken Stock
  (page 24)
50 g/2 oz Sultanas
15 ml/1 tbsp Lemon juice
15 ml/1 tbsp Chopped parsley

Mix half the honey with the curry powder. Season the chicken portions with salt and pepper and marinate in the mixture overnight.

Melt the butter or margarine and remaining honey and fry the chicken pieces until browned. Stir in the flour and cook for 1 minute, then stir in the stock, sultanas, lemon juice and season to taste with salt and pepper. Bring to the boil, cover and simmer for 20 minutes, stirring occasionally, adding a little extra stock if necessary. Sprinkle with parsley and serve with rice.

Quick Chicken Crunchies

Serves 4

400 g/14 oz Filo pastry
60 ml/4 tbsp Olive oil
450 g/1 lb Cooked chicken, cut into
  5 cm/2 in pieces
Oil for deep frying

Cover the pastry sheets you are not using with a damp cloth to avoid them drying out while you are working. Brush the pastry with oil, then fold in half lengthways. Place a piece of chicken on one end and fold over and over into a small parcel. Fry the chicken parcels in deep hot oil for 3 minutes until golden brown and crispy. Drain well on kitchen paper and keep them warm while you fry the remaining parcels.

Crunchy Chicken Bake

Serves 4

450 g/1 lb Cooked chicken, diced
15 ml/1 tbsp Lemon juice
120 ml/4 fl oz Mayonnaise
  (page 250)
Pinch of salt
2 Celery stalks, chopped
150 g/5 oz Canned condensed
  cream of chicken soup
2 Hard-boiled eggs, chopped
½ Onion, finely chopped
25 g/1 oz Flaked almonds
50 g/2 oz Cheddar cheese, grated
50 g/2 oz Potato crisps, crushed

Combine all the ingredients except the almonds, cheese and crisps and spoon into a baking dish. Top with the almonds, cheese and crisps and leave to chill in the fridge overnight.

Return to room temperature, then bake in a preheated oven at 200°C/ 400°F/gas mark 6 for 25 minutes until hot and bubbly.

Chicken and Broccoli Stir-Fry

Serves 4

60 ml/4 tbsp Oil

5 ml/1 tsp Sesame oil

50 g/2 oz Small corn cobs, sliced

225 g/8 oz Broccoli florets

225 g/8 oz Cooked chicken, cut into
strips

30 ml/2 tbsp Soy sauce

50 g/2 oz Mangetout

50 g/2 oz Beansprouts

50 g/2 oz Bamboo shoots, cut into
strips

Heat the oils and fry the sweetcorn
and broccoli for 5 minutes over a
high heat. Add the chicken and soy
sauce and stir-fry for 3 minutes. Add
the mangetout, beansprouts and
bamboo shoots and stir-fry for
3 minutes. Serve immediately.

Summer Chicken

Serves 4

450 g/1 lb Cooked chicken, cut into
strips

90 ml/6 tbsp Dry white wine

5 ml/1 tsp Lemon juice

½ Onion, grated

5 ml/1 tsp Tarragon

4 Oranges, peeled and segmented

1 Lettuce, shredded

1 Bunch of watercress

50 g/2 oz Walnuts, toasted

75g/3 oz Full fat soft cheese

150 ml/¼ pt Soured cream

5 ml/1 tsp Tabasco sauce

Salt and pepper

Place the chicken, wine, lemon juice,
onion, tarragon and oranges in a
bowl and mix well. Cover and leave
to marinate for 30 minutes. Arrange
the lettuce and watercress on a
serving plate. Remove the chicken
and orange segments from the marinade, mix with the walnuts and
spoon on to the lettuce. Mix the
cheese, soured cream and tabasco
sauce and season to taste with salt
and pepper. Stir in just enough
marinade to give a pouring consistency. Pour over the chicken
mixture and serve chilled.

Chicken Divan

Serves 4

275 g/10 oz Broccoli spears

50 g/2 oz Butter or margarine

25 g/1 oz Plain flour

250 ml/8 fl oz Chicken Stock
(page 24)

60 ml/4 tbsp Double cream

30 ml/2 tbsp Dry sherry

Salt and pepper

4 Cooked chicken breasts, cut in
half lengthways

50 g/2 oz Parmesan cheese,
grated

Blanch the broccoli in boiling water
for 5 minutes, then drain and arrange
on the base of a casserole dish. Melt
the butter in a frying pan, stir in the
flour and cook for 1 minute, stirring
continuously. Remove from the heat
and stir in the stock, bring to the boil,
then stir in the cream and sherry
and season to taste with salt and
pepper. Spoon half the sauce over

the broccoli, then lay the chicken on top and pour over the remaining sauce. Sprinkle with Parmesan and bake in a preheated oven at 180°C/350°F/gas mark 4 for 20 minutes until golden brown.

Chicken and Sweetcorn Samosas

Serves 4

| 15 g/½ oz Butter or margarine |
| 15 ml/½ oz Plain flour |
| 150 ml/¼ pt Milk |
| Salt and pepper |
| 1 Egg, beaten |
| 100 g/4 oz Cooked chicken, chopped |
| 50 g/2 oz Sweetcorn |
| 450 g/1 lb Puff Pastry (page 146) |

Melt the butter or margarine in a saucepan, stir in the flour and cook for 1 minute. Whisk in the milk and bring to the boil, stirring continuously, until the sauce thickens. Season to taste with salt and pepper, remove from the heat and beat in half the egg. Stir in the chicken and sweetcorn. Roll out the puff pastry as thinly as possible and divide into 8 small rectangles. Divide the chicken mixture between the rectangles, glaze the edges with the remaining egg and fold over to make square parcels. Seal the edges and glaze on both sides with egg. Chill for 30 minutes.

Fry in deep hot oil for 6 minutes until golden brown and well puffed, drain on kitchen paper and serve immediately.

Chicken Stuffed Pancakes

Serves 4

| 150 g/5 oz Plain flour |
| 1 Egg, beaten |
| 300 ml/½ pt Milk |
| Pinch of salt |
| 30 ml/2 tbsp Oil |
| 75 g/3 oz Butter or margarine |
| 100 g/4 oz Mushrooms, chopped |
| 300 ml/½ pt Chicken Stock (page 24) |
| 2.5 ml/½ tsp Mixed herbs |
| Salt and pepper |
| 225 g/8 oz Cooked chicken, chopped |

Beat 100 g/4 oz flour with the egg, milk and salt to a batter. Heat the oil in a frying pan and fry 8 pancakes.

Melt half the butter or margarine in a frying pan and fry the mushrooms until soft, then stir in the reserved flour and gradually add the stock. Bring to the boil, stirring continuously, add the herbs and season to taste with salt and pepper. Stir in the chicken, then remove from the heat and allow to cool.

Divide the sauce between the pancakes and fold over the edges to make square parcels. Place them, folded sides down, on a flat ovenproof dish, and place knobs of the remaining butter on top. Cover with foil and bake in a preheated oven at 200°C/400°F/gas mark 6 for 20 minutes until hot and golden.

Quick Lemon Chicken

Serves 4

25 g/1 oz Butter or margarine
25 g/1 oz Plain flour
300 ml/½ pt Chicken Stock (page 24)
300 ml/½ pt Milk
350 g/12 oz Cooked chicken, cut into strips
100 g/4 oz Cooked green beans
30 ml/2 tbsp Lemon juice
Pinch of thyme
Salt and pepper
175 g/6 oz Long-grain rice
15 ml/1 tbsp Chopped parsley
100 g/4 oz Carrots, peeled and cut into strips
25 g/1 oz Flaked almonds, toasted

Melt the butter or margarine, stir in the flour and cook gently for 1 minute, stirring. Whisk in the stock and milk, bring to the boil and simmer, stirring, until the sauce thickens. Stir in the chicken, beans, lemon juice and thyme and season to taste with salt and pepper. Cook for 10 minutes until heated through. Cook the rice in plenty of boiling salted water until just tender. Drain and toss with the parsley, then arrange in a ring on a warmed serving plate. Blanch the carrots in boiling salted water for 3 minutes. pour the chicken mixture into the centre of the rice and garnish with the carrots and almonds.

Nutty Chicken

Serves 4

25 g/1 oz Butter or margarine
2 Onions
100 g/4 oz Mushrooms, sliced
5 ml/1 tsp Soy sauce
225 g/8 oz Cooked chicken, chopped
225 g/8 oz Cooked pork, chopped
100 g/4 oz Bamboo shoots
150 ml/¼ pt Chicken Stock (page 24)
Salt and pepper
30 ml/2 tbsp Oil
12 Walnuts

Melt the butter or margarine. Chop 1 onion and slice the other into rings. Fry the chopped onion until soft but not browned, then add the mushrooms and fry for 1 minute. Stir in the soy sauce, then add the chicken, pork, bamboo shoots and stock and season to taste with salt and pepper. Bring to the boil and simmer for 20 minutes, stirring occasionally.

Heat the oil and fry the walnuts until golden. Remove from the pan and keep warm. Fry the onion rings until browned. Garnish the chicken with the walnuts and onion rings and serve with boiled rice.

French Mustard Poussin

Serves 4

75 g/3 oz Butter or margarine

2 Poussins

20 ml/1½ tbsp Dijon mustard

150 ml/¼ pt Chicken Stock
(page 24)

30 ml/2 tbsp Orange juice

30 ml/2 tbsp Double cream

15 ml/1 tbsp Chopped parsley

Melt the butter or margarine and fry the poussins until browned on all sides. Transfer them to a casserole dish just large enough to fit them. Mix the mustard into the pan, stirring to scrape up all the meat juices. Stir in the stock and orange juice, bring to the boil and pour over the poussins. Bake in a preheated oven at 180°C/350°F/gas mark 4 for 45 minutes until tender. Transfer the poussins to a warmed serving dish. Pour the sauce into a saucepan, bring almost to the boil and stir in the cream, then pour around the poussins and serve sprinkled with parsley.

Poussin à la Crème

Serves 4

75 g/3 oz Butter or margarine

2 Poussins with giblets, jointed into 4

2 Onions, chopped

100 g/4 oz Gammon, chopped

150 ml/¼ pt Dry white wine

150 ml/¼ pt Single cream

Pepper

Melt the butter or margarine and fry the leg portions gently for 2 minutes each side, then add the wing pieces. Chop the liver and add it with the onions and gammon and cook for 4 minutes, turning once. Stir in the wine and cook for 5 minutes, then slowly pour the cream over the poussins and simmer for 1 minute. Lift the poussins on to a warmed serving plate, stir the sauce well and pour over. Serve with boiled rice.

Turkey Filo Roll

Serves 4

225 g/8 oz Sausagemeat

5 ml/1 tsp Mixed herbs

50 g/2 oz Walnuts, finely chopped

Salt and pepper

1 Egg, beaten

200 g/7 oz Filo pastry

45 ml/3 tbsp Oil

2 Turkey breasts, sliced

Mix the sausagemeat, herbs and walnuts and season to taste with salt and pepper. Bind together with the egg. Cover the pastry sheets you are not using with a damp cloth to avoid them drying out while you are working. Brush the pastry sheets with oil and layer 4 or 5 sheets on a greased baking sheet. Place half the sausagemeat mixture down the centre of the sheets, top with the turkey, then with the remaining mixture. Carefully roll into a loose roll, tucking in the sides and the ends as you do so. Brush with oil and bake in a preheated oven at 190°C/375°F/gas mark 5 for 40 minutes to allow the inside to cook well.

Devilled Turkey Drummers

Serves 4

4 Turkey drumsticks
1 Garlic clove, cut lengthways
15 ml/1 tbsp Oil
8 Streaky bacon rashers, rinded
100 g/4 oz Apricot jam
250 ml/8 fl oz Tomato ketchup
60 ml/4 tbsp Soy sauce
45 ml/3 tbsp French mustard
60 ml/4 tbsp Worcestershire sauce
60 ml/4 tbsp Lemon juice
Salt and pepper

Stick a garlic sliver in the thick end of each drumstick and brush with oil. Roll up the bacon rashers. Melt the jam with the ketchup in a heavy saucepan. Stir in the soy sauce, mustard, Worcestershire sauce and lemon juice and season to taste with salt and pepper. Bring to the boil and cook for 1 minute. Place the drumsticks in an ovenproof dish and cover with the sauce, cover and bake in a preheated oven at 180°C/350°F/gas mark 4 for 2 hours until the drumsticks are well cooked through, basting occasionally with the sauce. Remove the lid and add the bacon rolls for the last 20 minutes of cooking.

Spiced Eastern Turkey

Serves 4

1.2 kg/2½ lb Turkey leg
5 ml/1 tsp Cumin
5 ml/1 tsp Coriander
5 ml/1 tsp Turmeric
2.5 ml/½ tsp Ground ginger
300 ml/½ pt Natural yoghurt
30 ml/1 tbsp Lemon juice
Salt and pepper
45 ml/3 tbsp Oil
225 g/8 oz Onion, sliced
45 ml/3 tbsp Desiccated coconut
30 ml/2 tbsp Plain flour
150 m/¼ pt Chicken Stock (page 24)
15 ml/1 tbsp Chopped parsley

Cut the meat off the bones and cut it into bite-sized pieces. Stir the spices into the yoghurt and lemon juice and season to taste with salt and pepper. Stir in the meat, cover and refrigerate for 3 hours.

Heat the oil and fry the onion until lightly browned. Add the coconut and flour and fry, stirring, for 1 minute. Stir in the turkey, marinade and the stock, bring to the boil and pour into a casserole dish. Cover and bake in a preheated oven at 160°C/325°F/gas mark 3 for 1¼ hours until the turkey is tender. Adjust the seasoning if necessary and sprinkle with parsley to serve.

Turkey and Bean Ragout

Serves 4

50 g/2 oz Butter or margarine

2 Onions, chopped

15 g/½ oz Plain flour

10 ml/2 tsp Chilli powder

400 g/14 oz Canned tomatoes, chopped

15 ml/1 tbsp Worcestershire sauce

30 ml/2 tbsp Tomato purée

300 ml/½ pt Turkey or Chicken Stock (page 24)

10 ml/2 tsp Caster sugar

1 Bay leaf

Salt and pepper

450 g/1 lb Cooked turkey, diced

200 g/7 oz Canned pimento, drained and chopped

200 g/7 oz Canned red kidney beans, drained

Melt half the butter and fry the onions until soft but not browned. Stir in the flour and chilli powder and cook for 1 minute, then stir in the tomatoes, Worcestershire sauce, tomato purée, stock, sugar and bay leaf and season to taste with salt and pepper. Bring to the boil, cover and simmer for 30 minutes. Fry the turkey in the remaining butter and stir it into the sauce with the pimento and beans and simmer for a further 10 minutes.

Turkey Roulade

Serves 4

50 g/2 oz Butter or margarine

50 g/2 oz Plain flour

300 ml/½ pt Milk

100 g/4 oz Strong cheese, grated

3 Eggs, separated

5 ml/1 tsp Mixed herbs

225 g/8 oz Cooked mixed vegetables, chopped

225 g/8 oz Cooked turkey, chopped

50 g/2 oz Cooked ham, chopped

Grated rind and juice of ½ lemon

100 g/4 oz Mushrooms, sliced

15 ml/1 tbsp Chopped chives

Salt and pepper

2 Tomatoes, sliced

Melt the butter, stir in the flour and cook for 1 minute. Whisk in the milk, bring to the boil and boil, stirring, until the sauce thickens. Remove from the heat and stir in the cheese. Divide the mixture in half and put half to one side. Stir the egg yolks, herbs and vegetables into one half. Whisk the egg whites until stiff, then fold them into the mixture and pile into a greased and lined 33 x 23 cm/13 x 9 in swiss roll tin. Bake in a preheated oven at 190°C/ 375°F/gas mark 5 for 30 minutes. Place the remaining sauce in a saucepan, stir in the turkey, ham, lemon rind and juice, mushrooms and chives. Cover and simmer gently for 15 minutes, then season to taste with salt and pepper. Turn the cooked soufflé on to a clean sheet of greaseproof paper and remove the lining paper. Spread the filling over and quickly roll up, using the paper to help. Roll on to a serving plate and garnish with the tomatoes.

Turkey Supreme

Serves 4

2.5 ml/½ tsp Curry powder
15 ml/1 tbsp Tomato purée
15 ml/1 tbsp Lemon juice
15 ml/1 tbsp Apricot jam
1 Onion, finely chopped
1 Garlic clove, chopped
450 g/1 lb Cooked turkey, chopped
Salt and pepper
150 ml/¼ pt Natural yoghurt
150 ml/¼ pt Mayonnaise
    (page 250)
15 ml/1 tbsp Chopped parsley
Pinch of paprika

Mix the curry powder, tomato purée, lemon juice and jam in a saucepan and bring slowly to the boil, stirring continuously. Add the onion and garlic and purée in a food processor or blender. Stir in the turkey and season to taste with salt and pepper. Fold in the yoghurt and mayonnaise and chill overnight in the fridge. Serve sprinkled with parsley and paprika.

Turkey Slices with Cider Cream

Serves 4

500 g/1¼ lb Turkey breast, sliced
    into 4
1 Egg, beaten
100 g/4 oz Breadcrumbs
100 g/4 oz Butter or margarine
300 ml/½ pt Dry cider
150 ml/¼ pt Double cream
Salt and pepper
2 Parsley sprigs

Dip the turkey breast slices in egg, then in breadcrumbs. Melt the butter or margarine and fry the turkey until golden brown and cooked through. Transfer to a warmed serving plate and keep it warm. Stir the cider into the pan and bring to the boil, stirring to scrape up the meat juices. Boil for 1 minute, then stir in the cream, season to taste with salt and pepper and heat through. Pour over the turkey and serve garnished with parsley.

Duck with Plum Sauce

Serves 4

400 g/14 oz Canned plums, drained
    and juice reserved
30 ml/2 tbsp Tomato purée
25 g/1 oz Soft dark brown sugar
15 ml/1 tbsp Red wine vinegar
5 ml/1 tsp Dijon mustard
1 Garlic clove, crushed
Salt and pepper
1 Duck, quartered

Place the plums, tomato purée, sugar, wine vinegar, mustard and garlic in a saucepan and warm gently to dissolve the sugar. Season to taste with salt and pepper, then purée in a food processor or blender. Thin, if necessary, with a little plum juice. Pour the sauce over the duck in a roasting tin and roast in a preheated oven at 190°C/375°F/gas mark 5 for 1½ hours until crisp and golden, basting from time to time with the sauce.

Honey Duck

Serves 4

450 g/1 lb Pork sausagemeat
50 g/2 oz Breadcrumbs
Grated rind and juice of 1 orange
2.5 ml/½ tsp Mixed herbs
Salt and pepper
2.25/5 lb Duck, oven-ready with giblets
300 ml/½ pt Water
15 ml/1 tbsp Honey
15 ml/1 tbsp Plain flour
1 Orange, sliced
1 Bunch of watercress

Mix together the sausagemeat, bread-crumbs, orange rind and herbs and season to taste with salt and pepper. Stuff the duck with the mixture and skewer down the loose skin. Place the duck on a rack in a roasting tin and prick the skin all over with a needle. Rub the skin with salt and roast in a preheated oven at 200°C/400°F/gas mark 6 for 30 minutes, then reduce the heat to 180°C/350°F/gas mark 4 and cook for a further 1½ hours until just cooked.

Meanwhile, bring the giblets and water to the boil in a saucepan and simmer for 45 minutes, then drain and reserve the stock for making gravy.

Mix the orange juice and honey and brush over the duck, then return it to the oven for 15 minutes. When ready, remove the duck to a warmed serving plate and keep it warm. Pour most of the fat out of the tin, leaving about 30 ml/2 tbsp. Stir in the flour and cook for 1 minute, then stir in the stock and boil, stirring, until smooth and thick. Season to taste with salt and pepper and pour into a sauce boat. Serve the duck garnished with orange slices and watercress.

Duck in Orange Liqueur Sauce

Serves 6

2 Ducks
4 Oranges
150 ml/¼ pt Red wine
15 ml/1 tbsp Caster sugar
300 ml/½ pt Giblet Stock (page 24)
Juice of ½ lemon
15 ml/1 tbsp Cornflour
15 ml/1 tbsp Water
45 ml/3 tbsp Orange liqueur

Place the ducks on their sides in a greased roasting tin and roast in a preheated oven at 200°C/400°F/gas mark 6 for 40 minutes. Turn them on the other side and roast for a further 30 minutes, then turn them on their backs and roast for a final 30 minutes until cooked, basting frequently.

Peel the oranges, remove the pith and divide into segments, reserving the juice which drips out as you work. Cut the rind into strips and boil in water for 5 minutes, then drain. Boil the wine and sugar until thickened, then add the reserved orange juice, stock and lemon juice, bring to the boil and boil for 5 minutes. Mix the cornflour and water and stir it into the sauce with the orange liqueur. Boil, stirring, until thickened, then pour the sauce over the ducks and garnish with the orange segments and rind.

Partridge with Red Cabbage

Serves 4

60 ml/4 tbsp Olive oil
4 Partridges
2 Onions, chopped
2 Apples, peeled, cored and chopped
2 Celery stalks, chopped
90 ml/6 tbsp Vinegar
25 g/1 oz Demerara sugar
15 ml/1 tbsp Orange juice
Salt and pepper
1 Bouquet garni

Heat the olive oil and fry the partridges until browned on all sides. Remove them from the pan. Fry the onions, apples and celery until just beginning to brown, then stir in the cider vinegar, sugar and orange juice and season to taste with salt and pepper. Transfer the mixture to a casserole dish and top with the partridges. Add the bouquet garni, cover tightly and bake in a preheated oven at 150°C/300°F/gas mark 2 for 3 hours until tender. Discard the bouquet garni before serving.

Grouse in Milk

Serves 2

25 g/1 oz Lard
1 Grouse
2 Bacon rashers, rinded and chopped
50 g/2 oz Belly of pork, diced
100 g/4 oz Mushrooms sliced
150 ml/¼ pt Milk
75 ml/5 tbsp Water
2.5 ml/½ tsp Ground mace
1 Bouquet garni
Salt and pepper

Heat the lard in a frying pan. Stuff the grouse with the bacon and brown it in the lard, then transfer it to a casserole dish. Fry the belly of pork until browned, then add the mushrooms, fry for 1 minute and spoon over the grouse. Bring the milk and water to the boil, stir in the mace and pour into the casserole. Add the bouquet garni and season to taste with salt and pepper. Cook in a preheated oven at 150°C/300°F/gas mark 2 for 4 hours until tender. Discard the bouquet garni before serving.

Pigeon with Mushrooms

Serves 4

100 g/4 oz Butter or margarine
3 Onions, chopped
4 Celery stalks, chopped
225 g/8 oz Mushrooms, sliced
4 Pigeons
Salt and pepper
120 ml/4 fl oz Brandy
100 g/4 oz Canned chestnut purée

Melt the butter in a large saucepan and fry the onions, celery and mushroom stalks until browned. Season the pigeons with salt and pepper and brown them in the pan, then cover and simmer gently for 30 minutes. Add the mushrooms and cook for 5 minutes, then add the brandy and simmer for 10 minutes. Season the chestnut purée with salt and pepper and place it in the bottom of a heated casserole dish. Sit the pigeons on top of the purée. Lift out the vegetables with a slotted spoon and place them round the pigeons. Bring the pan juices back to the boil, then pour them over the pigeons. Cook in a preheated oven at 180°C/350°F/gas mark 5 for 20 minutes before serving.

Pigeon Casserole

Serves 4

4 Pigeons
Salt and pepper
450 ml/¾ pt Dry white wine
2 Onions, chopped
2 Carrots, chopped
1 Bouquet garni
50 g/2 oz Butter or margarine
100 g/4 oz Belly of pork, rinded and diced
25 g/1 oz Plain flour
120 ml/4 fl oz Brandy
2 Garlic cloves, crushed
Salt and pepper

Season the pigeons with salt and pepper. Mix the wine, onions, carrots and bouquet garni and marinate the pigeons in the mixture overnight, turning 2 or 3 times.

Melt three-quarters of the butter in a flameproof casserole and fry the pork until crisp. Lift the pigeons out of the marinade, pat dry on kitchen paper and sprinkle with flour. Melt the remaining butter and brown the pigeons all over. Pour the brandy over them and set them alight to burn off the excess fat. Add the strained marinade and the garlic and season to taste with salt and pepper. Cover tightly and cook in a pre-heated oven at 150°C/300°F/gas mark 2 for 2½ hours. Serve with red cabbage and chestnuts.

Rabbit and Bacon Casserole

Serves 4

1 Rabbit, jointed and soaked
    overnight in salt water
25 g/1 oz Plain flour
50 g/2 oz Fresh breadcrumbs
Salt and pepper
Pinch of marjoram
Pinch of sage
30 ml/2 tbsp Milk
2 Large onions, sliced
300 ml/½ pt Chicken or Vegetable
    Stock (page 24)
225 g/8 oz Bacon rashers, rinded

Roll the rabbit pieces in the flour and
lay them in a casserole. Season the
breadcrumbs, moisten with the milk
and sprinkle over the rabbit pieces.
Lay the onions over the top and just
cover with boiling stock; you may
not need all the stock. Lay the bacon
on top, cover and bake in a preheated oven at 180°C/350°F/gas
mark 4 for 1½ hours, then remove
the lid for a further 30 minutes to
allow the top to brown.

Roast Pheasant

Serves 4

2 Pheasants
1 Garlic clove, crushed
Salt and pepper
100 g/4 oz Streaky bacon rashers,
    rinded
300 ml/½ pt Red wine
100 g/4 oz Butter or margarine
5 ml/1 tsp Marjoram
5 ml/1 tsp Chopped parsley

Clean and dry the pheasants, rub
with the crushed garlic and season
with salt and pepper. Place in a
roasting tin and cover with the bacon
rashers. Mix the wine, butter or
margarine and herbs and pour over
the pheasants. Roast in a preheated
oven at 180°C/350°F/gas mark 4 for
1 hour until the birds are tender,
basting occasionally with the sauce.
Lift the pheasants from the pan on to
a warmed serving dish and serve the
sauce in a sauce boat.

Pastry, Pies and Pizza

A hot pie makes a delicious and warming meal on a cold winter day, and can often be partly prepared in advance. Cold pies for slicing at a buffet or salad meal are guaranteed to be popular. Shortcrust pastry does not take long to make, but if you are busy and do not have much time to spare, make up a batch to freeze, or keep a packet of ready-made pastry in the freezer. Puff pastry, or other pastries which take a little more time and care to prepare, can also be made in advance, or bought in from the local supermarket.

Pizza is very popular either as a meal in itself with an adventurous salad, or as a snack. For those pressed for time, ready-made pizza bases are available either fresh or frozen, or you can try topping some crisp French bread.

Shortcrust Pastry

Makes 350 g/12 oz

225 g/8 oz Plain flour
Pinch of salt
50 g/2 oz Butter or margarine
50 g/2 oz Lard
30-45 ml/2-3 tbsp Water

Mix the flour and salt, then rub in the butter or margarine until the mixture forms a pastry which comes away cleanly from the sides of the bowl.

Wholemeal Shortcrust Pastry
If you use wholemeal flour, you may need a little extra water.

Suet Crust Pastry

Makes 350 g/12 oz

225 g/8 oz Plain flour
5 ml/1 tsp Baking powder
Pinch of salt
75 g/3 oz Shredded suet
30 ml/2 tbsp Water

Mix the flour, baking powder and salt, then stir in the suet. Mix with enough cold water to make a soft dough.

Hot Water Crust Pastry

Makes 450 g/1 lb

350 g/12 oz Plain flour
Pinch of salt
100 g/4 oz Lard
100 ml/4 fl oz Water

Mix the flour and salt in a warmed bowl. Melt the lard gently in a saucepan, add the water when just melted and bring to the boil. Stir the liquid into the flour with a wooden spoon and mix quickly until blended. Turn on to a floured surface and knead until smooth. Use at once and do not allow to cool.

Rough Puff Pastry

Makes 400 g/14 oz

225 g/8 oz Plain flour
2.5 ml/½ tsp Salt
75 g/3 oz Lard, cut into pieces
75 g/3 oz Butter, cut into pieces
90-120 ml/6-8 tbsp Water

Mix the flour and salt, then mix in the lard and butter and mix to a soft dough with the water. Roll out on a floured surface to a rectangle 30 x 15 cm/12 x 6 in. Fold the bottom third upwards and the top third downwards over it, turn the dough so that the fold is on the left and seal the edges. Roll, fold and seal twice more, keeping the folded edge on the left. If the pastry becomes too soft, chill between rollings.

Puff Pastry

Makes 900 g/2 lb

450 g/1 lb Plain flour
5 ml/1 tsp Salt
450 g/1 lb Butter
10 ml/2 tsp Lemon juice
250 ml/8 fl oz Ice-cold water

Mix the flour and salt and rub one-quarter of the butter into the flour, then mix the dough with the lemon juice and water. Turn on to a floured surface and knead until smooth. Leave to rest in a cool place for 15 minutes.

Roll out the dough on a floured surface to a rectangle 28 x15 cm/11 x 6 in. Roll out the butter into a 13 cm/ 5 in square and place on the top half of the dough, leaving a gap around the edges. Fold the pastry over, seal the edges and turn so that the folded edge is on the left. Roll the pastry into a rectangular 30 x 15 cm/12 x 6 in, keeping the edges straight. Fold the top third down and the bottom third up, then turn so that the folded edge is on the left. Seal the edges and roll out and turn once more, then wrap in polythene and chill for 20 minutes. Roll out 4 more times, leaving to rest for 20 minutes between each rolling.

Steak and Ale Pie

Serves 4

30 ml/2 tbsp Oil
750 g/1½ lb Chuck steak, cubed
1 Onion, chopped
4 Celery stalks, chopped
450 ml/¾ pt Beef Stock
  (page 24)
Salt and pepper
25 g/1 oz Plain flour
15 ml/1 tbsp Water
225 g/8 oz Puff Pastry
  (page 146)
1 Egg, beaten
300 ml/½ pt Brown ale

Heat the oil and fry the steak, onion and celery until just browned. Stir in the stock and season to taste with salt and pepper. Bring to the boil, cover and simmer for 1 hour until the meat is tender.

Mix the flour and water and stir this into the meat, then bring back to the boil, stirring continuously until the gravy thickens. Turn the meat and vegetables and half the gravy into a 900 ml/1½ pt pie dish and leave to cool.

Roll out the pastry and use to cover the pie. Brush with the beaten egg and bake in a preheated oven at 220°C/425°F/gas mark 7 for 10 minutes, then reduce the heat to 190°C/375°F/gas mark 5 for a further 20 minutes. Place the ale in a saucepan and boil rapidly until reduced by half. Before serving the pie, lift off the crust and stir the hot ale into the meat and vegetables. Replace the pie crust and serve.

Old-Fashioned Steak and Kidney Pie

Serves 4

25 g/1 oz Plain flour
Pinch of mustard powder
Pinch of ground mace
Salt and pepper
450 g/1 lb Braising steak, cubed
100 g/4 oz Ox kidney, cubed
100 g/4 oz Mushrooms, chopped
1 Onion, chopped
1 Garlic clove, crushed
300 ml/½ pt Beef Stock
  (page 24)
150 ml/¼ pt Port
2.5 ml/½ tsp Worcestershire sauce
1 Hard-boiled egg, sliced
225 g/8 oz Shortcrust Pastry
  (page 145)
1 Egg, beaten

Mix the flour, mustard and mace and season to taste with salt and pepper. Toss the steak and kidney in the seasoned flour, then place in a casserole dish with the mushrooms, onion and garlic. Mix the stock, port and Worcestershire sauce and pour over the meat. Cover and cook in a preheated oven at 150°C/300°F/gas mark 2 for 3 hours until the meat is tender. Remove from the oven, chill and skim any fat from the top.

Transfer the meat and gravy into a pie dish and lay the egg slices over the top. Roll out the pastry and use it to cover the pie. Brush with beaten egg and bake in a preheated oven at 200°C/400°F/gas mark 6 for 30 minutes until the pie is golden brown.

Steak and Mushroom Pie with Horseradish Pastry

Serves 6

15 ml/1 tbsp Oil
2 Onions, sliced
750 g/1½ lb Chuck steak, cubed
175 g/6 oz plain flour
45 ml/3 tbsp Prepared mustard
1 Garlic clove, crushed
100 g/4 oz Mushrooms, sliced
Pinch of thyme
Pinch of sage
Salt and pepper
300ml/½ pt Beef Stock (page 24)
40 g/1½ oz Lard
40 g/1½ oz Butter or margarine
5 ml/1 tsp Horseradish sauce
30 ml/2 tbsp Water
30 ml/2 tbsp Milk

Heat the oil and fry the onions until browned. Add the meat and brown well all over. Stir in 15 ml/1 tbsp flour, the mustard, garlic, mushrooms and herbs and season to taste with salt and pepper. Add the stock, cover and simmer until the meat is tender. Pour into a 1.2 litre/2 pt pie dish with an egg cup in the centre, cool quickly and refrigerate overnight.

Rub the lard, and butter or margarine into the remaining flour until the mixture resembles fine bread-crumbs, then stir in the horseradish. Mix in just enough water to make a smooth pastry. Roll out and use to cover the pie dish. Trim and crimp the edges and use the trimmings for decoration. Brush with milk and bake in a preheated oven at 200°C/400°F/gas mark 6 for 30 minutes until golden brown.

Beef Batter Pie

Serves 4

450 g/1 lb Minced beef
1 Onion, chopped
300 ml/½ pt Beef Stock (page 24)
10 ml/2 tsp Worcestershire sauce
Salt and pepper
225 g/8 oz Plain flour
5 ml/1 tsp Baking powder
25 g/1 oz Cornflour
75 g/3 oz Shredded suet
300 ml/½ pt Milk

Put the beef in a saucepan and fry gently until browned. Add the onion and fry until soft. Stir in the stock and Worcestershire sauce and season to taste with salt and pepper. Bring to the boil, simmer for 15 minutes, then transfer to a greased 1.2 litre/2 pt pie dish. Beat the flour, baking powder, cornflour, suet and milk to a thick batter and season to taste with salt and pepper. Pour over the meat and bake in a preheated oven at 180°C/350°F/gas mark 4 for 35 minutes until risen and golden brown.

Savoury Beef Roll

Serves 4

450 g/1 lb Minced beef
100 g/4 oz Sausagemeat
50 g/2 oz Breadcrumbs
1 Onion, chopped
Pinch of ground ginger
2.5 ml/½ tsp Mixed herbs
Salt and pepper
350 g/12 oz Shortcrust Pastry
  (page 145)
1 Egg, beaten

Mix together the beef, sausagemeat, breadcrumbs, onion, ginger and herbs and season to taste with salt and pepper. Shape into a roll, place in a greased baking tin, cover and bake in a preheated oven at 190°C/375°F/ gas mark 5 for 20 minutes.

Roll the pastry into a rectangle. Remove the meat from the oven, lay it on the pastry and quickly seal the pastry round the meat in a roll. Turn it seam downwards on a greaed baking sheet, decorate with pastry trimmings and brush with beaten egg. Return to the oven for 30 minutes until golden brown.

Corned Beef Pie

Serves 4

15 ml/1 tbsp Oil
2 Onions, chopped
450 g/1 lb Canned corned beef, flaked
100 g/4 oz Cooked carrots, sliced
100 g/4 oz Cooked peas
1 Egg, beaten
5 ml/1 tsp Tabasco sauce
Salt and pepper
350 g/12 oz Shortcrust Pastry (page 145)
15 ml/1 tbsp Milk

Heat the oil and fry the onions until soft but not browned. Remove from the heat and stir in the corned beef, carrots, peas, egg and tabasco sauce and season to taste with salt and pepper. Roll out the pastry and use half to line a greased 20 cm/8 in pie dish. Fill with the meat mixture, then top with remaining pastry and decorate with the trimmings. Brush with milk. Bake in a preheated oven at 200°C/400°F/gas mark 6 for 30 minutes.

Spiced Beef Puffs

Serves 4

15 ml/1 tbsp Oil
15 g/½ oz Butter or margarine
1 Onion, chopped
225 g/8 oz Minced beef
1 Green pepper, chopped
Pinch of ground ginger
Pinch of chilli powder
15 ml/1 tbsp Tomato purée
Salt and pepper
6 Stuffed olives
750 g/1½ lb Puff Pastry (page 146)
1 Egg, beaten
15 ml/1 tbsp Water

Heat the oil and butter or margarine and fry the onion until soft but not browned. Stir in the mince and cook until brown, then add the pepper, ginger, chilli powder and tomato purée and season to taste with salt and pepper. Cover and cook gently for 10 minutes. Add the stuffed olives and leave the mixture to cool.

Roll out the pastry and cut into 8 x 15 cm/6 in circles and prick them with a fork. Place spoonfuls of the beef mixture in the centre of each and dampen the edges. Fold in half, seal the edges and chill for 30 minutes.

Lay the puffs on a greased baking sheet and brush the tops with the mixed egg and water. Bake in a preheated oven at 220°C/425°F/gas mark 7 for 20 minutes until risen and golden brown.

Veal and Ham Pie

Serves 6

900 g/2 lb Pie veal, cubed

1 Veal shin bone, sawn into pieces

900 ml/1½ pts Chicken Stock
  (page 24)

Salt and pepper

15 ml/1 tbsp Chopped parsley

225 g/8 oz Cooked ham, diced

3 Hard-boiled eggs

Grated rind of 1 lemon

450 g/1 lb Puff Pastry
  (page 146)

1 Egg, beaten

Put the veal and bones in a large saucepan with the stock. Season to taste with salt and pepper and add the parsley. Cover and simmer for 2 hours, then leave to cool for 15 minutes. Scoop out the meat and cut into bite-sized pieces. Mix with the ham and put a layer of meats in a greased 1.2 litre/2 pt oval pie dish. Put the eggs on top and pack the remaining meat around and over them. Sprinkle with the lemon rind and add enough of the stock just to cover the meat. Roll out the pastry and cut an oval to fit the dish and a 2.5 cm/1 in strip to go round the edge. Moisten the edges and press the strip round the dish, then moisten the strip and seal the lid on top. Make a hole in the centre, roll out the pastry trimmings and use to decorate the pie. Brush with the beaten egg. Bake in a preheated oven at 230°C/ 450°F/gas mark 8 for 10 minutes, then reduce the heat to 200°C/ 400°F/gas mark 6 and bake for a further 20 minutes until the pastry is well risen and golden brown. Use a funnel to fill the pie with more hot stock, if needed. Serve hot or cold.

Tourte Bourguignonne

Serves 4

225 g/8 oz Pie veal, minced

100 g/4 oz Gammon, minced

100 g/4 oz Pork fat, minced

45 ml/3 tbsp Brandy

1 Onion, chopped

1 Garlic clove, chopped

2.5 ml/½ tsp Nutmeg

2.5 ml/½ tsp Cinnamon

2.5 ml/½ tsp Ground mace

Salt and pepper

350 g/12 oz Shortcrust Pastry
  (page 145)

1 Egg, separated

15 ml/1 tbsp Water

Mix all ingredients except the pastry, egg and water and leave in a cool place for at least 1 hour. Roll out the pastry and use half to line a greased 20 cm/8 in flan ring on a baking sheet. Brush the inside with egg white and fill with the meat mixture. Roll out the remaining pastry and use it to cover the pie, sealing the edges well, then roll out the trimmings and use them to decorate the top. Mix the egg yolk and water and brush it over the pie, then make 4 holes to allow steam to escape. Bake in a preheated oven at 190°C/ 375°F/gas mark 5 for 50 minutes. Serve hot or cold.

Terrine en Croûte

Serves 8

450 g/1 lb Streaky bacon rashers, rinded	
750 g/1½ lb Belly of pork	
450 g/1 lb Lean veal	
225 g/8 oz Pigs' liver	
1 Onion, chopped	
15 ml/1 tbsp Chopped parsley	
Pinch of mace	
1 Garlic clove, crushed	
3 Green peppercorns	
3 Juniper berries, crushed	
60 ml/4 tbsp Madeira	
150 ml/¼ pt Dry white wine	
1 Egg, beaten	
450 g/1 lb Puff Pastry (page 146)	

Stretch the rashers out thinly with a knife and use them to line a 1.2 litre/ 2 pt terrine, arranging them down on the sides and across the bottom and leaving the ends hanging over the sides. Mince together all the remaining ingredients except the Madeira, wine, egg and pastry and marinate in the Madeira and wine for 1 hour. Press the mixture firmly into the terrine, then lap the ends of the bacon rashers over the top to cover completely. Cover and stand the terrine in a pan of hot water. Bake in a preheated oven at 180°C/350°F/ gas mark 4 for 1½ hours.

Remove the terrine from the tin, uncover and leave to cool completely. Roll out the pastry into a square, set the terrine in the centre and wrap the pastry around neatly to form a parcel, sealing the edges with beaten egg. Set on a greased baking tray with the seam underneath and brush with egg. Roll out any pastry trimmings and use them to decorate the top, then brush with egg again. bake in a preheated oven at 220°C/ 425°F/gas mark 7 for 30 minutes until golden brown. Cool thoroughly before serving in slices.

Sausage Plait

Serves 4

350 g/12 oz Shortcrust Pastry (page 145)	
15 ml/1 tbsp French mustard	
450 g/1 lb Pork sausagemeat	
1 Onion, chopped	
5 ml/1 tsp Mixed herbs	
Salt and pepper	
2 Hard-boiled eggs, sliced	
1 Egg, beaten	

Roll out the pastry to a 30 cm/12 in square and spread with the mustard. Mix the sausagemeat, onion and herbs and season to taste with salt and pepper. Spread half the mixture down the centre third of the pastry, arrange the hard-boiled eggs on top and cover with the remaining sausage-meat. Cut diagonal slits in the sides of the pastry to within 2.5 cm/1 in of the filling. Brush the edges of the pastry with beaten egg, and fold alternate strips of pastry over the filling to make a plait. Seal the ends, place on a greased baking sheet and brush with egg. Bake in a preheated oven at 200°C/400°F/gas mark 6 for 20 minutes, then reduce the heat to 180°C/350°F/gas mark 4 and cook for a further 20 minutes.

Chicken and Pork Layer Pie

Serves 4-6

275 g/10 oz Plain flour

Pinch of salt

40 g/1½ oz Lard

75 g/3 oz Butter or margarine

2 Eggs, beaten

350 g/12 oz Lean pork, finely
  chopped

1 Onion, finely chopped

100 g/4 oz Belly of pork, rinded and
  finely chopped

2.5 ml/½ tsp Marjoram

Salt and pepper

100 g/4 oz Cooked chicken, cut into
  strips

Mix the flour and salt, then rub in the lard, and butter or margarine until the mixture resembles fine breadcrumbs. Reserve half an egg for glazing, and mix to a firm pastry with the remainder. Cover and chill until required.

Mix the pork, onion, belly pork and marjoram and season to taste with salt and pepper. Cut a 2.5 cm/1 in double strip of greaseproof paper and lay it along the length of a greased 450 g/1 lb loaf tin, sticking out at each end. Quarter the pastry, and roll it out into rectangles to fit the sides, base and top of the tin. Seal the base and sides together and fill the tin with half the pork mixture. Layer the chicken on top, then add the remaining pork and put on the pastry lid, pinching round the edge to seal and make a pattern. Roll out any trimmings and decorate the top of the pie with pastry leaves. Glaze well with the beaten egg and cut 3 steam vents in the top. Bake in a preheated oven at 200°C/400°F/gas mark 6 for 45 minutes, then reduce the heat to 160°C/325°F/gas mark 3 for a further 45 minutes. Leave to cool in the tin.

Fidget Pie

Serves 4

350 g/12 oz Lean back bacon,
  rinded

450 g/1 lb Potatoes, sliced

450 g/1 lb Cooking apples, peeled,
  cored and sliced

Salt and pepper

150 ml/¼ pt Chicken Stock
  (page 24)

225 g/8 oz Shortcrust Pastry
  (page 145)

1 Egg, beaten

Cut each bacon rasher into 3 pieces, and arrange layers of bacon, potatoes and apples in a large greased pie dish. Season to taste with salt and pepper and pour in the chicken stock. Roll out the pastry and cut a lid to fit the dish and a 2.5 cm/1 in strip round the edge, then moisten the strip and seal the lid on top, sealing the edges well. Roll out the trimmings and use to decorate the top. Brush with the beaten egg and bake in a preheated oven at 190°C/375°F/gas mark 5 for 20 minutes, then reduce the heat to 180°C/350°F/gas mark 4 and continue to cook for a further 45 minutes.

Pork Pie

Serves 4

750 g/12 oz Lean pork, cubed
Pinch of sage
Pinch of nutmeg
Salt
350 g/12 oz Pork bones
450 g/1 lb Hot Water Crust Pastry
 (page 146)
1 Egg, beaten
10 g/¼ oz Gelatine

Mix the pork, sage, nutmeg and salt, cover and chill. Put the bones in a saucepan, just cover with water, add a pinch of salt, bring to the boil and simmer gently for 2 hours. Drop a little stock on a chilled plate to see if it jells firmly.

Make up the pastry and put one-quarter of it aside in a warm place. Mould the remaining pastry over an inverted 18 cm/7 in deep cake tin or pie dish. Leave to cool, then ease off the tin and turn upright. Fill with the prepared meat and 30 ml/2 tbsp stock. Top with the remaining pastry and seal the edges. Make a hole in the centre and decorate with pastry trimmings. Place on a greased baking sheet and bake in a preheated oven at 180°C/350°F/gas mark 4 for 2¼ hours. Glaze with beaten egg 15 minutes before the end of cooking time. Leave to cool.

While the pie cools, soften the gelatine in 300 ml/½ pt stock, dissolve over a gentle heat, then bring to the boil. Use a funnel to pour the boiling stock into the pie through the centre hole. This helps the pie to keep well.

Chicken and Mushroom Pie

Serves 4

25 g/1 oz Butter or margarine
1 Onion, chopped
100 g/4 oz Mushrooms, sliced
25 g/1 oz Plain flour
150 ml/¼ pt Milk
150 ml/¼ pt Chicken Stock
 (page 24)
100 g/4 oz Shelled prawns
100 g/4 oz Cooked chicken, cubed
1 Hard-boiled egg, chopped
2.5 ml/½ tsp Paprika
Salt and pepper
350 g/12 oz Puff Pastry (page 146)
1 Egg, beaten

Melt the butter or margarine and fry the onion until soft but not browned. Stir in the mushrooms and cook for 1 minute, then stir in the flour and cook for a further 1 minute. Stir in the milk and stock, bring to the boil, stirring, and simmer until the sauce thickens. Stir in the prawns, chicken, egg and paprika, and season to taste with salt and pepper and leave to cool.

Roll out the pastry and use half to line a greased 18 cm/7 in pie dish. Fill with the chicken mixture and top with the remaining pastry. Seal the edges, roll out the trimmings and use to decorate the top. Glaze with beaten egg and bake in a preheated oven at 230°C/450°F/gas mark 8 for 10 minutes, then reduce the heat to 190°C/375°F/gas mark 5 for a further 20 minutes.

153

Lamb and Mushroom Pie

Serves 4

15 ml/1 tbsp Plain flour

Salt and pepper

450 g/1 lb Shoulder of lamb, cubed

2 Lambs' kidneys, chopped

15 ml/1 tbsp Oil

1 Onion, chopped

300 ml/½ pt Beef Stock (page 24)

100 g/4 oz Mushrooms, halved

225 g/8 oz Shortcrust Pastry
 (page 145)

1 Egg, beaten

Season the flour with salt and pepper and roll the lamb cubes and kidney in the flour. Heat the oil and fry the onion until soft but not browned. Add the meat and cook until lightly browned. Stir in the stock and mushrooms, bring to the boil, then simmer until the meat is tender. Season to taste with salt and pepper and turn into an ovenproof dish. Roll out the pastry and use it to cover the pie. Brush with beaten egg and bake in a preheated oven at 200°C/400°F/ gas mark 6 for 30 minutes.

Game Pie

Serves 4

750 g/1½ lb Hot Water Crust Pastry
 (page 146)

350 g/12 oz Pork sausagemeat

100 g/4 oz Lean bacon, cubed

175 g/6 oz Chuck steak, cubed

1 Pheasant, boned and chopped

Salt and pepper

150-300 ml/¼-½ pt Jellied stock, hot

1 Egg, beaten

Make up the pastry and use three-quarters of it to line a greased oval pie mould or round cake tin, pressing the pastry well into the sides of the tin. Line the pastry with a thin layer of sausagemeat. Mix the bacon, steak and pheasant meats and season with salt and pepper. Add about 60 ml/ 4 tbsp stock and pack the meat into the case. Cover with the remaining pastry and seal the edges. Decorate with the pastry trimmings, make a hole in the centre and brush with the beaten egg. Bake in a preheated oven at 220°C/425°F/gas mark 7 for 30 minutes then reduce the heat to 190°C/375°F/gas mark 5 for 30 minutes, then reduce it again to 180°C/350°F/gas mark 4 for a further 30 minutes. Cover the pie with grease-proof paper if it is becoming too brown. Remove the pie from the oven and fill with hot stock through a funnel, then leave to cool completely before removing from the tin.

Chestnut and Mushroom Pie

Serves 4

450 g/1 lb Chestnuts, shelled

25 g/1 oz Butter or margarine

25 g/1 oz Plain flour

250 ml/8 fl oz Milk

Salt and pepper

225 g/8 oz Button mushrooms

225 g/8 oz Shortcrust Pastry
 (page 145)

1 Egg, beaten

Place the chestnuts in a bowl and cover with boiling water. Leave for 5 minutes, drain and rub off the brown skins and chop roughly. Melt the butter or margarine, stir in the flour and cook for 1 minute. Whisk in the milk, bring to the boil and cook, stirring, until the sauce thickens. Season to taste. Put the sauce, chestnuts and mushrooms in a greased 20 cm/8 in pie dish. Roll out the pastry and use it to cover the dish. Brush with egg and bake in a preheated oven at 190°C/375°F/gas mark 5 for 30 minutes.

Country Winter Pie

Serves 4

50 g/2 oz Butter or margarine
175 g/6 oz Leeks, sliced
175 g/6 oz Carrots, sliced
175 g/6 oz Celery stalks, sliced
175 g/6 oz Parsnips, diced
225 g/8 oz Cooked ham, chopped
25 g/1 oz Plain flour
150ml/¼ pt Milk
150 ml/¼ pt Vegetable Stock (page 24)
Salt and pepper
350 g/12 oz Shortcrust Pastry
  (page 145)

Melt the butter or margarine and fry the vegetables until soft but not browned. Stir in the ham and flour and cook for 1 minute, then stir in the milk and stock, bring to the boil and simmer, stirring, until the sauce thickens. Season and leave to cool.

Roll out the pastry and use half to line a greased 20 cm/8 in pie dish. Fill with the vegetable mixture and top with the remaining pastry. Roll out the trimmings and use to decorate the top. Brush with beaten egg and cut a slit in the centre. Bake in a preheated oven at 200°C/400°F/gas mark 6 for 30 minutes.

Rabbit Pie

Serves 6-8

2 Rabbits, jointed
30 ml/2 tbsp Vinegar
600 ml/1 pt Chicken Stock (page 24)
1 Onion, chopped
1 Leek, sliced
1 Carrot, sliced
5 ml/1 tsp Thyme
15 ml/1 tbsp Chopped parsley
Salt and pepper
100 g/4 oz Gammon, diced
100 g/4 oz Mushrooms, sliced
1 Hard-boiled egg, chopped
50 g/2 oz Chestnuts, chopped
225 g/8 oz Shortcrust Pastry
  (page 145)
15 ml/1 tbsp Milk

Soak the rabbits in water with the vinegar overnight.

Drain the meat and transfer it to a saucepan, add enough stock just to cover the meat, add the onion, leek, carrot and herbs and season to taste with salt and pepper. Bring to the boil, then simmer gently for 30 minutes. Leave to cool slightly.

Lift out the rabbits and remove the meat from the bones. Mix the meat with the gammon, mushrooms, egg and chestnuts and place in a pie dish. Season to taste with a little extra parsley and thyme, if liked, and with salt and pepper. Pour in a little strained cooking liquor to about half way up the mixture. Roll out the pastry and use it to cover the pie. Decorate with the pastry trimmings and brush with milk. Bake in a preheated oven at 200°C/400°F/gas mark 6 for 45 minutes.

Pigeon and Steak Pie

Serves 6

100 g/4 oz Butter or margarine
100 g/4 oz Ham, chopped
15 ml/1 tbsp Chopped parsley
5 ml/1 tsp Cayenne pepper
Salt and pepper
1 Egg yolk
3 Pigeons, halved lengthways
450 g/1 lb Rump steak, cut into 6
3 Hard-boiled eggs, halved
300 ml/½ pt Jellied Chicken Stock
  hot (page 24)
225 g/8 oz Puff Pastry
  (page 146)
15 ml/1 tbsp Milk

Mix the butter or margarine, stir in the ham, parsley and cayenne pepper, season to taste with salt and pepper and bind the mixture with the egg yolk. Stuff the mixture into the breast cavity of each bird. Place the steak slices on the bottom of a 23 cm/9 in pie dish and lay the pigeon halves, breast side down, on top. Arrange the eggs in between and season with salt and pepper. Pour over the hot stock. Roll out the pastry and use to cover the pie. Roll out the trimmings and use to decorate the top. Glaze with milk and make a hole in the centre for steam to escape. Bake in a preheated oven at 220°C/425°F/gas mark 7 for 15 minutes, then reduce the heat to 180°C/350°F/gas mark 4 and bake for a further 1 hour.

Vegetable and Parsley Pie

Serves 4

40 g/1½ oz Butter or margarine
4 Carrots, sliced
25 g/1 oz Plain flour
300 ml/½ pt Milk
Salt and pepper
1 Cauliflower, broken into florets
100 g/4 oz Broccoli, broken into
  florets
50 g/2 oz Pearl barley, cooked
30 ml/2 tbsp Chopped parsley
225 g/8 oz Wholemeal Shortcrust
  Pastry (page 145)

Melt the butter or margarine and fry carrots for 5 minutes. Stir in the flour and cook for 1 minute, then stir in the milk, bring to the boil and simmer, stirring, until the sauce thickens. Season to taste with salt and pepper and remove from the heat. Blanch the cauliflower and broccoli in boiling salted water for 5 minutes, then drain. Mix the vegetables with the sauce, then add the pearl barley and parsley and spoon into a 1.2 litre/2 pt pie dish. Roll out the pastry and cut a circle large enough to cover the pie dish and a 2.5 cm/1 in strip to go round the rim. Damp the edge and press the strip round the rim, then damp the pastry rim and cover with the lid, sealing the edges carefully. Decorate with pastry trimmings and brush with milk. Bake in a preheated oven at 200°C/400°F/gas mark 6 for 30 minutes until golden brown.

Steak and Kidney Pudding

Serves 4

350 g/12 oz Suet Crust Pastry (page 145)
25 g/1 oz Plain flour
Salt and pepper
450 g/1 lb Beef steak, cut into 6 x 3 cm/2½ x 1¼ in strips
100 g/4 oz Kidney, roughly chopped
1 Onion, finely chopped (optional)
150 ml/¼ pt Beef Stock (page 24)

Roll out the pastry on a floured board and use it to line a greased pudding basin. Trim the edges. Season the flour with salt and pepper, roll the meat in it, then wrap the strips of meat round pieces of kidney. Put half the meat into the basin, add the onion, if using, and the stock, then fill with the remaining meat. Use the pastry trimmings to roll out a cover and seal it on the top of the pudding. Cover with a floured cloth, tie with string and put into a saucepan with enough boiling water to come half-way up the sides of the basin. Cover and boil for 2 to 3 hours, topping up with boiling water as necessary.

Savoury Pudding

Serves 4

100 g/4 oz Plain flour
100 g/4 oz Fine oatmeal
50 g/2 oz Breadcrumbs
175 g/6 oz Shredded suet
3 Onions, chopped
Pinch of thyme
Pinch of marjoram
Salt and pepper
1 Egg, beaten
30 ml/2 tbsp Milk

Mix all the ingredients together and season to taste with salt and pepper. Mix to a soft mixture with the egg and milk, adjusting the amount of milk used to give the right consistency. Spoon into a greased roasting tin and bake at 180°C/350°F/gas mark 4 for 1 hour. Serve with gravy.

Pizza Dough

Makes 450 g/1 lb

400 g/14 oz Plain flour
25 g/1 oz Yeast
15 ml/1 tbsp Sugar
250 ml/8 fl oz Warm water
20 ml/1½ tbsp Salt
30 ml/2 tbsp Oil

Sift the flour into a bowl and make a well in the centre. Crumble in the yeast, then add the sugar. Add the water, cover with a cloth and leave to rise in a warm place for 30 minutes. Add the salt and oil and beat into a smooth paste with a wooden spoon. Knead into a ball. Make a cross with a knife on the top, sprinkle with flour and leave until required.

Pizza Bread Dough

Makes 450 g/1 lb

450 g/1 lb Strong plain flour
1 Dried yeast sachet
15 ml/1 tbsp Salt
15 ml/1 tbsp Sugar
5 ml/1 tsp Ground caraway seeds
15 g/½ oz Lard
300 ml/½ pt Warm water

Sift the flour and salt into a bowl and add the yeast, salt, sugar and caraway seeds. Grate in the lard, add the warm water and knead to a firm dough. Cover and set aside in a warm place for about 30 minutes. Knead the dough again and cover until required.

Crumbly Yeast Dough

Makes 450 g/1 lb

400 g/14 oz Plain flour
15 ml/1 tbsp Sugar
40 g/1½ oz Salt
100 g/4 oz Butter or margarine, cubed
25 g/1 oz Yeast
250 ml/8 fl oz Warm milk
30 ml/2 tbsp Olive oil

Sift the flour on to a work surface, make a well in the centre and add the sugar and salt. Scatter the butter or margarine over the flour and rub in with the fingertips. Dissolve the yeast in the warm milk and add the oil. Mix into the dough and knead into a smooth paste. Shape into a ball, cut a cross in the top and sprinkle with flour. Set aside until required.

Rich Pizza Pastry

Makes 450 g/1 lb

400 g/14 oz Plain flour
5 ml/1 tsp Baking powder
5 ml/1 tsp Sugar
5 ml/1 tsp Salt
150 g/5 oz Butter or margarine
2 Eggs

Sift the flour and baking powder on to a work surface, mix in the sugar and salt then rub in the butter or margarine with the fingertips. Add the eggs and knead into a firm dough. Wrap in a damp cloth and chill in the fridge for 1 hour before using.

Four-Cheese Pizza

Serves 4

450 g/1 lb Rich Pizza Pastry (page 158)
60 ml/4 tbsp Tomato purée
8 Tomatoes, skinned and sliced
225 g/8 oz Ham, cut into strips
200 g/7 oz Canned button mushrooms, drained and sliced
20 Green olives
5 ml/1 tsp Oregano
Salt and pepper
50 g/2 oz Gorgonzola cheese, grated
50 g/2 oz Bel Paese cheese, grated
50 g/2 oz Mozzarella cheese, grated
50 g/2 oz Pecorino cheese, grated

Quarter the pastry, roll it out on a floured surface and use to line 4 greased pizza or flan tins. Spread the pastry with the tomato purée, then sprinkle on the tomatoes, ham, mushrooms and olives. Sprinkle with the oregano and season to taste with salt and pepper, then sprinkle on the cheeses. Bake in a preheated oven at 200°C/400°F/gas mark 6 for 20 minutes and serve immediately.

Note
You can vary the cheeses to suit your own taste.

Summer Calzone

Serves 4

25 g/1 oz Butter or margarine
100 g/4 oz Streaky bacon, diced
1 Onion, chopped
200 g/7 oz Frozen spinach, thawed and drained
Pinch of cayenne pepper
Pinch of nutmeg
Salt and pepper
300 g/11 oz Canned tomatoes, chopped
450 g/1 lb Crumbly Yeast Dough (page 158)
225 g/8 oz Cheese, grated
30 ml/2 tbsp Chopped chives

Melt the butter and fry the bacon and onion until soft but not browned. Add the spinach, cayenne pepper and nutmeg and season to taste with salt and pepper. Stir in the tomatoes, remove from the heat amd leave to cool.

Quarter the dough and roll it out on a floured surface into 4 circles. Spread the mixture on to half of each circle, then sprinkle with the cheese and chives. Fold over the pastry and seal the edges firmly. Place on a greased baking sheet and bake in a preheated oven at 200°C/400°F/gas mark 6 for 20 minutes.

Pizza Bolognese

Serves 4

60 ml/4 tbsp Olive oil
450 g/1 lb Minced beef or lamb
1 Onion, chopped
3 Garlic cloves, chopped
5 ml/1 tsp Cayenne pepper
5 ml/1 tsp Curry powder
15 ml/1 tbsp Oregano
225 g/8 oz Canned tomatoes, chopped
30 ml/2 tbsp Tomato purée
1 Red pepper, chopped
2.5 ml/½ tsp Mixed spice
Salt and pepper
450 g/1 lb Rich Pizza Pastry (page 158)
50 g/2 oz Breadcrumbs
8 Tomatoes, skinned and sliced
225 g/8 oz Emmenthal cheese, grated
15 ml/1 tbsp Chopped parsley

Heat the oil and fry the mince until browned, then add the onion and garlic and fry until soft. Stir in the cayenne pepper, curry powder, oregano, tomatoes, tomato purée and pepper. Season with mixed spice and salt and pepper to taste. Cook over a high heat until all the liquid has evaporated. Quarter the dough, roll it out on a floured surface and use to line 4 greased pizza or flan tins. Sprinkle with breadcrumbs, then spread the tomato slices over the dough. Spoon the mince mixture over the tomatoes, sprinkle with the cheese and bake in a preheated oven at 200°C/400°F/gas mark 6 for 20 minutes. Serve sprinkled with parsley.

Four Seasons Pizza

Serves 4

450 g/1 lb Rich Pizza Pastry (page 158)
60 ml/4 tbsp Tomato purée
15 ml/1 tbsp Oregano
100 g/4 oz Parmesan cheese, grated
8 Tomatoes, skinned and sliced
100 g/4 oz Shelled prawns
100 g/4 oz Ham, cut into strips
100 g/4 oz Salami
100 g/4 oz Mussels, shelled
200 g/7 oz Canned button mushrooms, drained and sliced
½ Red pepper, cut into strips
½ Green pepper, cut into strips
Salt and pepper
225 g/8 oz Mozzarella cheese

Quarter the pastry and roll it out into squares on a floured surface. Place the dough on a greased baking sheet. Spread with tomato purée, sprinkle with oregano and Parmesan cheese and arrange the tomato slices over the dough. Arrange the prawns in one quarter of each dough piece, the ham in another, the salami in the third and the mussels in the fourth. Make a cross across the centre of the dough using the mushrooms, red pepper and green peppers. Season to taste with salt and pepper and sprinkle with Mozzarella cheese. Bake in a preheated oven at 200°C/400°F/gas mark 6 for 20 minutes and serve immediately.

Focaccia

Serves 4

450 g/1 lb Pizza Bread Dough
  (page 158)
100 g/4 oz Ham, cut into strips
50 g/2 oz Stuffed olives
50 g/2 oz Black olives
4 Garlic cloves, chopped
30 ml/2 tbsp Olive oil
2 Egg yolks, beaten
15 ml/1 tbsp Caraway seeds
30 ml/2 tbsp Salt
15 ml/1 tbsp Coriander seeds

Quarter the dough, roll it out on a floured surface and use to line 4 greased pizza or flan tins. Arrange the ham and olives over the dough and sprinkle with garlic. Brush with oil and bake in a preheated oven at 200°C/400°F/gas mark 6 for 15 minutes. Remove from the oven and brush with the egg yolk, then sprinkle with caraway seeds, salt and coriander. Return to the oven for a further 5 minutes. Serve hot or cold.

Neapolitan Pizza

Serves 4

25 g/1 oz Butter or margarine
2 Onions, chopped
225 g/8 oz Ham, cubed
15 ml/1 tbsp Oregano
Salt and pepper
450 g/1 lb Crumbly Yeast Dough
  (page 158)
60 ml/4 tbsp Tomato purée
8 Tomatoes, skinned and sliced
100 g/4 oz Canned anchovy fillets
20 Black olives, stoned
225 g/8 oz Mozzarella cheese, sliced
15ml/1 tbsp Chopped parsley

Melt the butter and fry the onions until soft but not browned. Add the ham and cook for 2 minutes, then season with oregano, salt and pepper to taste. Remove from the heat and allow to cool.

Quarter the dough, roll it out on a floured surface and use to line 4 greased pizza or flan tins. Spread the dough with tomato purée and cover with the onions and ham, the tomatoes, anchovies and olives. Top with the Mozzarella cheese and bake in a preheated oven at 200°C/400°F/gas mark 6 for 20 minutes. Serve sprinkled with parsley.

Cheese and Egg

Speed is a great advantage of cooking with eggs and cheese, as a delicious meal can be put together in very little time. The variety of cheese available expands every week, it seems, so you can experiment with different types to suit your own tastes.

Cheese Pudding

Serves 4

300 ml/½ pt Milk
50 g/2 oz Breadcrumbs
2 Eggs, separated
40 g/1½ oz Cheshire cheese, grated
40 g/1½ oz Parmesan cheese, grated
15 ml/1 tbsp Butter or margarine, softened
Pinch of ground mace
Salt and pepper

Bring the milk to the boil and pour it over the breadcrumbs in a bowl. Leave to stand for 10 minutes. Beat in the egg yolks, then the cheeses and butter. Add the mace and season to taste with salt and pepper. Whisk the egg whites until just stiff, then stir a spoonful into the cheese mixture, then fold in the rest. Turn the mixture into a greased deep pie dish and bake in a preheated oven at 180°C/350°F/gas mark 4 for 30 minutes.

Cheese and Spinach Cutlets

Serves 4

450 g/1 lb Frozen chopped spinach
25 g/1 oz Butter or margarine
3 Egg yolks, beaten
225 g/8 oz Cheddar cheese, grated
Pinch of nutmeg
Salt and pepper
100 g/4 oz Breadcrumbs

Heat the spinach in a saucepan until thawed, then bring to the boil and simmer for 3 minutes until tender and dry. Drain well and stir in half the butter or margarine. Spread the mixture on a plate and leave to cool for 10 minutes, then mix in 2 egg yolks, the cheese and nutmeg and season to taste with salt and pepper. Chill for 15 minutes. Shape into 8 oval patties and pinch one end to make a cutlet shape. Coat with beaten egg yolk then breadcrumbs, then repeat. Grill gently until golden brown, turning once. Melt the remaining butter and sprinkle on the cutlets.

Gruyère Cheese Roll

Serves 4

6 Eggs

Salt and pepper

175 g/6 oz Gruyère cheese, grated

40 g/1½ oz Plain flour

25 g/1 oz Butter or margarine

150 ml/¼ pt Milk

30 ml/2 tbsp Double cream

30 ml/2 tbsp Chopped parsley

Separate 5 of the eggs. Season the yolks lightly with salt and pepper and beat until pale. Beat in two-thirds of the cheese and 25 g/1 oz flour. Whisk the egg whites with a pinch of salt until semi-stiff. Stir 45 ml/3 tbsp into the yolk mixture, then fold in the rest. Spread the mixture in a greased and lined Swiss roll tin and bake in a preheated oven at 180°C/350°F/gas mark 4 for 15 minutes until firm.

Meanwhile, melt the butter or margarine in a saucepan, stir in the remaining flour and cook for 1 minute. Whisk in the milk and cream and cook, stirring, until the sauce thickens. Remove from the heat. Beat the remaining whole egg and add it to the sauce with the remaining cheese and half the parsley. Remove the roll from the oven, turn out of the tin on to a sheet of greaseproof paper and peel off the lining paper. Spread the filling over the inverted roll, leaving 2.5 cm/1 in gap at the end. Roll up so that the cut end is underneath and place on the tin. Return the roll to the oven for 10 minutes and serve at once, sprinkled with the remaining parsley.

Délices au Gruyère

Serves 4

50 g/2 oz Butter or margarine

50 g/2 oz Plain flour

450 ml/¾ pt Milk, boiling

100 g/4 oz Gruyère cheese, grated

Pinch of nutmeg

2 Egg yolks

Salt and pepper

1 Egg, beaten

30 ml/2 tbsp Cold milk

15 ml/1 tbsp Olive oil

100 g/4 oz Breadcrumbs

Oil for deep frying

1 Lemon, cut into wedges

4 Parsley sprigs

Melt the butter in the top of a double saucepan, stir in half the flour and cook until smooth. Whisk in the boiling milk and simmer until thickened. Stir in the cheese and nutmeg and cook until the cheese has melted. Remove from the heat, stir in the egg yolks and season to taste with salt and pepper. Continue to cook over the hot water for 2 minutes without letting the mixture boil. Spread in a greased rectangular baking tin and leave to cool.

Just before serving, cut into rectangles and dip in the remaining flour. Beat the egg with the milk and oil, then dip the rectangles in the mixture and roll in the breadcrumbs. Fry in deep hot oil until golden brown and serve immediately garnished with lemon wedges and parsley.

Camembert Puffs with Conserve

Serves 4

350 g/12 oz Camembert, cut into 8 wedges and chilled

15 g/½ oz Plain flour

2 Eggs, beaten

100 g/4 oz Breadcrumbs

Oil for deep frying

60 ml/ 4 tbsp Gooseberry or cherry jam

Dust the chilled cheese wedges with flour, then dip in the egg and coat with breadcrumbs. Fry in deep hot oil for 4 minutes, then drain well and serve immediately with the cold conserve.

Light Cheese Soufflé

Serves 4

25 g/1 oz Butter or margarine

25 g/1 oz Plain flour

150 ml/¼ pt Milk

75 g/3 oz Cheddar cheese, grated

3 Eggs, separated

Salt and pepper

Pinch of cayenne pepper

Melt the butter or margarine, stir in the flour and cook for 1 minute. Whisk in the milk and cook, stirring, until the sauce thickens. Remove from the heat and cool slightly, then stir in the cheese. Gradually beat in the egg yolks and season to taste with salt and pepper. Whisk the egg whites until stiff, stir a spoonful into the cheese sauce, then fold in the rest. Turn the mixture into a greased soufflé dish and score a circular slit in the top of the mixture about 2 cm/¾ in from the edge. Bake in a preheated oven at 200°C/400°F/gas mark 6 for 30 minutes until well risen and golden brown. Serve immediately.

Leek and Stilton Flan

Serves 4

75 g/3 oz Plain flour

75g /3 oz Wholemeal flour

100 g/4 oz Butter or margarine

50 g/2 oz Stilton cheese, grated

30 ml/2 tbsp Water

450 g/1 lb Leeks, sliced

100 g/4 oz Streaky bacon, chopped

150 ml/¼ pt Single cream

2 Eggs, beaten

2.5 ml/½ tsp Made English mustard

Salt and pepper

Sift the flours into a bowl and rub in 75 g/3 oz butter or margarine and half the cheese until the mixture resembles fine breadcrumbs. Add the water gradually until the mixture forms a pastry which comes away cleanly from the sides of the bowl. Roll out and line a 23 cm/9 in flan ring.

Melt the remaining butter in a frying pan and fry the leeks gently for 15 minutes until soft. Cool, then place the leeks in the pastry case and sprinkle with the bacon. Mix the cream, eggs, mustard, salt and pepper and pour over the flan. Sprinkle with the remaining cheese and bake in a preheated oven at 200°C/400°F/gas mark 6 for 30 minutes. Serve hot with salad.

Vegetable and Cheese Flan

Serves 4

25 g/1 oz Lard
25 g/1 oz Butter or margarine
100 g/4 oz Wholemeal flour
30 ml/2 tbsp Water
5 ml/1 tsp Soft brown sugar
5 ml/1 tsp Oil
100 g/4 oz Curd cheese
2 Eggs, beaten
200 ml/7 fl oz Milk
Salt and pepper
10 ml/2 tsp Chopped parsley
100 g/4 oz Canned broad beans, drained
2 Tomatoes, sliced

Rub the fats into the flour until the mixture resembles fine breadcrumbs. Mix together the water, sugar and oil and use to bind the pastry. Leave it to rest in the fridge for 30 minutes, then use it to line a 20 cm/8 in flan ring.

Beat the cheese in a bowl until soft. Mix the eggs and milk, season to taste with salt, pepper and parsley, then beat this into the cheese. Arrange the beans in the base of the flan ring and pour the cheese mixture on top. Arrange the tomatoes over the flan. Bake in a preheated oven at 200°C/400°F/gas mark 6 for 30 minutes until brown and set.

Quiche Provençale

Serves 4

225 g/8 oz Plain flour
Pinch of salt
100 g/4 oz Butter or margarine
25 g/1 oz Lard
1 Egg yolk
30 ml/2 tbsp Iced water
1 Onion, sliced
1 Garlic clove, crushed
100 g/4 oz Mushrooms, sliced
1 Courgette, chopped
2 Tomatoes, skinned and chopped
5 ml/1 tsp Basil
5 ml/1 tsp Mixed herbs
Salt and pepper
2 Eggs, beaten
150 ml/¼ pt Single cream
50g/2 oz Cheddar cheese, grated
25 g/1 oz Gruyère cheese, grated

Mix the flour and the salt and rub in 75g/3 oz butter and the lard until the mixture resembles fine breadcrumbs. Stir in the egg yolk and enough water to make a firm dough. Roll out and use to line a 23 cm/9 in flan ring and chill for 30 minutes. Bake blind in a preheated oven at 190°C/375°F/gas mark 5 for 15 minutes. Melt the remaining butter or margarine and fry the onion and garlic for 5 minutes. Add the vegetables and herbs, season to taste with salt and pepper and cook for 10 minutes. Beat the eggs and cream together and stir in the cheeses. Spoon the cooked mixture over the flan case and pour in the eggs. Bake for 30 minutes until set and golden brown on top. Serve hot or cold.

Parsnip, Cheese and Almond Quiche

Serves 6

225 g/8 oz Wholemeal Shortcrust Pastry (page 145)

450 g/1 lb Parsnips, sliced

175 g/6 oz Carrots, sliced

300 ml/½ pt Single cream

Salt and pepper

3 Eggs, beaten

45 ml/3 tbsp Natural yoghurt

50 g/2 oz Cheddar cheese, grated

50 g/2 oz Flaked almonds

Roll out the pastry and use to line a 25 cm/10 in flan ring. Bake blind in a preheated oven at 200°C/400°F/gas mark 6 for 20 minutes. Put the parsnips, carrots and cream in a saucepan, season to taste with salt and pepper, bring to the boil and simmer for 20 minutes until the vegetables are tender. Purée in a food processor or blender until not quite smooth, then blend in the eggs and yoghurt. Pour the mixture into the flan case, sprinkle on the cheese and almonds and return to the oven for 20 minutes until risen and firm. Serve hot or cold.

Onion and Pepper Tart

Serves 4

175 g/6 oz Plain flour

Pinch of salt

75 g/3 oz Butter or margarine

30 ml/2 tbsp Cold water

15 ml/1 tbsp Oil

1 Onion, sliced

1 Red pepper, sliced

2 Eggs, beaten

150 ml/¼ pt Single cream

50 g/2 oz Cheese, grated

Salt and pepper

Mix the flour and salt, then rub in the butter or margarine until the mixture resembles fine breadcrumbs. Add the water gradually until the mixture forms a pastry which comes away cleanly from the sides of the bowl. Roll out and line a 20 cm/8 in flan ring. Heat the oil in a frying pan and fry the onion until soft but not browned. Add the pepper and cook for 5 minutes, then spread the mixture in the flan ring. Mix the eggs, cream and cheese and season to taste with salt and pepper. Pour over the flan and bake in a preheated oven at 200°C/400°F/gas mark 6 for 30 minutes until set and risen.

Quiche Lorraine

Serves 4

175 g/6 oz Plain flour

Salt and pepper

75 g/3 oz Butter or margarine

30 ml/2 tbsp Cold water

175 g/6 oz Streaky bacon, rinded
and chopped

2 Eggs, beaten

150 ml/¼ pt Single cream

175 g/6 oz Cheese, grated

Season the flour with salt and pepper, then rub in the butter or margarine until the mixture resembles fine breadcrumbs. Mix in enough water to mix to a firm dough. Roll out on a floured surface and use to line a 20 cm/8 in flan ring. Scatter the bacon over the pastry. Mix together the eggs, cream and cheese and pour the mixture into the case. Bake in a preheated oven at 220°C/425°F/gas mark 7 for 8 minutes, then reduce the heat to 190°C/375°F/gas mark 5 for a further 30 minutes until firm and golden brown. Serve hot or cold.

Eggs with Black Butter

Serves 4

4 Eggs

100 g/4 oz Butter or margarine

4 Bread slices

15 ml/1 tbsp Chopped parsley

2 Gherkins, chopped

10 ml/2 tsp Capers, chopped

Salt and pepper

20 ml/2 tbsp White wine vinegar

Poach the eggs and keep them warm but do not let them overcook. Melt half the butter or margarine and fry the bread until crispy, then drain it well on kitchen paper, arrange on a serving plate and top with the eggs. Heat the remaining butter or margarine until a deep nut brown. Quickly stir in the parsley, gherkins and capers and season to taste with salt and pepper, then pour over the eggs. Pour the wine vinegar into the pan, boil to reduce by half and pour it over the eggs. Serve with boiled potatoes and a green salad.

Baked Eggs in Peppers

Serves 4

2 Large green peppers

15 ml/1 tbsp Olive oil

75 g/3 oz Breadcrumbs

25 g/1 oz Butter or margarine

3 Tomatoes, skinned and chopped

1 Garlic clove, crushed

Salt and pepper

8 Eggs

Cut the peppers in half and remove the core and seeds. Blanch in boiling water for 6 minutes, then drain. Brush the peppers inside and out with olive oil and stand them in a shallow baking tin. Divide the breadcrumbs between the peppers, dot with half the butter, the chopped tomato and garlic and season to taste with salt and pepper. Break the eggs into the pepper halves, dot with the remaining butter and bake in a preheated oven at 180°C/350°C/gas mark 4 for 15 minutes.

Curried Egg Mousse

Serves 4

4 Hardboiled eggs

150 ml/¼ pt Mayonnaise (page 250)

10 ml/2 tsp Oil

1 Small onion, chopped

10 ml/2 tsp Curry powder

150 ml/¼ pt Chicken Stock
  (page 24)

5 ml/1 tsp Apricot jam

2.5 ml/½ tsp Tomato purée

Juice of ½ lemon

15 g/½ oz Gelatine

30 ml/2 tbsp Cold water

60 ml/4 tbsp Double cream,
  whipped

Salt and pepper

2 Watercress sprigs

Sieve the egg yolks and chop the whites, then fold them into the mayonnaise. Heat the oil and fry the onion until soft but not browned. Add the curry powder and cook for 1 minute. Add the stock, jam, tomato purée and lemon juice, bring to the boil and simmer for 5 minutes. Soften the gelatine in the cold water over a pan of hot water and strain into the mixture. Blend with the egg and mayonnaise. Fold in the cream and season to taste with salt and pepper. Pour into a rinsed 900 ml/1½ pt ring mould and leave to set. Unmould and serve garnished with watercress.

Piperade

Serves 4

50 g/2 oz Butter or margarine

2 Green peppers, sliced

2 Onions, sliced

1 Garlic clove, crushed

450 g/1 lb Tomatoes, skinned and
  chopped

Salt and pepper

6 Eggs, beaten

45 ml/3 tbsp Milk

4 Bacon rashers

Melt the butter or margarine and fry the peppers for 4 minutes. Add the onions and garlic and fry until soft but not browned. Add the tomatoes and cook until mushy, seasoning well with salt and pepper. Beat the eggs with the milk and pour them over the vegetables. Cook gently, stirring, until almost set. Meanwhile, grill the bacon until crisp and browned. Transfer the eggs to a warmed serving dish and serve topped with the bacon.

Eggs in Sage Jelly

Serves 4

4 Eggs

4 Sage sprigs

450 ml/¾ pt Chicken Stock
  (page 24)

15 g/½ oz Gelatine

8 Lettuce leaves, shredded

4 Cucumber slices

2 Stuffed olives, sliced

Soft boil the eggs for 5 minutes, then plunge them into cold water to stop them cooking further and shell them carefully. Reserve 4 sage leaves and heat the remaining sage in the stock. Bring to the boil and leave to infuse for 20 minutes. Remove the sage and stir in the gelatine until it dissolves, then strain a thin layer into individual ramekin dishes. Chill until firm, then lay a sage leaf in each dish and top with an egg. Strain on the remaining gelatine mixture and chill until set. Arrange the lettuce leaves on individual plates and turn out the moulds on top. Serve garnished with a thin slice of cucumber and a sliced stuffed olive.

Eggs with Cucumber Sauce

Serves 4

| 50 g/2 oz Butter or margarine |
| 1 Cucumber, peeled and chopped |
| 5 ml/1 tsp Plain flour |
| 150 ml/¼ pt Vegetable Stock (page 24), hot |
| 30 ml/2 tbsp Chopped dill |
| Salt and pepper |
| 60 ml/4 tbsp Double cream |
| 4 Hard-boiled eggs, sliced |

Melt the butter or margarine and fry the cucumber for 5 minutes. Stir in the flour and cook for 1 minute, then stir in the stock and half the dill and season to taste with salt and pepper. Bring to the boil and simmer for 10 minutes, then stir in the cream. Arrange the eggs on a warmed serving dish, pour over the sauce and serve sprinkled with the remaining dill.

Mushroom and Egg Pancakes

Serves 4

| 100 g/4 oz Plain flour |
| Pinch of salt |
| 1 Egg |
| 300 ml/½ pt Milk |
| 30 ml/2 tbsp Oil |
| 50 g/2 oz Butter or margarine |
| 100 g/4 oz Mushrooms, sliced |
| 1 Garlic clove, crushed |
| 15 ml/1 tbsp Chopped Parsley |
| 5 ml/1 tsp Thyme |
| 30 ml/2 tbsp Soured cream |
| 1 Hard-boiled egg, chopped |
| Salt and pepper |
| 25 g/1 oz Parmesan cheese, grated |

Mix the flour and salt, make a well in the centre and beat in the egg, then whisk in the milk until you have a smooth batter. Heat 15 ml/1 tbsp oil and fry the pancakes until golden brown on both sides, then layer them in greaseproof paper and keep them warm. Melt the butter or margarine and fry the mushrooms and garlic until soft, then stir in the herbs and continue to cook until the mushrooms are tender. Stir in the soured cream, egg and sprinkle with parsley. Divide the mixture between the pancakes, roll them up, brush with the remaining butter and sprinkle with Parmesan cheese. Brown for a few seconds under a hot grill before serving.

Herbed Eggs and Onions

Serves 4

75g /3 oz Butter or margarine
450 g/1 lb Onions, chopped
5 ml/1 tsp Plain flour
450 ml/¾ pt Vegetable Stock
    (page 24), hot
30 ml/2 tbsp Chopped sage
90 ml/6 tbsp Double cream
Salt and pepper
4 Hard-boiled eggs

Melt the butter or margarine and fry the onions until soft but not browned. Stir in the flour, then add the heated stock. Add the sage, cover and simmer for 10 minutes until the onions are cooked. Stir in the cream and season to taste with salt and pepper. Put the hard-boiled eggs in individual dishes and pour over the sauce.

Garlic Croûton Omelette

Serves 2

50 g/2 oz Butter or margarine
2 Bread slices, cubed
1 Garlic clove, crushed
5 Eggs, beaten
Salt and pepper
15 ml/1 tbsp Chopped parsley

Heat most of the butter or margarine and fry the bread cubes and garlic until crispy, stirring well. Remove from the pan and keep them warm. Melt the remaining butter. Season the eggs with salt and pepper and pour them into the pan. As the omelette is just setting, pour in the croûtons and continue to cook until the omelette is just set. Serve immediately, sprinkled with parsley.

Mexican Eggs

Serves 4

5 Eggs
75 g/3 oz Butter or margarine
2 Onions, chopped
1 Green pepper, chopped
300 g/11 oz Canned sweetcorn
    kernels, drained
15 ml/1 tbsp Tomato pickle
Salt and pepper
15 ml/1 tbsp Plain flour
250 ml/8 fl oz Milk
60 ml/4 tbsp Double cream
75 g/3 oz Cheddar cheese, grated

Soft boil the eggs, shell them and keep them in warm water. Melt 25 g/ 1 oz butter or margarine and fry the onions until soft and just beginning to brown, then add the pepper and corn and heat through. Stir in 25g/ 1 oz butter or margarine and the pickle. Shake over the heat until very hot, then set aside and keep it warm. Melt the remaining butter, stir in the flour and pour on the milk, whisking until sauce boils and thickens. Remove from the heat. Reserve a little of the cheese and stir the cream and remaining cheese into the sauce. Turn the corn mixture into an ovenproof dish, arrange the drained eggs on top and cover with the sauce. Sprinkle with the remaining cheese and brown under a hot grill.

Spanish Baked Eggs

Serves 4

25 g/4 oz Butter or margarine
2 Onions, chopped
4 Tomatoes, skinned and sliced
1 Garlic clove, crushed
8 Eggs
100 g/4 oz Parmesan cheese, grated
150 ml/¼ pt Double cream
Salt and pepper

Melt the butter or margarine and fry the onions until soft but not browned. Stir in the tomatoes and garlic and fry for 2 minutes. Transfer to a greased shallow ovenproof dish, break in the eggs, sprinkle with cheese and pour over the cream. Season to taste with salt and pepper and bake in a preheated oven at 180°C/350°F/gas mark 4 for 15 minutes until the egg whites are set.

Butter Eggs with Smoked Salmon

Serves 4

5 Eggs, beaten
Salt and pepper
300 ml/½ pt Double cream
100 g/4 oz Smoked salmon, diced
25 g/1 oz Butter or margarine
15 ml/1 tbsp Chopped parsley
Pinch of cayenne pepper

Season the eggs to taste with salt and pepper and beat in 15 ml/1 tbsp of cream and the smoked salmon. Melt the butter or margarine and scramble the egg mixture until just set. Transfer to a warmed serving dish. Bring the remaining cream to the boil and pour it over the eggs. Serve at once, garnished with parsley and cayenne pepper.

Pulses, Grains and Pasta

There is almost no limit to the versatility of these ingredients, which have only relatively recently become commonplace in our cooking. As a substitute for meat, or to enjoy in their own right, there are all sorts of pulses and grains to take advantage of in the kitchen. Pasta has long been popular, but fresh pastas are now widely available. Fresh pasta can always be substituted for dried in any recipe, but only needs cooking for 2 or 3 minutes, instead of about 10 minutes for dried pasta. You will need to test or taste the pasta to make sure that it is 'al dente' (just tender but with a hint of bite) as different pasta shapes will take different times to cook.

Home-Made Baked Beans

Serves 4

450 Haricot beans, soaked overnight and drained

2 Bay leaves

4 Cloves

30 ml/2 tbsp Black treacle or molasses

300 ml/½ pt Water

15 ml/1 tbsp Plain flour

15 ml/1 tbsp Milk

Pinch of basil

Salt and pepper

225 g/8 oz Tomatoes, skinned and chopped

Place the beans in a saucepan, just cover with fresh water and add the bay leaves and cloves. Bring to the boil and simmer for 1½ hours, then drain and discard the cloves and bay leaves.

Dilute the treacle or molasses with the water and mix the flour to a thin paste with the milk. Add this to the molasses with a pinch of basil and season with salt and pepper. Put the beans in a greased ovenproof casserole, cover with the tomatoes and sauce and bake in a preheated oven at 180°C/350°F/gas mark 4 for 1 hour until the beans are tender.

Note
If your children are keen on baked beans, you can make a quantity and freeze them.

Haricot Beans Provençale

Serves 4

225 g/8 oz Haricot beans, soaked overnight and drained

15 ml/1 tbsp Oil

2 Onions, sliced

1 Garlic clove, chopped

400 g/14 oz Canned tomatoes, drained

Salt and pepper

Place the beans in a saucepan and just cover with fresh water, bring to the boil and simmer for 1½ hours.

Heat the oil in a saucepan and fry the onions and garlic until soft but not browned. Add the tomatoes and drained beans and season to taste with salt and pepper. Continue to cook until heated through.

Cassoulet

Serves 4

450 g/1 lb Haricot beans, soaked overnight and drained

175 g/6 oz Belly of pork, rinded and chopped

4 Garlic cloves, chopped

1.2 litres/2 pts Water

30 ml/2 tbsp Oil

900 g/2 lb Shoulder of lamb, boned and cubed

6 Whole peppercorns

2 Bay leaves

2 Blades of mace

5 Parsley stalks

400 g/14 oz Canned tomatoes

30 ml/2 tbsp Tomato purée

100 g/4 oz Wholemeal breadcrumbs

Place the beans, pork and garlic in a flameproof casserole, pour on the water, bring to the boil, cover and simmer for 1 hour.

Heat the oil and fry the lamb until just browned, then add it to the casserole. Tie the herbs and spices together in a square of butter muslin or cotton and hang them from the edge of the casserole. Simmer gently for 2 hours, stirring occasionally, and adding extra water if necessary.

Stir in the tomatoes and tomato purée and cook for a further 1 hour until the sauce is thick and creamy. Sprinkle the breadcrumbs over the top of the casserole and bake in a preheated oven at 190°C/375°F/gas mark 5 until brown and crispy.

Pease Pudding

Serves 4

225 g/8 oz Split peas, soaked for 30 minutes and drained

1 Large onion, chopped

50 g/2 oz Butter or margarine

1 Egg, beaten

Salt and pepper

Place the peas in a saucepan and just cover with cold water. Bring to the boil and simmer until tender, then drain. Melt in the butter or margarine and fry the onion until soft but not browned. Stir in the peas and beaten egg, and season to taste with salt and pepper. Turn into a lightly greased casserole dish and bake at 180°C/350°F/gas mark 4 for 30 minutes. Serve hot, cut into slices with roast meats.

Aduki Burgers

Serves 4

175 g/6 oz Aduki beans, soaked
  overnight

2 Carrots, grated

25 g/1 oz Cashew nuts, chopped

50 g/2 oz Wholemeal breadcrumbs

Few drops of soy sauce

2.5 ml/½ tsp Yeast extract

Salt and pepper

1 Egg, beaten

30 ml/2 tbsp Oil

Drain and rinse the beans and cook in boiling salted water for 30 minutes. Drain well and mash. Add the carrots, nuts, breadcrumbs and seasonings and mash together. Add enough egg to bind the mixture and shape it into 4 burgers. Chill for 30 minutes before shallow frying in the oil. Serve hot with wholemeal baps and salad.

Boston Beans

Serves 4

30 ml/2 tbsp Oil

225 g/8 oz Belly of pork, rinded and
  cubed

1 Onion, chopped

1 Garlic clove, chopped

400 g/14 oz Canned tomatoes

10 ml/2 tsp Tomato purée

450 g/1 lb Haricot beans, soaked
  overnight and drained

600 ml/1 pt Vegetable Stock
  (page 24)

Heat the oil and fry the pork lightly in a large saucepan until browned. Lift out the meat with a draining spoon.

Fry the onion and garlic, then add the tomatoes, tomato purée, beans and meat. Stir well to break up the tomatoes. Add the stock, bring to the boil, partly cover and simmer for 40 minutes until the beans are tender and the sauce is thick and creamy.

Chick Pea Curry

Serves 4

50 g/2 oz Butter or margarine

1 Large onion, sliced

10 ml/2 tsp Curry powder

5 ml/1 tsp Turmeric

Pinch of ground ginger

15 ml/1 tbsp Desiccated coconut

60 ml/4 tbsp Boiling water

225 g/8 oz Canned chick peas

300 ml/½ pt Vegetable Stock
  (page 24)

15 g/½ oz Sultanas

1 Bay leaf

1 Red pepper, sliced

1 Leek, sliced

Salt and pepper

Melt the butter or margarine and fry the onion until soft but not browned. Stir in the spices and cook for 1 minute. Infuse the coconut in the boiling water for 10 minutes, then strain the liquid into the pan and discard the coconut. Add the chick peas, stock, sultanas and bay leaf, bring to the boil, cover and simmer for 25 minutes. Add the pepper and leek and cook for a further 20 minutes until the vegetables are tender and the sauce thick. Season to taste with salt and pepper and discard the bay leaf. Serve hot with boiled rice.

Swabian Lentils

Serves 4

400 g/14 oz Lentils, soaked
  overnight
600 ml/1 pt Vegetable Stock
  (page 24)
25 g/1 oz Butter or margarine
1 Onion, chopped
2 Carrots, diced
1 Leek, sliced
30 ml/2 tbsp Tomato purée
300 ml/½ pt Dry white wine
Juice of 1 lemon
300 ml/½ pt Crème fraîche
15 g/½ oz Wholewheat flour
30 ml/2 tbsp honey
60 ml/4 tbsp Cider vinegar
Salt and pepper
225 g/8 oz Pasta shapes
30 ml/2 tbsp Olive oil
Pinch of nutmeg
30 ml/2 tbsp Chopped chives

Drain the lentils, then bring to the boil in the stock and simmer for 15 minutes. Melt the butter or margarine and fry the onion, carrots and leek until soft. Stir in the tomato purée, wine and lemon juice, bring to the boil and stir into the lentils. Mix the crème fraîche with the flour and stir it into the lentils with the honey and cider vinegar and season to taste with salt and pepper. Heat gently but do not allow the mixture to boil.

Meanwhile, cook the pasta in plenty of boiling salted water until just tender, then drain and rinse in hot water. Heat the oil and toss the pasta until well coated, then season to taste with nutmeg, salt and pepper.

Turn the pasta on to a warmed serving plate, spoon the lentils on top and serve sprinkled with the chives.

Lentil Stew

Serves 4

225 g/8 oz Lentils, soaked
600 ml/1 pt Vegetable Stock
  (page 24)
225 g/8 oz Baby carrots
100 g/4 oz Mushrooms, sliced
2 Large onions, finely chopped
30 ml/2 tbsp Vinegar
2.5 ml/½ tsp Thyme
Salt and pepper
100 g/4 oz Self-raising flour
50 g/2 oz Shredded suet
½ Small onion, finely chopped
15 ml/1 tbsp Chopped parsley
30 ml/2 tbsp Water

Drain the lentils and place in a large saucepan with the stock, carrots, mushrooms, onions, vinegar and thyme. Season to taste with salt and pepper, bring to the boil and simmer for 30 minutes until the lentils are tender. Continue cooking, stirring frequently, until the lentils go mushy, adding more stock if necessary.

Make the dumplings by mixing all the remaining ingredients, adding enough water to make a firm dough. Roll the mixture into small dumplings and cook separately in boiling stock for about 30 minutes, then add them to the stew.

Lentils Grosvenor

Serves 4

25 g/1 oz Butter or margarine
2 Onions, chopped
1 Large carrot, chopped
2 Celery stalks, sliced
225 g/8 oz Lentils, soaked
600 ml/1 pt Water
Salt and pepper
15 ml/1 tbsp Chopped parsley

Melt the butter or margarine in a large saucepan and fry the onions, carrot and celery for 5 minutes, stirring continuously. Add the drained lentils and water, bring to the boil, cover and simmer for 20 minutes, stirring occasionally. When almost dry, check that everything is cooked. If not, add a little more water. When ready, season to taste with salt and pepper and sprinkle with parsley.

Lentil Dhal

Serves 4

225 g/8 oz Lentils
600 ml/1 pt Vegetable Stock
  (page 24)
2.5 ml/½ tsp Turmeric
25 g/1 oz Butter or margarine
1 Onion, chopped
1 Green pepper, chopped
2 Garlic cloves, whole
2.5 ml/½ tsp Chilli powder
2.5 ml/½ tsp Cumin seed

Put the lentils, stock and turmeric in a saucepan, bring to the boil and simmer for 20 minutes until almost tender and much of the liquid is absorbed. Meanwhile, melt the butter or margarine in a saucepan and fry the onion, pepper, garlic, chilli powder and cumin seed until the onion is golden brown. Remove the garlic, add the lentils and simmer gently, stirring, for 5 minutes.

Note
You can adjust the amount of stock to make the dhal the consistency you prefer.

Baked Polenta

Serves 4

450 ml/¾ pt Milk
100 g/4 oz Polenta
50 g/2 oz Butter or margarine
3 Eggs, separated
5 ml/1 tsp Salt
2.5 ml/½ tsp Baking powder

Bring the milk almost to the boil in a saucepan, then sprinkle in the polenta and stir until thickened. Melt half the butter and stir it into the pan, then remove from the heat and leave to cool for 5 minutes. Beat the egg yolks and salt until pale and stir them into the polenta. Whisk the egg whites and baking powder until stiff, then fold them into the polenta using a metal spoon. Turn the mixture into a greased 1.5 litre/2½ pt ovenproof dish and bake in a preheated oven at 180°C/350°F/gas mark 4 for 40 minutes until golden brown. Serve dotted with the remaining butter.

Vegetable Dhal

Serves 4

225 g/8 oz Lentils

1.2 litres/2 pts Vegetable stock (page 24)

1 Bay leaf

30 ml/2 tbsp Oil

1 Garlic clove, chopped

1 Large onion chopped

½ Red pepper, thinly sliced

½ Yellow pepper, thinly sliced

2.5 ml/½ tsp Turmeric

10 ml/2 tsp Curry powder

2.5 ml/½ tsp Coriander

1 Small cauliflower, broken into florets

100 g/4 oz Green beans, roughly chopped

Cook the lentils in the stock with the bay leaf for 20 minutes until soft, drain and remove the bay leaf. Heat the oil and fry the garlic and onion until soft but not browned, then stir in the peppers and spices and cook for 2 minutes. Stir in the cauliflower florets and cook for 3 minutes. Stir in the beans and lentils and cook for 5 minutes until the sauce is well combined but the vegetables remain crisp.

Herbed Vegetable Rice

Serves 4

50 g/2 oz Butter or margarine

1 Onion, chopped

225 g/8 oz Broccoli florets

225 g/8 ozs Cauliflower florets

2 Carrots, sliced

1 Leek, sliced

250 ml/8 fl oz Dry white wine

225 g/8 oz Brown rice

900 ml/1½ pts Vegetable Stock (page 24), hot

Salt and pepper

15 ml/1 tbsp Grated lemon rind

1 Garlic clove, crushed

25 g/1 oz Flaked almonds

3 Eggs, beaten

30 ml/2 tbsp Chopped parsley

30 ml/2 tbsp Chopped tarragon

30 ml/2 tbsp Chopped chervil

30 ml/2 tbsp Chopped sorrel

Melt the butter or margarine and fry the onion, broccoli and cauliflower florets until the onion is soft. Add the carrots, leek, wine and rice and stir well to coat in the butter. Add the stock, season to taste with salt and pepper and bring to the boil. Transfer to a casserole dish, cover and bake in a preheated oven at 200°C/400°F/ gas mark 6 for 25 minutes. Mix the lemon rind, garlic and almonds and sprinkle over the top. Pour over the eggs and sprinkle with the herbs. Return to the oven for a further 10 minutes, then serve immediately.

Kedgeree

Serves 4

350 g/12 oz Smoked haddock
350 g/12 oz Long-grain rice
5 ml/1 tsp Lemon juice
50 g/2 oz Butter or margarine, melted
2 Hard-boiled eggs, chopped
150 ml/¼ pt Single cream, hot
Salt and pepper
15 ml/1 tbsp Chopped parsley

Poach the haddock in a little salted water for 10 minutes, then strain the cooking liquor on to the rice in a saucepan, remove the fish bones and flake the flesh. Top up the liquid with water and the lemon juice and cook the rice until just tender. Drain and transfer to an ovenproof dish and place in a preheated oven at 150°C/ 300°F/gas mark 2 for 5 minutes to dry out. Stir in the butter or margarine, fish, most of the eggs and finally the hot cream. Season to taste with salt and pepper and serve sprinkled with parsley and the remaining egg.

Yellow Rice

Serves 4

750 ml/1¼ pts Water
200 g/7 oz Long-grain rice
1 Cinnamon stick
2.5 ml/½ tsp Turmeric
Salt
15 g/½ oz Butter or margarine
75 g/3 oz Raisins (optional)

Bring the water to the boil in a large saucepan. Sprinkle in the rice and stir in the remaining ingredients. Cover and cook for 15 minutes until the rice is just tender and all the water is absorbed. Remove the cinnamon stick. Add a little more water if the rice begins to dry out but do not let it go soggy. Serve hot with roasts, grills or barbecued dishes, or cold in rice salads.

Brown Rice with Leeks

Serves 4

25 g/1 oz Butter or margarine
15 ml/1 tbsp Oil
4 Leeks, sliced
225 g/8 oz Brown rice
450 ml/¾ pt Chicken Stock (page 24), hot
Salt and pepper
45 ml/3 tbsp Chopped chives
150 ml/¼ pt Natural yoghurt

Melt the butter or margarine with the oil and fry the leeks until soft. Stir in the rice and coat it thoroughly with the oil, then pour in the stock, bring back to the boil and season to taste with salt and pepper. Cover and simmer for 40 minutes until the rice is just tender and the stock is absorbed. Stir in the chives and serve with the yoghurt poured on the top.

Tomato Rice

Serves 4

225 g/8 oz Long-grain rice, soaked

45 ml/3 tbsp Oil

1 Onion, sliced

1 Garlic clove, crushed

25 g/1 oz Root ginger, grated

500 g/1¼ lb Canned tomatoes, chopped

Salt and pepper

15 ml/1 tbsp Coriander

Drain the rice thoroughly. Heat the oil and fry the onion until just beginning to brown, then add the garlic and ginger and fry for 2 minutes. Stir in the rice and fry for 2 minutes. Add the tomatoes and season to taste with salt and pepper. Cover and simmer for 20 minutes until the rice is just tender. Transfer to a warmed serving dish and sprinkle with coriander.

Rice with Yoghurt

Serves 4

225 g/8 oz Long-grain rice

30 ml/2 tbsp Oil

1 Bunch of spring onions, sliced

225 g/8 oz Tomatoes, skinned and sliced

150 ml/¼ pt Natural yoghurt

15 ml/1 tbsp Chopped dill

15 ml/1 tbsp Chopped chives

15 ml/1 tbsp Chopped tarragon

Salt and pepper

Cook the rice in boiling salted water until just tender. Drain and rinse in hot water. Heat the oil and fry the spring onions until just beginning to brown, then stir in the tomatoes and rice carefully. Mix the yoghurt and herbs, stir into the rice mixture and season to taste with salt and pepper. Heat through gently before serving.

Fruit and Vegetable Risotto

Serves 4

75 g/3 oz Butter or margarine

1 Onion, chopped

350 g/12 oz Long-grain rice

75 ml/5 tbsp Dry white wine

1 litre/1¾ pt Chicken Stock (page 24), warmed

25 g/1 oz Cooked peas

25 g/1 oz Cooked sliced green beans

25 g/1 oz Sultanas

25 g/1 oz Pimento, chopped

25 g/1 oz Button mushrooms, sliced

Salt and pepper

Melt 50 g/2 oz butter or margarine and fry the onion until soft. Add the rice and fry until well coated but not browned. Stir in the wine and cook gently, stirring until it is all absorbed. Add half the stock, bring to the boil, then simmer until it is all absorbed. Add a little more stock, cover and simmer until it is absorbed. Stir in the peas, beans, sultanas, pimento and mushrooms. Continue adding stock in small quantities until the rice is just tender. Season to taste with salt and pepper, stir in the remaining butter and serve hot and glistening.

Rice and Cabbage Roulade

Serves 4

1 Savoy cabbage
40 g/1½ oz Butter or margarine
2 Onions, chopped
1 Bunch of spring onions, sliced
25 g/1 oz Raisins
25 g/1 oz Flaked almonds
225 g/ 8 oz Cooked brown rice
2 Eggs, beaten
225 g/8 oz Mozzarella cheese, diced
30 ml/2 tbsp Chopped chives
1 Garlic clove, chopped
450 g/1 lb Tomatoes, skinned, seeded and chopped
Salt and pepper
15 ml/1 tbsp Chopped basil
100 g/4 oz Gouda cheese, grated

Separate the cabbage leaves and parboil in salted water for 5 minutes, then drain well. Remove the ribs, then spread them out on a work surface. Heat 25 g/1 oz butter or margarine and fry 1 onion and the spring onions until soft but not browned. Stir in the raisins, almonds and rice, remove from the heat and leave to cool. Fold the eggs, cheese and chives into the rice. Spread the stuffing equally between the cabbage leaves, then roll them up to make roulades. Place them in a single layer in an ovenproof dish. Melt the remaining butter or margarine and fry the remaining onion with the garlic until soft. Add the tomatoes, season to taste with salt and pepper and cook for 10 minutes. Purée the sauce in a food processor or blender, add the basil and pour over the cabbage. Sprinkle with Gouda and bake in a preheated oven at 200°C/400°F/gas mark 6 for 40 minutes until golden brown.

Seafood Risotto

Serves 4

15 ml/2 tbsp Oil
350 g/12 oz Long-grain rice
2 Onions, sliced
Salt and pepper
900 ml/1½ pts Chicken Stock (page 24), hot
50 g/2 oz Butter or margarine
100 g/4 oz Cooked prawns
100 g/4 oz Cooked mussels
5 ml/1 tsp Turmeric
Pinch of nutmeg
5 ml/1 tsp Soft brown sugar
5 ml/1 tsp Lemon juice
30 ml/2 tbsp Double cream
50 g/2 oz Parmesan cheese, grated

Heat the oil and turn the rice and onion until well coated. Season to taste with salt and pepper. Stir in one-third of the stock, bring to the boil and simmer until the liquid has been absorbed. Add more stock and simmer, continuing until the rice is tender and moist, then stir in half the butter. Melt the remaining butter in a saucepan and stir in the prawns, mussels, turmeric, nutmeg, sugar, lemon juice and cream. Heat through gently. Turn the rice into a warmed serving dish, pile the seafood mixture on top and serve sprinkled with Parmesan cheese.

Macaroni Tuscany

Serves 4

60 ml/4 tbsp Olive oil

450 g/1 lb Cooked veal or chicken, diced

1 Onion, chopped

225 g/8 oz Button mushrooms, sliced

15 g/½ oz Plain flour

250 ml/8 fl oz Chicken Stock (page 24)

150 ml/¼ pt Dry white wine

150 ml/¼ pt Crème fraîche

5 ml/1 tsp Worcestershire sauce

Salt and pepper

100 g/4 oz Blue cheese, crumbled

350 g/12 oz Macaroni

100 g/4 oz Pecorino cheese, grated

15 ml/1 tbsp Chopped chives

Heat the oil and fry the meat for 3 minutes, then remove and keep it warm. Fry the onion until soft but not browned, then add the mushrooms and fry for 1 minute. Sprinkle in the flour and cook for 1 minute, then stir in the stock and wine, bring to the boil and simmer, stirring, until the sauce has thickened. Fold in the crème fraîche and do not allow the mixture to boil again. Add the Worcestershire sauce and season to taste with salt and pepper. Stir in the blue cheese and meat and keep the sauce warm without allowing it to boil.

Meanwhile, cook the macaroni in boiling salted water for 15 minutes until just tender. Drain and rinse in hot water. Turn the macaroni on to a serving dish, pour over the sauce and sprinkle with Pecorino cheese and chives.

Macaroni with Four Cheeses

Serves 4

350 g/12 oz Macaroni

50 g/2 oz Butter or margarine

Pinch of nutmeg

100 g/4 oz Parmesan cheese, grated

300 ml/½ pt Béchamel Sauce (page 225)

Salt and pepper

75 g/3 oz Gouda cheese, diced

75 g/3 oz Gruyère cheese, diced

75 g/3 oz Mozzarella cheese, diced

Cook the pasta in boiling salted water until just tender, then drain and rinse in hot water and turn into a well greased ovenproof dish. Mix the nutmeg and half the Parmesan cheese into the béchamel sauce and season to taste with salt and pepper. Stir in the Gouda, Gruyère and Mozzarella cheeses and stir into the macaroni. Dot with butter and sprinkle with the remaining Parmesan. Bake in a preheated oven at 220°C/425°F/gas mark 7 for 15 minutes until brown and crispy on top.

Pasta Mix with Napolitana Sauce

Serves 4

400 g/14 oz Canned tomatoes, chopped
15 ml/1 tbsp Oil
1 Onion, chopped
15 ml/1 tbsp Tomato purée
10 ml/2 tsp Oregano
Pinch of sugar
450 g/1 lb Mixed pasta
400 g/14 oz Canned baked beans
225 g/8 oz Cooked ham, chopped
Salt and pepper
50 g/2 oz Breadcrumbs
50 g/2 oz Mozzarella cheese, grated

Put the tomatoes, oil, onion, tomato purée, oregano and sugar in a saucepan, bring to the boil and simmer for 25 minutes. Purée in a food processor or blender if you like a smooth sauce. Cook the pasta in boiling water for 15 minutes until just tender, then drain and rinse in hot water. Mix the pasta with the beans, ham and sauce and spoon into a large ovenproof dish. Season to taste with salt and pepper. Mix the breadcrumbs and cheese and sprinkle on the top. Bake in a preheated oven at 180°C/350°F/ gas mark 4 for 30 minutes until golden brown and crispy on top.

Pasta with Mushrooms and Soured Cream

Serves 4

25 g/1 oz Butter or margarine
30 ml/2 tbsp Oil
450 g/1 lb Mushrooms, chopped
2 Garlic cloves, crushed
15 ml/1 tbsp Anchovy essence
Salt and pepper
300 ml/½ pt Soured cream
90 ml/6 tbsp Chopped parsley
350 g/12 oz Pasta shapes

Melt the butter or margarine with the oil and fry the mushrooms and garlic for 5 minutes, stirring continuously. Season to taste with anchovy essence, salt and pepper and cook for 3 minutes, then stir in the soured cream and 60 ml/4 tbsp parsley and heat through gently without boiling.

Meanwhile cook the pasta in boiling salted water until just tender, then drain and rinse in hot water and turn into a serving dish. Pour the sauce over and sprinkle with parsley.

Creamy Pasta

Serves 4

225 g/8 oz Pasta shells
Salt and pepper
5 ml/1 tbsp Oil
25 g/1 oz Butter or margarine
100 g/4 oz Mushrooms, sliced
100 g/4 oz Cooked ham, cut into strips
150 ml/¼ pt Double cream
175 g/6 oz Cheese, grated
15 ml/1 tbsp Chopped parsley
25 g/1 oz Parmesan cheese, grated

Cook the pasta in boiling salted water with the oil until just tender, then drain and rinse in hot water. Melt the butter or margarine, add the mushrooms and ham and fry until soft. Add the pasta and cook over a gentle heat for 2 minutes. Mix the cream, cheese and parsley, stir into the pasta and season to taste with salt and pepper. Turn into a warmed serving dish and sprinkle with Parmesan cheese.

Pepper Vermicelli

Serves 4

| 30 ml/2 tbsp Olive oil |
| 1 Onion, sliced |
| 1 Red pepper, sliced |
| 1 Green pepper, sliced |
| 1 Yellow pepper, sliced |
| 30 ml/2 tbsp Red wine |
| 400 g/14 oz Canned tomatoes, chopped |
| 5 ml/1 tsp Sugar |
| Salt and pepper |
| 350 g/12 oz Vermicelli |
| 15 ml/1 tbsp Chopped parsley |

Heat the oil and fry the onion and peppers until soft. Stir in the wine and heat until it has evaporated, then add the tomatoes and sugar and simmer for 20 minutes. Season to taste with salt and pepper. Meanwhile, cook the vermicelli in boiling salted water until just tender, then drain and rinse in hot water and turn into a warmed serving dish. Mix in the hot sauce and serve sprinkled with parsley.

Pasta and Chicken

Serves 4

| 225 g/8 oz Broccoli florets |
| 75 g/3 oz Butter or margarine |
| 25 g/1 oz Plain flour |
| 450 ml/¾ pt Chicken Stock (page 24) |
| 150 ml/¼ pt Double cream |
| 5 ml/1 tsp Oregano |
| Salt and pepper |
| 350 g/12 oz Rigatoni |
| 450 g/1 lb Cooked chicken, cut into strips |
| 75 g/3 oz Parmesan cheese, grated |

Cook the broccoli in boiling salted water until just tender, then drain and chop. Heat 50 g/2 oz butter or margarine, stir in the flour and cook for 1 minute. Whisk in the chicken stock and cook, stirring, until the sauce thickens. Simmer for 5 minutes, then stir in the broccoli, cream and oregano and season to taste with salt and pepper.

Meanwhile, cook the rigatoni in boiling salted water until just tender, drain and rinse in hot water, then toss in the remaining butter or margarine. Put a layer of pasta in an ovenproof dish, followed by layers of chicken, sauce and a sprinkling of cheese. Bake in a preheated oven at 220°C/425°F/gas mark 7 for 20 minutes.

Japanese Tofu Pasta

Serves 4

25 g/1 oz Butter or margarine
175 g/6 oz Tofu, diced
1 Onion, chopped
1 Red pepper, diced
1 Green pepper, diced
15 g/1 oz Wholewheat flour
2 Tomatoes, skinned, seeded and chopped
2 Gherkins, diced
225 ml/8 fl oz Red wine
225 ml/8 fl oz Vegetable Stock (page 24)
350 g/12 oz Tagliatelle
5 ml/1 tsp Paprika
2.5 ml/½ tsp Curry powder
Salt and pepper
150 ml/¼ pt Crème fraîche
15 ml/1 tbsp Chopped chives

Melt the butter or margarine and fry the tofu for 2 minutes, then add the onion and peppers and fry until beginning to soften. Stir in the flour and cook for 1 minute, then add the tomatoes and gherkins and stir in the wine and stock, bring to the boil, cover and simmer for 10 minutes.

Meanwhile, cook the tagliatelle in boiling salted water until just tender, drain and rinse in hot water. Turn on to a warmed serving plate. Add the paprika and curry powder to the sauce and season to taste with salt and pepper. Stir in the crème fraîche, pour the sauce over the pasta and serve sprinkled with chives.

Ham and Tagliatelle

Serves 4

60 ml/4 tbsp Oil
1 Onion, chopped
2 Garlic cloves, crushed
100 g/4 oz Parma ham, chopped
1 Chilli pepper, chopped
400 g/14 oz Canned tomatoes, chopped
60 ml/4 tbsp Dry white wine
Salt and pepper
350 g/12 oz Tagliatelle
50 g/2 oz Parmesan or Pecorino cheese, grated

Heat the oil and fry the onion and garlic until soft, then add the ham, chilli pepper, tomatoes and wine and season to taste with salt and pepper. Simmer for 15 minutes. Meanwhile, cook the tagliatelle in boiling salted water until just tender, then drain and rinse in hot water. Toss the tagliatelle with the ham sauce and serve sprinkled with Parmesan cheese.

Spaghetti with Mozzarella

Serves 4

4 Tomatoes, skinned, seeded and chopped
60 ml/4 tbsp Capers, chopped
225 g/8 oz Mozzarella cheese, chopped
2 Egg yolks
150 ml/¼ pt Double cream
350 g/12 oz Spaghetti
Salt and pepper

Mix together the tomatoes, capers,

cheese, egg yolks and cream. Cook the spaghetti in boiling salted water until just tender, then drain and rinse in hot water. Stir the tomato mixture gently into the spaghetti over a low heat until the cheese melts, then serve immediately.

Spaghetti with Rich Veal Sauce

Serves 4

25 g/1 oz Butter or margarine
15 ml/1 tbsp Oil
1 Onion, chopped
1 Garlic clove, chopped
100 g/4 oz Pie veal, chopped
100 g/4 oz Mushrooms, sliced
75 ml/5 tbsp Dry white wine
400 g/14 oz Canned tomatoes, chopped
30 ml/2 tbsp Tomato purée
5 ml/1 tsp Oregano
5 ml/1 tsp Thyme
Salt and pepper
350 g/12 oz Spaghetti
15 ml/1 tbsp Soured cream

Heat the butter or margarine with the oil and fry the onion and garlic until soft. Add the meat and fry until browned, then stir in the mushrooms followed by the wine. Bring to the boil and boil until the mixture has reduced by three-quarters. Then stir in the tomatoes, tomato purée, oregano and thyme and season to taste with salt and pepper. Simmer for 30 minutes until the sauce is thick and shiny. Meanwhile, cook the spaghetti in boiling salted water until just tender, then drain and rinse in hot water and turn into a serving dish.

Stir the soured cream into the sauce and pour it over the spaghetti.

Pepper Spaghetti

Serves 4

60 ml/4 tbsp Olive oil
350 g/12 oz Steak, diced
100g/4 oz Streaky bacon, rinded and diced
1 Onion, chopped
1 Red pepper, chopped
1 Green pepper, chopped
400 g/14 oz Canned tomatoes, chopped
50 g/2 oz Green olives, stoned
150 ml/¼ pt Beef Stock (page 24)
15 ml/1 tbsp Cornflour
2.5 ml/½ tsp Cayenne pepper
2.5 ml/½ tsp Curry powder
Salt and pepper
30 ml/2 tbsp Chopped chives
350 g/12 oz Spaghetti

Heat the oil and fry the steak until browned. Add the bacon and onion and fry until soft, then add the peppers and cook until soft. Stir in the tomatoes, olives and stock. Mix the cornflour with a little stock, then stir into the sauce, bring to the boil and simmer, stirring, until the sauce thickens. Add the cayenne pepper and curry powder and season to taste with salt and pepper. Stir in the chives and meat and heat gently.

Meanwhile cook the spaghetti in boiling salted water for 15 minutes until just tender. Drain and rinse in hot water. Turn the spaghetti into a warmed serving dish, pour over the sauce and serve immediately.

Spaghetti Pancakes with Vegetable Filling

Serves 4

150 g/5 oz Wholewheat spaghetti

5 Eggs, beaten

Pinch of nutmeg

50 g/2 oz Parmesan cheese, grated

Salt and pepper

60 ml/4 tbsp Oil

25 g/1 oz Butter or margarine

1 Onion, chopped

1 Red pepper, sliced

1 Courgette, sliced

150 g/5 oz Mangetout

3 Tomatoes, skinned, seeded and chopped

225 ml/8 fl oz Vegetable Stock (page 24)

15 ml/1 tbsp Cornflour

30 ml/2 tbsp Water

30 ml/2 tbsp Soy sauce

30 ml/2 tbsp Cider vinegar

15 ml/1 tbsp Honey

30 ml/2 tbsp Chopped chives

Break the spaghetti roughly into 7.5 cm/3 in lengths, then cook it in boiling salted water until just tender, drain and rinse in hot water. Beat the eggs with the nutmeg and cheese and season to taste with salt and pepper. Stir in the spaghetti. Heat 15 ml/1 tbsp oil and fry a quarter of the spaghetti batter on both sides, then remove from the pan, keep it warm, and fry 3 more pancakes.

Heat the butter or margarine and fry the onion until soft. Add the pepper, courgette and mangetout and fry for 2 minutes, stirring. Add the tomatoes and stock, cover and simmer for 5 minutes. Mix the cornflour and water and stir it into the vegetable mixture until the mixture thickens. Add the soy sauce, vinegar and honey and season to taste with salt and pepper. Divide the mixture between the pancakes and fold them in half. Serve sprinkled with chives.

Spaghetti alla Carbonara

Serves 4

30 ml/2 tbsp Oil

1 Onion, chopped

1 Garlic clove, crushed

25 g/1 oz Butter or margarine

175 g/6 oz Bacon, rinded and chopped

90 ml/6 tbsp Dry white wine

350 g/12 oz Spaghetti

3 Eggs

75 g/3 oz Parmesan cheese, grated

15 ml/1 tbsp Chopped parsley

Salt and pepper

Heat the oil and fry the onion and garlic until soft but not browned. Add the butter and bacon and fry until crisp. Add the wine, bring to the boil and simmer until the wine has evaporated. Meanwhile, cook the spaghetti in boiling salted water until just tender, then drain and rinse in hot water. Beat the eggs with the cheese and parsley and season to taste with salt and pepper. Toss the spaghetti with the egg mixture, then mix in the bacon mixture. The heat from the spaghetti will be sufficient to cook the eggs. Serve immediately.

Spaghetti with Garlic Butter

Serves 4

600 ml/1 pt Water
6 Garlic cloves, peeled
100 g/4 oz Butter or margarine
90 ml/6 tbsp Chopped parsley
350 g/12 oz Spaghetti
Salt and pepper
100 g/4 oz Parmesan cheese

Bring the water to the boil, add the garlic and boil for 5 minutes, then drain and crush the garlic. Melt the butter and stir in the garlic and parsley and cook over a low heat for 2 minutes. Meanwhile, cook the spaghetti in boiling salted water until just tender, then drain and rinse in hot water. Toss the spaghetti in the garlic butter, season to taste with salt and pepper and turn into a warmed serving dish. Serve sprinkled with cheese.

Beef Lasagne

Serves 4

15 ml/1 tbsp Olive oil
1 Onion, chopped
1 Garlic clove, chopped
450 g/1 lb Minced beef
400 g/14 oz Canned tomatoes, chopped
60 ml/4 tbsp Tomato purée
10 ml/2 tsp Oregano
Salt and pepper
25 g/1 oz Butter or margarine
15 g/½ oz Plain flour
300 ml/½ pt Milk
175 g/6 oz Lasagne slices
225 g/8 oz Mozzarella cheese, sliced
50 g/2 oz Parmesan cheese, grated

Heat the oil and fry the onion and garlic until soft but not browned, then stir in the meat and fry until browned. Add the tomatoes, tomato purée and oregano and season to taste with salt and pepper. Simmer for 15 minutes until cooked through.

Meanwhile, melt the butter or margarine in a saucepan, stir in the flour and cook for 1 minute. Whisk in the milk and cook, stirring, until the sauce thickens. Season to taste with salt and pepper. Cook the lasagne in boiling salted water until just tender, then drain and rinse in cold water, making sure that the sheets are separate.

Spoon alternate layers of meat, lasagne and sauce into a shallow ovenproof dish, finishing with a layer of sauce. Cover with the Mozzarella and sprinkle with Parmesan. Bake in a preheated oven at 190°C/375°F/gas mark 5 for 20 minutes until browned and bubbling on top.

Kidney Bean and Vegetable Lasagne

Serves 4

6 Lasagne slices
50 g/2 oz Butter or margarine
60 g/2½ oz Wholemeal flour
600 ml/1 pt Milk
Salt and pepper
100 g/4 oz Strong cheese, grated
30 ml/2 tbsp Oil
1 Leek, sliced
1 Garlic clove, chopped
1 Celery stalk, sliced
50 g/2 oz Mushrooms, sliced
15 ml/1 tbsp Sherry
Few drops of soy sauce
450 ml/¾ pt Vegetable Stock
  (page 24)
225 g/8 oz Canned kidney beans,
  rinsed and drained
225 g/8 oz Courgettes, sliced

Drop the lasagne slices one at a time into plenty of boiling salted water, and simmer for 10 minutes, then drain and rinse separately in cold water. Melt the butter or margarine in a large pan and fry 50 g/2 oz flour for 1 minute. Gradually stir in the milk and bring to the boil, stirring. Remove from the heat and season well with salt and pepper. Stir in half the cheese.

Heat the oil and fry the leek, garlic, celery and mushrooms until soft and just browned. Stir in the sherry, then the remaining flour. Add the soy sauce to the stock and stir this into the pan, bring to the boil, add the kidney beans and simmer for 15 minutes. Place half the courgettes on the base of an ovenproof dish. Pour half the vegetable sauce over the top. Lay half the lasagne on top, then pour on the remaining sauce. Cover with lasagne, then the cheese sauce, and finally the remaining grated cheese. Bake in a preheated oven at 190°C/375°F/gas mark 5 for 30 minutes.

Spinach-Stuffed Cannelloni

Serves 4

225 g/8 oz Frozen spinach, thawed
100 g/4 oz Cream cheese
Salt and pepper
12 Cannelloni tubes
40 g/1½ oz Butter or margarine
40 g/1½ oz Plain flour
600 ml/1 pt Milk
2.5 ml/½ tsp Nutmeg
25 g/1 oz Wholemeal breadcrumbs

Purée the spinach and cream cheese in a food procesor or blender, and season to taste with salt and pepper. Fill the cannelloni tubes with the mixture and place them in a shallow ovenproof dish. Melt the butter or margarine in a saucepan, stir in the flour and cook for 1 minute. Whisk in the milk and cook, stirring, until thickened. Add the nutmeg and season to taste with salt and pepper. Pour the sauce over the cannelloni, sprinkle with breadcrumbs and bake in a preheated oven at 200°C/400°F/gas mark 6 for 40 minutes until golden brown.

Prawn Cannelloni

Serves 4

25 g/1 oz Butter or margarine

1 Bunch of spring onions, sliced

450 g/1 lb Shelled prawns

225 g/8 oz Canned tomatoes, drained, juice reserved and chopped

100 g/4 oz Button mushrooms, sliced

150 ml/¼ pt Dry white wine

15 g/½ oz Plain flour

Pinch of mixed spice

Salt and pepper

450 g/1 lb Cannelloni

75 ml/5 tbsp Tomato purée

225 g/8 oz Mozzarella cheese, sliced

Melt the butter or margarine and fry the onions until soft but not browned. Add the prawns, tomatoes and mushrooms. Blend the wine with the flour and stir it into the pan. Bring to the boil, stirring, and simmer until the sauce thickens. Add the spice and season to taste with salt and pepper. Leave to cool.

Cook the cannelloni in boiling salted water for 5 minutes until just tender, then drain and rinse in hot water. Stuff with the prawn mixture and lay in a greased ovenproof dish. Mix the tomato purée with the juice from the tomatoes and pour it over the cannelloni then place the cheese on top. Bake in a preheated oven at 200°C/ 400°F/gas mark 6 for 15 minutes.

Vegetables

Though some vegetables, such as the newest carrots or the first new potatoes are at their best simply boiled and served with a knob of butter or a sprinkling of fresh herbs, it is very dull just to serve all vegetables plain boiled! Try out some of the interesting options offered here for all your favourite vegetables, and some you may not have tried.

Scalloped Artichokes

Serves 4

6 Jerusalem artichokes, peeled and sliced
50 g/2 oz Butter or margarine
50 g/2 oz Breadcrumbs
300 ml/½ pt Béchamel Sauce (page 225)
Pinch of cayenne pepper

Boil the artichokes in lightly salted water for 15 minutes, then drain. Butter 4 scallop shells or soufflé dishes, melt the remaining butter and stir in the breadcrumbs. Line the dishes with about two-thirds of the breadcrumb mixture. Mix the artichokes with enough sauce to coat them well, season to taste with cayenne pepper and divide them between the dishes. Cover with the reserved breadcrumbs and bake in a preheated oven at 180°C/350°F/gas mark 4 until golden brown on top.

Malaysian Asparagus

Serves 4

10 ml/2 tsp Soy sauce
5 ml/1 tsp Root ginger, finely chopped
1 Garlic clove, crushed
15 ml/1 tbsp Oil
450 g/1 lb Asparagus, sliced
150 ml/¼ pt Single cream
10 ml/2 tsp Cornflour
Pinch of salt

Mix the soy sauce, ginger and garlic and leave to stand for 30 minutes. Heat the oil and fry the asparagus with the sauce for 2 minutes, then cover and steam until the asparagus is tender. Meanwhile, mix the cream, cornflour and salt in a bowl over a pan of hot water and stir until the sauce thickens. When the asparagus is ready, pour over the cream sauce and serve immediately.

190

French Beans with Bacon

Serves 4

25 g/1 oz Butter or margarine
½ Leek, sliced
3 Streaky bacon rashers, rinded
and cut into strips
225 g/8 oz French beans, cut into
2.5 cm/1 in pieces
¼ Iceberg lettuce, shredded

Melt the butter in a large pan and fry the leek until soft but not browned. Add the bacon and fry until browned. Blanch the beans in boiling water for 1 minute, then drain and add to the pan. Stir-fry for 2 minutes, then stir in the lettuce and cook for 30 seconds. Turn on to a warmed serving dish and serve immediately.

Green Beans with Pears

Serves 4

450 ml/¾ pt Vegetable Stock
(page 24)
4 Hard pears, peeled, cored and
sliced
Twist of lemon peel
225 g/8 oz Green beans, sliced
15 ml/1 tbsp Tarragon vinegar
30 ml/2 tbsp Demarara sugar
Salt and pepper

Bring the stock to the boil, then add the pears and lemon peel and simmer for 10 minutes. Add the beans and simmer for 20 minutes. Add the vinegar and sugar and season to taste with salt and pepper. Continue simmering until the liquid is almost all absorbed. Serve immediately.

French Beans with Almonds

Serves 4

350 g/12 oz French beans
25 g/1 oz Butter
50 g/2 oz Flaked almonds
Pepper

Cook the beans in boiling salted water for 7 minutes, then drain. Melt the butter and fry the almonds until just browned. Mix them with the beans, season with pepper and serve immediately.

Polish Beetroot

Serves 4

15 ml/1 tbsp Butter or margarine
1 Onion, chopped
15 ml/1 tbsp Plain flour
60 ml/4 tbsp Milk
900 g/2 lb Beetroot
5 ml/1 tsp Horseradish, grated
Salt and pepper
Pinch of sugar
15 ml/1 tbsp Vinegar
30 ml/2 tbsp Natural yoghurt

Melt the butter or margarine and fry the onion until soft but not browned. Add the flour and cook, stirring, until slightly browned, then remove from the heat and gradually stir in the milk. Bring to the boil, stirring continuously. Add the remaining ingredients except the yoghurt and simmer for about 6 minutes. Pour into a warmed serving dish and top with the yoghurt.

Beetroot au Gratin

Serves 4

6 Cooked beetroot, sliced
150 ml/¼ pt Single cream
Grated rind of ½ lemon
15 ml/1 tbsp Chopped parsley
25 g/1 oz Breadcrumbs
25 g/1 oz Parmesan cheese, grated
50 g/2 oz Butter or margarine
Salt and pepper

Arrange the beetroot in an ovenproof dish. Pour over the cream. Mix the lemon rind, parsley, breadcrumbs and cheese and sprinkle over the beetroot. Dot with butter and season to taste with salt and pepper. Place under a hot grill until brown and bubbling.

Deep-Fried Sprouts

Serves 4

100 g/4 oz Plain flour
Pinch of salt
1 Egg, beaten
150 ml/¼ pt Milk
450 g/1 lb Brussels sprouts
Oil for deep frying
300 ml/½ pt Béchamel Sauce
   (page 225)

Beat together the flour, salt, egg and milk to make a batter and leave in a cool place. Cook the sprouts in boiling salted water for about 5 minutes until they are just tender, then drain them. Dip the sprouts in the batter and fry in batches in hot oil for a few minutes until crisp and golden. Drain well and serve with béchamel sauce.

Broccoli in Lemon Sauce

Serves 4

450 g/1 lb Broccoli florets
300 ml/½ pt Cooking liquor
Grated rind and juice of 1 lemon
5 ml/1 tsp Sugar
Salt
30 ml/2 tbsp Cornflour
30 ml/2 tbsp Water

Cook the broccoli in boiling salted water for 10 minutes, then drain and reserve 300 ml/½ pt cooking liquid. Keep the broccoli warm while making the sauce.

Add the lemon rind, juice and sugar to the cooking liquid and season to taste with salt. Mix the cornflour and water to a paste, then stir it into the liquid, bring to the boil, stirring continuously, and simmer until the sauce becomes thick and clear. Pour the sauce over the broccoli and serve.

Broccoli with Black Bean Sauce

Serves 4

225 g/8 oz Broccoli florets
45 ml/3 tbsp Oil
2 Chilli peppers, chopped
½ Leek, chopped
½ Red pepper, chopped
50 g/2 oz Cooked black beans, chopped
200 ml/7 fl oz Vegetable Stock
   (page 24)
15 ml/1 tbsp Soy sauce
15 ml/1 tbsp Cornflour

Steam the broccoli for 7 to 8 minutes, then remove to a serving dish and keep it warm. Heat the oil in a large pan and fry the chilli peppers, leek and pepper until soft, then add the beans, stock and soy sauce and cook for 2 minutes. Blend the cornflour with a little cold water, then add to the sauce and cook for 1 minute. Pour the sauce over the broccoli and serve.

Red Cabbage with Apple

Serves 4

| 1 Red cabbage , shredded |
| 2 Cooking apples, peeled, cored and cubed |
| 50 g/2 oz Butter or margarine |
| 2-3 Cloves |
| Salt and pepper |
| 15 ml/1 tbsp Redcurrant jelly |
| 15 ml/1 tbsp Vinegar |
| 30 ml/2 tbsp Plain flour |

Put the cabbage in a large saucepan with just enough water to cover, add the apples, butter or margarine and cloves and season with salt and pepper. Bring to the boil and simmer gently for 2 hours until the cabbage is tender and the apples have virtually disappeared.

Warm the jelly, add the vinegar and mix with the flour. Add a little juice from the pot, then stir into the cabbage mixture and heat until the sauce thickens.

Cabbage and Bacon Pie

Serves 4

| 1 White cabbage |
| Salt |
| 45 ml/3 tbsp Oil |
| 225 g/8 oz Bacon, rinded and chopped |
| 1 Onion, chopped |
| 2 Garlic cloves, crushed |
| 2 Eggs |
| 150 ml/¼ pt Milk |
| 50 g/2 oz Breadcrumbs |
| 100 g/4 oz Gruyère cheese, grated |
| Pepper |

Remove 8 large leaves from the cabbage and cook in boiling salted water for 5 minutes, then drain. Heat 15 ml/1 tbsp oil and fry the bacon until the fat begins to run. Add the onion and garlic and fry until lightly browned. Remove from the pan. Chop half the inner leaves of the cabbage. Heat the remaining oil and fry the leaves for 5 minutes, stirring well. Meanwhile, beat the eggs with the milk, breadcrumbs and cheese and season to taste with salt and pepper. Stir the fried cabbage, the bacon and onion into the egg mixture. Layer most of the whole cabbage leaves over the base of an ovenproof dish, fill with the cabbage mixture and top with the remaining leaves. Bake in a preheated oven at 180°C/ 350°F/gas mark 4 for 45 minutes, then unmould on to a warmed serving plate and serve with sausages.

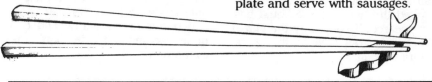

Cabbage Beanfeast

Serves 4

1 Small green cabbage, shredded
4 Small sausages, sliced
25 g/1 oz Butter or margarine
100 g/4 oz Cooked haricot beans

Cook the cabbage in boiling salted water until just tender. Drain. Fry the sausages in the butter or margarine until crisp. Add the cabbage and beans, stir well, cover and cook for 3 minutes. Turn on to a warmed serving dish and serve immediately.

Glazed Carrots

Serves 4

675 g/1½ lb Carrots
50 g/2 oz Butter or margarine
15 ml/1 tbsp Sugar
2.5 ml/½ tsp Salt
450 ml/¾ pt Vegetable Stock
  (page 24)

If the carrots are young, leave them whole; old carrots should be scraped and quartered. Melt the butter or margarine in a saucepan and add the carrots, sugar and salt. Pour in enough stock to come half-way up the carrots, bring to the boil and simmer for 15 minutes, shaking the pan occasionally until the carrots are cooked through and the liquid has disappeared, leaving only the glaze. Stir the carrots well in the glaze before serving.

Herbed Carrots

Serves 4

50 g/2 oz Butter or margarine
8 Large carrots, thinly sliced
1 Onion, chopped
15 ml/1 tbsp Cornflour
300 ml/½ pt Vegetable Stock
  (page 24)
5 ml/1 tsp Mixed herbs
Salt and pepper

Melt the butter or margarine in a saucepan and fry the carrots and onion for 5 minutes. Stir in the cornflour and cook for 1 minute. Stir in the stock and simmer, stirring, until the sauce thickens. Add the herbs, season to taste with salt and pepper and simmer for about 20 minutes until the carrots are tender, adding a little more stock if necessary.

Sweet and Sour Carrots

Serves 4

450 g/1 lb Young carrots, cut into
  chunks
45 ml/3 tbsp Vinegar
10 ml/2 tsp Soft brown sugar
25 g/1 oz Butter or margarine

Place the carrots in a saucepan and just cover with water, bring to the boil and cook for about 15 minutes until tender. Add the vinegar, sugar and butter or margarine and continue cooking until the liquid has evaporated.

Carrots Bourguignonne

Serves 4

450 g/1 lb Carrots, sliced
75 g/3 oz Butter or margarine
2 Large onions, sliced
30 ml/2 tbsp Plain flour
300 ml/½ pt Vegetable Stock
(page 24)
Salt and pepper

Place the carrots in a saucepan and just cover with water, bring to the boil and cook for about 15 minutes until tender, then drain. Meanwhile, melt the butter or margarine and fry the onions until soft. Add the carrots, mix in the flour and stir until it browns. Add the stock, season to taste with salt and pepper, simmer for 15 minutes and serve.

Cauliflower Fritters

Serves 4

100 g/4 oz Plain flour
Pinch of salt
1 Egg, beaten
150 ml/¼ pt Milk
350 g/12 oz Cauliflower florets
Oil for deep frying

Beat together the flour, salt, egg and milk to make a batter and leave in a cool place. Cook the cauliflower in boiling salted water for about 10 minutes until just tender, then drain. Dip the cauliflower in the batter and fry in batches in hot oil for a few minutes until crisp and golden. Drain well before serving.

Indian Cauliflower

Serves 4

45 ml/3 tbsp oil
1 Onion, sliced
2.5 ml/½ tsp Turmeric
1 Cauliflower, broken into florets
Salt
2 Green chillies, seeded
1 Red pepper, sliced
1 Green pepper, sliced
1 Yellow pepper, sliced

Heat the oil and fry the onion until soft. Add the turmeric and cook for 1 minute. Add the cauliflower and season to taste with salt. Cover and cook gently for 10 minutes until the cauliflower is almost cooked. Stir in the chillies and peppers and cook for a further 5 minutes until tender. Serve with curries.

Cauliflower Polonaise

Serves 4

1 Cauliflower, broken into florets
50 g/2 oz Butter or margarine
1 Garlic clove, crushed
50 g/2 oz Breadcrumbs
15 ml/1 tbsp Chopped parsley
1 Hard-boiled egg, finely chopped

Cook the cauliflower in plenty of boiling salted water for 10 minutes until just tender. Drain and place in a warmed serving dish. Meanwhile, melt the butter and fry the garlic for 1 minute. Add the breadcrumbs and fry until lightly browned, stir in the parsley and egg, heat through and pour over the cauliflower.

Braised Celery Hearts with Orange

Serves 4

25 g/1 oz Butter or margarine
1 Onion, chopped
1 Carrot, sliced
2 Celery hearts
300 ml/½ pt Chicken Stock (page 24)
Grated rind and juice of 1 orange
Salt and pepper

Melt the butter in a saucepan and fry the onion until soft but not browned. Stir in the carrot, celery and stock. Add the orange rind and juice and season to taste with salt and pepper. Pour into an ovenproof dish, cover and bake in a preheated oven at 170°C/325°F/gas mark 3 for 1½ hours. Serve hot with lamb or pork.

Braised Celery Mirepoix

Serves 4

1 Head of celery, trimmed and washed
50 g/2 oz Butter or margarine
2 Carrots, chopped
½ Turnip, chopped
2 Onions, chopped
1 Bouquet garni
1 Blade of mace
6 White peppercorns
1 Bay leaf
450 ml/¾ pt Vegetable Stock (page 24)
Salt and pepper

Leave the celery head whole and tie so it does not disintegrate during cooking. Melt the butter or margarine in a large saucepan and fry the vegetables until lightly browned. Add the herbs and spices, and just cover the vegetables with stock. Season to taste with salt and pepper, bring to the boil and lay the head of celery on top, basting well with stock. Cover tightly and simmer gently for about 1½ hours until the celery is tender. Drain the vegetables, discard the bouquet garni and bay leaf and keep the vegetables warm. Reduce the liquid by boiling rapidly, and pour it over the vegetables.

Italian Celery

Serves 4

350 g/12 oz Celery, diced
25 g/1 oz Butter or margarine
1 Onion, finely chopped
1 Garlic clove, chopped
½ Green pepper, finely chopped
4 Tomatoes, skinned and cut into wedges
15 ml/1 tbsp Chopped parsley
Pinch of basil
Pinch of cayenne pepper
Salt and pepper

Cook the celery in boiling water until tender, then drain. Melt the butter and fry the onion, garlic and pepper until soft. Stir in the celery, tomatoes, parsley, basil and cayenne pepper and season to taste with salt and pepper. Cook for 10 minutes until tender.

Celeriac au Gratin

Serves 4

1 Celeriac, sliced
25 g/1 oz Butter or margarine
25 g/1 oz Plain flour
450 ml/¾ pt Milk
Salt and pepper
50 g/2 oz Cheese, grated
25 g/1 oz Breadcrumbs

Cook the celeriac in boiling salted water for 4 minutes, then drain and turn into a greased ovenproof dish. Melt the butter or margarine, stir in the flour and cook for 1 minute. Whisk in the milk, bring to the boil and cook, stirring, until the sauce thickens. Remove from the heat, stir in half the cheese and pour in the dish. Mix the remaining cheese with the breadcrumbs and sprinkle on top. Bake in a preheated oven at 190°C/375°F gas mark 5 for 15 minutes until brown.

Fennel with Cheese

Serves 4

3 Fennel, sliced
50 g/2 oz Butter or margarine
100 g/4 oz Gruyère cheese, grated

Cook the fennel in boiling water for 12 minutes until tender, then drain. Rub half the butter or margarine over an ovenproof dish and lay the fennel in the dish. Dot with the remaining butter or margarine and sprinkle with the cheese. Bake in a preheated oven at 180°C/350°F/gas mark 4 for 20 minutes until brown.

Stuffed Courgettes

Serves 4

6 Courgettes
50 g/2 oz Butter or margarine
1 Onion, chopped
2.5 ml/½ tsp Paprika
30 ml/2 tbsp Tomato purée
4 Tomatoes, chopped
2.5 ml/½ tsp Oregano
2.5 ml/½ tsp Basil
175 g/6 oz Cooked long-grain rice
100 g/4 oz Strong Cheddar cheese, grated

Trim the stalks and boil the courgettes, whole and unpeeled, for 5 minutes. Drain, rinse in cold water and cut in half lengthways. Scoop out and discard the seeds. Scoop out and reserve most of the flesh, leaving a wall inside the skin. Melt the butter or margarine in a saucepan and fry the onion until soft but not browned. Add the courgette flesh and all the other ingredients except the cheese, and simmer gently for 5 minutes. Fill the courgettes with the mixture, place them in a greased ovenproof dish, sprinkle with the cheese and bake in a preheated oven at 190°C/375°F/gas mark 5 for 20 minutes until browned and crispy on top.

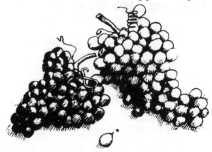

Chestnuts

Serves 4

900 g/2 lb Chestnuts
3 Cloves
1 Small onion
1 Celery stalk
1 Bay leaf
1 Blade of mace
600 ml/1 pt Vegetable Stock
    (page 24)
Salt and cayenne pepper

Make a small cut in the top of each chestnut shell. Put them in a saucepan and cover with cold water, bring to the boil and boil for 2 minutes. Drain, peel and skin the chestnuts while they are still hot, otherwise the skins will not come off. Stick the cloves in the onion and put it in the pan with the chestnuts and all the other ingredients, adding enough boiling stock to cover. Simmer for about 1 hour, drain and keep the chestnuts warm in a serving dish while you return the stock to the pan. Boil the liquid to reduce it by half. Season to taste with salt and cayenne pepper and pour over the chestnuts.

Bacon and Leek Toastie

Serves 4

50 g/2 oz Butter or margarine
4 Leeks, sliced
Salt and pepper
100 g/4 oz Strong cheese, grated
4 Bread slices
8 Streaky bacon rashers

Melt the butter or margarine and fry the leeks until soft. Season to taste with salt and pepper and stir in the cheese. Cover and simmer gently until the leeks are tender. Toast the bread and lay the toast on a warmed serving plate. Grill the bacon until crisp. Spoon the leeks over the toast and top with the bacon rashers.

Mangetout Stir-Fry

Serves 4

15 ml/1 tbsp Oil
½ Red pepper, thinly sliced
½ Yellow pepper, thinly sliced
2.5 cm/1 in Piece root ginger
50 g/2 oz Cashew nuts
225 g/8 oz Mangetout
100 g/4 oz Beansprouts
30 ml/2 tbsp Dry sherry
Few drops soy sauce
5 ml/1 tsp Tomato purée

Heat the oil in a frying pan and fry the peppers and ginger for 2 minutes, then stir in the cashew nuts and stir-fry until browned. Stir in the mangetout and beansprouts and stir-fry for 2 minutes. Mix together the sherry, soy sauce and tomato purée, stir into the vegetables and serve immediately.

Orange Baked Marrow

Serves 4

1 Marrow, peeled and thickly sliced
25 g/1 oz Butter or margarine
30 ml/2 tbsp Honey
30 ml/2 tbsp Orange juice
15 ml/1 tbsp Lemon juice
5 ml/1 tsp Cinnamon
2.5 ml/½ tsp Ground ginger
5 ml/1 tsp Grated orange peel

Scallop the edges of the marrow, then lay the slices in a greased ovenproof dish. Melt the butter and stir in the honey and orange and lemon juice. Pour over the marrow. Sprinkle with the spices and orange peel and bake in a preheated oven at 180°C/350°F/gas mark 4 for 40 minutes, basting occasionally. Serve with rich meat or poultry.

Stuffed Mushrooms

Serves 4

Split peas, soaked for 30 minutes and drained
100 g/4 oz Wholemeal breadcrumbs
1 Carrot, chopped
1 Onion, chopped
1 Potato, chopped
15 ml/1 tbsp Oil
2.5 ml/½ tsp French mustard
2.5 ml/½ tsp Yeast extract
10 ml/2 tsp Chopped parsley
1 Sage leaf, chopped
15 ml/1 tbsp Dry sherry
15 ml/1 tbsp Water
8 Large open mushrooms

Boil the peas in water until soft, then drain and mash. Reserve half the breadcrumbs, then mix all the remaining ingredients, except the mushrooms, with the peas. Chop the mushroom stalks and stir them into the mixture. Lay the mushrooms, black side up, in a shallow ovenproof dish. Divide the stuffing between the mushrooms and sprinkle with the reserved breadcrumbs. Bake in a preheated oven at 190°C/375°F/gas mark 5 for 20 minutes until crispy.

Fried Mushrooms Kiev

Serves 4

24 Cup mushrooms
100 g/4 oz Unsalted butter, softened
2 Garlic cloves, crushed
30 ml/2 tbsp Chopped parsley
Salt and pepper
2 Eggs, beaten
75 g/3 oz Breadcrumbs
Oil for deep frying
Parsley sprigs

Remove the stalks from the mushrooms and chop them finely. Keep the caps whole. Mix the stalks with the butter, garlic and parsley and season to taste with salt and pepper. Spoon the mixture into the mushroom caps and press them together in pairs and secure with cocktail sticks. Dip the mushrooms in egg then breadcrumbs, then egg and breadcrumbs again. Chill for 1 hour. Fry the mushrooms in deep hot oil until golden brown. Drain well, remove the cocktail sticks and serve garnished with parsley.

Italian Mushrooms

Serves 4

| 45 ml/3 tbsp Olive oil |
| 1 Onion, chopped |
| 1 Garlic clove, chopped |
| 350 g/12 oz Button mushrooms, sliced |
| 400 g/14 oz Canned tomatoes, drained and chopped |
| 60 ml/4 tbsp Dry white wine |
| 2.5 ml/½ tsp Oregano |
| 1 Bouquet garni |
| Salt and pepper |
| 15 ml/1 tbsp Chopped parsley |

Heat the oil and fry the onion and garlic until browned. Add the mushrooms and toss well in the oil, then stir in the tomatoes, wine, oregano and bouquet garni and season to taste with salt and pepper. Simmer gently for 15 minutes, remove the bouquet garni, sprinkle with parsley and serve hot.

Parsnip Balls

Serves 4

| 25 g/1 oz Butter or margarine |
| 450 g/1 lb Parsnips, boiled and mashed |
| 15 ml/1 tsp Milk |
| Salt and pepper |
| 2 Eggs, beaten |
| 100 g/4 oz Breadcrumbs |
| Oil for deep-frying |

Melt the butter or margarine, add the parsnips and milk and season to taste with salt and pepper. Stir over a low heat until it begins to bubble, then remove from the heat and beat in 1 egg. Allow to cool, then shape into small balls. Roll in beaten egg and then in breadcrumbs and fry in deep hot oil until golden brown.

Baked Potatoes in Soured Cream

Serves 4

| 450 g/1 lb Potatoes, sliced |
| 300 ml/½ pt Vegetable Stock (page 24) |
| 5 ml/1 tsp Ground caraway |
| Salt and pepper |
| 2 Onions, chopped |
| 1 Bunch of spring onions, sliced |
| 450 ml/¾ pt Soured cream |
| 2 Eggs, beaten |
| 100 g/4 oz Emmenthal cheese, grated |
| 4 Tomatoes, skinned, seeded and sliced |
| 30 ml/2 tbsp Chopped chives |
| 25 g/1 oz Butter, cut into pieces |

Place the potatoes in a shallow oven-proof dish. Pour over the stock, then add the caraway and season to taste with salt and pepper. Sprinkle with onions and spring onions and bake in a preheated oven at 200°C/400°F/gas mark 6 for 25 minutes. Meanwhile, mix the soured cream, eggs and cheese. Spread the tomatoes over the potatoes and pour over the cream. Sprinkle with chives and dot with butter. Return to the oven for a further 20 minutes.

Fried Potatoes and Onions

Serves 4

45 ml/3 tbsp Oil
450 g/1 lb Potatoes, thinly sliced
4 Onions, sliced
Salt and pepper

Heat the oil in a frying pan, then layer the potatoes and onions in the pan, seasoning each layer well with salt and pepper. Fry gently, turning so that the potatoes and onions are cooked through and crispy and browned on the top and bottom. Serve with grilled meats and gherkins.

Chip and Chutney Cheesey Spuds

Serves 4

4 Large baking potatoes, scrubbed
15 ml/1 tbsp Oil
300 ml/½ pt Thick White Sauce
  (page 223)
175 g/6 oz Cheddar cheese, grated
60 ml/4 tbsp Mild chutney
450 g/1 lb Cooked chipolata
  sausages, chopped
Salt and pepper

Prick the potato skins with a fork and brush with oil. Bake in a preheated oven at 200°C/400°F/gas mark 6 for 2 hours until tender.

When the potatoes are almost ready, place all the remaining ingredients in a saucepan and heat through. Cut the potatoes open and pile the chutney mixture over the top.

Baked Potatoes with Chick Peas

Serves 4

4 Large potatoes, scrubbed
100 g/4 oz Canned chick peas,
  drained
50 g/2 oz Butter or margarine, cubed
Salt and pepper
50 g/2 oz Cheese, grated

Prick the potatoes all over with a fork and bake in a preheated oven at 200°C/400°F/gas mark 6 for about 1 hour until soft. Purée the chick peas. Cut the cooked potatoes in half and scoop out the flesh. Mash well, then mix in the butter or margarine and chick peas and season. Pile back into the potato shells, sprinkle with grated cheese and return the potatoes to the oven for 10 minutes to brown.

Potato Layer

Serves 4

900 g/2 lb Potatoes, thinly sliced
2 onions, sliced
50 g/2 oz butter, grated
225 g/8 oz Cheddar cheese, grated
300 ml/½ pt Milk
Salt and pepper

Layer the potatoes, onions, butter and cheese in an ovenproof dish, ending with a layer of cheese. Season the milk with salt and pepper and pour it over the potatoes. Bake in a preheated oven at 190°C/375°F/gas mark 5 for 1½ hours until the potatoes are cooked through and crispy on top.

Potato Scones

Serves 4

450 g/1 lb Cooked potato, mashed
25 g/1 oz Butter or margarine
50 g/2 oz Cheese, grated
65 g/2½ oz 81% extraction flour
Salt and pepper
30 ml/2 tbsp Oil

Mix the potato, butter, cheese and flour and season to taste with salt and pepper. Divide into pieces, shape into flat rounds and fry in the oil for about 3 minutes each side until golden. Serve immediately.

Sauerkraut and Potatoes

Serves 4

450 g/1 lb Potatoes, sliced
30 ml/2 tbsp Oil
2 Onions, sliced
100 g/4 oz Bacon, chopped
450 g/1 lb Bottled sauerkraut
Salt and pepper
15 ml/1 tbsp Cornflour

Cook the potatoes in boiling salted water until just tender. Do not drain. Meanwhile, heat the oil and fry the onions and bacon until soft and browned. When the potatoes are ready, stir in the sauerkraut, onions and bacon and season to taste with a little salt and plenty of black pepper. Mix the cornflour with a little cold water then stir it into the pan, bring to the boil, stirring, then simmer for 20 minutes until thick. Serve with frankfurters and gherkins.

Pumpkin Bake

Serves 4

450 g/1 lb Pumpkin, rinded and
  chopped
100 g/4 oz Butter or margarine
100 g/4 oz Onions, chopped
175g/6 oz Carrots, chopped
100 g/4 oz Celery, chopped
175 g/6 oz Breadcrumbs
5 ml/1 tsp Basil
5 ml/1 tsp Thyme
Salt and pepper
450 ml/¾ pt Natural yoghurt
45 ml/3 tbsp Sesame oil
1 Egg, beaten
30 ml/ 2 tbsp Chopped chives
50 g/2 oz Sesame seeds, toasted

Steam the pumpkin until tender, then drain. Melt the butter or margarine and fry the onions, carrots and celery until soft but not browned. Add the breadcrumbs and herbs and season to taste with salt and pepper. Put half the pumpkin in a greased ovenproof dish, spread with the stuffing mixture and top with the remaining pumpkin. Stir the yoghurt, oil and cheese over a low heat until the cheese melts. Season with a little salt. Stir a spoonful of the sauce into the egg, then stir the egg into the sauce and add the chives. Pour the sauce over the pumpkin and sprinkle with the sesame seeds. Bake in a preheated oven at 180°C/350°F/gas mark 4 for 30 minutes.

Spinach Florentine

Serves 4

| 25 g/1 oz Butter or margarine |
| 40 g/1½ oz Plain flour |
| 450 ml/¾ pt Milk |
| Salt and pepper |
| 225 g/8 oz Frozen spinach, thawed and finely chopped |
| 4 Eggs |

Melt the butter or margarine, stir in the flour and cook for 1 minute. Whisk in the milk and cook, stirring, until the sauce thickens. Season to taste. Mix one-third of the sauce with the spinach and adjust the seasoning if necessary. Pour the mixture into a shallow ovenproof dish and make 4 wells in the mixture. Break an egg into each one, cover with the remaining sauce and bake in a preheated oven at 190°C/375°F/gas mark 5 for 25 minutes.

Turnips with Parsley Sauce

Serves 4

| 450 g/1 lb Turnips, quartered |
| 50 g/2 oz Butter or margarine |
| 15 ml/1 tbsp Dijon mustard |
| 150 ml/¼ pt Double cream |
| Salt and pepper |
| 75 ml/5 tbsp Chopped parsley |

Cook the turnips in boiling water until tender, then drain. Melt the butter or margarine, then stir in the turnips, mustard and cream and season to taste. Bring almost to the boil then serve sprinkled with parsley.

Sweetcorn Fritters

Serves 4

| 2 Eggs, separated |
| Salt and pepper |
| 225 g/8 oz Frozen or canned sweetcorn |
| 5 ml/1 tsp Baking powder |
| 50 g/2 oz Breadcrumbs |
| Oil for frying |

Whisk the egg yolks with salt and pepper and stir in the sweetcorn and baking powder. Whisk the egg whites until stiff, then fold them into the mixture with the breadcrumbs. Fry spoonfuls of the mixture in hot shallow oil for a few minutes, turning once during cooking. Serve hot with chicken dishes.

Stuffed Tomatoes

Serves 4

| 4 Large tomatoes |
| 100 g/4 oz Cream cheese |
| 60 ml/4 tbsp Natural yoghurt |
| 30 ml/2 tbsp Finely chopped cucumber |
| 15 ml/1 tbsp Chopped mint |
| Salt and pepper |

Cut a slice off the top of each tomato and hollow out the inside. Discard the seeds and juice and chop the flesh. Beat the cream cheese and yoghurt, then stir in the tomato, cucumber and mint and season to taste with salt and pepper. Fill the tomatoes with the mixture and serve.

Vegetable Fritters

Serves 4

225 g/8 oz Broccoli florets
225 g/8 oz Cauliflower florets
225 g/8 oz Carrots, cubed
225 g/8 oz Celeriac, cubed
100 g/4 oz Wholemeal flour
200 ml/7 fl oz Beer
15 ml/1 tbsp Olive oil
5 ml/1 tsp Sugar
Pinch of salt
1 Egg, separated
45 ml/3 tbsp Oil
25 g/1 oz Butter or margarine
1 Onion, chopped
100 g/4 oz Canned tomatoes
15 g/½ oz Plain flour
30 ml/2 tbsp Tomato purée
150 ml/¼ pt Dry white wine
150 ml/¼ pt Vegetable Stock (page 24)
150 ml/¼ pt Single cream
15 ml/1 tbsp Oregano
Salt and pepper

Blanch the vegetables in boiling salted water for 5 minutes, then drain well. Mix the wholemeal flour with the beer, olive oil, sugar, salt and egg yolk and leave to stand for 15 minutes. Whisk the egg white until stiff, then fold into the batter. Turn the vegetables in the batter and fry in shallow oil until golden brown. Drain well and keep them warm.

To make the sauce, heat the butter or margarine and fry the onion until soft but not browned. Add the tomatoes, flour and tomato purée, then stir in the wine and stock. Bring to the boil, cover and simmer for 5 minutes, stirring frequently. Add the cream and oregano and season to taste with salt and pepper. Pour on to individual plates, top with the vegetables and serve immediately.

Tomatoes Duxelle

Serves 4

4 Large tomatoes
25 g/1 oz Butter or margarine
1 Onion, finely chopped
50 g/2 oz Mushrooms, finely chopped
25 g/1 oz Breadcrumbs
15 ml/1 tbsp Chopped parsley
1 Egg yolk, beaten
Salt and pepper

Cut the stalk ends off the tomatoes and scoop out the seeds. Melt the butter and fry the onion until soft, add the mushrooms and cook for 2 minutes. Stir in the breadcrumbs, parsley and egg yolk and season to taste with salt and pepper. Fill the tomato shells with the mixture, replace the lids and place in an ovenproof dish. Bake at 190°C/375°F/ gas mark 5 for 25 minutes.

Ratatouille

Serves 4

25 g/1 oz Butter or margarine	
45 ml/3 tbsp Olive oil	
2 Onions, thinly sliced	
2 Garlic cloves, crushed	
3 Medium aubergines, thinly sliced	
1 Green pepper, chopped	
1 Red pepper, chopped	
5 Courgettes	
400 g/14 oz Canned tomatoes	
5 ml/1 tsp Basil	
5 ml/1 tsp Rosemary	
2 Bay leaves	
Salt and pepper	
30 ml/2 tbsp Chopped parsley	

Melt the butter or margarine with the oil in a flameproof casserole, and fry the onions and garlic until soft but not browned. Add the aubergines, peppers and courgettes and fry for 5 minutes, stirring frequently. Add the tomatoes and their juice and the herbs and season to taste with salt and pepper. Sprinkle with parsley and bring to the boil, cover and simmer for 45 minutes until the vegetables are cooked.

Variation

Line some individual tins with short-crust pastry, fill with baking beans and bake blind in a preheated oven at 200°C/400°F/gas mark 6 for 10 minutes. Fill with hot ratatouille and serve hot.

Vegetarian Dishes

An increasing number of people are becoming vegetarian and finding that the idea of daily nut roast is more than a little outdated! Even more people are cutting down on their intake of red meats in particular, and perhaps choosing to have a 'vegetarian' day each week. But even those who never intend to give up eating meat will find recipes here to enjoy.

Vegetarian Chop Suey

Serves 4

30 ml/2 tbsp Oil
100 g/4 oz Onions, sliced
150 g/5 oz Celery, chopped
1 Green pepper, sliced
1 Red pepper, sliced
100 g/4 oz Mushrooms, sliced
225 g/8 oz Mung bean sprouts
10 ml/2 tsp Brewer's yeast
15 ml/1 tbsp Soy sauce
25 g/1 oz Flaked almonds

Heat the oil and fry the onions and celery until soft but not browned. Add the peppers and mushrooms, cover and heat through thoroughly. Add the sprouts, yeast and soy sauce and heat through. Turn into a warmed serving bowl and serve sprinkled with almonds.

Vegetable Curry

Serves 4

45 ml/3 tbsp Oil
2 Onions, sliced
5 ml/1 tsp Chilli powder
5 ml/1 tsp Coriander
25 g/1 oz Root ginger, grated
2 Aubergines, sliced
175 g/6 oz Peas
100 g/4 oz Potatoes, cubed
225 g/8 oz Canned tomatoes, chopped

Heat the oil and fry the onions until just browned. Add the chilli powder, coriander and ginger and fry for 2 minutes. Add the aubergines, peas and potatoes and fry for 5 minutes. Stir in the tomatoes and season to taste with salt and pepper. Bring to the boil, cover and simmer for 30 minutes until the vegetables are tender.

Chick Pea and Mushroom Curry

Serves 4

50 g/2 oz Split peas, soaked
  overnight
30 ml/2 tbsp Oil
25 g/1 oz Margarine
2 Garlic cloves, crushed
2 Onions, chopped
15 ml/1 tbsp Curry powder
45 ml/3 tbsp Tomato purée
50 g/2 oz Creamed coconut, grated
225 g/8 oz Button mushrooms,
  quartered
450 g/1 lb Canned chick peas
Salt and pepper

Cook the split peas in boiling water until tender, then drain. Heat the oil and margarine and fry the garlic and onions until soft but not browned. Stir in the curry powder to taste and cook for 1 minute, then stir in the tomato purée, coconut and mushrooms and cook for 5 minutes. Add the chick peas and season to taste with salt and pepper. Cover and simmer for 10 minutes. Serve with rice.

Green Bean Casserole

Serves 4

450 g/1 lb French beans, chopped
3 Onions
225 g/8 oz Canned water chestnuts,
  sliced
450 g/1 lb Canned beansprouts,
  sliced
275 g/10 oz Canned condensed
  mushroom soup
100 g/4 oz Cheddar cheese, grated
15 ml/1 tbsp Oil

Cook the beans in boiling salted water until just tender but still crisp. Chop 2 of the onions and slice the other one. Layer the beans, chopped onions, water chestnuts and beansprouts in an ovenproof dish and pour over the soup. Sprinkle with the cheese. Heat the oil and fry the remaining onion until browned and spoon on top of the casserole. Bake in a preheated oven at 180°C/350°F/gas mark 4 for 25 minutes.

Savoury Choux Fritters

Serves 4

300 ml/½ pt Vegetable Stock (page 24)
50 g/2 oz Margarine
Pinch of nutmeg
Salt and pepper
150 g/5 oz Wholemeal flour
40 g/1½ oz Cornflour
100 g/4 oz Wheatgerm
4 Eggs, beaten
100 g/4 oz Parmesan cheese, grated
30 ml/2 tbsp Chopped chives
Oil for deep frying

Place the stock, margarine and nutmeg in a saucepan and season to taste with salt and pepper. Bring just to the boil, then stir in the flour, cornflour and wheatgerm and beat until the mixture comes cleanly away from the sides of the pan. Beat in the eggs a little at a time, then beat in the cheese and chives. Heat the oil and drop spoonfuls of the mixture into the hot oil and fry until golden. Drain well and serve hot or cold.

Soya Dumplings in Beer

Serves 4

225 g/8 oz Soya granules
750 ml/1¼ pts Vegetable Stock (page 24)
175 g/6 oz Low fat quark
2 Eggs, beaten
60 ml/4 tbsp Olive oil
15 ml/1 tbsp Made mustard
5 ml/1 tsp Marjoram
1 Garlic clove, chopped
30 ml/2 tbsp Whisky
Salt and pepper
25 g/1 oz Breadcrumbs (optional)
Oil for deep frying
1 Onion, sliced
1 Leek, sliced
2 Carrots, cut into strips
½ Celeriac, cut into strips
30 ml/2 tbsp Tomato purée
25 g/1 oz Wholemeal flour
150 ml/¼ pt Brown ale
30 ml/2 tbsp Honey
30 ml/2 tbsp Cider vinegar
5 ml/1 tsp Marjoram
5 ml/1 tsp Thyme

Mix the soya granules with 400 ml/ 14 fl oz stock, the quark, eggs, half the oil, the mustard, marjoram, garlic and whisky and season to taste with salt and pepper. Add the breadcrumbs, if necessary, to bind the mixture together. Shape into dumplings and fry in deep hot oil until browned, then drain well, place on a warmed serving plate and keep them warm.

Meanwhile, heat the remaining oil and fry the vegetables until soft but not browned. Stir in the tomato purée and flour and cook for 1 minute, then stir in the remaining stock and the beer. Add the honey, cider vinegar and herbs and season to taste with salt and pepper. Bring to the boil, cover and simmer for 10 minutes, then pour over the dumplings and serve immediately.

Mixed Curried Beans

Serves 4

100 g/4 oz Margarine
2 Onions, chopped
2 Garlic cloves, crushed
15 ml/1 tbsp Coriander
5 ml/1 tsp Garam masala
5 ml/1 tsp Chilli powder
400 g/14 oz Canned tomatoes, chopped
5 ml/1 tsp Sugar
300 g/11 oz Canned red kidney beans, drained
300 g/11 oz Canned borlotti beans, drained
300 g/11 oz Canned haricot beans, drained
Salt and pepper

Melt the margarine and fry the onions until just browned. Add the garlic and fry for 1 minute, then add the coriander, garam masala and chilli powder and fry for a few seconds. Stir in the tomatoes and sugar and simmer for 10 minutes. Stir in the beans, season to taste with salt and pepper and heat through thoroughly before serving.

Country Hot Pot

Serves 4

175 g/6 oz Dried soya cubes
300 ml/½ pt Vegetable Stock (page 24)
50 g/2 oz Margarine
1 Onion, chopped
1 Leek, sliced
2 Carrots, cubed
4 Potatoes, cubed
30 ml/2 tbsp Tomato purée
25 g/1 oz Wholemeal flour
250 ml/8 fl oz Red wine
5 ml/1 tsp Marjoram
5 ml/1 tsp Thyme
225 g/8 oz Button mushrooms
150 ml/¼ pt Single cream
100 g/4 oz Blue cheese, crumbled
Salt and pepper
15 ml/1 tbsp Chopped parsley

Soak the soya cubes in the stock for 30 minutes, then drain. Heat the margarine and fry the soya until just browned, then add the vegetables and fry for 2 minutes. Stir in the tomato purée and flour, then the wine, marinade, herbs and mushrooms, bring to the boil and simmer for 30 minutes. Stir in the cream and cheese, season to taste with salt and pepper and serve sprinkled with parsley.

Hungarian Soya Goulash

Serves 4

175 g/6 oz Dried soya cubes
600 ml/1 pt Vegetable Stock (page 24)
250 ml/8 fl oz Red wine
45 ml/3 tbsp Olive oil
225 g/8 oz Mushrooms, sliced
2 Onions, sliced
1 Red pepper, sliced
1 Green pepper, sliced
30 ml/2 tbsp Tomato purée
2 Tomatoes, skinned, seeded and chopped
Grated rind of 1 lemon
2 Garlic cloves, crushed
5 ml/1 tsp Marjoram
5 ml/1 tsp Paprika
Salt and pepper
250 ml/8 fl oz Soured cream
30 ml/2 tbsp Chopped chives

Cover the soya cubes with the stock and wine and leave to marinate for 30 minutes, then drain well. Heat the oil and fry the soya cubes for 2 minutes, then add the mushrooms, onions and peppers and fry until soft. Stir in the tomato purée and flour, then tomatoes and marinade and bring to the boil. Add the lemon rind, garlic, marjoram and paprika and season to taste with salt and pepper. Simmer for 30 minutes, then serve garnished with soured cream and chives.

Stuffed Aubergines

Serves 4

| 2 Large aubergines, halved |
| 45 ml/3 tbsp Olive oil |
| 2 Garlic cloves, crushed |
| 1 Onion, chopped |
| 4 Tomatoes, skinned, seeded and chopped |
| 250 ml/8 fl oz Vegetable Stock (page 24) |
| 225 g/8 oz Soya granules |
| 175 g/6 oz Low fat quark |
| 30 ml/2 tbsp Tomato purée |
| 5 ml/1 tsp Basil |
| 5 ml/1 tsp Oregano |
| 2 Eggs, beaten |
| 15 ml/1 tbsp Chopped chives |
| 15 ml/1 tbsp Chopped parsley |
| 100 g/4 oz Emmenthal cheese, grated |
| Salt and pepper |

Cook the aubergines in boiling salted water for 5 minutes, then drain. Heat the oil and fry the garlic and onion until soft but not browned, then add the tomatoes and stock, bring to the boil, cover and simmer for 5 minutes. Prepare the soya granules according to the instructions on the packet. Mix with the quark, tomato purée, spices, eggs, herbs and cheese and season to taste with salt and pepper. Fill the aubergines with the mixture and place them in an ovenproof dish. Pour over the tomato sauce and bake in a preheated oven at 200°C/400°F/gas mark 6 for 20 minutes. Serve immediately.

Pepperoni with Herbes de Provence

Serves 4

| 4 Green peppers |
| 2 Onions, chopped |
| 225 g/8 oz Mushrooms, chopped |
| 2 Eggs, beaten |
| 100 g/4 oz Emmenthal cheese, grated |
| 50 g/2 oz Breadcrumbs |
| 30 ml/2 tbsp Chopped parsley |
| Pinch of nutmeg |
| Salt and pepper |
| 4 Tomatoes, skinned, seeded and chopped |
| 225 g/8 oz Crème fraîche |
| 250 ml/8 fl oz Dry white wine |
| 15 ml/1 tbsp Herbes de Provence (basil, rosemary, garlic) |

Cut a lid off each pepper and remove the seeds. Mix the onions, mushrooms, eggs, cheese, breadcrumbs, parsley and nutmeg and season to taste with salt and pepper. Fill the peppers with the mixture and stand them in an ovenproof dish just large enough to hold them. Mix the tomatoes, crème fraîche and wine, season with the herbs, then pour over the peppers and bake in a preheated oven at 200°C/400°F/gas mark 6 for 20 minutes.

Tofu Ragout

Serves 4

225 g/8 oz Tofu, cut into strips
750 ml/1¼ pts Vegetable Stock (page 24)
30 ml/2 tbsp Oil
25 g/1 oz Margarine
1 Onion, chopped
1 Green pepper, chopped
100 g/4 oz Mushrooms, sliced
225 ml/8 fl oz Dry white wine
150 ml/¼ pt Crème fraîche
15 ml/1 tbsp Cornflour
30 ml/2 tbsp Water
Pinch of nutmeg
5 ml/1 tsp Soy sauce
Salt and pepper
50 g/2 oz Parmesan cheese, grated
30 ml/2 tbsp Chopped parsley

Soak the tofu in 500 ml/18 fl oz hot stock for 15 minutes. Remove, drain well and toss in a little flour. Heat the oil and fry the tofu until golden. Meanwhile, melt the margarine and fry the onion and pepper until soft but not browned. Add the mushrooms, wine, remaining stock, crème fraîche and tofu. Simmer over a low heat for 10 minutes but do not allow to boil. Combine the cornflour and water and stir into the ragout to thicken slightly. Add the nutmeg and soy sauce and season to taste with salt and pepper. Stir in the Parmesan cheese and serve sprinkled with parsley.

Soya Risotto

Serves 4

50 g/2 oz Margarine
1 Onion, chopped
2 Carrots, diced
½ Celeriac, diced
1 Leek, sliced
1 Courgette, diced
250 ml/8 fl oz Dry white wine
Juice of 1 lemon
2.5 ml/½ tsp Worcestershire sauce
8 Soya sausages
225 g/8 oz Brown rice
1 litre/1¾ pts Vegetable Stock (page 24)
4 Tomatoes, skinned, seeded and chopped
225 g/8 oz Crème fraîche
Salt and pepper
15 ml/1 tbsp Chopped chives

Melt the margarine and fry the vegetables until soft. Stir in the wine, lemon juice and Worcestershire sauce, bring to the boil, cover and simmer for 5 minutes. Add the sausages and rice and fry until the rice is coated. Pour in 150 ml/¼ pt stock, bring to the boil and simmer, uncovered, until the liquid is absorbed. Add some more stock and continue gradually adding the stock until the rice is tender. Add the tomatoes and crème fraîche, season to taste with salt and pepper and reheat, but do not allow the risotto to boil. Serve sprinkled with chives.

Buckwheat Pancakes with Cherries and Butterscotch Sauce

Serves 4

100 g/4 oz Buckwheat flour
3 Eggs, beaten
Salt
250 ml/8 fl oz Milk
75 g/3 oz Sugar
30 ml/2 tbsp Oil
25 g/1 oz Margarine
450 ml/¾ pt Red wine
225 g/8 oz Cherries, stoned
Pinch of ground cloves
2.5 ml/½ tsp Cinnamon
15 ml/1 tbsp Green peppercorns, crushed
5 ml/1 tsp Cornflour
75 ml/5 tbsp Water

Beat the flour into the eggs and add the salt, milk and 10 ml/2 tsp sugar. Heat the oil and pour in some batter. Cook until set, then toss and cook the other side. Keep the pancakes warm while you cook the remainder.

Heat the margarine with half the remaining sugar for about 4 minutes until the sauce is smooth and bubbly. Boil the wine with the remaining sugar and the cherries for 2 minutes. Stir in the cloves, cinnamon and peppercorns and thicken with the mixed cornflour and water. Cook until glossy. Fill the pancakes with the cherry mixture and pour over the sauce.

Potato Fritters Aix-la-Chapel

Serves 4

450 g/1 lb Potatoes
225 g/8 oz Wholemeal flour
1 Egg, beaten
Pinch of nutmeg
Salt and pepper
60 ml/4 tbsp Oil
50 g/2 oz Margarine
1 Onion, chopped
1 Small white cabbage, shredded
250 ml/8 fl oz Dry white wine
250 ml/8 fl oz Vegetable Stock (page 24)
15 ml/1 tbsp Cider vinegar
5 ml/1 tsp Caraway seeds
Pinch of sugar
Chopped chives

Cook the potatoes in boiling salted water until tender, then drain and mash. Stir in the flour, egg and nutmeg and season to taste with salt and pepper, then roll into thick fritters. Heat the oil and fry the fritters until golden brown on all sides.

Meanwhile, melt the margarine and fry the onion until soft but not browned. Add the cabbage and fry for 2 minutes, then pour in the wine, stock, cider vinegar, caraway seeds and sugar. Bring to the boil, then simmer for 30 minutes. Serve the cabbage, sprinkled with chives, with the hot fritters.

Mushroom and Almond Croustade

Serves 4

100 g/4 oz Breadcrumbs
100 g/4 oz Ground almonds
50 g/2 oz Margarine
100 g/4 oz Flaked almonds
1 Garlic clove, crushed
2.5 ml/½ tsp Mixed herbs
450 g/1 lb Button mushrooms
450 ml/¾ pt Soya milk
1 Bay leaf
25 g/1 oz Plain flour
150 ml/¼ pt Dry white wine
Pinch of nutmeg
Salt and pepper
15 ml/1 tbsp Chopped parsley

Mix the breadcrumbs and ground almonds and rub in the margarine until the mixture resembles breadcrumbs. Add the flaked almonds, garlic and herbs. Press the mixture into a greased pie dish and bake in a preheated oven at 230°C/450°F/gas mark 8 for 15 minutes until crisp. Keep it warm.

Meanwhile, put the mushrooms, milk and bay leaf in a saucepan, bring to the boil and simmer for 5 minutes until the mushrooms are tender. Remove the bay leaf. Blend the flour with the wine and stir in a little of the hot milk, then mix the flour into the sauce, stirring well. Simmer for 5 minutes, then add the nutmeg and season to taste with salt and pepper. Spoon on to the warm base and serve sprinkled with parsley.

Leek and Cheese Roly Poly

Serves 4

400 g/14 oz Wholewheat flour
3 Eggs
30 ml/2 tbsp Oil
250 ml/8 fl oz Water, lukewarm
Salt and pepper
5 ml/1 tsp Ground caraway seeds
2.5 ml/½ tsp Honey
30 ml/2 tbsp Cider vinegar
50 g/2 oz Margarine
2 Onions, chopped
2 Leeks, sliced
2 Garlic cloves, crushed
250 ml/8 fl oz Quark or cream cheese
100 g/4 oz Emmenthal cheese, grated
45 ml/3 tbsp Breadcrumbs
A pinch of nutmeg
30 ml/2 tbsp snipped chives
1 Egg yolk mixed with a little water

Sift the flour and add 1 egg, the oil, water and 5 ml/1 tsp salt. Add the caraway, honey and cider vinegar and knead to a dough. Cover and leave for 30 minutes.

Meanwhile, heat the margarine and fry the onions, leeks and garlic until translucent. Leave to cool. Beat the quark with the remaining eggs, then fold in the vegetables, cheese, breadcrumbs, nutmeg and chives and season.

Roll out the dough to 5 mm/¼ in thick, spread with the quark mixture, then roll the dough into a tube, transfer it to a greased baking sheet and bake in a preheated oven at 200°C/400°F/gas mark 6 for 30 minutes. Brush with egg yolk and water and bake for a further 10 minutes.

Mushroom Kebabs

Serves 4

16 Large button mushrooms

2 Red peppers, cut into 6

1 Courgette, sliced

1 Banana, sliced

Salt and pepper

50 g/2 oz Margarine, melted

Thread the mushrooms, peppers, courgette and banana on to 4 skewers, beginning and ending with a mushroom. Season to taste with salt and pepper and brush with melted margarine. Cook under a low grill for 15 minutes until the pepper and courgette are tender, turning and basting frequently.

Vegeburgers

Serves 4

4 Wholemeal rolls, halved

60 ml/4 tbsp Tartare sauce

4 Lettuce leaves

4 Radicchio leaves

1 Tomato, sliced

100 g/4 oz Tofu, sliced

25 g/1 oz Plain flour

1 Egg, beaten

50 g/2 oz Breadcrumbs

30 ml/2 tbsp Oil

1 Onion, sliced

½ Box of cress

60 ml/4 tbsp Crème fraîche

30 ml/2 tbsp French mustard

15 ml/1 tbsp Soy sauce

Salt and pepper

Toast the rolls and spread the bottom halves with tartare sauce. Layer with the lettuce and raddichio leaves and tomato. Coat the tofu slices in flour, then dip in egg and breadcrumbs. Heat the oil and fry the slices until golden brown. Drain well and place on top of the tomato. Garnish with the onion and cress. Mix the crème fraîche, mustard and soy sauce and season. Spread over the burgers and top with the second half of the roll.

Spinach and Herb Loaf

Serves 4

25 g/1 oz Margarine

1 Onion, chopped

450 g/1 lb Spinach, roughly chopped

225 g/8 oz Breadcrumbs

300ml/½ pt Vegetable Stock (page 24)

15 ml/1 tbsp Chopped parsley

15 ml/1 tbsp Chopped chives

5 ml/1 tsp Tarragon

2 Garlic cloves, crushed

Salt and pepper

250 ml/8 fl oz Crème fraîche

4 Eggs, beaten

25 g/1 oz Wholewheat flour

Melt the margarine and fry the onion until soft but not browned. Stir in the spinach and fry for 2 minutes. Add the breadcrumbs to the stock with the spinach mixture, herbs and garlic and season to taste with salt and pepper. Fold in the crème fraîche, eggs and flour and knead to a firm mixture. Transfer to a greased 900 g/ 2 lb loaf tin and bake in a preheated oven at 220°C/425°F/gas mark 7 for 40 minutes.

Cheese Round

Serves 4

2 Onions, chopped
175 g/6 oz Strong cheese, grated
15 ml/1 tbsp Chopped parsley
30 ml/2 tbsp Mustard pickle
Salt and pepper
400 g/14 oz Shortcrust Pastry
  (page 145)
1 Egg, beaten
15 ml/1 tbsp Sesame seeds

Mix the onions, cheese, herbs and pickle and season to taste with salt and pepper. Roll out the pastry on a floured surface to a large rectangle. Spread the filling over the pastry to within 1 cm/½ in of the edge, then roll up like a swiss roll and make cuts along the roll to three-quarters of the width. Shape into a ring and seal the ends with egg. Place on a greased baking sheet, brush with egg and sprinkle with sesame seeds. Bake in a preheated oven at 200°C/400°F/gas mark 6 for 30 minutes.

Savoury Onion Dumplings

Serves 4

4 Large onions
25 g/1 oz Margarine
30 ml/2 tbsp Chopped parsley
50 g/2 oz Breadcrumbs
2 Eggs, beaten
2.5 ml/½ tsp Paprika
Salt and pepper
450 g/1 lb Shortcrust Pastry
  (page 145)

Hollow out the onions, leaving the shells about 1 cm/½ in thick and cook the shells in boiling water for 6 minutes, then drain. Chop the onion centres. Melt the margarine and fry the chopped onion until soft but not browned, then remove from the heat and mix in the parsley, breadcrumbs, 1 egg and paprika and season to taste with salt and pepper. Press the stuffing into the onion shells. Roll out the pastry and cut into 4 rounds. place the onions in the centre of each round and pull up the pastry to cover, brushing the edges with beaten egg to seal. Place on a greased baking sheet, brush with egg and bake in a preheated oven at 190°C/375°F/gas mark 5 for 40 minutes.

Pitta Crunch

Serves 4

4 Vegetarian sausages, sliced
4 Red dessert apples, cored and
  sliced
450 g/1 lb Cottage cheese
50 g/2 oz Celery, chopped
Pepper
4 Wholemeal pitta breads

Grill the sausages until crispy, then drain on kitchen paper and cut into small pieces. Mix the sausages, apples, cheese and celery and season well with freshly ground black pepper. Warm the pitta breads under the grill, cut in half and gently open up. Stuff with the filling and heat through in a preheated oven at 180°C/350°F/gas mark 4 for 10 minutes before serving.

Spinach and Cheese Quenelles

Serves 4

| 225 g/8 oz Spinach, chopped |
| 225 g/8 oz Low fat cheese |
| 75 g/3 oz Breadcrumbs |
| 15 g/½ oz Wheatgerm |
| 1 Egg, beaten |
| 1 Small onion, chopped |
| 1 Garlic clove, crushed |
| 25 g/1 oz Parmesan cheese, grated |
| 2.5 ml/½ tsp Basil |
| Pinch of nutmeg |
| Salt and pepper |
| 50 g/2 oz Wholemeal flour |
| Tomato Sauce (page 230) |

Mix together all the ingredients except the flour and tomato sauce and season to taste with salt and pepper. Roll into 2.5 cm/1 in balls, roll lightly in flour and chill. Bring a saucepan of salted water to the boil, then drop in the spinach balls and simmer until they rise to the surface. Remove with a slotted spoon and serve with tomato sauce.

Vegetable Soufflé

Serves 4

| 225 g/8 oz Potatoes, diced |
| 2 Carrots, chopped |
| 100 g/4 oz Parsnips, chopped |
| 100 g/4 oz Cauliflower florets |
| 100 g/4 oz Broccoli florets |
| 75 ml/5 tbsp Single cream |
| 3 Eggs, separated |
| 100 g/4 oz Cheddar cheese, grated |
| Salt and pepper |

Cook the vegetables in boiling salted water until tender, then drain and mash. Beat in the cream, egg yolks and cheese and season to taste with salt and pepper. Whisk the egg whites until stiff, then fold into the vegetables. Spoon into a greased 18 cm/7 in soufflé dish and bake in a preheated oven at 200°C/400°F/gas mark 6 for 20 minutes until well risen and lightly brown. Serve immediately.

Cucumber and Cheese Mousse

Serves 4

| 1 Cucumber, diced |
| Salt |
| 175 g/6 oz Cream cheese |
| 5 ml/1 tsp Chopped onion |
| Salt and pepper |
| 15 g/½ oz Gelatine |
| 150 ml/¼ pt Water |
| 30 ml/2 tbsp White wine vinegar |
| 15 ml/1 tbsp Caster sugar |
| Pinch of ground mace |
| 150 ml/¼ pt Double cream, whipped |
| 225 g/8 oz Cooked, shelled prawns |

Sprinkle the cucumber with salt and leave pressed between 2 plates for 30 minutes. Mix the cheese and onion and season to taste with salt and pepper. Dissolve the gelatine in the water over a pan of hot water and stir it into the cheese. Drain the cucumber and mix with the wine vinegar, sugar and mace. Fold the cucumber and cream into the cheese, spoon into a greased 900 ml/1½ pt ring mould and leave to set. Turn out and fill the centre with prawns.

Barley Cake Garni

Serves 4

500 g/2 oz Margarine

1 Onion, chopped

1 Red pepper, chopped

225 g/8 oz Barley

900 ml/1½ pts Vegetable Stock
 (page 24)

150 ml/¼ pt Dry white wine

2 Garlic cloves, crushed

Salt and pepper

450 ml/¾ pt Béchamel Sauce
 (page 225)

225 g/8 oz Emmenthal cheese,
 grated

25 g/1 oz Breadcrumbs

30 ml/2 tbsp Chopped chives

30 ml/2 tbsp Chopped parsley

Pinch of nutmeg

3 Eggs, separated

1 Boiled potato, sliced

2 Tomatoes, skinned, seeded and
 sliced

½ Cucumber, sliced

4 Radishes, sliced

15 g/½ oz Gelatine

Melt the margarine and fry the onion and pepper until soft but not browned. Add the barley and fry for 1 minute, then stir in 600 ml/1 pt stock, the wine and garlic and season to taste with salt and pepper. Bring to the boil, cover and simmer for 40 minutes, then take off the lid and boil until all the liquid has evaporated. Leave to cool.

Fold in the béchamel sauce, cheese, breadcrumbs, chives, parsley and nutmeg and season to taste with salt and pepper. Stir in the egg yolks.

Whisk the egg whites until stiff, then fold them into the mixture. Spoon the mixture into a greased 20 cm/8 in cake tin and bake in a preheated oven at 200°C/400°F/gas mark 6 for 40 minutes. Leave to cool.

Decorate the cake with potato, tomatoes, cucumber and radishes. Dissolve the gelatine in the remaining stock and pour over the top. Leave to cool before serving.

Nut Roast

Serves 4

50 g/2 oz Margarine

3 Onions

350 g/12 oz Mixed nuts, chopped

225 g/8 oz Breadcrumbs

600 ml/1 pt Vegetable Stock
 (page 24)

10 ml/2 tsp Yeast extract

10 ml/2 tsp Mixed herbs

Salt and pepper

1 Tomato, sliced

Melt the margarine. Chop 2 onions and fry them until soft but not browned. Remove from the heat and stir in the nuts, most of the breadcrumbs, the stock, yeast extract and herbs and season to taste with salt and pepper. Press the mixture into a greased shallow baking dish, sprinkle with the reserved breadcrumbs and bake in a preheated oven at 180°C/350°F/gas mark 4 for 50 minutes until golden brown. Slice the remaining onion into rings and serve the loaf garnished with onion rings and tomato slices.

Oat Cutlets Milanese

Serves 4

50 g/2 oz Margarine

3 Onions, chopped

750 ml/1¼ pts Vegetable Stock
(page 24)

175 g/6 oz Rolled oats

15 ml/1 tbsp Mixed herbs

Salt and pepper

3 Eggs, beaten

30 ml/1 tbsp Made mustard

30 ml/2 tbsp Chopped chives

25 g/1 oz Breadcrumbs

45 ml/3 tbsp Oil

1 Red pepper, chopped

100 g/4 oz Sweetcorn

90 ml/6 tbsp Tomato ketchup

100 g/4 oz Crème fraîche

5 ml/1 tsp Curry powder

5 ml/1 tsp Paprika

Few drops of tabasco sauce

Pinch of sugar

Melt half the margarine and fry 2 onions until soft but not browned. Add 600 ml/1 pt stock, the oats and herbs and season to taste with salt and pepper. Bring to the boil, cover and simmer for 30 minutes. Remove from the heat and allow to cool, then stir in the eggs, mustard, chives and breadcrumbs and shape into cutlets. Heat the oil and fry the cutlets until golden brown on both sides then place them on a warmed serving plate and keep them warm.

Meanwhile, melt the remaining margarine and fry the remaining onion and the pepper until soft but not browned. Add the sweetcorn, tomato ketchup and remaining stock, then stir in the crème fraîche, curry powder, paprika, tabasco and sugar and season to taste with salt and pepper. Heat through gently, but do not allow the sauce to boil. Pour over the cutlets and serve.

Peanut Roast

Serves 4

225 g/8 oz Peanuts, finely chopped

100 g/4 oz Wholemeal breadcrumbs

50 g/2 oz Rolled oats

1 Onion, finely chopped

1 Carrot, grated

2.5 ml/½ tsp Sage

Salt and pepper

10 ml/2 tsp Yeast extract

10 ml/2 tsp Hot water

250 ml/8 fl oz Milk

25 g/1 oz Cheddar cheese, grated

400 g/14 oz Canned tomatoes,
chopped

1 Garlic clove, crushed

2.5 ml/½ tsp Mixed herbs

2.5 ml/½ tsp Sugar

Mix the nuts, breadcrumbs, oats, onion, carrot and sage and season to taste with salt and pepper. Dissolve the yeast extract in the hot water, then stir it into the nut mixture and add enough milk to give a soft consistency. Turn into a greased 900 g/2 lb loaf tin, sprinkle with grated cheese and bake in a preheated oven at 190°C/375°F/gas mark 5 for 45 minutes.

Put the tomatoes, garlic, herbs and sugar in a saucepan, bring to the boil and simmer for 10 minutes. Serve hot with the peanut roast.

Turlu Guvec

Serves 4

| 1 Aubergine, peeled and cubed |
| Salt and pepper |
| 1 Green pepper, sliced |
| 100 g/4 oz Okra, stalks removed |
| 4 Courgettes, sliced |
| 225 g/8 oz Green beans, chopped |
| 225 g/8 oz Peas |
| 400 g/14 oz Canned tomatoes, chopped |
| 1 Bunch parsley, chopped |
| 10 ml/2 tsp Paprika |
| 60 ml/4 tbsp Oil |
| 4 Tomatoes, sliced |

Sprinkle the aubergine with salt in a colander and leave for 1 hour, then rinse and drain. Mix all the vegetables with the parsley, paprika and oil in a large casserole and season to taste with salt and pepper. Arrange the tomato slices on top and bake in a preheated oven at 190°C/375°F/gas mark 5 for 1¼ hours until most of the liquid has been absorbed and the tomatoes are browned on top.

Millet Pilaf

Serves 4

| 350 g/12 oz Millet |
| 30 ml/2 tbsp Olive oil |
| 1 Onion, chopped |
| 2 Garlic cloves, crushed |
| 900 ml/1½ pts Vegetable Stock (page 24) |
| 1 Red pepper, sliced |
| 50 g/2 oz Sultanas |
| 50 g/2 oz Shelled pistachio nuts |

Place the millet in a heavy-based pan and shake over a high heat until the millet begins to pop. Remove the millet from the pan. Heat the oil and fry the onion and garlic until soft but not browned. Add the millet and stock, bring to the boil, cover and simmer for 10 minutes. Add the pepper and sultanas and cook for a further 10 minutes until the millet is softened and the stock is absorbed. Serve sprinkled with pistachios.

Filo Vegetable Pie

Serves 4

| 900 g/2 lb Courgettes, chopped |
| 250 ml/8 fl oz Oil |
| 225 g/8 oz Feta cheese, crumbled |
| 3 Eggs, beaten |
| 25 g/1 oz Breadcrumbs |
| 15 ml/1 tbsp Chopped dill |
| Salt and pepper |
| 400 g/14 oz Filo pastry |

Place the courgettes in a pan with half the oil, cover and simmer gently until very soft, then leave to cool. Add the cheese, eggs, breadcrumbs and dill and season to taste with salt and pepper. Cover the pastry sheets you are not using with a damp cloth to prevent them drying out. Brush the pastry sheets with oil and layer two-thirds of the pastry over a greased baking sheet. Cover with the filling, then top with the remaining oiled pastry sheets and seal the edges together well. Brush the top with oil, then bake in a preheated oven at 180°C/350°F/gas mark 4 for 35 minutes until golden brown.

Stir-Fry Pancake Stack

Serves 4

50 g/2 oz Cashew nuts, ground
300 ml/½ pt Milk
50 g/2 oz Plain flour
1 Egg, beaten
60 ml/4 tbsp Oil
½ Red pepper, sliced
½ Green pepper, sliced
1 Garlic clove, chopped
1 Leek, sliced OR
6 Spring onions, chopped
1 Courgette, sliced
50 g/2 oz Cooked, shelled prawns
1 Tomato, sliced
225 g/8 oz Beansprouts
30 ml/2 tbsp Soy sauce
45 ml/3 tbsp Sherry

Beat the nuts, milk, flour and egg to a batter. Heat a little oil in a frying pan and use the batter to make 6 pancakes. Set aside. Blanch the peppers in boiling water for 2 minutes then drain and rinse with cold water. Heat the remaining oil and fry the garlic until browned, stir in the leek or spring onions, then add the courgette, peppers and prawns and cook for 1 minute, then add the tomatoes, beansprouts, soy sauce and sherry, stir well and heat through.

Place one pancake in a flat ovenproof dish, spread one-quarter of the cooked mixture on top and then place another pancake on top. Continue layering pancakes and filling, finishing with a pancake. Cover with foil and bake in a preheated oven at 190°C/375°F/gas mark 5 for 10 minutes. Cut into wedges and serve immediately.

Quick Tofu Quiche

Serves 4

175 g/6 oz Wholemeal flour
25 g/1 oz Soft brown sugar
25 g/1 oz Margarine
8 g/¼ oz Yeast
30 ml/ 2 tbsp Cold water
1 Egg, beaten
Pinch of salt
15 ml/1 tbsp Oil
1 Onion, chopped
1 Garlic clove, chopped
50 g/2 oz Mushrooms, chopped
Few drops of soy sauce
225 g/8 oz Tofu, mashed
75 g/ 3oz Cheese, grated
150 ml/¼ pt Water
1 Carrot, grated
25 g/i oz Sesame seeds

Mix the flour and sugar and rub in the margarine. Dissolve the yeast in the water and add the egg and salt. Mix into the dry ingredients and knead until the dough is firm. Use to line a 20 cm/8 in flan ring. Heat the oil and fry the onion, garlic, mushrooms and soy sauce until soft, but not browned. Turn them into the pastry case. Mix together the tofu, cheese and water and pour them over the vegetables. Sprinkle with the carrot and sesame seeds. Leave to rest for 10 minutes, then bake in a preheated oven at 200°C/400°F/gas mark 6 for 25 minutes.

Tyropitakia

Serves 4

225 g/8 oz Feta cheese
225 g/8 oz Ricotta or cottage
  cheese
30 ml/2 tbsp Chopped parsley
10 ml/2 tsp Chopped mint
Pepper
2 Eggs, beaten
400 g/14 oz Filo pastry
60 ml/4 tbsp Oil

Mix the cheese with the herbs and season to taste with pepper. Stir in the eggs. Cut the filo pastry into 13 cm/5 in wide strips, and cover the strips you are not using with a damp cloth to avoid them drying out while you are working. Take one strip at a time, brush it lightly with oil and fold it in half lengthways. Place a teaspoonful of the cheese mixture on the end of the strip and fold over into triangles. Place the finished triangles on a greased baking sheet, brush the tops with a little oil and bake in a preheated oven at 180°C/350°F/ gas mark 4 for 35 minutes until golden brown.

Corn Pudding

Serves 4

15 g/½ oz Plain flour
300 ml/½ pt Milk
350 g/12 oz Canned sweetcorn,
  drained
1 Egg white, whipped
Salt and pepper

Mix the flour to a paste with a little milk, then mix together all the ingredients and season to taste with salt and pepper. Turn into a greased soufflé dish, cover with foil and bake in a preheated oven at 180°C/350°F/ gas mark 4 for 30 minutes until the centre is set.

Nut and Vegetable Medley

Serves 4

1 Aubergine, sliced
Salt
15 ml/1 tbsp Oil
2 Leeks, sliced
1 Large potato, sliced
50 g/2 oz Mushrooms, sliced
½ Small cabbage, sliced
400 g/14 oz Canned tomatoes
5 ml/1 tsp Paprika
75 g/3 oz Smoked cheese, sliced
50 g/2 oz Breadcrumbs
50 g/2 oz Cashew nuts, ground
25 g/1 oz Margarine, melted
Salt and pepper

Lay the aubergine on a plate, sprinkle with salt, cover and leave for 30 minutes. Heat the oil and fry the leeks until soft. Place the potatoes in a layer in a base of an ovenproof dish. Add the leeks, then the mushrooms and cabbage. Drain the aubergine and place on top. Purée the tomatoes and juice with the paprika in a food processor or blender and pour over the vegetables. Layer the cheese on top. Mix the breadcrumbs and nuts with the melted margarine and season to taste with salt and pepper. Sprinkle over the vegetables and bake in a preheated oven at 180°C/350°F/gas mark 4 for 1¼ hours.

Crunchy Croquettes

Serves 4

25 g/1 oz Margarine
1 Onion, chopped
450 g/1 lb Cooked peas
200 g/7 oz Breadcrumbs
30 ml/2 tbsp Chopped parsley
5 ml/1 tsp Green peppercorns,
  crushed
30 ml/2 tbsp Rolled oats
Pinch of nutmeg
15 ml/1 tbsp Soy sauce
15 ml/1 tbsp Made mustard
Salt and pepper
4 Eggs, beaten
150 g/5 oz Wholemeal flour
Oil for frying

Melt the margarine and fry the onion until golden brown. Purée the peas in a food processor or blender. Mix the peas, onion, breadcrumbs, parsley, peppercorns, oats, nutmeg, soy sauce and mustard and season to taste with salt and pepper. Bind with 2 eggs. Shape into rissoles, then roll in flour, dip in the remaining eggs and then the remaining breadcrumbs. Fry in hot oil until golden brown, drain and serve immediately.

Sweet Potato and Parsnip Cakes

Serves 4

450 g/1 lb Sweet potatoes, diced
225 g/8 oz Parsnips, diced
15 ml/1 tbsp Plain flour
2.5 ml/½ tsp Nutmeg
Salt and pepper
30 ml/2 tbsp Milk
50 g/2 oz Rolled oats
50 g/2 oz Coarse oatmeal
30 ml/2 tbsp Oil

Cook the sweet potatoes and parsnips in boiling salted water for 15 minutes until just tender, then drain and purée in a food processor or blender with the flour and nutmeg or mash with a potato masher. Season to taste with salt and pepper and shape into 8 rounds. Brush with milk and roll in the oats and oatmeal. Heat the oil and fry the cakes for 10 minutes until golden on both sides. Serve warm with green salad.

Sauces and Stuffings

Here is a range of sauces — savoury and sweet — which can be used in conjunction with so many other recipes, as accompaniments or to liven up a simple meal. Sauces you use regularly can sometimes be frozen so they are ready at a moment's notice. A small sauce whisk is usually the best utensil to use when making sauces as it will keep the sauces free from lumps.

White Sauce

Makes 300 ml/½ pt

15 g/½ oz Butter or margarine
15 g/½ oz Plain flour
300 ml/½ pt Milk, hot
Salt and pepper

Melt the butter or margarine in a saucepan, add the flour and cook for 1 minute, stirring continuously and without letting the flour brown. Continue stirring as you add the milk, bring to the boil and simmer gently for 5 minutes. Season to taste with salt and pepper.

This sauce is used as the basis for many other sauces.

Mushroom Sauce

Makes 300 ml/½ pt

100 g/4 oz Mushrooms
300 ml/½ pt Milk
25 g/1 oz Butter or margarine
25 g/1 oz Plain flour
Salt and pepper

Simmer the mushrooms in the milk for 2 minutes. Strain and chop the mushrooms. Melt the butter or margarine in a saucepan, add the flour and cook for 2 to 4 minutes, stirring constantly and without letting the flour brown. Stir in the flavoured milk, bring to the boil, stirring continuously, and simmer gently for 5 minutes. Add the chopped mushrooms and season to taste with salt and pepper.

Cheese Sauce

Makes 300 ml/½ pt

300 ml/½pt White Sauce (page 223)
50 g/2 oz Cheddar cheese, grated
5 ml/1 tsp Made mustard

Make up the white sauce, remove from the heat and stir in the grated cheese and mustard.

Mustard Sauce

Makes 300 ml/½ pt

300 ml/½ pt White Sauce (page 223)
15 ml/1 tbsp French mustard
5 ml/1 tsp White vinegar
5 ml/1 tsp Sugar
15 g/½ oz Butter or margarine, cut
 into pieces

Make the white sauce. Mix together the mustard, vinegar and sugar and whisk it into the hot sauce. Reheat to almost boiling and whisk in the butter but do not allow the sauce to boil.

Parsley Sauce

Makes 300 ml/½ pt

300 ml/½ pt White Sauce (page 223)
15 ml/1 tbsp Finely chopped
 parsley
25 g/1 oz Butter or margarine, cut
 into pieces

Make the white sauce. Rinse the chopped parsley and add it to the hot sauce. Bring to the boil then remove from the heat and whisk in the butter.

Prawn Sauce

Makes 300 ml/½ pt

15 g/½ oz Butter or margarine
15 g/½ oz Plain flour
150 ml/¼ pt Milk, hot
150 ml/¼ pt Fish Stock (page 24)
50 g/2 oz Cooked and shelled
 prawns
5 ml/1 tsp Lemon juice
Cayenne pepper

Melt the butter or margarine in a saucepan, add the flour and cook for 2 to 3 minutes, stirring constantly and without letting the flour brown. Continue stirring as you add the milk and stock, bring to the boil and simmer gently for 5 minutes. Add the prawns amd lemon juice and season to taste with cayenne pepper.

Béchamel Sauce

Makes 300 ml/½ pt

300 ml/½ pt Milk
1 Small onion
1 Sprig parsley
6 White peppercorns
1 Bay leaf
15 g/½ oz Butter or margarine
15 g/½ oz Plain flour
Salt and pepper
15 ml/1 tbsp Single cream (optional)

Bring the milk just to boiling point and add the onion, parsley, peppercorns and bay leaf. Remove from the heat, cover and leave to infuse for 15 minutes.

Melt the butter or margarine in saucepan, stir in the flour and cook for 2 to 3 minutes, stirring continuously. Strain the flavoured milk into the flour and butter, stirring continuously until the sauce thickens. Continue to cook for 3 minutes. Strain the sauce through a fine sieve, season to taste with salt and pepper and stir in the cream, if liked, but do not allow the sauce to boil.

Hollandaise Sauce

Makes 300 ml/½ pt

10 ml/2 tsp Lemon juice
10 ml/2 tsp Wine vinegar
15 ml/1 tbsp Water
5 Peppercorns
1 Bay leaf
3 Egg yolks
175 g/6 oz Butter or margarine
Salt and pepper

Put the lemon juice, wine vinegar, water, peppercorns and bay leaf into a saucepan. Bring to the boil and simmer gently until the liquid is reduced by half. Leave to cool, then strain.

Put the egg yolks and vinegar mixture into a double saucepan or basin standing over a pan of simmering water and whisk until thick and foamy. Whisk in the butter a piece at a time until the sauce is thick and shiny and the consistency of mayonnaise. Season with salt and pepper and serve at once with vegetable and egg dishes.

Note
Take care when making the sauce otherwise the eggs may curdle.

Barbecue Sauce

Makes 450 ml/¾ pt

50 g/2 oz Butter or margarine
1 Onion, chopped
5 ml/1 tsp Tomato purée
30 ml/2 tbsp Red wine vinegar
30 ml/2 tbsp Soft brown sugar
10 ml/2 tsp Mustard powder
30 ml/2 tbsp Worcestershire sauce
150 ml/¼ pt Water

Melt the butter or margarine and fry the onion until soft but not browned. Stir in the remaining ingredients, bring to the boil and simmer for 10 minutes. Serve with grilled meats, sausages or beefburgers.

Apple Sauce

Makes 450 ml/¾ pt

450 g/1 lb Cooking apples, peeled, cored and sliced

50 g/2 oz Sugar

Grated rind and juice of ½ lemon

45 ml/3 tbsp Water

25 g/1 oz Butter or margarine

Place the apples, sugar, lemon rind and water in a saucepan and simmer until very soft. Purée in a food processor or blender or pass through a sieve. Reheat with the lemon juice and butter until hot and serve with pork, duck or goose.

Black Butter Sauce

Makes 100 ml/4 fl oz

100 g/4 oz Butter

30 ml/2 tbsp Vinegar

Salt and pepper

Heat the butter until nut brown then remove it from the heat. Add the vinegar and season to taste with salt and pepper. Reheat without boiling and serve hot with fish.

Bread Sauce

Makes 300 ml/½ pt

300 ml/½ pt Milk

1 Small onion

2 Cloves

75 g/3 oz Breadcrumbs

15 g/½ oz Butter or margarine

Salt and pepper

Bring the milk to the boil with the onion and cloves, cover and simmer gently for 15 minutes. Strain over the breadcrumbs in a clean pan. Stir in the butter or margarine and season to taste with salt and pepper. Reheat but do not allow the sauce to boil.

Brown Sauce

Makes 300 ml/½ pt

50 g/2 oz Butter or margarine

2 Onions, finely chopped

15 g/½ oz Wholewheat flour

300 ml/½ pt Beef Stock (page 24)

5 ml/1 tsp Worcestershire sauce

Salt and pepper

Melt the butter or margarine in a large saucepan and fry the onions until well browned. Add the flour and cook, stirring continuously, until browned. Gradually stir in the stock and cook for 5 minutes. Season to taste with Worcestershire sauce, salt and pepper.

Cranberry Sauce

Makes 450 ml/¾ pt

175 g/6 oz Sugar

150 ml/¼ pt Water

225 g/8 oz Cranberries

Bring the sugar and water to the boil and simmer for 4 minutes. Add the cranberries, cover and simmer gently for about 5 minutes until all the cranberries have popped. Cool and serve chilled with poultry.

Chestnut Sauce

Makes 450 ml/¾ pt

100 g/4 oz Chestnuts
Salt and pepper
15 ml/1 tbsp Cornflour
300 ml/½ pt Milk

Remove the outside coating of the nuts and soak them in boiling water for 5 minutes. Remove the skins, place in a saucepan and just cover with water. Bring to the boil and boil for 1 hour. Drain and purée the chestnuts in a food processor or blender, then season to taste with salt and pepper. Make a paste with the cornflour and a little milk. Pour the remainder of the milk into a saucepan and bring it to the boil, then stir in the cornflour paste and chestnuts, bring to the boil and simmer for 5 minutes.

Cucumber Sauce

Makes 450 ml/¾ pt

75 g/3 oz Butter or margarine
1 Cucumber, peeled, seeds removed and sliced
1 Small onion, chopped
15 g/½ oz Plain flour
300 ml/½ pt Water, hot

Melt the butter or margarine in a saucepan and fry the cucumber and onion until browned. Mix the flour into the water and add to the pan, stirring well until the sauce thickens. Cook for a further 3 minutes.

Curry Sauce

Makes 450 ml/¾ pt

50 g/2 oz Butter or margarine
1 Onion, finely chopped
15 ml/1 tbsp Curry powder
15 g/½ oz Plain flour
300 ml/½ pt Milk
150 ml/¼ pt Chicken Stock (page 24)
30 ml/2 tbsp Sweet chutney, chopped
Salt and pepper

Melt the butter or margarine and fry the onion until soft but not browned. Stir in the curry powder and flour and cook for 2 minutes. Stir in the milk and stock, bring to the boil and simmer until thickened, stirring continuously. Add the chutney and season to taste with salt and pepper. Serve with plain vegetables or chicken.

Horseradish Sauce

Makes 150 ml/¼ pt

30 ml/2 tbsp Fresh horseradish, grated
5 ml/1 tsp Caster sugar
10 ml/2 tsp White vinegar
Pinch of salt
Pinch of mustard
150 ml/¼ pt Double cream. lightly whipped

Mix together the horseradish, sugar, vinegar, salt and mustard. Fold the mixture into the whipped cream and chill before serving with beef or smoked fish dishes.

Dill Sauce

Makes 300 ml/½ pt

6 Dill sprigs
150 ml/¼ pt Single cream
1 Egg yolk
5 ml/1 tsp Dijon mustard
Pinch of salt
150 ml/¼ pt Olive oil
10 ml/2 tsp White wine vinegar

Chop 15 ml/1 tbsp dill leaves and put the remaining sprigs and the cream in a saucepan, bring to the boil, then remove from the heat and leave to infuse for 15 minutes. Strain and leave to cool.

Whisk the egg yolk, mustard and salt, then gradually whisk in the oil a little at a time. Stir in the wine vinegar. Stir in the cream and chopped dill and serve with vegetable dishes.

Italian Sauce

Makes 450 ml/¾ pt

25 g/1 oz Butter or margarine
2 Shallots, chopped
50 g/2 oz Mushrooms, sliced
1 Bay leaf
2.5 ml/½ tsp Chopped parsley
15 ml/1 tbsp Plain flour
300 ml/½ pt Dry white wine
150 ml/¼ pt Chicken or Vegetable
  Stock (page 24)

Melt the butter or margarine and fry the shallots, mushrooms, bay leaf and parsley for about 3 minutes. Stir in the flour, wine and stock, bring to the boil and simmer for 5 minutes until the sauce has reduced and thickened. Remove the bay leaf before serving with meat or fish dishes.

Madeira Sauce

Makes 450 ml/¾ pt

25 g/1 oz Butter or margarine
25 g/1 oz Plain flour
150 ml/¼ pt Milk, hot
150 ml/¼ pt Vegetable Stock
  (page 24)
150 ml/¼ pt Madeira
Salt and pepper

Melt the butter or margarine in a saucepan, add the flour and cook for 2 to 3 minutes, stirring continuously. Continue stirring as you add the milk and stock, bring to the boil and stir until quite smooth, then add the Madeira and cook for a further 4 minutes. Season to taste with salt and pepper and serve with hot ham or bacon dishes.

Marrow Sauce

Makes 450 ml/¾ pt

1 Small marrow, peeled and diced
150 ml/¼ pt Brown Sauce (page 226)

Boil the marrow with a little water until tender. Drain and mash to a pulp. Stir it into the sauce and bring to the boil, stirring. Add a little hot water if necessary to make a pouring consistency. Serve with haricot beans or lentils.

Spanish Sauce

Makes 450 ml/¾ pt

| 25 g/1 oz Butter or margarine |
| 50 g/2 oz Bacon, finely chopped |
| 1 Onion, sliced |
| 1 Carrot, sliced |
| 50 g/2 oz Mushrooms, sliced |
| 25 g/1 oz Plain flour |
| 300 ml/½ pt Vegetable Stock (page 24) |
| 2 Tomatoes, skinned and quartered |
| 30 ml/2 tbsp Sherry |
| Salt and pepper |

Melt the butter or margarine in a saucepan and fry the bacon, onion, carrot and mushrooms until just browned. Stir in the flour and cook slowly until the mixture is smooth and browned. Add the stock, stir well, and simmer for 30 minutes. Add the tomatoes and sherry and cook for a further 10 minutes. Strain, season to taste with salt and pepper and reheat before serving.

Spinach Sauce

Makes 450 ml/¾ pt

| 450 g/1 lb Spinach |
| 15 ml/1 tbsp Plain flour |
| 15 ml/1 tbsp Butter or margarine |
| Salt and pepper |

Steam the spinach very gently with no added water, then purée in a food processor or blender. Mix the flour and butter or margarine and stir it into the sauce until thickened. Season to taste with salt and pepper and serve with roast meat or poultry.

Mint Sauce

Makes 150 ml/¼ pt

| 60 ml/4 tbsp Chopped fresh mint |
| 10 ml/2 tsp Sugar |
| 15 ml/1 tbsp Water, boiling |
| 30 ml/2 tbsp Vinegar |

Mix the mint, sugar and water and stir until the sugar melts. Add the vinegar and leave to stand for at least 2 hours before serving with lamb.

Orange Mint Sauce

Makes 150 ml/¼ pt

| 1 Bunch of mint |
| 15 ml/1 tbsp Boiling water |
| 10 ml/2 tsp Caster sugar |
| 30 ml/ 2tbsp White wine vinegar |
| 60 ml/4 tbsp Orange juice |

Chop the mint in a food processor or blender, then add the remaining ingredients and blend again. Serve with lamb or other meats.

Tartare Sauce

Makes 150 ml/¼ pt

| 150 ml/¼ pt Mayonnaise (page 250) |
| 5 ml/1 tsp Chopped gherkin |
| 5 ml/1 tsp Chopped parsley |
| 5 ml/1 tsp Chopped, drained capers |
| 5 ml/1 tsp Chopped chives |
| 10 ml/2 tsp Lemon juice |

Mix all the ingredients together and leave to stand for at least 1 hour before serving with fried fish or meat.

229

Tomato Sauce

Makes 300 ml/½ pt

6 Tomatoes
1 Onion, finely chopped
1 Bay leaf
120 ml/4 fl oz Water
25 g/1 oz Plain flour
250 ml/8 fl oz Vegetable Stock
  (page 24)
50 g/2 oz Butter or margarine, cut
  into pieces
10 ml/2 tsp Sugar
Salt and pepper

Place the tomatoes, onion, bay leaf and water in a saucepan, bring to the boil and simmer for 30 minutes until the tomatoes are tender. Purée in a food processor or blender and pass through a sieve, then return the purée to the pan. Mix the flour to a paste with a little of the stock, then add this with the remaining stock to the tomato purée. Reheat and season to taste with sugar, salt and pepper, cooking gently until the sauce thickens. Strain before serving.

Tomato and Lentil Sauce

Makes 300 ml/½ pt

100 g/4 oz Lentils
15 ml/1 tbsp Oil
1 Onion, sliced
½ Green pepper, sliced
400 g/14 oz Canned tomatoes
5 ml/1 tsp Mixed herbs
5 ml/1 tsp Basil
Salt and pepper

Place the lentils in a saucepan and just cover with water. Bring to the boil and simmer for 30 minutes until tender, then drain. Heat the oil in a saucepan and fry the onion and pepper until soft but not browned. Add the tomatoes and simmer for 10 minutes. Add the lentils and herbs and season to taste with salt and pepper. Purée in a food processor or blender and serve with pasta.

Yoghurt Sauce with Herbs

Makes 150 ml/¼ pt

1 Garlic clove, crushed
150 ml/¼ pt Natural yoghurt
15 ml/1 tbsp Chopped dill
15 ml/1 tbsp Chopped tarragon
Salt and pepper

Crush the garlic clove well and beat it into the yoghurt until well combined. Mix in the herbs and season to taste with salt and pepper. Chill before serving with grilled or roast meats.

Minted Yoghurt

Makes 150 ml/¼ pt

½ Cucumber, peeled and grated
150 ml/¼ pt Natural yoghurt
1 Garlic clove, crushed
30 ml/2 tbsp Chopped mint
Salt and pepper

Squeeze any excess water out of the cucumber, then purée all the ingredients together. Chill before serving with roast lamb.

Sweet White Sauce

Makes 300 ml/½ pt

50 g/2 oz Butter or margarine
10 ml/2 tsp Cornflour
5 ml/1 tsp Caster sugar
300 ml/½ pt Milk

Melt the butter or margarine in a saucepan and stir in the flour. Cook for 1 minute, then stir in the sugar and milk, bring to the boil, stirring continuously, and cook for a further 3 minutes.

Nut Sauce

Makes 300 ml/½ pt

300 ml/½ pt Sweet White Sauce
  (page 231)
15 g/1 tbsp Mixed nuts, finely
  chopped

Make the white sauce, stir in the nuts and heat through for 3 or 4 minutes.

Custard Sauce

Makes 300 ml/½ pt

300 ml/½ pt Milk
1 Egg yolk, beaten
25 g/1 oz Caster sugar

Bring the milk to the boil, then allow it to cool for about 3 minutes. Mix in the egg yolk and return the milk to the heat, stirring gently but not allowing the custard to boil. Add the sugar and serve.

Sweet Jam Sauce

Makes 300 ml/½ pt

300 ml/½ pt Water
5 ml/1 tsp Cornflour
45 ml/3 tbsp Raspberry or
  strawberry jam
5 ml/1 tsp Lemon juice

Mix the water and cornflour and bring it to the boil, stirring. Add the jam and lemon juice and boil for 1 minute, then rub the sauce through a fine sieve. Serve hot or cold.

Carob Syrup

Makes 300 ml/½ pt

100 g/4 oz Carob powder
200 ml/8 fl oz Water

Mix the carob and water in a small saucepan, bring to the boil and simmer, stirring, for 8 minutes or until the syrup is smooth. Leave to cool, cover and store in the fridge.

Carob Sauce

Makes 200 ml/8 fl oz

100 ml/4 fl oz Carob Syrup
  (page 231)
20 g/¾ oz Butter or margarine
60 ml/4 tbsp Honey
1 Egg, beaten
5 ml/1 tsp Vanilla essence

Mix all the ingredients and cook over a low heat until thick and smooth. Leave to cool, then store in the fridge.

Chocolate Sauce

Makes 300 ml/½ pt

300 ml/½ pt Milk
10 ml/2 tsp Cocoa
1 Egg yolk
15 ml/1 tbsp Caster sugar
A few drops of vanilla essence

Bring the milk and cocoa to the boil. Beat the egg yolk well with the sugar. Pour the boiling milk on to the egg and sugar mixture, whisking well. Return the mixture to the pan and stir over a low heat until the sauce boils. Add a few drops of vanilla essence and serve.

Lemon Sauce

Makes 600 ml/1 pt

5 ml/1 tsp Cornflour
600 ml/1 pt Milk
1 Egg yolk
Grated rind and juice of 1 lemon
50 g/2 oz Caster sugar

Mix the cornflour with all but 30 ml/2 tbsp milk. Beat the remaining milk with the egg yolk. Bring the cornflour, milk, lemon rind and juice and sugar to the boil. Remove from the heat and stir in the egg yolk and milk. Reheat but do not allow to boil.

Sauce Cassis

Makes 450 ml/¾ pt

225 g/8 oz Canned blackcurrants
Water
10 ml/2 tsp Cornflour

Purée the fruit in a food processor or blender, then make up to 450 ml/¾ pt with water in a saucepan. Mix the cornflour with 15 ml/1 tbsp purée then mix this into the purée. Bring to the boil, stirring, then serve warm or pour on fruit and leave to set.

Orange Sauce

Makes 600 ml/1 pt

5 ml/1 tsp Cornflour
600 ml/1 pt Milk
1 Egg yolk
Grated rind and juice of 1 orange
25 g/1 oz Caster sugar

Mix the cornflour with all but 30 ml/2 tbsp milk. Beat the remaining milk with the egg yolk. Bring the cornflour, milk, orange rind and juice and sugar to the boil. Remove from the heat and stir in the egg yolk and milk. Reheat but do not allow to boil.

Fluffy Almond Sauce

Makes 600 ml/1 pt

25 g/1 oz Ground almonds
600 ml/1 pt Milk
15 ml/1 tbsp Plain flour
15 ml/1 tbsp Caster sugar
1 Egg, separated

Beat the almonds, milk, flour, sugar and egg yolk together in a saucepan, bring to the boil and cook, stirring until the sauce thickens. Allow to cool slightly, then whisk well. Whisk the egg white until stiff, then fold it into the sauce and serve warm.

Chive Butter

Makes 50 g/2 oz

50 g/2 oz Unsalted butter or
  margarine
30 ml/2 tbsp Chopped chives
Juice of ½ lemon
Salt and pepper

Purée all the ingredients together in
food processor or blender. Chill
before serving with grilled meats.

Garlic Butter

Makes 50 g/2 oz

50 g/2 oz Unsalted butter or
  margarine
2 Garlic cloves, crushed
30 ml/2 tbsp Chopped parsley
Juice of ½ lemon

Purée all the ingredients together in
a food processor or blender. Chill
before serving with grilled pork or on
garlic bread.

Peanut Butter

Makes 225 g/8 oz

225 g/8 oz Peanuts
10 ml/2 tsp Oil

Purée the peanuts in a food processor or blender for 20 seconds
until they form a paste. Scrape down,
add the oil and process for a further
20 seconds. Store in a screw-top jar
in the fridge.

Herb Butter

Makes 100 g/4 oz

100 g/4 oz Unsalted butter or
  margarine
10 ml/2 tsp Chopped mint
10 ml/2 tsp Chopped dill
10 ml/2 tsp Chopped tarragon
10 ml/2 tsp Chopped chives
15 ml/1 tbsp Lemon juice
Salt and pepper

Purée together all the ingredients in
a food processor or blender, seasoning to taste with salt and pepper. Chill
before serving with grilled or roast
meats.

Sage Butter

Makes 50 g/2 oz

50 g/2 oz Unsalted butter or
  margarine
15 ml/1 tbsp Chopped sage
5 ml/1 tsp Lemon juice
5 ml/1 tsp Finely chopped onion
Salt and pepper

Purée all the ingredients together in
a food processor or blender. Chill
before serving with grilled meats.

Apple and Walnut Stuffing

Makes 225 g/8 oz

25 g/1 oz Breadcrumbs
50 g/2 oz Walnuts, chopped
1 Onion, chopped
2 Eating apples, peeled and
  chopped
30 ml/2 tbsp Chopped parsley
25 g/1 oz Butter or margarine,
  melted
1 Egg, beaten
Salt and pepper

Mix all the ingredients together thoroughly and season to taste with salt and pepper. Use to stuff poultry or pork or make into small balls and bake or fry.

Celery and Apple Stuffing

Makes 100 g/4 oz

25 g/1 oz Breadcrumbs
1 Cooking apple, peeled and
  chopped
2 Celery stalks, finely chopped
25 g/1 oz Mushrooms, chopped
1 Egg, beaten
Pinch of paprika
Salt and pepper

Mix the breadcrumbs, apple, celery and mushrooms. Season the egg with paprika, salt and pepper and use it to bind the stuffing ingredients. Use to stuff pork or other meats.

Herb Stuffing

Makes 175 g/6 oz

100 g/4 oz Breadcrumbs
50 g/2 oz Suet
30 ml/2 tbsp Chopped parsley
2.5 ml/½ tsp Mixed herbs
Pinch of grated lemon rind
Pinch of cayenne pepper
Salt and pepper
1 Egg, beaten

Mix all the ingredients together well. Use to stuff chicken, meat or vegetables or to make stuffing balls for frying.

Kidney and Mushroom Stuffing

Makes 225 g/8 oz

15 g/½ oz Butter or margarine
100 g/4 oz Lambs' kidney
25 g/1 oz Mushrooms, chopped
15 g/½ oz Pistachio nuts,
  chopped
25 g/1 oz Cooked long-grain rice
Pinch of thyme
Pinch of rosemary

Melt the butter or margarine and fry the kidney until just soft, then chop. Return them to the pan with the mushrooms, nuts, rice and herbs and stir well. Use to stuff meat or poultry.

Tomato and Pepper Stuffing

Makes 100 g/4 oz

| 25 g/1 oz Butter or margarine |
| 1 Small leek, sliced |
| 1 Garlic clove, crushed |
| ½ Red pepper, chopped |
| 15 ml/1 tbsp Chopped parsley |
| 25 g/1 oz Breadcrumbs |
| 2 Tomatoes, skinned and chopped |
| Salt and pepper |

Melt the butter or margarine and fry the leek until soft. Add the garlic and fry until browned, then remove from the heat. Blanch the pepper in boiling water for 2 minutes, then drain and mix into the garlic mixture. Stir in the parsley, breadcrumbs and tomatoes and season to taste with salt and pepper. Use to stuff meat or poultry.

Herby Sausagemeat

Makes 225 g/8 oz

| 25 g/1 oz Breadcrumbs |
| 5 ml/1 tsp Mixed herbs |
| 1 Onion, finely chopped |
| 1 Garlic clove, finely chopped |
| 225 g/8 oz Belly of pork, finely chopped |
| 2.5 ml/1 tsp French mustard |
| 15 ml/1 tbsp Lemon juice |
| 1 Egg, beaten |

Mix all the ingredients together well and bind with the beaten egg. The finished sausagemeat holds its shape well and can be used for stuffings and sausage rolls.

Salads and Salad Dressings

Salads need not mean just lettuce, tomato and sliced cucumber! Even the humble lettuce now has a whole family of new relations in the shops—from lollo rosso to oak leaf and frissée—so salads can be as adventurous as you like, and use any ingredients you prefer. Don't be afraid to experiment, and use these recipes as a guide to some excellent taste combinations. If you don't make your own mayonnaise, just use any good quality brand.

Avocado and Bacon Salad

Serves 4

6 Streaky bacon rashers, rinded and chopped

2 Avocado pears, peeled and stoned

15 ml/1 tbsp Lemon juice

30 ml/2 tbsp Olive oil

Salt and pepper

Fry the bacon pieces until crisp. Slice 1½ avocados and place the remainder in a food processor or blender. Purée with the lemon juice, oil and salt and pepper to taste until thick. Arrange the avocado slices around a serving dish and pile the purée in the centre. Sprinkle the bacon pieces on top and chill before serving.

Red Bean and Broccoli Salad

Serves 4

225 g/8 oz Broccoli florets

425 g/15 oz Canned red kidney beans, drained

1 Red onion, sliced into rings

2 Celery stalks, chopped

150 ml/¼ pt French Dressing (page 249)

Salt and pepper

Blanch the broccoli in boiling salted water for 2 minutes, then drain well and mix with the remaining salad ingredients. Toss in the French dressing and season to taste with salt and pepper.

Asparagus and Soya Bean Salad

Serves 4

100 g/4 oz Soya beans, soaked
   overnight
200 g/7 oz Canned asparagus tips,
   drained and chopped
2 Celery stalks, chopped
1 Carrot, grated
30 ml/2 tbsp Oil and Vinegar
   Dressing (page 249)
15 ml/1 tbsp Chopped basil
Salt and pepper

Drain the beans, then put them in a saucepan, cover with water, bring to the boil and simmer for 2 hours until cooked. Drain and leave to cool.

Mix all the remaining ingredients with the cold beans and season to taste with salt and pepper.

Mexican Salad

Serves 4

225 g/8 oz Cauliflower florets
450 g/1 lb Canned red kidney beans,
   drained
4 Onions, sliced into rings
100 g/4 oz Canned tomatoes, finely
   chopped
2.5 ml/½ tsp Chilli sauce
2.5 ml/½ tsp Soy sauce
10 ml/2 tsp Cumin seeds

Cook the cauliflower florets in boiling water for 3 minutes, then drain and mix with the kidney beans and onions. Mix together the tomatoes, sauces and cumin seeds. Toss the salad in the dressing and serve.

Quick Bean Salad

Serves 4

Cooked French beans, cut into
   2.5 cm/1 in pieces
425 g/15 oz Canned kidney beans,
   drained and rinsed
425 g/15 oz Canned butter beans,
   drained and rinsed
45 ml/3 tbsp Oil
30 ml/2 tbsp White wine vinegar
2.5 ml/½ tsp French mustard
Salt and pepper
2 Tomatoes, cut into 8
15 ml/1 tbsp Chopped parsley

Pile the beans into a salad bowl. Mix the oil, wine vinegar and mustard and season to taste with salt and pepper. Toss the salad in the dressing. Arrange the tomatoes round the edge of the bowl and sprinkle the parsley on top.

Carrot and Orange Salad

Serves 4

8 Carrots, grated
2 Oranges, peeled and diced
100 g/8 oz Walnuts, chopped
30 ml/2 tbsp Chopped chervil
15 ml/1 tbsp Lemon juice
15 ml/1 tbsp Groundnut oil
Salt and pepper

Mix the carrots, oranges, walnuts and chervil. Whisk together the lemon juice and oil, season to taste with salt and pepper and pour over the salad.

237

Bean Sprout and Fruit Salad

Serves 4

175 g/6 oz Pasta shapes

Salt

200 g/7 oz Canned pineapple
chunks

120 ml/4 fl oz Oil

30 ml/2 tbsp Orange juice

15 ml/1 tbsp Soy sauce

Pinch of ground ginger

2 Carrots, shredded

½ Cucumber, sliced

175 g/6 oz Beansprouts

Cook the pasta in boiling salted water until just tender, then drain. Drain the pineapple, reserving the juice. Mix 30 ml/2 tbsp juice with the oil, orange juice, soy sauce and ginger and mix with the pasta while the pasta is still warm. Leave to cool. Add the carrots, cucumber and pineapple chunks and toss, then add the beansprouts and mix in lightly.

Israeli Carrot Salad

Serves 4

300 ml/½ pt Orange juice

6 Carrots, grated

½ White cabbage, shredded

100 g/4 oz Raisins

50 g/2 oz Sesame seeds

1 Orange, peeled and sliced

Purée the orange juice and carrots in a food processor or blender. Mix in the cabbage, raisins and sesame seeds, turn into a serving bowl and garnish with the orange slices.

Sprout and Chestnut Salad

Serves 4

8 Brussels sprouts, chopped

1 Dessert apple, chopped

100 g/4 oz Cooked chestnuts, chopped

5 ml/1 tsp Chopped parsley

15 ml/1 tbsp Mayonnaise

Salt and pepper

Mix all the ingredients together well and season to taste with salt and pepper.

Broccoli Niçoise

Serves 4

450 g/1 lb Broccoli florets

200 g/7 oz Canned tuna fish,
drained and flaked

2 Hard-boiled eggs, cut into wedges

50 g/2 oz Canned anchovy fillets,
drained

8 Black olives, stoned

150 ml/¼ pt French Dressing
(page 249)

Cook the broccoli in boiling salted water until just tender, then drain and rinse in cold water. Arrange the broccoli over the base of a serving dish and place the tuna on top. Arrange the eggs, anchovy fillets and olives on the tuna and pour over the French dressing.

Cauliflower Salad

Serves 4

1 Small cauliflower, divided into florets

60 ml/4 tbsp French Dressing (page 249)

3 Celery stalks, chopped

2 Red pimentos, chopped

2 Gherkins, chopped

1 Shallot, finely chopped

10 ml/2 tsp Orange juice

Salt and pepper

Marinate the cauliflower in the French dressing for 2 hours, then drain and mix with the remaining ingredients and season to taste with salt and pepper.

Minted Courgette Salad

Serves 4

450 g/1 lb Courgettes, finely chopped

10 ml/2 tsp Salt

50 g/2 oz Flaked almonds

100 g/4 oz Sultanas

90 ml/6 tbsp Olive oil

30 ml/2 tbsp Lemon juice

15 ml/2 tbsp Chopped mint

Pepper

Put the courgettes in a colander, sprinkle with the salt and leave for 1 hour, then rinse, drain and pat dry. Mix with the almonds and sultanas. Mix the oil, lemon juice and mint and toss the salad in the dressing. Season well with pepper.

Cucumber Riata

Serves 4

½ Cucumber, peeled and grated

150 ml/¼ pt Natural yoghurt

30 ml/2 tbsp Chopped chives

Mix the cucumber and yoghurt and sprinkle with the chives. Serve with curry as a side dish.

Lemon Fennel Salad

Serves 4

1 Lemon

30 ml/2 tbsp Olive oil

30 ml/2 tbsp Natural yoghurt

10 ml/2 tsp Sugar

Salt and pepper

1 Head of fennel, sliced

6 Black olives, stoned

Cut the lemon in half. Cut half into thick slices and trim away the peel. Purée the flesh with 15 ml/1 tsp juice from the other half lemon, the oil, yoghurt, sugar, salt and pepper. Process until thick. Toss the fennel slices in the dressing and garnish with the olives.

Green Salad with Blue Cheese

Serves 4

100 g/4 oz White cabbage, shredded
100 g/4 oz Broccoli florets
100 g/4 oz Courgettes, thinly sliced
1 Green pepper, sliced
1 Celery stalk, sliced
150 ml/¼ pt Blue Cheese Dressing
   (page 250)
50 g/2 oz Blue cheese, crumbled

Mix all the salad ingredients together well and pour on the dressing. Top with the crumbled blue cheese and chill well before serving.

Mushroom and Watercress Salad

Serves 4

60 ml/4 tbsp Oil
15 ml/1 tbsp White wine vinegar
Salt and pepper
350 g/12 oz Mushrooms, sliced
100 g/4 oz Watercress leaves
15 ml/1 tbsp Chopped parsley
15 ml/1 tbsp Chopped chives

Beat the oil and vinegar and season to taste with salt and pepper. Toss the mushrooms, watercress and parsley. Pour over the dressing just before serving, toss well and sprinkle with chives.

Potato and Frankfurter Salad

Serves 4

900 g/2 lb Small new potatoes
6 Frankfurters
5 Spring onions, sliced
50 g/2 oz Flaked almonds, toasted
15 ml/1 tbsp Chopped chives
½ Red pepper, chopped
90 ml/6 tbsp Mayonnaise (page 250)
45 ml/3 tbsp Natural yoghurt
Few drops of tabasco sauce
Salt and pepper

Cook the potatoes in boiling salted water until just cooked, then drain. Cook the frankfurters according to the instructions on the packet, then cut them into bite-sized pieces. Mix the potatoes, frankfurters, onions, almonds, chives and pepper. Mix the mayonnaise, yoghurt and tabasco sauce and season to taste with salt and pepper. Toss the salad in the dressing and turn into a serving dish.

Bacon and Potato Salad

Serves 4

4 Bacon rashers, rinded
75 g/3 oz Cheddar cheese, diced
2 Cocktail gherkins, chopped
1 Onion, finely chopped
350 g/12 oz Boiled potatoes, diced
5 ml/1 tsp Chopped parsley
30 ml/2 tbsp Olive oil
15 ml/1 tbsp Vinegar

Grill the bacon until crisp, then dice it and leave to cool. Mix together the cheese, gherkins, onion, potatoes and parsley, then mix in the cooled bacon. Mix together the oil and vinegar and sprinkle over the salad.

Provençale Potato Salad

Serves 4

50 g/2 oz Canned anchovy fillets
2.5 ml/½ tsp Mixed herbs
5 ml/1 tsp Chopped parsley
15 ml/1 tbsp Olive oil
450 g/1 lb Potatoes, sliced
1 Onion, sliced
225 g/8 oz Tomatoes, sliced

Mash the anchovies with the herbs and parsley. Arrange one-third of the potatoes over the base of a greased 1.2 litre/2 pt ovenproof dish, cover with half the onion and half the tomatoes, spread with half the anchovy paste, then repeat the layers. Top with potatoes. Dot with butter, then bake in a preheated oven at 190°C/375°F/gas mark 5 for 1 hour until cooked through and golden brown. Leave to cool before serving.

Spring Potato Salad with Tofu Dressing

Serves 4

50 g/2 oz Green lentils
Water
1 Bay leaf
1 Garlic clove, roughly chopped
225 g/8 oz New potatoes, diced
½ Cucumber, diced
2 Tomatoes, cut into 8
3 Hard-boiled eggs, cut into 8
100 g/4 oz Tofu
10 ml/2 tsp White wine vinegar
5 ml/1 tsp French mustard
2.5 ml/½ tsp Soft brown sugar
5 ml/1 tsp Olive oil
15 ml/1 tbsp Chopped tarragon
Salt and pepper

Put the lentils in a small saucepan, just cover with water and add the bay leaf and garlic. Bring to the boil and simmer for about 20 minutes until soft, then drain and discard the bay leaf. Boil the potatoes until tender, then drain. Combine the lentils, potatoes, cucumber and tomatoes in a salad bowl and arrange the eggs round the edge. Purée the tofu, wine vinegar, mustard, sugar, oil and tarragon in a food processor or blender and pour over the salad. Season to taste with salt and freshly ground black pepper.

Domates Salata

Serves 4

350 g/12 oz Cooked new potatoes, diced

225 g/8 oz Tomatoes, skinned, seeded and chopped

1 Onion, finely chopped

50 g/2 oz Black olives, stoned

45 ml/3 tbsp Mayonnaise (page 250)

30 ml/2 tbsp Milk

Black pepper

Toss all the vegetables together. Mix the mayonnaise with the milk and season to taste with freshly ground black pepper. Toss lightly with the vegetables and chill before serving.

Red Cabbage Slaw

Serves 4

1 Small white cabbage, shredded

2 Carrots, grated

1 Red pepper, chopped

2.5 ml/½ tsp Celery seed

120 ml/4 fl oz Cider vinegar

30 ml/2 tbsp Honey

45 ml/3 tbsp Mayonnaise (page 250)

Mix the salad ingredients together well. Mix the cider vinegar, honey and mayonnaise and toss the salad in the dressing.

Cold Herbed Rice

Serves 4

100 g/4 oz Long-grain rice

Salt and pepper

30 ml/2 tbsp Olive oil

10 ml/2 tsp White wine vinegar

5 ml/1 tsp Lemon juice

45 ml/3 tbsp Chopped parsley

45 ml/3 tbsp Chopped chives

Cook the rice in boiling salted water until just tender, then drain and rinse in cold water. Mix in the oil, wine vinegar and lemon juice and leave to cool, then stir in the herbs.

Rice and Vegetable Salad

Serves 4

100 g/4 oz Long-grain rice

Salt

90 ml/6 tbsp French Dressing (page 249)

1 Carrot, grated

50 g/2 oz Cooked peas

2 Celery stalks, chopped

1 Red-skinned apple, cored and chopped

15 ml/1 tbsp Chopped chives

10 ml/2 tsp Chopped parsley

Pepper

Cook the rice in boiling salted water until just tender, then drain and rinse in hot water. Mix with enough dressing to moisten it well, then stir in the vegetables, apples, chives and parsley and season lightly with salt and pepper. Turn into a serving bowl and chill before serving.

Hot Spinach Salad

Serves 4

450 g/1 lb Spinach, trimmed
60 ml/4 tbsp Olive oil
50 g/2 oz Flaked almonds
4 Streaky bacon rashers, rinded and
  chopped
45 ml/3 tbsp Lemon juice
Salt and pepper

Arrange the spinach in a salad bowl.
Heat the oil and fry the almonds and
bacon until golden brown. Add the
lemon juice and season to taste with
salt and pepper. Pour over the spinach,
toss well and serve immediately.

Sweetcorn Salad

Serves 4

450 g/1 lb Canned sweetcorn
½ Onion, chopped
50 g/2 oz Sultanas
1 Orange pepper, chopped
60 ml/4 tbsp Oil
15 ml/1 tbsp White wine vinegar
15 ml/1 tbsp Worcestershire sauce
15 ml/1 tbsp Tomato ketchup
15 ml/1 tbsp Soft brown sugar
15 ml/1 tbsp Chopped chives

Mix the sweetcorn, onion, sultanas
and pepper. Mix the dressing ingredients and toss the salad in the
dressing. Serve sprinkled with chives.

Sunshine Salad

Serves 4

2 Hard-boiled eggs
200 g/7 oz Canned sweetcorn,
  drained
50 g/2 oz Mushrooms, chopped
100 g/4 oz Carrots, grated
5 ml/1 tsp Lemon juice
2.5 ml/½ tsp French mustard
15 ml/1 tbsp Soured cream
15 ml/1 tbsp Chopped parsley
Pepper

Separate the yolks from the whites of
the eggs. Chop the whites, mix with
the sweetcorn and mushrooms and
turn into a serving dish. Mix the
carrots with the lemon juice then
arrange them round the bowl. Mix
the mustard, crumbled egg yolks and
soured cream and pour the dressing
over the salad. Serve garnished with
parsley and seasoned to taste with
pepper.

Californian Fruit Salad

Serves 4

1 Iceberg lettuce, shredded
200 g/7 oz Canned pineapple
  chunks, drained
200 g/7 oz Canned peaches, drained
4 Celery stalks, chopped
25 g/1 oz Flaked almonds
30 ml/2 tbsp Mayonnaise (page 250)

Arrange the lettuce in the base of a
salad bowl. Mix the remaining ingredients together well and spoon into
the bowl.

Rainbow Salad

Serves 4

120 ml/4 fl oz Olive oil
60 ml/4 tbsp Lemon juice
2.5 ml/½ tsp Caster sugar
Salt and pepper
2 Carrots, grated
100 g/4 oz Button mushrooms,
  sliced
½ Cucumber, seeded and cut into
  matchsticks
5 Tomatoes, quartered
4 Celery stalks, sliced
2 Spring onions, chopped
15 ml/1 tbsp Chopped chives
15 ml/1 tbsp Chopped parsley
½ Onion, cut into rings

Mix the oil, lemon juice, sugar, salt and pepper. Toss the carrots with 30 ml/2 tbsp dressing and arrange in a strip on a flat platter. Lay the mushrooms, cucumber, tomatoes, celery and spring onions in strips alongside. Sprinkle each with one of the garnishes, either chives, parsley or onion rings. Serve the remaining dressing in a jug.

Waldorf Salad

Serves 4

2 Red dessert apples, sliced
30 ml/2 tbsp Lemon juice
50 g/2 oz Walnuts, chopped
½ Head of Chinese leaf, sliced
90 ml/6 tbsp Olive oil
45 ml/3 tbsp White wine vinegar
5 ml/1 tsp Caster sugar
Salt and pepper

Sprinkle the sliced apples with lemon juice, then mix them with the walnuts and Chinese leaf. Whisk or purée the oil, wine vinegar, sugar, salt and pepper until thick and well blended. Toss the salad in the dressing just before serving.

Danish Chef's Salad

Serves 4

½ Cos lettuce, sliced
1 Bunch of radishes, sliced
¼ Cucumber, sliced
1 Onion, sliced
225 g/8 oz Cooked ham, shredded
100 g/4 oz Danish Blue cheese,
  cubed
Salt and pepper
Pinch of mustard powder
Pinch of caster sugar
60 ml/4 tbsp Oil
30 ml/2 tbsp White wine vinegar

Layer the lettuce, radishes, cucumber, onion, ham and cheese in a glass serving bowl and toss lightly. Put the seasonings, oil and wine vinegar in a screw-top jar and shake well to mix. Shake again and toss lightly with the salad just before serving.

Crunchy Pear Salad

Serves 4

1 Small iceberg lettuce, shredded
2 Pears, halved and cored
15 ml/1 tbsp Lemon juice
2 Celery stalks, chopped
50 g/2 oz Walnuts, chopped
50 g/2 oz Raisins
225 g/8 oz Cottage cheese
150 ml/¼ pt Mayonnaise (page 250)

Arrange the lettuce on a serving plate. Brush the pears with the lemon juice to prevent them from going brown and arrange them on the plate. Mix the remaining ingredients well and pile them on to the pears.

Pineapple Sauerkraut Salad

Serves 4

100 g/4 oz Bottled sauerkraut
4 Pineapple slices, diced
4 Tomatoes, skinned, seeded and chopped
1 Box of cress
450 ml/¾ pt Natural yoghurt
Juice of 1 orange
15 ml/1 tbsp Worcestershire sauce
Salt and pepper

Mix the sauerkraut, pineapple, tomatoes and cress. Mix the yoghurt with the orange juice and Worcestershire sauce and season to taste with salt and pepper. Toss the salad in the dressing and serve.

Pineapple Slaw

Serves 4

450 g/1 lb Firm white cabbage, shredded
1 Pineapple, cored and cubed
1 Dessert apple, cored and quartered
75 g/3 oz Walnut halves
60 ml/4 tbsp Mayonnaise (page 250)
120 ml/ 4 fl oz Natural yoghurt
10 ml/2 tsp Honey
15 ml/1 tbsp Lemon or orange juice
Salt and pepper

Mix the cabbage, pineapple and apple. Reserve a few walnuts for garnish and mix in the remainder. Mix the mayonnaise and yoghurt, then stir in the honey and lemon or orange juice and season to taste with salt and pepper. Toss the slaw with the dressing, cover and refrigerate. Toss again and garnish just before serving.

Madrid Salad

Serves 4

| 8 Hard-boiled eggs, cut into wedges |
| 1 Radicchio, shredded |
| 1 Small iceberg lettuce, shredded |
| 2 Large tomatoes, diced |
| 100 g/4 oz Black olives, stoned |
| 30 ml/2 tbsp Pickled capers |
| 225 g/8 oz Goats' cheese, flaked |
| 175 g/6 oz Feta cheese, flaked |
| 1 Large onion, sliced |
| 90 ml/6 tbsp Olive oil |
| 90 ml/6 tbsp Red wine vinegar |
| 5 ml/1 tsp Oregano |
| 15 ml/1 tbsp Chopped lemon balm |
| 15 ml/1 tbspChopped chives |
| 15 ml/1 tbsp Chopped mint |
| Salt and pepper |

Gently toss together all the salad ingredients. Mix the oil with the remaining dressing ingredients and season to taste with salt and pepper. Toss the salad in the dressing and serve.

Scandinavian Herring Salad

Serves 4

| 4 Cooked beetroot, diced |
| 4 Cooked potatoes, diced |
| 3 Gherkins, diced |
| 4 Rollmop herrings with onions in the centre, chopped |
| 30 ml/2 tbsp Mayonnaise (page 250) |
| Salt and pepper |

Mix the ingredients together well and season to taste with salt and pepper.

Smoked Haddock Salad

Serves 4

| 225 g/8 oz Smoked haddock, flaked |
| Salt and pepper |
| 15 ml/1 tbsp Chopped dill |
| 150 ml/¼ pt Mayonnaise (page 250) |
| ½ Iceberg lettuce, shredded |
| 1 Bunch of watercress |
| 2 Hard-boiled eggs, quartered |
| 1 Cooked beetroot, diced |

Season the fish to taste. Mix the dill with the mayonnaise and stir in the fish. Arrange the lettuce and watercress round a serving dish and pile the fish in the centre. Garnish with the hard-boiled eggs and beetroot just before serving.

Smoked Cod Mayonnaise

Serves 4

| 450 g/1 lb Smoked cod fillets, cooked and flaked |
| 300 ml/½ pt Mayonnaise (page 250) |
| 225 g/8 oz Potato salad |
| 1 Hard-boiled egg, sliced |
| 30 ml/2 tbsp Chopped dill |

Mix the fish with the mayonnaise and pile on to a serving plate. Surround with the potato salad and lay the egg rings decoratively on top. Sprinkle with chopped dill and serve with a green salad.

Variations
This recipe can also be made with cod, haddock, hake or any other white fish.

Lobster Mayonnaise

Serves 4

1 Cooked lobster

1 Cos lettuce, heart reserved and shredded

300 ml/½ pt Mayonnaise (page 250)

2 Hard-boiled eggs, cut into wedges

Remove the flesh from the shell and cut it into equal size pieces. Keep the flesh from the claws whole and put it to one side with the coral for garnishing. Mix the shredded lettuce with the lobster meat and enough mayonnaise to moisten. Pile this into a deep dish or salad bowl. Arrange the hard-boiled eggs around the bowl. Separate the heart of the lettuce and use the leaves with the claw meat and coral to decorate the top of the salad. Pour over the remaining mayonnaise.

Creole Potato Salad

Serves 4

450 g/1 lb Potatoes

100 g/4 oz Shrimps

4 Hard-boiled eggs, chopped

1 Green pepper, chopped

45 ml/3 tbsp French Dressing (page 249)

Salt and pepper

Cook the potatoes in boiling salted water until tender, then drain and chop. Mix with the shrimps while still warm. Mix in the eggs, pepper and French dressing and season to taste with salt and pepper.

Prawn and Mushroom Pasta Salad

Serves 4

175 g/6 oz Pasta shapes

1 Avocado, peeled, stoned and sliced

15 ml/1 tbsp Lemon juice

225 g/8 oz Shelled prawns

100 g/4 oz Button mushrooms, sliced

30 ml/2 tbsp Mayonnaise (page 250)

30 ml/2 tbsp Soured cream

1 Garlic clove, crushed

10 ml/2 tsp Chopped chives

Salt and pepper

Cook the pasta in boiling salted water until just tender, then drain and rinse in cold water. Toss the avocado in the lemon juice, then add it to the pasta. Reserve a few prawns for garnish, then add the remainder to the pasta with the mushrooms. Mix the mayonnaise, cream, garlic and chives and season to taste with salt and pepper. Fold the dressing into the pasta and turn into a serving dish. Chill before serving garnished with the reserved prawns.

Chicken and Spinach Salad

Serves 4

175 g/6 oz Red lentils
60 ml/4 tbsp Corn oil
15 ml/1 tbsp Olive oil
45 ml/3 tbsp Apple juice
1 Garlic clove, crushed
5 ml/1 tsp Wholegrain mustard
Salt and pepper
350 g/12 oz Spinach, trimmed
4 Cooked chicken breasts, skinned
    and sliced
100 g/4 oz Walnuts, toasted

Soak the lentils in hot water for 15 minutes, then drain them and place in a saucepan with 600 ml/1 pt fresh cold water. Bring to the boil, then simmer for 5 minutes. Drain. Mix the oils, apple juice, garlic and mustard and season to taste with salt and pepper. Toss the lentils in a little of the dressing. Arrange the spinach leaves on a serving plate and arrange the chicken on top, leaving a circle in the centre into which to spoon the lentils. Sprinkle with nuts and pour over the remaining dressing.

Smoked Chicken Salad

Serves 4

2 Red-skinned apples, cubed
15 ml/1 tbsp Lemon juice
225 g/8 oz Smoked chicken, cut into
    strips
2 Celery stalks, chopped
1 Red pepper, sliced
½ Green pepper, sliced
50 g/2 oz Walnut halves
60 ml/4 tbsp Olive oil
30 ml/2 tbsp White wine vinegar
10 ml/2 tsp French mustard
Salt and pepper

Toss the apples in the lemon juice to prevent them from going brown. Mix the apples, chicken, celery, peppers and walnuts. Whisk the oil, wine vinegar and mustard and season to taste with salt and pepper. Toss the salad in the dressing just before serving.

Chicken and Almond Salad

Serves 4

350 g/12 oz Cooked chicken, diced
50 g/2 oz Almonds, roasted
300 g/11 oz Canned pineapple
    chunks, drained
½ Green pepper, chopped
½ Red pepper, chopped
2 Small chicory hearts, chopped
30 ml/2 tbsp Mayonnaise (page 250)
Pepper

Mix all the ingredients together and toss in the mayonnaise. Season to taste with pepper.

Curried Chicken Salad

Serves 4

350 g/12 oz Cooked chicken, sliced
2 Bananas, sliced
15 ml/1 tbsp Lemon juice
50 g/2 oz Sultanas
50 g/2 oz Dried apricots, chopped
50 g/2 oz Cashew nuts
45 ml/3 tbsp Mayonnaise (page 250)
½ Onion, finely chopped
5 ml/1 tsp Curry powder
1 Apple, peeled and grated
10 ml/2 tsp Sweet chutney
Salt and pepper

Place the chicken in a serving bowl and mix with the bananas, lemon juice, sultanas, apricots and nuts. Mix together the mayonnaise, onion, curry powder, apple and chutney and season to taste with salt and pepper. Toss the salad in the dressing just before serving.

Curried Ham and Yoghurt Salad

Serves 4

100 g/4 oz Mushrooms, sliced
225 g/8 oz Cooked ham, diced
25 g/1 oz Raisins
1 Dessert apple, cored and chopped
15 ml/1 tbsp Lemon juice
150 ml/¼ pt Natural yoghurt
5 ml/1 tsp Curry powder
15 ml/1 tbsp Chopped parsley
50 g/2 oz Chutney

Mix the mushrooms, ham and raisins. Toss the apple in the lemon juice,

then add it to the mixture. Mix the yoghurt with the curry powder and pour over the salad. Sprinkle with parsley and serve with chutney.

Oil and Vinegar Dressing

Makes 150 ml/¼ pt

100 ml/4 fl oz Oil
50 ml/2 fl oz Vinegar
Salt and pepper

Whisk the ingredients together well.

French Dressing

Makes 150 ml/¼ pt

100 ml/4 fl oz Oil
50 ml/2 fl oz Vinegar
15 ml/1 tbsp Dijon mustard
10 ml/2 tsp Sugar
Salt and pepper

Whisk the ingredients together well.

Vinaigrette Dressing

Makes 150 ml/¼ pt

100 ml/4 fl oz Oil
50 ml/2 fl oz Vinegar
15 ml/1 tbsp Mustard
10 ml/2 tsp Sugar
15 ml/1 tbsp Finely chopped onion
15 ml/1 tbsp Chopped parsley

Whisk the ingredients together well.

Mayonnaise

Makes 450 ml/¾ pt

1 Egg
1 Egg yolk
2.5 ml/½ tsp Salt
2.5 ml/½ tsp Mustard powder
30 ml/2 tbsp Lemon juice
15 ml/1 tbsp White wine vinegar
375 ml/13 fl oz Oil

Purée the egg, egg yolk, salt, mustard, lemon juice, wine vinegar and one-third of the oil in a food processor or blender. While the blender is running, slowly pour in the remaining oil.

Note
If you do not have a food processor or blender, you can use a whisk, making sure you pour the oil gradually and keep whisking all the time.

Blue Cheese Dressing

Makes 150 ml/¼ pt

½ Onion, chopped
5 ml/1 tsp Worcestershire sauce
50 g/2 oz Blue cheese, crumbled
150 ml/ ¼ pt Mayonnaise (page 250)
Salt and pepper

Mix the onion, Worcestershire sauce and cheese into the mayonnaise and season to taste with salt and pepper.

Thousand Island Dressing

Makes 200 ml/7 fl oz

150 ml/¼ pt Mayonnaise (page 250)
30 ml/2 tbsp Milk
15 ml/1 tbsp Tomato purée
15 ml/1 tbsp Finely chopped red pepper
15 ml/1 tbsp Finely chopped green pepper
15 ml/1 tbsp Finely chopped gherkin
1 Hard-boiled egg, finely chopped

Mix all the ingredients together well and chill until required.

Cheese Mayonnaise

Makes 150 ml/¼ pt

100 g/4 oz Cream cheese
5 ml/1 tsp Dijon mustard
30 ml/2 tbsp Oil
30 ml/2 tbsp Milk
30 ml/2 tbsp Vinegar
Salt and pepper

Beat the cheese until smooth, then work in the mustard. Gradually beat in the oil, followed by the milk and vinegar and season to taste with salt and pepper.

Dill Mayonnaise with Soured Cream

Makes 300 ml/½ pt

150 ml/¼ pt Mayonnaise (page 250)
90 ml/6 tbsp Soured cream
15 ml/1 tbsp Lemon juice
30 ml/2 tbsp Chopped dill
Pinch of mustard powder
Few drops of chilli sauce

Whisk the ingredients together well.

Soured Cream Dressing

Makes 150 ml/¼ pt

2 Hard-boiled egg yolks, sieved
150 ml/¼ pt Soured cream
5 ml/1 tsp Tarragon vinegar
Salt and pepper

Mix the egg yolks to a smooth paste with the soured cream, add the vinegar and season to taste with salt and pepper.

Sharp Yoghurt Dressing

Makes 150 ml/¼ pt

100 ml/4 fl oz Natural yoghurt
30 ml/2 tbsp Soured cream
2.5 ml/½ tsp Made English mustard
15 ml/1 tbsp Lemon juice
Salt and pepper

Mix all the ingredients together well and season to taste with salt and pepper. Chill until needed.

Creamy Mustard Mayonnaise

Makes 150 ml/¼ pt

75 ml/5 tbsp Natural yoghurt
60 ml/4 tbsp Single cream
15 ml/1 tbsp Dijon mustard
Salt and pepper

Mix all the ingredients together well and season to taste with salt and pepper. Chill until required.

Green Onion Dressing

Makes 150 ml/¼ pt

120 ml/4 fl oz Mayonnaise (page 250)
60 ml/4 tbsp Natural yoghurt
1 Spring onion, cut into
  3 cm/1 in lengths
10 ml/2 tsp White wine vinegar
5ml/1 tsp Lemon juice
5 ml/1 tsp Chopped parsley leaves
Pinch of sugar
Pinch of salt
Pinch of cayenne pepper
½ Garlic clove

Place all the ingredients except the garlic into a food processor or blender. Squeeze the garlic over the mixture through a garlic press. Process until the onions and parsley leaves are finely chopped. Cover and chill for 1 hour before use.

Curry Dressing

Makes 450 ml/¾ pt

15 ml/1 tbsp Oil
1 Small onion, chopped
15 ml/1 tbsp Curry powder
150 ml/¼ pt Vegetable Stock
    (page 24)
15 ml/1 tbsp Apricot jam
5 ml/1 tsp Lemon juice
150 ml/¼ pt Mayonnaise (page 250)
150 ml/¼ pt Soured cream
Salt and pepper

Heat the oil and fry the onion until soft but not browned. Add the curry powder and cook for 2 minutes, then stir in the Stock and bring to the boil. Add the jam and lemon juice and simmer for 5 minutes, then leave to cool.

Stir the mayonnaise and soured cream into the sauce and season to taste with salt and pepper.

Soy Dressing

Makes 120 ml/4 fl oz

60 ml/4 tbsp Soy sauce
15 ml/1 tbsp Corn oil
15 ml/1 tbsp Lemon juice
2.5 ml/½ tsp Ground ginger
20 ml/1½ tbsp Honey, warmed

Stir all the ingredients together in a jug and use for seasoning kebabs and stir-fries.

Hot Desserts

British cookery can boast some of the best hot desserts you can prepare — we really excel at the great British pudding. Here are some delicious versions of old favourites as well as some unusual and exotic new desserts.

Cointreau Banana Melts

Serves 4

100 g/4 oz Desiccated coconut
2 Bananas, mashed
75 g/3 oz Soft brown sugar
Few drops of vanilla essence
30 ml/2 tbsp Cointreau
Pinch of baking powder
Oil for deep-frying

Reserve one-quarter of the coconut, then mix together all the remaining ingredients. Roll teaspoonfuls of the mixture into balls, roll in the coconut, then fry in deep hot oil for 3 minutes. Drain well and serve immediately.

Fruit in Rum Batter

Serves 4

300 ml/½ pt Milk
60 ml/4 tbsp Rum
Pinch of salt
30 ml/2 tbsp Caster sugar
225 g/8 oz Plain flour
5 ml/1 tsp Baking powder
30 ml/2 tbsp Oil
200 g/7 oz Canned pineapple pieces, drained
200 g/7 oz Canned peach slices, drained
Oil for deep-frying
Sugar for sprinkling
Cinnamon

Beat the milk with the rum, salt, sugar, flour, baking powder and oil to a batter. Pat the fruit dry on kitchen paper then dip it into the batter and fry in deep hot oil for 3 minutes. Sprinkle with sugar and cinnamon and serve immediately.

Italian Cream Fritters

Serves 4

3 Eggs
25 g/1 oz Caster sugar
75 g/3 oz Cornflour
Grated rind of 1 lemon
450 ml/¾ pt Milk
25 g/1 oz Butter or margarine
Pinch of salt
75 g/3 oz Breadcrumbs
Oil for frying
Caster sugar for sprinkling
90 ml/6 tbsp Apricot jam

Mix 2 eggs with the sugar in a saucepan, then beat in the cornflour and lemon rind. Stir in the milk, butter or margarine and salt and bring to the boil, stirring. Cook over a low heat for 3 minutes, stirring continuously. Pour into a wetted 18 cm/7 in square tin and leave in a cool place to set.

Cut into squares, and dip the squares in beaten egg then in breadcrumbs. Fry in hot oil until golden, then drain on kitchen paper and serve sprinkled with caster sugar with a spoonful of apricot jam on top.

Nursery Slices

Serves 4

600 ml/1 pt Milk
175 g/6 oz Semolina
50 g/2 oz Sultanas
100 g/4 oz Caster sugar
2 Eggs, beaten
50 g/2 oz Butter or margarine
Butter or margarine for frying

Bring the milk almost to the boil in a saucepan, then stir in 100 g/4 oz semolina and cook over a low heat, stirring, for 2 minutes. Add the sultanas and continue to cook until the mixture is thick and creamy. Remove from the heat and stir in 50 g/2 oz caster sugar, and eggs. Pour into a greased 900 g/2 lb loaf tin and leave to set.

When cold, turn out of the tin and cut into thick slices. Roll each slice in the remaining semolina and fry on both sides in butter until golden brown. Drain and serve hot sprinkled with caster sugar.

Tipsy Apple Doughnuts

Serves 4

3 Apples, peeled, cored and thickly
   sliced

15 ml/1 tbsp Rum or brandy

250 ml/8 fl oz Water, warm

45 ml/3 tbsp Condensed milk

Pinch of salt

1 Egg, separated

225 g/8 oz Plain flour

2.5 ml/½ tsp Baking powder

Caster sugar for sprinkling

Cinnamon

Oil for deep-frying

Lay the apples on a plate, sprinkle with the rum or brandy and leave to soak for 15 minutes. Mix the water, condensed milk, salt and egg yolk, then mix in the flour and baking powder. Whisk the egg white until stiff, then fold it into the mixture to make a very thick batter. Dip the apple slices in the batter, then fry in deep hot oil. Drain well and serve sprinkled with sugar and cinnamon.

Banoffee Pie

Serves 4

175 g/6 oz Canned condensed milk

50 g/2 oz Butter or margarine

25 g/1 oz Caster sugar

225 g/8 oz Digestive biscuits,
   crushed

1 Large banana, sliced

150 ml/¼ pt Double cream,
   whipped

Stand the unopened tin of condensed milk in a saucepan of simmering water and simmer for 1½ hours, topping up with boiling water as necessary. Carefully remove from the heat, leave to cool for 10 minutes then open the tin.

Melt the butter or margarine and mix in the sugar and biscuit crumbs. Press into the base of a greased 20 cm/8 in cake tin. Spread the sliced banana over the base and pour on the condensed milk, which will have turned toffeeish. Spread the whipped cream over the top. Serve warm.

Variation
You can use natural yoghurt on the top for a slightly less rich dessert.

Spotted Dick

Serves 4

225 g/8 oz Shredded suet

450 g/1 lb Plain flour

5 ml/1 tsp Baking powder

100 g/4 oz Caster sugar

350 g/12 oz Dates, stoned and
   chopped

45 ml/3 tbsp Milk

Mix all the dry ingredients together thoroughly, then work to a light dough with the milk. Spoon into a greased 600 ml/1 pt pudding basin and cover with pleated greaseproof paper. Place the basin in a saucepan and fill with water to come half way up the sides. Bring to the boil and boil for 3 hours, topping up with boiling water as necessary. Serve with custard.

255

Christmas Pudding

Serves 8

50 g/2 oz Plain flour

Pinch of salt

100 g/4 oz Breadcrumbs

10 ml/2 tsp Mixed spice

100 g/4 oz Shredded suet

175 g/6 oz Soft brown sugar

50 g/2 oz Mixed peel

225 g/8 oz Raisins

225 g/8 oz Sultanas

225 g/8 oz Currants

50 g/2 oz Flaked almonds, chopped

Grated rind of 1 lemon

30 ml/2 tbsp Black treacle or
molasses

1 Egg, beaten

60 ml/4 tbsp Brandy

30 ml/2 tbsp Orange juice

Mix all the dry ingredients together well, then stir in the remaining ingredients and mix until well combined. Turn into a greased 1.2 litre/2 pt pudding basin, cover with pleated greaseproof paper and a cloth and steam for 4 hours, topping up with boiling water as necessary. Cover with clean paper and cloth and store in a cool, dry place. Steam for 2 hours topping up with boiling water as necessary.

Fat-Free Christmas Pudding

Serves 6

225 g/8 oz Wholemeal breadcrumbs

100 g/4 oz Muscovado sugar

100 g/4 oz Sultanas

100 g/4 oz Raisins

25 g/1 oz Almonds, finely
chopped

25 g/1 oz Brazils, finely chopped

1 Apple, peeled, cored and
grated

1 Banana, chopped

10 ml/2 tsp Cinnamon

Grated rind and juice of 1 lemon

Pinch of salt

2 Eggs, beaten

150 ml/¼ pt Milk

Mix together all the dry ingredients, then stir in the eggs. Add enough milk to make a firm but not stiff mixture. Spoon the mixture into a greased 1.2 litre/2 pt pudding basin, cover with pleated greaseproof paper and a cloth and steam for 4½ hours, topping up with boiling water as necessary.

Fig Pudding

Serves 4

50 g/2 oz Plain flour

50 g/2 oz Shredded suet

50 g/2 oz Breadcrumbs

25 g/1 oz Caster sugar

Pinch of salt

100 g/4 oz Figs, chopped

Pinch of bicarbonate of soda

30 ml/2 tbsp Milk

Mix together all the ingredients, using enough milk to make a soft mixture. Spoon into a greased 600 ml/1 pt pudding basin and steam for 2 hours, topping up with boiling water as necessary. Serve with custard.

Date and Lemon Pudding

Serves 4

2 Lemons
75 ml/5 tbsp Water
75 g/3 oz Caster sugar
100 g/4 oz Soft margarine
100 g/4 oz Self-raising flour
50 g/2 oz Soft brown sugar
2 Eggs, beaten
25 g/1 oz Breadcrumbs
100 g/4 oz Dates, stoned and chopped

Grate the lemon rinds, quarter the lemons and place the flesh in a food processor or blender and purée. Make up to 300 ml/½ pt with water, add the caster sugar and place in a saucepan. Dissolve the sugar over a low heat then boil rapidly for 3 minutes.

Mix the margarine, flour, brown sugar, eggs, breadcrumbs and dates until smooth. Turn into a well greased 1.2 litre/2 pt pudding basin, pour over the sauce, cover with pleated foil, tie securely and steam for 1½ hours until the top is dry and spongy, topping up with boiling water as necessary. Turn out with care as the sauce will pour round the pudding.

Golden Surprise Pudding

Serves 4–6

225 g/8 oz Golden syrup
1 Lemon
175 g/6 oz Self-raising flour
Pinch of salt
5 ml/1 tsp Baking powder
100 g/4 oz Shredded suet
100 g/4 oz Breadcrumbs
30-45 ml/2-3 tbsp Water

Put 45 ml/3 tbsp golden syrup in the bottom of a greased 900 ml/1½ pt pudding basin. Grate the rind from the lemon, remove the pith and slice the flesh thinly. Lay the lemon slices over the syrup. Mix the flour, salt, baking powder, suet, lemon rind and half the suet. Mix to a light dough with a little water. Roll out the dough and cut into 4 pieces, increasing in size. Roll out the smallest piece and lay it in the bottom of the basin. Spoon some syrup over the dough and sprinkle with breadcrumbs. Repeat with the remaining layers, finishing with the final layer of dough. Cover with pleated greaseproof paper and foil and steam the pudding for 2 hours, topping up with boiling water as necessary. Turn out and serve hot with custard.

Ginger Pudding

Serves 4

225 g/8 oz Plain flour
Pinch of salt
5 ml/1 tsp Ground ginger
75 g/3 oz Shredded suet
50 g/2 oz Caster sugar
100 g/4 oz Golden syrup, warmed
1 Egg, beaten
Pinch of bicarbonate of soda
45 ml/3 tbsp Milk, warmed
45 ml/3 tbsp Golden syrup

Mix the flour, salt, ginger, suet and sugar. Mix the syrup and egg and use to bind the dry ingredients. Dissolve the bicarbonate of soda in the milk and mix in to give a dropping consistency. Spoon the extra syrup into a greased 1.2 litre/2 pt pudding basin, then spoon in the mixture. Cover with pleated greaseproof and foil and steam for 2 hours, topping up with boiling water as necessary. Turn out on to a serving plate and serve with custard.

Steamed Orange Pudding

Serves 4

120 g/5 oz Caster sugar
100 g/4 oz Butter or margarine
2 Eggs
100 g/4 oz Plain flour
2.5 ml/½ tsp Baking powder
15 ml/1 tbsp Orange juice
30 ml/2 tbsp Orange pulp
Grated rind of 1 orange
300 ml/½ pt Boiling water
10 ml/2 tsp Arrowroot

Cream 100 g/4 oz sugar with the butter and eggs, then beat in the flour and baking powder, followed by the orange juice and pulp. Pour the mixture into a greased 1.2 litre/2 pt pudding basin, cover with pleated greaseproof paper and steam for 1½ hours, topping up with boiling water as necessary.

Mix the remaining sugar with the orange rind in a saucepan and heat gently until the sugar has dissolved. Mix the arrowroot with a little cold water, then stir it into the pan, bring to the boil and boil until the mixture thickens. Add a little more sugar and orange juice to taste, if necessary and serve the sauce with the orange pudding.

Rhubarb Pudding with Brown Sugar Sauce

Serves 4

225 g/8 oz Self-raising flour
Pinch of salt
2.5 ml/½ tsp Ground ginger
100 g/4 oz Butter or margarine
175 g/6 oz Soft brown sugar
225 g/8 oz Rhubarb, chopped
2 Eggs, beaten
30 ml/2 tbsp Single cream

Mix the flour, salt and ginger, then rub in half the butter or margarine until the mixture resembles fine breadcrumbs. Stir in 100 g/4 oz sugar, the rhubarb and eggs. Spoon the mixture into a greased 1.2 litre/ 2 pt pudding basin, cover with pleated greaseproof paper and foil and steam for 1½ hours, topping up with boiling water as necessary.

To make the sauce, melt the remaining butter and stir in the remaining sugar and the cream until the sugar has dissolved. Serve the sauce warm with the hot pudding.

Apricot and Orange Pancakes

Serves 4

25 g/1 oz Ground almonds
100 g/4 oz Plain flour
Pinch of salt
1 Egg
300 ml/½ pt Milk
Grated rind of 1 orange
25 g/1 oz Butter or margarine, melted
Oil for frying
2 Oranges
50 g/2 oz Dried apricots, soaked overnight then chopped

Beat together the almonds, flour, salt, egg, milk, orange rind and melted butter or margarine to a batter. Heat some oil in a frying pan and use the batter to make 6 to 8 pancakes. As they are cooked, place them in a stack separated by sheets of greaseproof paper and keep them warm.

Peel the oranges and remove all the pith and pips. Purée with the apricots in a food processor or blender, use the mixture to fill the pancakes then roll them up and place them in a shallow ovenproof dish. Cover with foil and reheat in a preheated oven at 200°C/400°F/gas mark 6 for 20 minutes. Serve hot with cream.

French Apple Flan

Serves 4

175 g/6 oz Plain flour
Pinch of salt
100 g/4 oz Butter or margarine
175 g/6 oz Caster sugar
1 Egg yolk
15 ml/1 tbsp Water
900 g/2 lb Cooking apples, peeled, cored and chopped
2 Red dessert apples, sliced
Juice of 1 lemon
15 ml/1 tbsp Apricot jam, sieved

Mix the flour and salt, then rub in 75 g/3 oz butter or margarine until the mixture resembles fine breadcrumbs. Stir in 30 ml/1 tbsp sugar, then bind together to a pastry with the egg yolk and a little cold water. Cover and chill the pastry.

Melt the remaining butter or margarine in a saucepan, add the cooking apples and half the remaining sugar. Cover and simmer for 10 minutes. Strain and purée the apples in a food processor or blender, and save the juice. Sprinkle the sliced apples with lemon juice to stop them going brown. Roll out the pastry and use to line a greased 18 cm/7 in flan ring. Prick the base with a fork and spoon in the apple purée, then arrange the apple slices in overlapping circles on the top. Dissolve the remaining sugar in the apple juice, 30 ml/2 tbsp lemon juice and the jam. Bring to the boil and boil for 5 minutes, then brush generously over the apple slices. Bake in a preheated oven at 200°C/400°F/gas mark 6 for 40 minutes until golden brown. Serve hot or cold with cream.

Crunchy Apricot Pudding

Serves 4

900 g/2 lb Canned apricot halves in syrup, drained and halved

100 g/4 oz Butter or margarine

Pinch of salt

5 ml/1 tsp Cinnamon

2.5 ml/½ tsp Nutmeg

90 ml/6 tbsp Honey

6 Bread slices

50 g/2 oz Cornflakes

Mix 150 ml/¼ pt apricot syrup with the butter, salt, cinnamon, nutmeg and honey in a large saucepan and heat gently until well mixed. Toast the bread and cut it into 1 cm/½ in cubes. Add the bread, apricots and cornflakes to the syrup and toss all the ingredients together lightly. Spoon the mixture into a large greased ovenproof dish and bake in a pre-heated oven at 180°C/350°F/gas mark 4 for 30 minutes. Serve hot or cold with cream or ice cream.

Baked Stuffed Apples with Lemon Butter Sauce

Serves 4

4 Cooking apples

100 g/4 oz Dates, stoned and chopped

15 ml/1 tbsp Golden syrup

15 g/½ oz Butter or margarine

25 g/1 oz Demerara sugar

15 ml/1 tbsp Cornflour

Juice of 1 lemon

Water

Core the apples and make a horizontal score in the skins all round. Stuff the centre with the dates and bake in a preheated oven at 180°C/350°F/gas mark 4 for 45 minutes.

Place the golden syrup, butter, demerara sugar and cornflour in a saucepan. Make the lemon juice up to 150 ml/¼ pt with water and add this to the pan. Bring to the boil, stirring continuously, then simmer for 10 minutes and serve with the baked apples.

Fluffy Apple Pudding

Serves 4

600 ml/1 pt Milk

100 g/4 oz White breadcrumbs

15 g/½ oz Butter or margarine

Grated rind of 1 lemon

25 g/1 oz Caster sugar

2 Eggs, separated

1 Cooking apple, peeled, cored and sliced

15 ml/1 tbsp Soft brown sugar

Heat the milk in a saucepan, then remove from the heat and stir in the breadcrumbs, butter or margarine, lemon rind and caster sugar. Leave to stand for 20 minutes until most of the milk is absorbed. Add the egg yolks and beat well. Whisk the egg whites until stiff then fold them into the mixture. Place the apple slices in the base of a greased shallow oven-proof dish. Sprinkle with brown sugar and pour the milk mixture on top. Bake in a preheated oven at 180°C/350°F/gas mark 4 for 30 minutes until well risen and golden brown.

Apple Betty

Serves 4

750 g/1½ lb Cooking apples, peeled, cored and sliced	
30 ml/2 tbsp Water	
1 Lemon	
1 Orange	
100 g/4 oz Sultanas	
25 g/1 oz Soft brown sugar	
100 g/4 oz Wholemeal breadcrumbs	
50 g/2 oz Walnuts, finely chopped	
25 g/1 oz Butter or margarine, chopped	
2.5 ml/½ tsp Cinnamon	

Cook the apples in the water for 10 minutes until just soft. Grate the rind from the lemon. Cut the lemon and orange into quarters and purée the flesh in a food processor or blender. Add the sultanas, half the brown sugar and the lemon rind and blend to mix. Add the apple. Place half the mixture in the base of a deep oven-proof dish. Mix the breadcrumbs and nuts and spread half of the mixture over the top followed by half the remaining sugar. Then add the rest of the apple mixture, the remaining breadcrumb mixture and the sugar. Dot the butter on top and sprinkle with cinnamon. Bake in a preheated oven at 190°C/375°F/gas mark 5 for 35 minutes until crisp on top. Serve hot with cream or custard.

Apple Charlotte

Serves 4-6

450 g/1 lb Cooking apples, peeled, cored and sliced	
Grated rind and juice of 1 lemon	
100 g/4 oz Caster sugar	
10 White bread slices, crusts removed	
75 g/3 oz Butter or margarine, melted	

Place the apples, lemon rind and juice and caster sugar in a saucepan and simmer to a thick purée, then leave to cool. Cut 1 bread slice into a round to fit the bottom of a greased 1.2 litre/2 pt soufflé dish. Dip the bread in melted butter and lay it in the dish, filling any gaps with small pieces of bread. Cut another round to fit the top of the dish and keep it aside. Dip the remaining slices in butter and use to line the sides of the mould, making sure there are no gaps. Spoon in the purée and cover with the reserved bread, dipped in butter. Cover with foil and bake in a preheated oven at 180°C/350°F/gas mark 4 for 40 minutes until golden brown. Sprinkle with caster sugar and serve with cream.

Apple Crunch

Serves 4

900 g/2 lb Cooking apples, peeled, cored and sliced

50 g/2 oz Granulated sugar

2.5 ml/½ tsp Cinnamon

175 g/6 oz Plain flour

5 ml/1 tsp Baking powder

100 g/4 oz Butter or margarine

100 g/4 oz Soft brown sugar

50 g/2 oz Mixed nuts, chopped

Place the apples in a greased ovenproof dish and sprinkle with granulated sugar and cinnamon to taste. Mix the flour and baking powder and rub in the butter or margarine until the mixture resembles fine breadcrumbs. Stir in the sugar and nuts and spread the mixture over the apples. Bake in a preheated oven at 220°C/ 425°F/gas mark 7 for 30 minutes until brown and crisp. Serve hot or cold with ice cream.

Crunchy Topped Apple Layer Pie

Serves 4-6

450 g/1 lb Cooking apples, peeled, cored and sliced

30 ml/2 tbsp Orange juice

15 ml/1 tbsp Caster sugar

100 g/4 oz Butter or margarine

175 g/6 oz Plain flour

Pinch of salt

30-45 ml/2-3 tbsp Water

25 g/1 oz Ground almonds

15 ml/1 tbsp Honey

15 ml/1 tbsp Hot water

Arrange the apples on the base of a greased 20 cm/8 in ovenproof dish and sprinkle with the orange juice and caster sugar. Rub the butter or margarine into the flour and salt until the mixture resembles fine breadcrumbs, then mix to a smooth pastry with the water. Roll out to fit the dish and place on top of the apples. Mix the almonds, honey and hot water and spread evenly over the pastry. Bake in a preheated oven at 190°C/375°F/gas mark 5 for 30 minutes until the top is crispy. Serve hot with custard.

Luxury Bread and Butter Pudding

Serves 4

300 ml/½ pt Milk

150 ml/¼ pt Double cream

2.5 ml/½ tsp Vanilla essence

2 Eggs, beaten

50 g/2 oz Caster sugar

25 g/1 oz Butter or margarine, softened

8 Bread slices, quartered

50 g/2 oz Raisins

Grated rind of 1 lemon

Mix the milk, cream and vanilla essence in a saucepan, bring to the boil, then remove from the heat and leave to cool. Beat the eggs and sugar until pale and thick, then whisk in the milk. Spread the butter on the bread and layer in a greased 1.2 litre/ 2 pt pie dish with the raisins and lemon rind. Pour in the custard and bake in a preheated oven at 180°C/ 350°F/gas mark 4 for 40 minutes until set and golden brown on top.

Baked Fruit Dumplings

Serves 4

275 g/10 oz Plain flour
Pinch of salt
75 g/3 oz Butter or margarine
50 g/2 oz Lard
15 ml/1 tbsp Caster sugar
45-60 ml/3-4 tbsp Water
4 Cooking apples, peeled and cored
50 g/2 oz Soft brown sugar
5 ml/1 tsp Cinnamon
30 ml/2 tbsp Milk

Mix the flour and salt, then rub in the fats until the mixture resembles fine breadcrumbs. Stir in 5 ml/1 tsp sugar and add just enough water to bind to a pastry. Roll out and cut into 4 rounds, each large enough to cover an apple. Place an apple in the centre of each round and fill the cores with mixed sugar and cinnamon. Dampen the edges of the pastry and draw it up to cover each apple, sealing the edges together well. Place the dumplings on a greased baking sheet with the joins underneath. Brush with milk and sprinkle with caster sugar. Bake in a preheated oven at 200°C/400°F/gas mark 6 for 40 minutes.

Crundel Pudding

Serves 4

60 g/2½ oz Butter or margarine
75 g/3 oz Plain flour
60 g/2½ oz Caster sugar
450 ml/¾ pt Milk
1 Egg, beaten

Rub the butter or margarine into the flour, then stir in the caster sugar. Heat the milk gently until warm, then add the beaten egg and stir well into the dried ingredients. Bake in a preheated oven at 180°C/350°F/gas mark 4 for 45 minutes.

Hot Chocolate Soufflé

Serves 4

75 g/3 oz Butter or margarine
50 g/2 oz Plain flour
15 ml/1 tbsp Cocoa
2.5 ml/½ tsp Cinnamon
450 ml/¾ pt Milk
4 Eggs, separated
50 g/2 oz Caster sugar
15 ml/1 tbsp Icing sugar

Melt the butter, stir in the flour, cocoa and cinnamon and blend well over a low heat. Stir in the milk, stirring continuously until the sauce thickens. Remove from the heat and leave to cool slightly. Beat the egg yolks into the sauce. Whisk the egg whites lightly, then add the caster sugar and whisk again until they hold soft peaks. Fold into the sauce, and turn the mixture into a greased 1.2 litre/2 pt soufflé dish with a collar of paper round the sides. Stand the dish in a roasting tin filled with water to come half way up the sides of the dish, and bake in a preheated oven at 190°C/375°F/gas mark 5 for 45 minutes until well risen. Sprinkle with icing sugar and serve immediately.

Carrot Pudding

Serves 4

50 g/2 oz Butter or margarine
25 g/1 oz Lard
175 g/6 oz Plain flour
45 ml/3 tbsp Water
50 g/2 oz Carrots, grated
50 g/2 oz Breadcrumbs
300 ml/½ pt Milk, hot
50 g/2 oz Caster sugar
Grated rind and juice of 1 lemon
25 g/1 oz Raisins, chopped
10 ml/2 tbsp Mixed spice
2 Eggs, beaten

Rub the butter or margarine and the lard into the flour until the mixture resembles fine breadcrumbs, then mix to a pastry with the water. Roll out the pastry and use to line a 20 cm/8" pie dish. Mix the remaining ingredients, pour into the pie dish and bake in a preheated oven at 190°C/375°F/gas mark 5 for 40 minutes until set.

Rich Chocolate Pudding

Serves 4

100 g/4 oz Soft brown sugar
100 g/4 oz Self-raising flour
5 ml/1 tsp Baking powder
40 g/1½ oz Cocoa
100 g/4 oz Butter or margarine
2 Eggs
10 ml/2 tsp Caster sugar
5 ml/1 tsp Cornflour
150 ml/¼ pt Water

Mix the brown sugar, flour, baking powder and 25 g/1 oz cocoa, then rub in the butter or margarine and mix in the eggs. Turn the mixture into a greased 1.2 litre/2 pt casserole dish. Mix the caster sugar, cornflour and water with the remaining cocoa, pour on top of the pudding mixture and leave to stand for 5 minutes. Bake in a preheated oven at 190°C/375°F/gas mark 5 for 45 minutes. Turn out on to a serving dish. The pudding will be moist and soggy on the top with a crisper base. Serve with cream or custard.

Coffee Custard Pudding

Serves 4

100 g/4 oz Butter or margarine
175 g/6 oz Soft brown sugar
1 Egg, beaten
75 ml/5 tbsp Strong black coffee
100 g/4 oz Plain flour
5 ml/1 tsp Baking powder
25 g/1 oz Hazelnuts, chopped
300 ml/½ pt Milk

Cream the butter and 100 g/4 oz sugar, then beat in the egg and coffee. Stir in the flour and hazelnuts. Spoon the mixture into a greased 1.2 litre/2 pt pudding basin. Mix the remaining sugar with the milk and pour over the pudding. Bake in a preheated oven at 160°C/325°F/gas mark 3 for 1½ hours until set and springy. Serve with cream or custard.

Note
The pudding separates into a soft sponge with a delicious sauce.

Rimside Tart

Serves 4

| 100 g/4 oz Butter or margarine |
| 225 g/8 oz Plain flour |
| 45 ml/3 tbsp Water |
| 50 g/2 oz Breadcrumbs |
| 90 ml/6 tbsp Marmalade |
| 225 g/8 oz Currants |

Rub the butter or margarine into the flour until the mixture resembles fine breadcrumbs. Mix in the water to a smooth pastry. Roll out the pastry and use it to line 2 greased 18 cm/7 in sandwich tins. Roll out the trimmings and cut into strips. Mix together the breadcrumbs, marmalade and currants, adding a little water, if necessary, to keep the mixture fairly moist. Divide the filling between the tins and cover with the strips of pastry in a lattice pattern. Bake in a preheated oven at 200°C/400°F/gas mark 6 for 25 minutes.

Jack Tart

Serves 4

| 90 g/3½ oz Butter or margarine |
| 40 g/1½ oz Lard |
| 175 g/6 oz Plain flour |
| 30 ml/2 tbsp Water |
| 60 ml/ 4 tbsp Raspberry jam |
| 50 g/2 oz Caster sugar |
| 100 g/4 oz Rolled oats |
| Few drops of almond essence |

Rub 40 g/1½ oz butter or margarine and the lard into the flour and mix to a pastry with water. Roll out the pastry and use to line a greased 20 cm/8 in pie dish. Spread the jam over the pastry. Melt the remaining butter and stir in the sugar, oats and almond essence. Spoon over the jam, spread with a fork and bake in a preheated oven at 200°C/400°F/gas mark 6 for 25 minutes until lightly browned.

Orange Delight

Serves 4

| 100 g/4 oz Butter or margarine |
| 50 g/2 oz Lard |
| 275 g/10 oz Plain flour |
| 45 ml/3 tbsp Water |
| 60 ml/4 tbsp Lemon curd |
| 2 Oranges, peeled and sliced |
| 25 g/1 oz Cornflour |
| 2.5 ml/½ tsp Salt |
| 2.5 ml/½ tsp Baking powder |
| 50 g/2 oz Caster sugar |
| 1 Egg |

Rub half the butter or margarine and the lard into 225 g/8 oz flour until the mixture resembles fine breadcrumbs. Mix to a pastry with the water. Roll out the pastry and use it to line 2 greased 18 cm/7 in sandwich tins. Spread the pastry with the lemon curd, then layer the orange slices over the top. Mix the remaining flour with the cornflour, salt and baking powder. Cream the remaining butter or margarine with the sugar and egg. Stir in the flour mixture and beat until smooth. Spread the mixture over the oranges. Bake in a preheated oven at 190°C/375°F/gas mark 5 for 30 minutes.

Two-Layer Lemon Bake

Serves 4

50 g/2 oz Butter or margarine
100 g/4 oz Caster sugar
45 ml/3 tbsp Lemon juice
5 ml/1 tsp Grated lemon rind
2 Eggs, separated
50 g/2 oz Semolina
450 ml/¾ pt Milk

Melt the butter, then stir in the sugar, lemon juice and rind. Remove from the heat and beat in the egg yolks and semolina. Stir in the milk and mix to a smooth batter. Whisk the egg whites until stiff, then fold them into the mixture. Pour into a greased ovenproof dish and stand the dish in a roasting tin filled with water to come half way up the sides of the dish. Bake in a preheated oven at 180°C/350°F/gas mark 4 for 45 minutes. Serve hot or cold.

Spicy Pear Pudding

Serves 4

120 g/5 oz Butter or margarine
120 g/5 oz Soft brown sugar
3 Pears, peeled, halved and cored
6 Walnuts, whole
25 g/1 oz Walnuts, ground
2 Eggs
100 g/4 oz Self-raising flour
5 ml/1 tsp Mixed spice
15 ml/1 tbsp Milk
25 g/1 oz Oats

Butter the base of an ovenproof dish and sprinkle with 15 ml/1 tbsp sugar.

Place a walnut in the dip in each pear half and arrange the pears, flat side down, on the base of the dish. Cream the remaining butter and sugar until smooth, then mix in the ground walnuts, eggs, flour, spice, milk and oats. Spoon the mixture over the pears and bake in a preheated oven at 190°C/375°F/gas mark 5 for 35 minutes until well risen and golden brown. Turn out of the dish and serve hot with cream or custard.

Queen of Puddings

Serves 4

4 Eggs, separated
600 ml/1 pt Milk
100 g/4 oz Breadcrumbs
90 ml/6 tbsp Raspberry jam
75 g/3 oz Caster sugar

Beat 1 whole egg and 3 egg yolks, then stir in the milk and bread-crumbs. Spread the jam over the bottom of a greased 20 cm/8 in pie dish, spoon the egg mixture over the top and leave to stand for 30 minutes.

Bake in a preheated oven at 150°C/300°F/gas mark 2 for 1 hour until set.

Whisk the egg whites until stiff, then fold in half the sugar. Whisk again, then fold in the remaining sugar. Pile the meringue on top of the custard, sprinkle with sugar and return to the oven for 20 minutes until the meringue is set and lightly browned.

Austrian Lattice Pie

Serves 4

| 350 g/12 oz Raspberries |
| 60 g/2½ oz Caster sugar |
| 15 g/½ oz Butter or margarine |
| 5 ml/1 tsp Cinnamon |
| 225 g/8 oz Shortcrust Pastry (page 145) |
| 50 g/2 oz Ground almonds |
| 1 Egg white, lightly beaten |

Place the raspberries, 50 g/2 oz sugar, the butter and cinnamon in a saucepan and heat gently until the fruit is soft. Roll out the pastry and use to line a greased 18 cm/7 in flan ring. Sprinkle the base with ground almonds and spread the raspberry mixture on top. Roll out the pastry trimmings, cut into 1 cm/½ in strips and make a lattice pattern on top of the pie. Brush over the whole pie with egg white and sprinkle with the remaining sugar. Bake in a preheated oven at 190°C/375°F/gas mark 5 for 30 minutes until golden and well cooked. Serve warm with cream.

Baked Rice Pudding

Serves 4

| 50 g/2 oz Pudding rice |
| 600 ml/1 pt Milk |
| 25 g/1 oz Caster sugar |
| Grated rind of ½ lemon |
| Nutmeg |
| 15 g/½ oz Butter or margarine |

Put the rice into a greased 900 ml/ 1½ pt ovenproof dish and stir in the milk. Leave to soak for 30 minutes. Stir in the sugar and lemon rind, sprinkle with nutmeg and dot with butter or margarine. Bake in a pre-heated oven at 150°C/300°F/gas mark 2 for 30 minutes, stir well, then bake for a further 2 hours.

Toffee Fruit Cobbler

Serves 4

| 60 g/2½ oz Butter or margarine |
| 175 g/6 oz Self-raising flour |
| 150 ml/¼ pt Milk |
| 2 Cooking apples, peeled, cored and sliced |
| 15 ml/1 tbsp Water |
| 400 g/14 oz Canned raspberries, drained |
| 150 ml/¼ pt Double cream |
| 25 g/1 oz Demerara sugar |

Rub 50 g/2 oz butter or margarine into the flour until the mixture resembles fine breadcrumbs. Mix to a soft dough with the milk, roll out on a floured surface and cut into small rounds. Place them on a greased baking sheet and bake in a preheated oven at 220°C/425°F/gas mark 7 for 10 minutes.

Meanwhile, cook the apples in the water for 10 minutes until soft, then drain any excess juice, stir in the raspberries and spoon the fruit into a flameproof bowl. Split the scones, spread with the remaining butter and arrange round the edge of the dish. Pour the cream in the centre and sprinkle with the sugar. Place under a hot grill for a few minutes until the sugar has caramelised, then serve immediately.

Rhubarb Batter

Serves 4

450 g/1 lb Rhubarb, chopped
45 ml/3 tbsp Orange juice
225 g/8 oz Honey
25 g/1 oz Butter
1 Egg, beaten
2.5 ml/½ tsp Vanilla essence
30 ml/2 tbsp Soured cream
100 g/4 oz Wholewheat flour
Pinch of salt
2.5 ml/½ tsp Bicarbonate of soda

Spread the rhubarb over the base of a greased 20 cm/8 in pie dish. Mix the orange juice and half the honey and trickle it over the rhubarb. Dot with the butter. Mix the egg, the remaining honey, the vanilla essence and soured cream. Stir in the flour, salt and bicarbonate of soda and spread the batter over the rhubarb. Bake in a preheated oven at 180°C/350°F/gas mark 4 for 30 minutes until brown.

Treacle Tart

Serves 4

175 g/6 oz Plain flour
10 ml/2 tsp Caster sugar
75 g/3 oz Butter or margarine
1 Egg yolk
225 g/8 oz Golden syrup
50 g/2 oz Breadcrumbs
15 ml/1 tbsp Lemon juice

Mix the flour and sugar and rub in the butter or margarine until the mixture resembles coarse breadcrumbs. Mix to a firm pastry with the egg yolk,

cover and chill for 30 minutes. Roll out the pastry on a floured surface and use to line a greased 20 cm/8 in pie dish. Warm the syrup, then stir in the breadcrumbs and lemon juice and leave to cool. Pour into the pastry base and bake in a preheated oven at 180°C/350°F/gas mark 4 for 35 minutes until set and golden.

Walnut and Apple Flan

Serves 4

100 g/4 oz Butter or margarine
175 g/6 oz Plain flour
100 g/4 oz Caster sugar
1 Egg yolk
15 ml/1 tbsp Cold water
450 g/1 lb Cooking apples, peeled, cored and sliced
25 g/1 oz Walnuts, chopped
2 Eggs
2.5 ml/½ tsp Cinnamon

Rub the butter or margarine into the flour until the mixture resembles fine breadcrumbs. Stir in half the sugar and mix to a smooth pastry with the egg yolk. Roll out and use to line a greased 23 cm/9 in flan ring. Chill while preparing the filling.

Arrange the apples in the base of the flan. Mix the walnuts, eggs, cinnamon and remaining sugar together well and spoon over the apples. Bake in a preheated oven at 200°C/400°F/gas mark 6 for 30 minutes. Serve warm.

Hot Walnut Pudding with Butterscotch Sauce

Serves 4

4 Eggs, separated
175 g/6 oz Caster sugar
100 g/4 oz Walnuts, chopped
Grated rind and juice of 1 orange
100 g/4 oz Self-raising flour
100 g/4 oz Butter or margarine, softened
100 g/4 oz Soft brown sugar
25 g/1 oz Plain flour
90 ml/6 tbsp Milk

Beat the egg yolks with the caster sugar until thick, then add the walnuts and orange rind and juice and stir in the self-raising flour. Whisk the egg whites until stiff, then fold them into the mixture and turn it into a greased and lined 18 cm/7 in square cake tin. Bake in a preheated oven at 180°C/350°F/gas mark 4 for 45 minutes.

To make the sauce, beat the butter, brown sugar and plain flour together, then heat gently until the butter melts and the mixture bubbles. Cook for 4 minutes, stirring continuously. Stir in the milk and bring to the boil, stirring, until the sauce is thick and smooth. Serve the pudding warm with the hot sauce.

Trigona

Serves 4

225 g/8 oz Walnuts, chopped
100 g/4 oz Breadcrumbs
5 ml/1 tsp Cinnamon
350 g/12 oz Sugar
300 ml/½ pt Water
150 ml/¼ pt Honey
1 Egg yolk
225 g/8 oz Filo pastry
175 g/6 oz Butter or margarine, melted

Mix the walnuts, breadcrumbs and cinnamon. Boil 50 g/2 oz sugar with 50 ml/2 fl oz water and 15 ml/1 tbsp honey for 5 minutes. Remove from the heat and stir in the walnut mixture and the egg yolk. Cut the pastry into 13 cm/5 in strips and cover the sheets you are not using with a damp cloth to avoid them drying out while you are working. Brush the pastry strips with butter, fold in half lengthways and brush again. Place a teaspoonful of the filling on one end and fold into a triangle, then fold over and over to the end of the strip. Place the finished triangles on a greased baking sheet and brush with the rest of the butter. Bake in a preheated oven at 180°C/350°F/gas mark 4 for 30 minutes.

To make the sauce, boil the remaining water with the remaining honey and sugar until it thickens to a syrup. Pour the warmed syrup over the triangles.

Cold Desserts

This collection of cold desserts will give you a great choice when looking for something for a warm summer day, to follow a rich main course, or a sweet you can prepare in advance so that you can enjoy your time with guests. There are plenty of light mousses as well as richer desserts to try out for special occasions.

Brandied Berry Compôte

Serves 4-6

100 g/4 oz Gooseberries
225 g/8 oz Blackcurrants
225 g/8 oz Redcurrants
225 g/8 oz Blackberries
225 g/8 oz Raspberries
60 ml/4 tbsp Blackcurrant juice
30 ml/2 tbsp Lemon juice
45 ml/3 tbsp Brandy
25 g/1 oz Icing sugar
50 g/2 oz Almonds, toasted
2 Mint sprigs
150 ml/¼ pt Double cream, whipped

Place the prepared fruit in a serving bowl. Mix the blackcurrant juice, lemon juice and brandy and pour it over the fruit. Sprinkle with the icing sugar and chill for at least 3 hours. Sprinkle with toasted almonds, garnish with mint and serve with cream.

Apricot Orange Mousse

Serves 4

225 g/8 oz Dried apricots, soaked overnight
30 ml/2 tbsp Apricot brandy
175 g/6 oz Frozen concentrated orange juice
150 ml/¼ pt Whipping cream, whipped
3 Egg whites, whisked
25 g/1 oz Flaked almonds
8 Ratafia biscuits

Simmer the apricots in water until soft, then drain and purée with the apricot brandy and orange juice in a food processor or blender. Fold in the cream, then the egg whites. Spoon into a glass bowl and sprinkle with flaked almonds. Serve with ratafia biscuits.

Hazelnut Pavlova

Serves 4

3 Egg whites
175 g/6 oz Caster sugar
75 g/3 oz Hazelnuts, ground
Few drops of white wine vinegar
300 ml/½ pt Whipping cream,
  whipped
225 g/8 oz Soft fruit (strawberries,
  raspberries, kiwi fruits, canned
  mandarins, etc.)

Whisk the egg whites until they form soft peaks. Add half the sugar and whisk again until stiff. Fold in the remaining sugar, nuts and wine vinegar using a metal spoon. Pipe or spoon the meringue into a circle about 20 cm/8 in in diameter on a greased and lined baking sheet. Bake in a pre-heated oven at 190°C/375°F/gas mark 5 for 20 minutes until brown and crisp on top. Turn off the oven and leave the door ajar, but leave the meringue in the oven until cool.

When ready to serve, spread half the cream in the base of the pavlova, cover with the fruit and pipe stars of cream around the edge.

Blackberry Soufflé

Serves 4

450 g/1 lb Blackberries
120 ml/4 fl oz Water
4 Eggs, separated
100 g/4 oz Caster sugar
15 g/½ oz Gelatine
300 ml/½ pt Whipping cream,
  whipped

Reserve a few of the blackberries for decoration and cook the remainder in 75 ml/5 tbsp of water for 10 minutes. Purée in a food processor or blender.

Whisk the egg yolks and sugar in a large bowl over a pan of hot water until thick and creamy, then remove from the heat and whisk until cool. Dissolve the gelatine in a bowl in 45 ml/3 tbsp water and stand it over hot water to melt. Whisk the egg whites until stiff. Stir the gelatine into the fruit purée, then fold this into the egg yolk mixture. Fold in half the whipped cream then the egg whites. Make a collar of greaseproof paper round an 18 cm/7 in soufflé dish, pour the mixture into the dish and leave to set in the fridge for 5 to 6 hours or overnight.

Remove the greaseproof collar, pipe rosettes of cream on top and decorate with the reserved blackberries.

Note
You can use other soft fruits such as raspberries or strawberries for this recipe.

Chocolate Pudding

Serves 4

50 g/2 oz Plain chocolate
30 ml/2 tbsp Water
25 g/1 oz Caster sugar
2.5 ml/½ tsp Vanilla essence
600 ml/1 pt Double cream, whipped
25 g/1 oz Flaked almonds, toasted

Melt the chocolate and water over a low heat. Stir in the sugar and vanilla essence and leave to cool slightly. Fold in the whipped cream, turn into a serving dish and chill for at least 4 hours. Sprinkle with the almonds before serving.

Chocolate Mousse

Serves 4

450 g/1 lb Plain chocolate
Grated rind and juice of 1 orange
50 g/2 oz Butter or margarine
30 ml/2 tbsp Brandy
2 Eggs, separated
2 Egg yolks
150 ml/¼ pt Whipping cream, whipped
25 g/1 oz Milk chocolate, grated

Melt the plain chocolate in a bowl over a pan of hot water, then stir in the orange rind and juice and the butter or margarine. Remove from the heat and stir in the brandy. Beat the egg yolks together well, then strain the chocolate mixture into the eggs, beating well all the time. Leave to cool.

Beat the egg whites until stiff, then gently fold them into the chocolate mixture. Pour into individual glass dishes and chill for at least 2 hours before serving. Decorate with cream and grated chocolate.

Mocha Delight

Serves 4

100 g/4 oz Brown breadcrumbs
175 g/6 oz Demerara sugar
5 ml/1 tsp Instant coffee powder
50 g/2 oz Drinking chocolate
150 ml/¼ pt Double cream
150 ml/¼ pt Single cream
25 g/1 oz Plain chocolate

Mix the breadcrumbs, sugar, coffee and drinking chocolate. Whip the creams together lightly. Layer the breadcrumb mixture and cream alternately in a glass bowl, finishing with a layer of cream. Sprinkle with grated chocolate and chill for at least 12 hours.

Cider Syllabub

Serves 4

90 ml/6 tbsp Dry cider
Grated rind and juice of 1 lemon
75 g/3 oz Caster sugar
300 ml/½ pt Double cream, whipped
8 Shortbread fingers

Mix the cider, lemon rind and juice and caster sugar and leave to stand for at least 2 hours. Stir in the whipped cream and whisk until the mixture stands in soft peaks. Spoon into individual glasses and chill. Serve with shortbread fingers.

Coffee Cream Charlotte

Serves 4

30 ml/2 tbsp Apricot jam, sieved
19 Boudoir biscuits
4 Eggs, separated
100 g/4 oz Icing sugar
60 ml/4 tbsp Coffee essence
45 ml/3 tbsp Rum
300 ml/½ pt Double cream, lightly
  whipped
150 ml/¼ pt Whipping cream,
  whipped
50 g/2 oz Plain chocolate, grated

Warm the jam slightly and brush it over the sides of a 15 cm/6 in cake tin. Trim the ends of the biscuits and stand them round the edge. Whisk the egg whites until very stiff. Whisk the egg yolks, icing sugar, coffee essence and rum, then fold in the egg whites and cream. Spoon the mixture into the cake tin and freeze for 5 hours.

When ready to serve, carefully loosen round the sides of the tin with a palette knife and turn out. Decorate with whirls of whipped cream and grated chocolate.

Hazelnut and Gooseberry Fool

Serves 4

450 g/1 lb Gooseberries
60 g/2½ oz Sugar
15 ml/1 tbsp Custard powder
300 ml/½ pt Milk
150 ml/¼ pt Hazelnut yoghurt
25 g/1 oz Hazelnuts, chopped
8 Shortbread biscuits

Cook the gooseberries with 50 g/2 oz sugar and a little water until soft, then purée in a food processor or blender. Mix the custard powder with the remaining sugar and a little milk. Bring the remaining milk to the boil, pour on to the custard mixture then return to the heat and stir until the custard boils and thickens. Leave to cool.

Mix the custard, gooseberry purée and hazelnut yoghurt together, pour into individual glasses and decorate with the chopped hazelnuts. Serve with shortbread biscuits.

Simple Lemon Soufflé

Serves 4-6

1 Lemon jelly tablet
300 ml/½ pt Water
Grated rind and juice of 1 lemon
150 ml/¼ pt Double cream
15 ml/1 tbsp Milk
2 Eggs, separated
150 ml/¼ pt Whipping cream,
  whipped
50 g/2 oz Plain chocolate, grated

Dissolve the jelly in 150 ml/¼ pt water over a low heat, then make up to 450 ml/¾ pt with cold water. Add the lemon rind and juice and put in a cool place until the jelly is beginning to set. Whip the cream and milk until thick. Whisk the egg whites until very stiff. When the jelly is just beginning to set, whisk in the egg yolks until fluffy, then fold in the cream and egg whites. Spoon into individual bowls and leave to set. When cold, decorate with whipped cream and grated chocolate.

Melon Surprise

Serves 4

| 1 Melon |
| Grated rind and juice of 1 lemon |
| 15 g/½ oz Gelatine |
| 45 ml/3 tbsp Water |
| 5 ml/1 tsp Ground ginger |
| 15 ml/1 tbsp Honey |
| 300 ml/½ pt Natural yoghurt |

Halve the melon and discard the seeds. Scoop out the flesh with a melon baller and put aside. Scoop out any remaining flesh and purée in a food processor or blender with the lemon rind and juice. Measure the pulp and make up to 150 ml/¼ pt with water if necessary. Dissolve the gelatine in the water over a pan of hot water and stir it into the pulp with the ginger and honey. Fold in the yoghurt and all but 12 of the melon balls. Spoon into individual dishes, garnish with the remaining melon balls and sprinkle with ginger. Chill before serving.

Boodles

Serves 4

| 24 Boudoir biscuits, broken into pieces |
| Grated rind and juice of 2 oranges |
| Grated rind and juice of 1 lemon |
| 25 g/1 oz Caster sugar |
| 300 ml/½ pt Double cream, whipped |

Arrange the biscuits in the base of a serving dish. Mix the orange and lemon juice with the sugar and sprinkle it over the biscuits. Spoon the cream on top and sprinkle with the orange and lemon rind. Chill well before serving.

Fruit and Nut Oranges

Serves 4

| 4 Large oranges |
| 300 ml/½ pt Double cream |
| 30 ml/2 tbsp Orange juice |
| 75 g/3 oz Walnuts, chopped |
| 50 g/2 oz Glacé cherries, finely chopped |
| 50 g/2 oz Plain chocolate, grated |
| 5 ml/1 tsp Orange liqueur |

Cut a slice from the top of each orange and cut out the flesh with a sharp knife. Chop the flesh and spoon it back into the orange shells. Whip the cream with the orange juice, then stir in the nuts, glacé cherries, chocolate and liqueur. Spoon the mixture into the oranges and chill before serving.

Brandied Peaches

Serves 4

4 Ripe peaches
30 ml/2 tbsp Lemon juice
25 g/1 oz Caster sugar
60 ml/4 tbsp Brandy
300 ml/½ pt Whipping cream,
whipped

Blanch the peaches in boiling water, then remove the skins. Toss the peaches in the lemon juice, place in a serving dish and prick with a fork. Sprinkle with sugar and brandy. Cover and chill for several hours until the flavours are absorbed. Serve with whipped cream.

Peach Cream

Serves 4

25 g/1 oz Short-grain rice
300 ml/½ pt Milk
350 g/14 oz Canned peaches, sliced
15 g/½ oz Gelatine
300 ml/½ pt Double cream, whipped

Put the rice and milk in a saucepan, bring to the boil and simmer until the rice is soft and thick. Mix 45 ml/3 tbsp peach juice with the gelatine and dissolve over hot water. Reserve some peach slices for decoration and purée the remaining peaches and the juice in a food processor or blender. Pour in the gelatine and blend again, then lightly blend in half the cream and the cooked rice and pour the mixture into a serving dish or mould and allow to set. Decorate with the remaining cream and the peach slices.

Pineapple and Ginger Trifle

Serves 4

1 Jamaican ginger cake
225 g/8 oz Canned pineapple in
natural juice
30 ml/2 tbsp Custard powder
100 g/4 oz Sugar
2 Eggs, separated
450 ml/¾ pt Milk

Slice the cake and arrange in a flameproof dish. Pour over the pineapple juice, then chop the fruit and add it to the dish. Mix the custard powder, 25 g/1 oz sugar, the egg yolks and a little milk. Bring the remaining milk to the boil in a saucepan, pour into the custard mixture, then return to the pan, bring back to the boil and simmer for 2 minutes, stirring. Pour the custard over the cake and pineapple. Whisk the egg whites until stiff, then whisk in the remaining sugar. Pipe a pineapple design on top of the custard, or pile it on to the trifle and peak the meringue using the back of a spoon. Place the dish under a hot grill until the meringue is golden brown.

Raspberry Crowdie

Serves 4

50 g/2 oz Coarse oatmeal

600 ml/1 pt Double cream,
    whipped

25 g/1 oz Caster sugar

15 ml/1 tbsp Whisky

100 g/4 oz Raspberries

Toss the oatmeal in a heavy-based pan over a moderate heat for 3 minutes, then leave to cool slightly. Stir the oatmeal into the cream with the sugar, whisky and berries. Spoon into individual bowls and serve.

Rhubarb Fool

Serves 4

1.5 kg/3 lb Rhubarb, sliced

225 g/8 oz Soft brown sugar

90 ml/6 tbsp Water

45 ml/3 tbsp Lemon juice

225 g/8 oz Marshmallows

300 ml/½ pt Whipping cream,
    whipped

8 Brandy snaps

Cook the rhubarb, sugar and water gently until soft. Add the lemon juice and marshmallows and heat gently until dissolved, then beat well, pour into a serving dish and leave to cool. Fold in the whipped cream and chill until required. Serve with brandy snaps.

Strawberry and Cointreau Crush

Serves 4

225 g/8 oz Strawberries

25 g/1 oz Caster sugar

30 ml/2 tbsp Cointreau

300 ml/½ pt Double cream,
    whipped

Reserve 4 strawberries for decoration, then crush the remainder with the sugar. Whisk the Cointreau into the double cream, then fold in the strawberry mixture. Spoon into individual glass dishes and top with a strawberry. Chill until required.

Green Fruit Salad

Serves 4

1 Apple, cored and sliced

225 g/8 oz Seedless grapes

225 g/8 oz Kiwi fruit, sliced

1 Melon, cut into balls

100 g/4 oz Granulated sugar

150 ml/¼ pt Water

15 ml/1 tbsp Lemon juice

15 ml/1 tbsp Green Chartreuse

Mix the prepared fruits in a serving bowl. Bring the sugar and water to the boil and boil for 3 minutes. Leave to cool, then stir in the lemon juice and Chartreuse and pour over the fruit. Chill until required, stirring occasionally.

Granny's Favourite

Serves 4

600 ml/1 pt Milk
50 g/2 oz Semolina
25 g/1 oz Caster sugar
60 ml/4 tbsp Blackberry jelly
150 ml/¼ pt Double cream, whipped

Warm the milk in a saucepan, sprinkle on the semolina, bring to the boil, stirring constantly, and simmer until thick. Remove from the heat and stir in the sugar. Leave to cool slightly, then pour into individual dishes and leave to set. Warm the jelly slightly and pour over the top of the semolina, then leave to cool. Serve decorated with whipped cream.

Butterscotch Puddings

Serves 4

50 g/2 oz Butter or margarine
75 g/3 oz Demerara sugar
75 g/3 oz Fine semolina
300 ml/½ pt Milk
150 ml/¼ pt Whipping cream, whipped
6 Strawberries, sliced

Melt the butter, stir in the sugar and semolina and cook gently for 3 minutes. Gradually stir in the milk and continue stirring until the mixture boils and thickens. Simmer for 3 minutes, then pour into individual glasses and chill. When cold, decorate with cream and strawberries.

Burgundy Wine Trifle

Serves 4

225 g/8 oz Plums, stoned
150 ml/¼ pt Water
1 Blackcurrant jelly tablet
60 ml/4 tbsp Burgundy
4 Macaroons
150 ml/¼ pt Double cream, whipped
25 g/1 oz Hazelnuts, toasted and chopped

Place the plums and water in a saucepan and simmer until soft. Pour the fruit into a measuring jug and add enough of the juice, and water if necessary, to make up 450 ml/¾ pt. Return the fruit and juice to the saucepan, bring to the boil, add the jelly and stir until dissolved. Add the burgundy and leave to cool. Crumble the macaroons into a serving dish, pour the jelly over and leave to set. When set, top with the cream and sprinkle with the hazelnuts.

277

Frosted Chocolate Pudding

Serves 4

100 g/4 oz Plain chocolate
225 g/8 oz Cottage cheese, sieved
2 Eggs, separated
50 g/2 oz Caster sugar
5 ml/1 tsp Vanilla essence
2.5 ml/½ tsp Almond essence
225 g/8 oz Plain cake, cubed
150 ml/¼ pt Whipping cream, whipped

Melt the chocolate in a bowl over a pan of hot water. Remove from the heat and beat in the cottage cheese and egg yolks. Whisk the egg whites until stiff and beat in the sugar. Fold into the chocolate mixture with the essences, then fold in the cake cubes. Stand the bowl over the pan of simmering water and cook for 15 minutes. Spoon into glasses and chill. Serve with whipped cream.

Orange Brulée

Serves 4

4 Oranges
30 ml/2 tbsp Orange liqueur
300 ml/½ pt Soured cream
300 ml/½ pt Double cream, whipped
100 g/4 oz Demerara sugar

Peel the oranges, remove the pith and slice thinly. Place in a shallow flame-proof dish and sprinkle with the orange liqueur. Blend the creams together and spread over the oranges. Chill for at least 2 hours, then sprinkle with the sugar and brown under a hot grill until the sugar has just melted. Chill until required.

Coffee and Banana Krispie Pie

Serves 4

25 g/1 oz Butter or margarine
30 ml/2 tbsp Golden syrup
50 g/2 oz Rice Krispies
175 g/6 oz Marshmallows
45 ml/3 tbsp Hot water
15 ml/1 tbsp Instant coffee powder
300 ml/½ pt Double cream, whipped
3 Bananas, sliced

Melt the butter and syrup, then remove from the heat and stir in the cereal. Press the mixture into a 20 cm/8 in pie dish and chill. Put the marshmallows, water and coffee powder into a bowl over a pan of hot water. Simmer until the marshmallows have melted, stirring occasionally, then leave to cool. Fold the cream into the coffee mixture with 2 sliced bananas. Cool until thick, then pour onto the crisp base and chill until firm. Decorate with the remaining banana.

Oranges in Grand Marnier

Serves 4

6 Oranges
175 g/6 oz Caster sugar
150 ml/¼ pt Cold water
30 ml/2 tbsp Grand Marnier
Juice of ½ lemon

Cut away all the peel and pith from the oranges, slice crossways and arrrange in a serving dish. Cut away the pith from 6 pieces of rind and slice finely. Put in a saucepan, cover with water, bring to the boil then simmer for 15 minutes and drain well. Put the sugar in a heavy-based saucepan and stir over a low heat until the sugar has dissolved and caramelised. Remove from the heat and carefully stir in the cold water, which will make the mixture bubble. When the bubbling has stopped, return to the heat and stir until the caramel has dissolved and a syrup has formed. Add the prepared peel, bring to the boil and simmer for 3 minutes. Cool slightly, then stir in the lemon juice and Grand Marnier. Spoon the sauce over the oranges, cover and chill until required.

Paradise Pears

Serves 4

150 ml/¼ pt Red wine
150 ml/¼ pt Water
100 g/4 oz Caster sugar
4 Pears, peeled but with stalks on
5 ml/1 tsp Arrowroot

Mix the wine, water and sugar in a heavy-based saucepan and dissolve over a gentle heat, then boil until syrupy, without stirring. Stand the pears, stalks upwards, in the pan. Cut a circle of greaseproof paper with holes in for the stalks to poke through and place it over the pears. Boil for 5 minutes, basting occasionally until the pears are just tender. Carefully remove the pears to a serving dish. If the syrup is thin, boil it again, then stir in the arrowroot mixed with a little cold water. Boil for about 7 minutes until thick and clear, then allow to cool. Pour over and around the pears and serve.

Summer Pudding with Chantilly Cream

Serves 4-6

6 Stale white bread slices
100 g/4 oz Caster sugar
75 ml/5 tbsp Water
750 g/1½ lb Soft summer fruits (raspberries, strawberries, blackcurrants, redcurrants)
150 ml/¼ pt Double cream, whisked
½ Egg white, whisked
15 g/½ oz Icing sugar
Few drops of vanilla essence

Remove the bread crusts, cut into strips and use most of them to line a greased 1.2 litre/2 pt pudding basin, covering the basin tightly. Dissolve the sugar in water over a low heat, then add the fruit and simmer for 10 minutes. Spoon the hot fruit into the basin, reserving a little of the juice, and cover with the reserved bread. Put a saucer on top of the basin, and weigh down, then refrigerate overnight.

Mix the whipped cream and whisked egg white and fold in the icing sugar and vanilla essence. Chill.

When ready to serve, turn out the pudding on to a serving plate and spoon the reserved juice over any parts of the bread which have not absorbed the fruit juice. Serve with the chantilly cream.

Peaches in Bitter-Sweet Cream

Serves 4

150 ml/¼ pt Water

100 g/4 oz Granulated sugar

4 Peaches, peeled and sliced

75 ml/5 tbsp Double cream, lightly whipped

150 ml/¼ pt Natural yoghurt

25 g/1 oz Demerara sugar

25 g/1 oz Soft brown sugar

Put the water and granulated sugar in a saucepan and heat gently, stirring, until the sugar has dissolved. Bring to the boil and simmer for 5 minutes. Add the peaches, cover and simmer for 5 minutes until tender. Remove the peaches from the syrup and transfer them to a large serving dish. Mix together the cream and yoghurt and spread it over the peaches. Mix the demerara and soft brown sugars and sprinkle them thickly over the cream. Cover and chill for several hours until the sugar melts on the top.

Caribbean Bananas

Serves 4

4 Bananas

50 g/2 oz Soft brown sugar

30 ml/2 tbsp Orange juice

Pinch of nutmeg

Pinch of cinnamon

30 ml/2 tbsp Rum

25 g/1 oz Butter or margarine

Cut the bananas in half lengthways and place in a baking dish. Mix the sugar, orange juice, spices and rum and pour over the fruit. Dot with butter and bake in a preheated oven at 230°C/450°F/gas mark 8 for 15 minutes, basting from time to time. Serve hot with cream or ice cream.

Cheese Mandarin Puffs

Serves 4-6

150 ml/¼ pt Water

50 g/2 oz Unsalted butter or margarine

60 g/2½ oz Plain flour

2 Eggs, beaten

300 ml/½ pt Double cream

75 g/3 oz Cheddar cheese, grated

15 ml/1 tbsp Orange liqueur

300 g/11 oz Canned mandarin oranges, drained

Heat the water and butter in a saucepan, bring to the boil, then remove from the heat and beat in the flour. Beat over a low heat until the mixture comes away from the sides of the pan. Cool slightly, then beat in the eggs. Spoon the pastry into a piping bag with a 1 cm/½ in plain nozzle and pipe 20 bun shapes on a greased baking sheet. Bake in a preheated oven at 220°C/425°F/gas mark 7 for 25 minutes until well risen and golden brown. Slit the side of each puff to allow the steam to escape, then leave to cool.

Whip half the cream until stiff, then stir in the cheese and liqueur. Pipe the cream into the puffs, press a few mandarin segments into each one and pile the puffs on a large dish. Serve with the remaining cream.

Chocolate Fruit and Nut Dessert

Serves 4-6

100 g/4 oz Hazelnuts, toasted and
chopped
100 g/4 oz Blanched almonds,
chopped
25 g/1 oz Pine nuts
50 g/2 oz Mixed peel, chopped
50 g/2 oz Plain flour
25 g/1 oz Cocoa
Pinch of ground cloves
Pinch of cinnamon
Pinch of white pepper
100 g/4 oz Caster sugar
100 g/4 oz Honey
25 g/1 oz Unsalted butter or
margarine
15 ml/1 tbsp Icing sugar

Mix the nuts and mixed peel and stir
in the flour, cocoa and spices. Dissolve the sugar, honey and butter or
margarine in a heavy-based saucepan, then boil, without stirring until a
drop in cold water will form a soft
ball between the fingers. Immediately
stir the syrup into the fruit and nut
mixture and press it into a greased
and lined 20 cm/8 in cake tin. Bake in
a preheated oven at 150°C/300°F/
gas mark 2 for 35 minutes. Leave to
cool in the tin for 30 minutes, then
turn out and leave until cold. Dust
with icing sugar and serve cut into
thin wedges.

Apple Strudel

Serves 4

5 Crisp apples, peeled, cored and
chopped
100 g/4 oz Almonds, toasted and
chopped
100 g/4 oz Raisins
15 ml/1 tbsp Cinnamon
Pinch of salt
Pinch of nutmeg
225 g/8 oz Caster sugar
5 ml/1 tsp Vanilla essence
6 Filo pastry sheets
100 g/4 oz Butter or margarine,
melted
15 ml/1 tbsp Icing sugar

Stir together the apples, almonds,
raisins, cinnamon, salt, nutmeg, sugar
and vanilla essence. Lay a sheet of
filo pastry on a clean tea towel and
brush with melted butter. Lay a
second sheet beside it, overlapping
the edges and brush with butter. Lay
2 more sheets on top in the opposite
direction and brush with butter. Lay
the final 2 sheets on top, in the
opposite direction, and brush with
butter. Fold the edges in 1 cm/½ in.
Spread the fruit mixture evenly over
the pastry, right up to the folded
edges. Roll up carefully from the
narrow end, using the towel to help.
Roll on to a greased and lined baking
sheet with the join underneath and
tuck in the ends. Brush with the
remaining butter and bake in a
preheated oven at 180°C/350°F/gas
mark 4 for 30 minutes until crisp and
golden. Lift carefully from the paper
on to a wire rack to cool and serve
sprinkled with icing sugar.

Banana and Ginger Cheesecake Flan

Serves 4

75 g/3 oz Butter or margarine

225 g/8 oz Gingernut biscuits, crushed

225 g/8 oz Cottage cheese, sieved

150 ml/¼ pt Natural yoghurt

30 ml/2 tbsp Honey

3 Bananas, mashed

Juice of ½ lemon

15 g/½ oz Gelatine

30 ml/2 tbsp Water

6 Slices of preserved ginger

150 ml/¼ pt Whipping cream, whipped

Melt the butter or margarine, remove from the heat and stir in the biscuit crumbs. Press into the base and sides of a 20 cm/8 in flan ring. Leave to cool. Mix the cottage cheese, yoghurt, honey, bananas and lemon juice. Dissolve the gelatine in the water, then stir it into the mixture, pour it into the flan case and leave to set. Arrange the slices of ginger on top and decorate with piped stars of whipped cream. Chill before serving.

Apricot Cream Meringue

Serves 4

3 Eggs, separated

225 g/8 oz Caster sugar

450 g/1 lb Canned apricots

150 ml/¼ pt Milk

5 ml/1 tsp Cornflour

2.5 ml/½ tsp Vanilla essence

Whisk the egg whites until stiff, then whisk in three-quarters of the sugar. Spoon or pipe into a circle on wetted greaseproof paper on a baking sheet and build up the edges to form a case. Bake in a preheated oven at 140°C/275°F/gas mark 1 for 1 hour until the meringue is crisp, then turn off the oven and leave the meringue in the oven until it cools. Mix the milk with 150 ml/¼ pt juice from the apricots, stir in the cornflour and heat gently. Whisk the egg yolks and remaining sugar and pour on a little of the hot liquid. Return to the pan and stir over a low heat until creamy. Leave to cool, then stir in the vanilla essence. Just before serving, arrange half the drained fruit in the meringue case, cover with the custard and top with the remaining apricots.

Honey Meringues

Serves 4

6 Egg whites

350 g/12 oz Caster sugar

30 ml/2 tbsp Honey

100 g/4 oz Hazelnuts, chopped

10 ml/2 tsp Brandy

300 ml/½ pt Double cream, whipped

Whisk the egg whites until stiff, then whisk in half the sugar and fold in the remainder. Pipe or drop teaspoons of the mixture on to a lightly greased baking sheet. Bake in a preheated oven at 140°C/275°F/gas mark 1 for 50 minutes, then leave to cool. Fold the honey, hazelnuts and brandy into the cream and sandwich the meringues together with the cream filling.

Coffee Meringue Tarts

Serves 4

225 g/8 oz Shortcrust Pastry
(page 145)

300 ml/½ pt Custard Sauce
(page 231)

25 ml/1½ tbsp Coffee essence

1 Egg yolk

1 Egg white

50 g/2 oz Caster sugar

Roll out the pastry and use it to line
12 small tartlet tins. Prick well with a
fork and chill. Bake blind in a preheated oven at 200°C/400°F/gas
mark 6 for 10 minutes. Beat the
custard, 15 ml/1 tbsp coffee essence
and the egg yolk. Divide the mixture
between the tartlets and leave to set.
Whisk the egg white until stiff, whisk
in half the sugar until stiff, then fold in
the remaining sugar with the remaining coffee essence. Return to a cool
oven and bake at 160°C/325°F/gas
mark 3 for 20 minutes until pale
golden and firm. Leave to cool.

Apple Gingerbread Surprise

Serves 4

175 g/6 oz Butter or margarine

175 g/6 oz Soft brown sugar

2 Dessert apples, peeled, cored and
sliced

100 g/4 oz Self-raising flour

2.5 ml/½ tsp Salt

8 ml/1½ tsp Ground ginger

5 ml/1 tsp Grated nutmeg

Grated rind and juice of 1 lemon

2 Eggs

Cream 50 g/2 oz butter or margarine
with 50 g/2 oz sugar and spread over
the bottom and sides of a 20 cm/8 in
cake tin. Arrange the apple slices
over the base. Mix the flour, salt and
spices. Cream the remaining butter
and sugar with the lemon rind and
juice until light and fluffy, then beat in
the eggs. Fold in the flour mixture
and spread the mixture over the
apples. Bake in a preheated oven
at 180°C/350°F/gas mark 4 for
45 minutes. Turn out and allow to
cool. Serve with cream.

Chocolate Cream Tart

Serves 4

50 g/2 oz Butter or margarine

50 g/2 oz Caster sugar

15 ml/1 tbsp Golden syrup

175 g/6 oz Sweet biscuits, crushed

175 g/6 oz Plain chocolate

3 Eggs, separated

10 ml/2 tsp Brandy

150 ml/¼ pt Double cream,
whipped

25 g/1 oz Walnuts, chopped

Melt the butter or margarine, sugar
and syrup and stir in the biscuit
crumbs. Press into a 20 cm/8 in flan
ring and bake in a preheated oven at
180°C/350°F/gas mark 4 for 15
minutes. Chill until firm and crisp.
Melt the chocolate. Remove from
the heat and stir in the egg yolks and
brandy. Leave to cool, then fold in
the cream. Whisk the egg whites until
stiff, then fold them into the mixture.
Pour into the crumb case and chill
until firm. Sprinkle with walnuts
before serving.

Cheesecake Torte

Serves 4

150 ml/¼ pt Double cream, whipped
25 g/1 oz Cornflour
450 g/1 lb Cottage cheese, sieved
4 Egg whites
175 g/6 oz Caster sugar
5 ml/1 tsp Vanilla essence
25 g/1 oz Butter or margarine
100 g/4 oz Digestive biscuits, crushed
50 g/2 oz Flaked almonds, toasted
2 Kiwi fruit, sliced
150 ml/¼ pt Whipping cream, whipped

Mix the cream with the cornflour and cottage cheese. Whisk the egg whites until stiff, then whisk in the sugar and fold into the cheese mixture with the vanilla essence. Rub the butter or margarine over a 23 cm/9 in loose-bottomed cake tin and sprinkle with the biscuit crumbs. Pour in the cheese mixture and bake in a pre-heated oven at 180°C/350°F/gas mark 4 for 1 hour. Cool slightly before removing from the tin. Sprinkle with toasted almonds and decorate with the kiwi fruit and piped cream.

Lemon Fridge Cake

Serves 4

6 Eggs
150 g/5 oz Caster sugar
15 ml/1 tbsp Water
100 g/4 oz Self-raising flour
1 Egg yolk
150 ml/¼ pt Icing sugar
15 g/½ oz Gelatine
Grated rind and juice of 1 lemon
150 ml/¼ pt Double cream, whipped

Cream 3 eggs with the caster sugar until pale and thick, then add the water and fold in the flour. Spoon into 2 greased 20 cm/8 in round cake tins and bake in a preheated oven at 180°C/350°F/gas mark 4 for 12 minutes. Turn out and cool on a wire rack.

Whisk the remaining eggs and the egg yolk with the icing sugar until frothy. Dissolve the gelatine in the lemon juice over a pan of hot water, then stir this into the egg yolks with the lemon rind. Fold in the whipped cream. Place one sponge back in the cake tin, spoon in the soufflé mixture, place the other sponge on top and chill until required.

Linzertorte

Serves 4

175 g/6 oz Soft margarine

50 g/2 oz Caster sugar

50 g/2 oz Ground almonds

Grated rind of 1 lemon

1 Egg

225 g/8 oz Plain flour

2.5 ml/½ tsp Cinnamon

450 g/1 lb Raspberries

100 g/4 oz Granulated sugar

30 ml/2 tbsp Redcurrant jelly

30 ml/2 tbsp Icing sugar

Cream the margarine, sugar, nuts and lemon rind, egg and 15 g/½ oz flour until well mixed, then stir in the remaining flour and cinnamon to form a soft dough. Turn on to a floured surface and knead lightly until smooth. Roll out two-thirds of the dough and use it to line a greased 20 cm/8 in flan ring, placed on a baking sheet. Chill for 30 minutes. Roll out the remaining pastry and cut into 1 cm/½ in strips. Cook the raspberries with the sugar until soft, then spoon into the pastry case and arrange the pastry strips across the top in a lattice pattern. Bake in a pre-heated oven at 190°C/375°F/gas mark 5 for 30 minutes. Brush with redcurrant jelly to glaze and leave to cool. Serve sprinkled with icing sugar.

Note
You can use raspberry jam instead of the cooked raspberries or substitute canned fruit instead.

Pear and Hazelnut Shortcake

Serves 8

100 g/4 oz Butter or margarine

50 g/2 oz Caster sugar

75 g/3 oz Hazelnuts, skinned and ground

140 g/5 oz Plain flour

15 ml/1 tbsp Water

2 Pears, sliced

150 ml/¼ pt Double or whipping cream, whipped

15 ml/1 tbsp Icing sugar

Beat the butter until soft, then beat in the sugar, nuts and flour. Add the water and mix to a soft dough. Divide the dough in half and form each into a ball. Pat each ball into a circle about 18 cm/7 in in diameter, place the circles on a greased baking sheet and bake in a preheated oven at 190°C/375°F/gas mark 5 for 10 minutes until just brown around the edges. Cut one round into 8 segments. Allow to cool on the tray.

Do not assemble the shortcake until an hour before it is needed. Place the whole round on a serving plate. Spread half the cream on top, then cover with the pears. Put the remaining cream in a piping bag with a large star nozzle and pipe 8 large rosettes on top of the pears. Lay each triangle of pastry on top of the rosettes of cream so that it rests at an angle. Sprinkle with sifted icing sugar and serve immediately.

Orange Savarin

Serves 4-6

15 g/½ oz Fresh yeast OR
15 ml/1 tbsp Dried yeast

85 ml/3 fl oz Warm milk

100 g/4 oz Granulated sugar

60 g/2½ oz Butter or margarine

100 g/4 oz Strong plain flour

2 Eggs, beaten

150 ml/¼ pt Water

1 Orange

10 ml/2 tsp Rum or brandy

2-3 drops Pink food colouring
(optional)

150 ml/¼ pt Double or whipping
cream, whipped

Mix the yeast and milk with 2.5 ml/ ½ tsp sugar and leave for 10 minutes until frothy. Rub the butter or margarine into the flour, then mix in the yeast mixture and eggs. Pour into a 20 cm/8 in savarin or ring mould, cover with a damp cloth and leave to rise in a warm place for 45 minutes. Bake in a preheated oven at 230°C/450°F/gas mark 8 for 30 minutes.

Meanwhile make the sauce by dissolving the sugar in the water over a gentle heat. Use a potato peeler to remove 4 strips of orange rind and put these in the sugar syrup. Bring to the boil, boil for 1 minute, then add the rum or brandy and remove from the heat. Colour the syrup with a few drops of food colouring, if liked. Turn the savarin out of the mould, pour the sauce over and leave to soak in. Slice half the orange and cut the rest into small pieces. Arrange the slices round the edge and the pieces in the centre of the savarin. Serve with the whipped cream.

Ice Creams and Sorbets

There is something rather special about home-made ice cream — it always tastes so special. It does take a little time to prepare as you usually need to whip the cream a few times while it is freezing, but it is well worth the extra trouble.

Iced Apricot Cream

Serves 4

450 g/1 lb Fresh apricots
15 ml/1 tbsp Water
Thin strip of orange rind
50 g/2 oz Caster sugar
25 g/1 oz Icing sugar
300 ml/½ pt Double cream, whipped
75 g/3 oz Almond macaroon or ratafia biscuits, crumbled
2 Egg whites
150 ml/¼ pt Whipping cream, whipped

Reserve 2 apricots for decoration and quarter them. Place the remaining apricots, water, orange rind and caster sugar in a saucepan, bring to the boil and simmer gently until the fruit is soft. Remove the orange rind, then purée the mixture in a food processor or blender. Fold the icing sugar into the double cream. Reserve 15 ml/1 tbsp crumbled biscuits and fold the remainder into the cream with the apricot purée. Whisk the egg whites until stiff, then fold them into the mixture. Turn the mixture into a freezer container and freeze until set.

Turn out the apricot cream, sprinkle with the reserved crumbs and decorate with the whipped cream and reserved apricots.

Frozen Banana Cream

Serves 4

2 Ripe bananas, mashed
20 ml/1½ tbsp Lemon juice
30 ml/2 tbsp Honey
200 ml/7 fl oz Double cream, whipped

Purée the bananas, lemon juice and honey in a food processor or blender. Fold the mixture into the whipped cream, pour into an ice cube tray and freeze until firm but not hard.

Vanilla Ice Cream

Makes 900 ml/1½ pts

2 Eggs
100 g/4 oz Caster sugar
600 ml/1 pt Milk, warmed
300 ml/½ pt Double cream
7.5 ml/1½ tsp Vanilla essence

Beat the eggs and sugar until liquid then stir in the milk and strain into a bowl over a pan of simmering water. Stir over a gentle heat for 20 minutes until the custard is as thick as single cream. Pour into a clean bowl, cover and leave to cool.

Half whip the cream, then mix it lightly with the egg custard and vanilla essence. Turn into a freezer container and freeze for 1 hour. Turn out into a chilled bowl and beat until smooth. Return it to the container and freeze until firm.

Orange Almond Ice Cream

Serves 4

4 Eggs
75 ml/5 tbsp Honey
2 Drops vanilla essence
150 ml/¼ pt Whipping cream,
  whipped
45 ml/3 tbsp Orange liqueur
25 g/1 oz Butter or margarine
25 g/1 oz Flaked almonds

Whisk the eggs with the honey and vanilla essence until creamy, then fold in the cream and liqueur. Turn into a freezer container and freeze for 1 hour. Turn out into a chilled bowl and beat until smooth, then return it to the container and freeze until firm.

Just before serving, melt the butter or margarine and fry the flaked almonds until just beginning to brown. Sprinkle on top of the ice cream.

Fruity Ice Cream

Makes 600 ml/1 pt

300 ml/½ pt Cold puréed soft
  or stewed fruit
300 ml/½ pt Double cream
5 ml/1 tsp Lemon juice

Sieve the fruit purée if it contains any lumps or pips. Half whip the cream, then blend in the purée and lemon juice. Pour into a freezer container and freeze for 1 hour. Turn out into a chilled bowl and beat until smooth. Return it to the container and freeze until firm.

Chocolate Ice Cream

Serves 6-8

4 Egg yolks
100 g/4 oz Caster sugar
600 ml/1 pt Milk, warmed
75 g/3 oz Plain chocolate, grated
5 ml/1 tsp Vanilla essence
150 ml/¼ pt Double cream,
  whipped

Beat the egg yolks and sugar until liquid then stir in the milk and strain into a bowl over a pan of simmering water. Stir over a gentle heat for 20 minutes until the custard is as thick as single cream. Pour into a clean bowl and whisk in the chocolate and vanilla essence until smooth. Leave to cool.

Fold the whipped cream into the custard. Turn it into a freezer container and freeze for 1 hour. Turn out into a chilled bowl and beat until smooth, then return it to the container and freeze for a further 1 hour. Beat again, return it to the container and freeze until firm.

Chocolate Mint Ice Cream

Serves 4

4 Egg yolks
175 g/6 oz Caster sugar
300 ml/½ pt Milk
100 g/4 oz Plain chocolate, grated
30 ml/2 tbsp Crème de menthe
50 g/2 oz Chocolate mint crisps, grated
250 ml/8 fl oz Double cream
30 ml/2 tbsp Iced water

Beat the egg yolks and sugar until pale, then whisk in the milk. Cook the mixture over a low heat, stirring until the custard is thick enough to coat the back of a wooden spoon. Remove from the heat and leave to cool for 5 minutes. Mix the chocolate into the custard and stir until it has melted, then chill. Stir in the crème de menthe and chocolate crisps. Whip the cream with the iced water until it forms soft peaks. Fold the cream and chocolate custard together, pour into a freezer container and freeze until beginning to set. Whisk well, then return to the container and freeze until firm.

Christmas Pudding Ice Cream

Serves 8

50 g/2 oz Butter or margarine
175 g/6 oz Raisins
100 g/4 oz Sultanas
50 g/2 oz Currants
50 g/2 oz Mixed peel
2.5 ml/½ tsp Almond essence
Grated rind and juice of 1 orange
Grated rind of 1 lemon
1 Cooking apple, peeled, cored and finely chopped
100 g/4 oz Canned pineapple, drained and crushed
5 ml/1 tsp Mixed spice
50 g/2 oz Caster sugar
50 g/2 oz Walnuts, chopped
30 ml/2 tbsp Brandy or rum
1 litre/1¾ pts Soft scoop ice cream

Mix together all the ingredients except the ice cream in a large saucepan, bring to the boil, cover and simmer gently for 30 minutes. Leave to cool.

Spoon the ice cream into a bowl and whisk. Fold in the fruit mixture and pour into a freezer container until set.

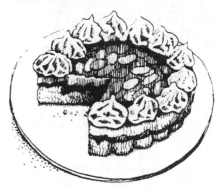

Kiwi Fruit Ice Cream

Serves 4

6 Eggs, separated

225 g/8 oz Caster sugar

30 ml/2 tbsp Boiling water

600 ml/1 pt Double cream,
  whipped

8 Kiwi fruit

60 ml/4 tbsp Kirsch

5 ml/1 tsp Vanilla essence

Whisk the egg whites with 30 ml/2 tbsp sugar. Whisk the egg yolks with the remaining sugar and the boiling water. Fold the two mixtures together, then fold in the cream. Reserve 1 kiwi fruit for decoration and slice it thinly. Purée the remaining kiwi fruit in a food processor or blender and sieve to remove any pips. Stir the fruit into the mixture with the kirsch and vanilla essence. Pour into a freezer container and freeze until firm. Serve garnished with slices of kiwi fruit.

Pineapple Ice Cream Pie

Serves 4-6

50 g/2 oz Butter or margarine

100 g/4 oz Digestive biscuits,
  crushed

275 g/10 oz Canned pineapple in
  natural juice, drained

5 ml/1 tsp Cornflour

Juice of ½ lemon

5 ml/1 tsp Honey

1 litre/1¾ pts Soft scoop ice cream

25 g/1 oz Flaked almonds

Melt the butter or margarine and stir in the biscuits. Press into a 20 cm/8 in flan ring and place in the fridge.

Blend the cornflour with a little pineapple juice, then heat the rest of the juice with the lemon juice and honey. Add the hot liquid to the cornflour mixture and return to the pan over a low heat to thicken. Allow to cool. Reserve a few pieces for decoration, then purée the remaining pineapple in a food processor or blender and add to the sauce. Place scoops of the ice cream in the biscuit base, arranging them round in a pyramid. Pour over the pineapple sauce and freeze for 30 minutes. Remove, sprinkle with nuts and decorate with the reserved pineapple pieces. Serve immediately.

Lemon Ice Box Pudding

Serves 4

6 Eggs, separated

225 g/8 oz Caster sugar

Grated rind and juice of 2 lemons

600 ml/1 pt Double cream,
  whipped

225 g/8 oz Rich Tea biscuits,
  crushed

Place the egg yolks in a large warmed bowl and whisk, gradually adding the sugar, until the volume will increase no further, then beat in the lemon rind and juice. Fold in the cream. Whisk the egg whites until stiff, then fold them into the mixture. Sprinkle half the biscuits over the base of a deep china flan dish, spread with the mousse mixture and top with the remaining biscuits. Freeze for at least 12 hours. Transfer to the fridge for 30 minutes before serving.

Raspberry Bombe

Serves 4

225 g/8 oz Raspberries

25 g/1 oz Icing sugar

300 ml/½ pt Double cream

150 ml/¼ pt Single cream

100 g/4 oz Meringues, broken into
pieces

Reserve a few raspberries for decoration and purée the remainder with the icing sugar in a food processor or blender. Sieve to remove the pips. Whip the creams together until they form soft peaks, then fold in the meringues. Lightly fold in half the raspberry purée to give a marbled effect, then turn into a 1.2 litre/2 pt pudding basin, cover and freeze until firm. Transfer to the fridge 30 minutes before serving, pour over the remaining purée and decorate with the reserved raspberries.

Strawberry Ice Cream Gâteau

Serves 6

1.2 litre/2 pts Vanilla Ice Cream
(page 288)

1½ quantity Victoria Sandwich
mixture (page 337)

90 ml/6 tbsp Strawberry jam

225 g/8 oz Strawberries, sliced

300 ml/½ pt Double cream,
whipped

Make the ice cream and after beating it, freeze it in 2 x 18 cm/7 in sandwich tins. Make the cake in 3 x 18 cm/7 in cake tins and leave to cool.

Warm the jam and sieve it, if

necessary, then spread it over 2 of the cakes. Spread most of the strawberries on top, reserving a few for decoration. Layer half the ice cream on one jam-covered cake, place the other jam-covered cake on top and top with the remaining ice cream. Place the plain cake on top, cover with the whipped cream and decorate with the reserved fruit.

Variations

You can use raspberries for this cake, or canned peaches, apricots or kiwi fruit are also suitable, used with an appropriately flavoured jam.

Pineapple Ice

Serves 4

1 Pineapple, halved lengthways

175 g/6 oz Granulated sugar

450 ml/¾ pt Water

1 Egg white

Remove the core from the pineapple and scoop out the flesh, keeping the shells intact. Purée the flesh in a food processor or blender and chill the shells in the fridge. Dissolve the sugar in the water in a saucepan, then bring to the boil and boil for 5 minutes. Leave to cool.

Mix the pineapple pulp into the syrup, pour into a freezer container and freeze for 3 hours.

Whisk the egg white until stiff, then whisk in the ice cream. Return to the freezer container and freeze until firm.

Transfer to the fridge 10 minutes before serving and scoop into the pineapple shells to serve.

Apple Sorbet with Mint

Serves 4

4 Dessert apples, peeled, cored and
  finely chopped
225 ml/8 fl oz White wine
100 ml/4 fl oz Water
75 ml/5 tbsp Honey
Juice of 1 lemon
6 Mint leaves, finely chopped

Purée the apples, wine and water, then stir in the honey and lemon juice. Freeze for 1 hour. Stir well, then freeze again and continue to stir the sorbet occasionally while it is freezing. Just before it sets, stir in the mint. Whisk the sorbet and serve in individual glasses.

Grapefruit Parfait

Serves 4

3 Egg whites
2.5 ml/½ tsp Salt
225 g/8 oz Granulated sugar
150 ml/¼ pt Water
175 g/6 oz Frozen concentrated
  grapefruit juice
300 ml/½ pt Whipping cream,
  whipped

Whisk the egg whites with the salt until they stand in soft peaks. Dissolve the sugar in the water over a low heat, then bring to the boil and boil rapidly for 3 minutes. Pour slowly on to the egg whites, whisking until the mixture is stiff, then whisk in the fruit juice and stir in the cream. Freeze overnight. Serve with fruit salad and cream.

Orange and Ginger Sorbet

Serves 4

450 ml/¾ pt Orange juice
4 chunks Stem ginger
6 Egg whites
1 Orange, peeled and sliced

Purée the orange juice and ginger in a food processor or blender. Pour into a shallow container and freeze until the mixture begins to harden. Remove from the freezer and mix well. Whisk the egg whites until stiff, then fold them into the orange mixture. Return to the freezer and leave to harden. Transfer to the fridge 30 minutes before serving and serve garnished with orange slices.

Lemon Water Ice

Serves 4

450 g/1 lb Cube sugar
600 ml/1 pt Water
Peeled rind and juice of 2 lemons
2 Egg whites
Mint leaves to garnish

Place the sugar, water, peeled lemon rind and juice in a saucepan and stir over a low heat until the sugar has dissolved. Bring to the boil and boil for 6 minutes, then leave to cool and strain.

Whisk the egg whites until stiff, then fold in the lemon syrup, pour into a freezer container and freeze for 1 hour. Turn out into a chilled bowl and whisk, then freeze and whisk again. Serve garnished with mint leaves.

Confectionery

There are lots of simple and different sweets here for you to try, and they make super gifts for family and friends if you package them attractively.

When making pastes or pouring hot sugar, you will need a suitable working surface. They used to be made on marble or enamel but plastic laminate is equally good.

Barley Sugar

Makes 450 g/1 lb

450 g/1 lb Loaf or caster sugar
300 ml/½ pt Water
Pinch of cream of tartar
Few drops of lemon essence

Dissolve the sugar, water and cream of tartar in a heavy-based saucepan. Boil, without stirring, to 155°C/315°F or until the syrup is pale golden. Make sure the hotplate is no larger than the pan or that gas flames do not rise up the sides of the pan. Stir in the lemon essence. Pour the mixture onto an oiled work surface and leave to cool a little. Fold the sides to the centre to make a tube shape, then cut into narrow strips with scissors and twist them into spirals. When cold, store in an airtight container.

Acid Drops

Makes 450 g/1 lb

450 g/1 lb Loaf or caster sugar
300 ml/½ pt Water
Pinch of cream of tartar
Caster sugar for dusting

Dissolve the sugar and water in a heavy-based saucepan. Boil, with stirring, to 155°C/315°F or until the syrup is pale golden. Make sure the hotplate is no larger than the pan or that gas flames do not rise up the sides of the pan. Pour the mixture onto an oiled work surface and sprinkle with the cream of tartar. Fold the sides to the centre to mix them together. Roll the sugar into sticks, cut it into little drops and roll them in caster sugar.

Candied Ginger

Makes 450 g/1 lb

450 g/1 lb Sugar
175 ml/6 fl oz Water
100 g/4 oz Root ginger, grated

Line a large tin with greased baking parchment. Boil the sugar and water in a heavy-based saucepan until the sugar begins to candy round the edges, then stir in the grated ginger. Pour out immediately on to the paper and leave to cool, then cut into fancy shapes.

Candied Lemon

Makes 450 g/1 lb

450 g/1 lb Sugar
175 ml/6 fl oz Water
15 ml/1 tbsp Lemon essence

Line a large tin with greased baking parchment. Boil the sugar and water in a heavy-based saucepan until the sugar begins to candy round the edges, then stir in the lemon essence. Pour out immediately on to the paper and leave to cool, then cut into fancy shapes.

Peppermint Candy

Makes 450 g/1 lb

450 g/1 lb Sugar
175 ml/6 fl oz Water
15 ml/1 tbsp Peppermint essence

Line a large tin with greased baking parchment. Boil the sugar and water in a heavy-based saucepan until the sugar begins to candy round the edges, then stir in the peppermint essence. Pour out immediately on to the paper and leave to cool, then cut into fancy shapes.

Caramels

Makes 450 g/1 lb

450 g/1 lb Loaf or caster sugar
150 ml/¼ pt Water
25 g/1 oz Butter or margarine
Pinch of cream of tartar

Bring the sugar and water to the boil in a heavy-based saucepan. Add the butter and cream of tartar and mix well. Boil to 143°C/290°F or until a drop cracks when dropped into cold water. Pour into a greased 18 cm/7 in tin to set. Cut into squares before it is quite cold and wrap them in grease-proof paper.

Butterscotch

Makes 450 g/1 lb

450 g/1 lb Demerara sugar
150 ml/¼ pt Water
50 g/2 oz Butter or margarine

Dissolve the sugar and water in a heavy-based saucepan. Boil, without stirring to 137°C/280°F or until a drop forms a ball when dropped into cold water. Stir in the butter a piece at a time then pour into a greased 18 cm/7 in tin and leave to cool before marking into squares.

Chocolate Fudge

Makes 450 g/1 lb

450 g/1 lb Caster sugar
10 ml/2 tsp Cocoa
150 ml/¼ pt Milk
50 g/2 oz Butter or margarine
45 ml/3 tbsp Water
Few drops of vanilla essence

Place all the ingredients in a heavy-based saucepan and boil to 115°C/ 240°F or until a drop will just set when dropped into cold water. Remove from the heat and beat with a wooden spoon until creamy and almost cold. Pour into a greased 18 cm/7 in tin and leave to set before cutting into squares.

Butterscotch Fudge

Makes 450 g/1 lb

450 g/1 lb Caster sugar
150 ml/¼ pt Evaporated milk
150 ml/¼ pt Milk
50 g/2 oz Butter or margarine
45 ml/3 tbsp Water
Few drops of butterscotch essence

Place all the ingredients in a heavy-based saucepan and boil to 115°C/ 240°F or until a drop will just set when dropped into cold water. Remove from the heat, add the essence and beat well until the mixture thickens. Pour into a greased 18 cm/ 7 in tin and leave to set before cutting into squares.

Toffee

Makes 450 g/1 lb

450 g/1 lb Soft brown sugar
50 g/2 oz Butter or margarine

Dissolve the sugar and butter in a heavy-based saucepan. Boil to 143°C/ 290°F or until a drop will crack when dropped into cold water. Pour into a greased 18 cm/7 in tin and leave to set. Cut into squares and store in an airtight container.

Toffee Apples

Makes 12

175 g/6 oz Golden syrup
350 g/12 oz Soft brown sugar
25 g/1 oz Butter or margarine
150 ml/¼ pt Water
5 ml/1 tsp Vinegar
12 Eating apples, washed, dried and with a wooden skewer pushed into each

Dissolve all the ingredients except the apples in a heavy-based saucepan. Boil to 143°C/290°F or until a drop cracks when dropped into cold water. Remove from the heat and twist the apples in the toffee to cover them. Dip them in cold water, then stand them on a greased baking sheet to set. Wrap carefully if the apples are not to be eaten straight away, otherwise the toffee will soften.

Toffee Brazils

Makes 900 g/2 lb

100 g/4 oz Butter or margarine
450 g/1 lb Soft brown sugar
225 g/8 oz Black treacle
450 g/1 lb Brazils, shelled and
   halved

Melt the butter in a saucepan, add the sugar and treacle and boil to 143°C/290°F or until a drop cracks when dropped into cold water. Turn into a greased 20 cm/8 in tin and allow to cool a little. When the toffee is beginning to set, press the nuts into it, and mark into squares with a knife. Snap the toffee into pieces when cold and store in an airtight container.

Everton Toffee

Makes 450 g/1 lb

100 g/4 oz Butter or margarine
225 g/8 oz Soft brown sugar
225 g/8 oz Black treacle

Dissolve the butter and sugar with the treacle in a heavy-based saucepan. Boil to 143°C/290°F or until a drop cracks when dropped into cold water. Pour into a greased 18 cm/7 in tin, mark into squares and leave to set.

Fondant

Makes 450 g/1 lb

450 g/1 lb Caster sugar
150 ml/¼ pt Water
5 ml/1 tsp Glucose
Few drops of flavouring of choice
Few drops of colouring of choice

Rinse out a saucepan with cold water, dissolve the sugar and water over a low heat, stirring, then add the glucose. Boil to 110°C/230°F or until a drop in cold water will form a soft ball between the fingers. Pour into a large greased tin and leave until cool enough to handle. Work it with a wooden spoon until the fondant becomes white and creamy, adding a few drops of flavouring or colouring if required, then knead it until smooth. Leave to stand for 2 to 3 hours before using to make into sweets.

Before use, place the fondant in a bowl and stand the bowl in a tin of hot water for a few minutes, then knead the fondant until soft enough to use.

Coconut Fondants

Makes 30

225 g/8 oz Fondant (page 296)
100 g/4 oz Desiccated coconut
Few drops of red food colouring

Warm the fondant in a basin, then stir in the desiccated coconut. Place small balls of half the mixture on to greased baking parchment to dry. Colour the remainder with a few drops of food colouring and make them into balls in the same way.

Coffee Fondants

Makes 30

225 g/8 oz Fondant (page 296)
Few drops of coffee essence OR
5 ml/1 tspVery strong black coffee

Warm the fondant in a basin, then stir in the coffee essence or cold black coffee. Place small balls of the mixture on to greased baking parchment to dry.

Almond Crunch

Makes 36

60 g/2½ oz Butter or margarine
60 ml/4 tbsp Honey
75 g/3 oz Flaked almonds

Melt the butter in a heavy-based saucepan, stir in the honey and almonds and cook over a medium heat, stirring continuously, for 7 minutes until the mixture is golden brown. Spread the mixture in a greased 20 cm/8 in square tin and cut into squares at once with a sharp greased knife. Leave to cool, chill in the fridge then store in a covered container.

Chocolate Pineapple

Makes 350 g/12 oz

200 g/7 oz Plain chocolate
300 g/11 oz Canned pineapple
    chunks, drained
Crystallised violets to garnish

Melt the chocolate in a bowl over a pan of hot water. Hold the pineapple chunks with two forks, dip them into the chocolate and coat evenly. Leave to dry on greaseproof paper and decorate with crystallised violets.

Coffee Brazils

Makes 450 g/1 lb

450 g/1 lb Ground almonds
100 g/4 oz Icing sugar
Few drops of coffee essence OR
5 ml/1 tsp Very strong black coffee
25 g/1 oz Butter or margarine
100 g/4 oz Caster sugar
15 ml/1 tbsp Water
450 g/1 lb Brazil nuts, shelled

Mix the ground almonds and icing sugar with the coffee essence or black coffee. Mix in the butter or margarine and work to a smooth paste. Dissolve the sugar in the water, then boil for 5 minutes to a syrup. Cover the nuts with the almond paste and press them into compact shapes. Spear them with a fine skewer (a hat pin is ideal if you can find one!), then dip them into the boiling syrup, twist to remove drips and leave them on greased baking parchment to harden.

Variations
You can use walnuts for this recipe, or substitute melted chocolate for the coffee essence to make chocolate nuts.

Rum Truffles

Makes 12

| 75 g/3 oz oz Plain chocolate |
| 1 Egg yolk |
| 15 g/½ oz Butter or margarine |
| 5 ml/1 tsp Rum |
| 5 ml/1 tsp Single cream |
| 50 g/2 oz Chocolate vermicelli |

Melt the chocolate in a bowl over a pan of hot water. Beat in the egg yolk, butter or margarine, rum and cream until thick, then chill in the fridge until firm. Shape into 12 balls and toss in the vermicelli. Place in petit four cases to serve.

Marrons Glacé

Makes 350 g/12 oz

| 450 g/1 lb Chestnuts |
| 450 g/1 lb Caster sugar |
| 150 ml/¼ pt Water |
| Few drops of vanilla essence |

Peel the chestnuts and boil them in water for a few minutes till the skins come off easily, then boil them gently until they are soft but not broken. Dissolve the sugar in the water with the vanilla essence, then boil until the mixture thickens to a syrup. Add the chestnuts and bring back to the boil for 4 minutes. Carefully remove the chestnuts from the syrup with a slotted spoon, bring the syrup back to the boil and continue boiling until the syrup thickens again. Replace the chestnuts and boil again for 3 minutes. Drain and serve, or store in the syrup in an airtight jar.

Coconut Ice

Makes 500 g/1¼ lb

| 450 g/1 lb Granulated sugar |
| 150 ml/¼ pt Milk |
| 175 g/6 oz Desiccated coconut |
| Few drops of vanilla essence |
| Few drops of red food colouring |

Dissolve the sugar and milk in a heavy-based saucepan, then boil to 115°C/240°F or until the mixture begins to thicken. Remove from the heat and stir in the coconut and vanilla essence. Pour half the mixture into a greased loaf tin. Stir the food colouring into the other half and pour it on top. When cold, turn out and cut into bars.

Date Bon-Bons

Makes 20

| 225 g/8 oz Dates, stoned and chopped |
| 50 g/2 oz Butter or margarine softened |
| 60 ml/4 tbsp Honey |
| 1 Egg, beaten |
| 2.5 ml/½ tsp Vanilla essence |
| 100 g/4 oz Sunflower seeds, chopped |
| 50 g/2 oz Desiccated coconut |

Mix the dates, butter or margarine, honey, egg and vanilla essence in a saucepan, bring to the boil and cook, stirring, for 1 minute. Stir in the seeds. Chill, then shape into balls and roll in coconut. Store in the fridge.

Fruit and Nut Caramels

Makes 36

75 g/3 oz Butter or margarine
150 g/5 oz Golden syrup
175 g/6 oz Honey
100 g/4 oz Walnuts, chopped
100 g/4 oz Dates, stoned and
  chopped

Melt the butter or margarine in a heavy-based saucepan, add the syrup and honey, bring to the boil and boil to 137°C/270°F or until a drop in cold water forms a soft ball between the fingers. Remove from the heat, stir in the walnuts and dates and beat until opaque. Pour into a greased and lined shallow 20 cm x 13 cm/8 in x 5 in tin and leave to cool. When almost set, cut through into squares. Store in waxed paper.

Maple Glazed Nuts

Makes 300 g/11 oz

120 ml/4 fl oz Maple syrup
2.5 ml/½ tsp Cinnamon
10 ml/2 tsp Butter or margarine
Pinch of salt
5 ml/1 tsp Vanilla essence
225 g/8 oz Walnut halves

Stir the syrup, cinnamon, butter or margarine and salt over a medium heat until the mixture is lightly browned and syrupy. Stir in the vanilla essence, then add the nuts and turn them over until evenly covered with glaze. Spread on greaseproof paper to cool.

Caramel Grapes

Makes 450 g/1 lb

450 g/1 lb Caster sugar
300 ml/½ pt Water
Pinch of cream of tartar
225 g/8 oz Grapes, washed, dried and
  divided into pairs

Dissolve the sugar and cream of tartar in the water in a heavy-based saucepan, then boil to 150°C/300°F or until a drop will harden in cold water. Remove from the heat and quickly dip the pairs of grapes into the syrup, holding them with a fork. Place them on a greased baking sheet to harden, then put them into paper petit four cases to serve.

Note
The caramel will turn sticky if not eaten on the same day.

Variations
You can also use cherries for this recipe.

Peppermint Creams

Makes 24

225 g/8 oz Icing sugar
1 Egg white, whisked until stiff
2.5 ml/½ tsp Peppermint essence

Mix the ingredients together to a stiff paste. Add a few drops of water if it is too dry. Roll out on a floured surface to about 1 cm/½ in thick and cut into small rounds. ' Leave on baking parchment to dry.

Peanut Brittle

Makes 450 g/1 lb

350 g/12 oz Granulated sugar	
225 g/8 oz Golden syrup	
150 ml/¼ pt Water	
10 ml/2 tsp Glucose powder	
25 g/1 oz Butter or margarine	
75 g/3 oz Peanuts, toasted	
2.5 ml/½ tsp Lemon essence	
10 ml/2 tsp Bicarbonate of soda	

Dissolve the sugar and syrup in the water in a heavy-based saucepan. Bring to the boil and simmer to 150°C/300°F or until a drop will harden in cold water. Add the butter, nuts and lemon essence, then stir in the bicarbonate of soda; the mixture will froth for a few minutes. Pour it on to a greased baking tray and leave to cool. Break into pieces when set.

Popcorn

Makes 2 x 1.2 litre/2 pt bowls

150 ml/¼ pt Oil	
60 ml/4 tbsp Popping corn	
30 ml/2 tbsp Caster, brown sugar or honey	

Heat the oil in a large, lidded saucepan, add the corn and replace the lid tightly. Shake the pan gently over a medium heat for about 2 minutes until all the popping stops, then drain the popcorn on kitchen paper and sprinkle with sugar or honey, or use salt, maple syrup or any flavour you choose. Do not open the lid while the corn is still popping.

Marshmallows

Makes 750 g/1½ lb

450 g/1 lb Caster sugar	
25 g/1 oz Golden syrup	
300 ml/½ pt Water	
30 ml/2 tbsp Gelatine	
2 Egg whites, whisked	
Few drops of vanilla essence	
Few drops of pink food colouring	
30 ml/2 tbsp Icing sugar	
15 ml/1 tbsp Cornflour	

Dissolve the sugar and syrup in half the water in a heavy-based pan, then boil to 130°C/260°F or until the mixture is beginning to set. Dissolve the gelatine in the remaining water, remove the syrup from the heat and stir in the gelatine mixture. Whisk in the egg whites, add the vanilla essence and colouring and continue whisking until the mixture is thick and stiff. Pour into a greased and lined 23 cm/9 in square tin and leave exposed to the air for 24 hours. Cut into squares, roll in the icing sugar and cornflour and store in an airtight container.

Nut Surprise

Makes 24

100 g/4 oz Milk chocolate	
75 g/3 oz Butter or margarine	
75 g/3 oz Demerara sugar	
25 g/1 oz Golden syrup	
175 g/6 oz Mixed nuts, chopped	
1 Egg yolk	
Few drops of vanilla essence	
25 g/1 oz Plain flour	

Melt the chocolate in a bowl over a pan of hot water, then spread it over the base of a greased and lined 22 cm x 18 cm/9 in x 7 in baking tin. Cream the butter or margarine, sugar and syrup, then stir in the nuts, egg yolk, vanilla essence and flour. Press over the chocolate and bake in a preheated oven at 180°C/350°F/gas mark 4 for about 15 minutes. Allow to cool in the tin, then cut into squares.

Marzipan Petit Fours

Makes 450 g/1 lb

225 g/8 oz Icing sugar

225 g/8 oz Caster sugar

450 g/1 lb Ground almonds

2 Eggs, beaten

5 ml/1 tsp Vanilla essence

Few drops of lemon juice (optional)

Few drops of food colouring

Cloves and angelica to decorate

Mix the icing and caster sugars and the ground almonds. Stir in the eggs and vanilla essence and mix to a stiff dough. If the dough is too stiff, add a few drops of lemon juice. Knead lightly. Colour small pieces of the marzipan and roll into fruit shapes. Use cloves or pieces of angelica as stems. Place the petit fours in paper cases to serve.

Almond Paste
You can use the uncoloured marzipan to cover cakes or for cake decorations.

Nougat

Makes 675 g/1½ lb

100 g/4 oz Blanched almonds, lightly toasted and chopped

25 g/1 oz Angelica, chopped

50 g/2 oz Glacé cherries, chopped

450 g/1 lb Caster sugar

225 g/8 oz Powdered glucose

150 ml/¼ pt Water

2 Egg whites, whisked until stiff

Rice paper

Mix the almonds, angelica and cherries. Dissolve the sugar and glucose in the water in a heavy-based saucepan, then boil to 132°C/270°F or until syrupy. Stir in the egg whites, then beat until the mixture thickens. This will take some time. Stir in the fruit and nuts. Turn into a greased 20 cm/8 in tin, cover with a piece of rice paper and press down well. Leave to set and cut into bars when cold.

Variation
Dip the ends of the nougat in melted chocolate for a really delicious treat.

Icings, Frostings and Fillings

Here are all the basic recipes you need for a range of cake icings and fillings as well as some more unusual options which are ideal for jazzing up a plain cake or making a special cake that bit more special.

Butter Icing

Makes 350 g/12 oz

100 g/4 oz Butter
225 g/8 oz Icing sugar
5-10 ml/1-2 tsp Hot water

Beat the butter until soft, then beat in the icing sugar. Add the hot water and mix again to make the icing sugar soft enough to spread or pipe.

Note
You can flavour the icing sugar with 15 ml/1 tbsp lemon or orange juice; 15 ml/1 tbsp finely grated orange or lemon rind; 10 ml/2 tsp coffee; 30 ml/2 tbsp cocoa powder mixed to a paste with 30 ml/2 tbsp boiling water; 50 g/2 oz melted chocolate.

Rich Butter Icing

Covers 2 x 20 cm/8 in cakes

50 g/2 oz Butter or margarine, softened
Pinch of salt
450 g/1 lb Icing sugar
75 ml/5 tbsp Double cream
5 ml/1 tsp Vanilla essence

Cream the butter or margarine with the salt. Sift the icing sugar and warm the cream, but do not allow it to boil. Beat the sugar and hot cream into the butter alternately, blending well. Beat in the vanilla essence and continue beating until the icing is cold, creamy and thick enough to spread.

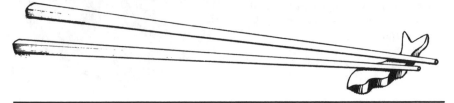

Caramel Icing

Covers 1 x 20 cm/8 in cake

75 g/3 oz Butter or margarine
75 ml/5 tbsp Single cream
25 g/1 oz Caster sugar
175 g/6 oz Icing sugar

Melt the butter or margarine and cream together in one saucepan. Heat the caster sugar gently in another saucepan until it turns golden brown. Pour the cream into the sugar and heat, stirring, until the caramel has dissolved. Beat in the icing sugar until smooth, then use immediately.

Chocolate Icing

Covers tops of 2 x 20 cm/8 in cakes

50 g/2 oz Plain chocolate, grated
15 ml/1 tbsp Milk
275 g/10 oz Icing sugar
100 g/4 oz Butter or margarine, softened
Few drops of vanilla essence

Place the chocolate in a bowl over a pan of hot water, add the milk and stir until the chocolate has melted, then leave to cool. Gradually beat in the icing sugar, then beat in the butter or margarine and vanilla essence and use at once.

Glacé Icing

Makes 100 g/4 oz

100 g/4 oz Icing sugar
15 ml/1 tbsp Hot water
Few drops of flavouring (optional)
Few drops of food colouring (optional)

Sift the icing sugar into a bowl and add the water, a little at a time, until the icing is smooth. Add flavouring and colouring to taste. Pour over the cake and spread with a knife dipped in hot water. Do not move the cake until the icing has set.

Variations

For Almond Icing, use almond essence and a few drops of lemon juice.

For Lemon Icing, add grated lemon rind and juice and a few drops of yellow food colouring.

For Orange Icing, substitute orange rind and orange colouring.

For Pineapple Icing, use pineapple essence and a few drops of yellow colouring.

For Chocolate Icing, blend 10 ml/2 tsp cocoa with 15 ml/1 tbsp water and mix into the icing.

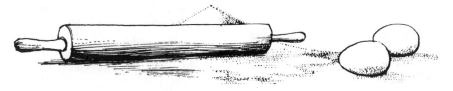

Fondant Icing

Covers 1 x 18 cm/7 in cake

350 g/12 oz Icing sugar
15 ml/1 tbsp Liquid glucose
1 Egg white
Icing sugar and cornflour for
    dusting

Sift the icing sugar into a bowl, make a well in the centre and mix in the glucose with a palette knife then with the hands. Turn on to a work surface sprinkled with icing sugar and work into a ball. Roll out the icing until it is 7 cm/3 in larger than the cake. Brush the almond paste on the cake with egg white. Lift the icing and mould it over the cake with fingers dipped in cornflour and icing sugar. Trim the edges to neaten.

Note
There is a recipe for almond paste on page 306.

Royal Icing

Covers the top and sides of 1 x 20 cm/
    8 in cake

5 ml/1 tsp Lemon juice
2 Egg whites
450 g/1 lb Icing sugar
Few drops of glycerine (optional)
Few drops of blue food colouring
    (optional)

Mix the lemon juice and egg whites and gradually beat in the icing sugar until the icing is smooth and white and will coat the back of a spoon. A few drops of glycerine will prevent the icing becoming too brittle. A few drops of blue food colouring will prevent the icing developing a yellowish tinge when stored. Cover with a damp cloth and leave to stand for 20 minutes to allow any air bubbles to rise to the surface.

This consistency can be poured on to the cake and smoothed with a knife dipped in hot water. For piping, mix in extra icing sugar so that the icing is stiff enough to stand in peaks.

American Frosting

Covers 1 x 15 cm/6 in cake

175 g/6 oz Granulated sugar
30 ml/2 tbsp Water
Pinch of cream of tartar
1 Egg white
Few drops of flavouring (optional)
Few drops of food colouring
    (optional)

Put the sugar and water in a large bowl over a pan of hot water and stir until the sugar dissolves. Add the cream of tartar and egg white. Place the pan over the heat and bring to the boil. Whisk for 5 minutes or until the mixture forms peaks. Take the bowl off the pan and add flavouring and colouring if liked. Continue whisking until the frosting has a thick consistency, then spread on the cake with a round-bladed knife.

Lady Baltimore Frosting

Fills and covers 2 x 20 cm/8 in cakes

50 g/2 oz Raisins, chopped
50 g/2 oz Glacé cherries, chopped
50 g/2 oz Mixed nuts, chopped
4 Dried figs, chopped
2 Egg whites
350g/12 oz Caster sugar
Pinch of cream of tartar
75 ml/5 tbsp Cold water
Pinch of salt
5 ml/1 tsp Vanilla essence

Mix the raisins, cherries, nuts and figs. Place the egg whites, sugar, cream of tartar, water and salt in a bowl over boiling water and beat for about 7 minutes until the mixture forms soft peaks. Remove from the heat and beat in the vanilla essence. Combine 150 ml/¼ pt frosting with the fruit and nuts and use to fill a plain cake. Use the remaining frosting to cover the top and sides of the cake.

Chocolate Frosting

Makes 100 g/4 oz

25 g/1 oz Chocolate, grated
30 ml/2 tbsp Cream
75 g/3 oz Icing sugar

Stand the chocolate in a bowl over a pan of hot water, add the cream and stir until all the chocolate has melted. Add the sugar and whisk until smooth. Use while warm and allow to set.

Honey Butter Frosting

Covers 1 x 20 cm/8 in cake

75 g/3 oz Butter or margarine
175 g/6 oz Icing sugar
15 ml/1 tbsp Honey
15 ml/1 tbsp Lemon juice

Beat the butter until soft, then beat in half the icing sugar. Beat in the honey and lemon juice, followed by the remaining icing sugar.

Apricot Topping

Makes 300 ml/½ pt

450 g/1 lb Fresh apricots, skinned, stoned and chopped
Thin slice lemon rind, chopped
60 ml/4 tbsp Honey

Mix the apricots, lemon and honey in a saucepan and heat gently until the honey has dissolved and the fruit is juicy. Purée the mixture in a food processor or blender, then return it to the saucepan and cook gently for 8 minutes, stirring to prevent the topping burning. Leave to cool and store in an airtight jar in the fridge.

Variation
You can use dried apricots, soaked, skinned and chopped.

Butterscotch Topping

Makes 375 ml/¾ pt

150 ml/¼ pt Honey
60 ml/4 tbsp Water
25 g/1 oz Butter or margarine
50 g/2 oz Mixed nuts, finely
  chopped

Boil the honey and water together over a low heat to 112°C/234°F or until a drop in cold water forms a soft ball. Remove from the heat and stir in the butter and nuts. Place in an air-tight jar, leave to cool and store in the fridge.

Coconut-Chocolate Topping

Covers 1 x 20 cm/8 in cake

225 g/8 oz Milk chocolate, grated
90 ml/6 tbsp Boiling water
225 g/8 oz Desiccated coconut

Purée the chocolate and water in a food processor or blender. Add the coconut and process until well mixed.

Melba Topping

Makes 450 ml/¾ pt

900 g/2 lb Fresh raspberries
120 ml/4 fl oz Honey
120 ml/4 fl oz Water

Sieve the raspberries and put to one side. Boil the honey and water together gently for 12 minutes, then add the raspberries and cook for another 1 minute. Leave to cool, then chill before using.

Blender Cream

Makes 300 ml/½ pt

150 ml/¼ pt Milk
150 g/5 oz Unsalted butter, cubed

Place the milk in a saucepan, add the butter and heat gently until the butter melts, but do not allow the mixture to boil. Pour into a food processor or blender and blend well. Pour into a jug, cover and chill in the fridge for several hours or overnight before use.

Almond Paste

Covers top and sides of 1 x 23 cm/ 9 in cake

175 g/6 oz Caster Sugar
175 g/6 oz Icing Sugar
350 g/12 oz Ground almonds
2 Eggs, beaten
Few drops of almond essence
5 ml/½ tsp Lemon juice

Mix the sugars and stir in the almonds. Make a well in the centre and beat in the eggs, one at a time. Add the almond essence and lemon juice and knead the paste until smooth. Place in a polythene bag if not being used at once.

Confectioners' Custard

Makes 350 ml/12 fl oz

25 g/1 oz Butter or margarine
25 g/1 oz Plain flour
300 ml/½ pt Milk
50 g/2 oz Caster sugar
1 Egg
1 Egg yolk
Pinch of salt
Few drops of vanilla essence

Melt the butter or margarine in a saucepan, stir in the flour and cook for 1 minute. Whisk in the milk and cook, stirring, for 5 minutes until the sauce is smooth and glossy. Remove from the heat, add the sugar and beat for a few minutes, then add the eggs, salt and vanilla essence. Beat the custard well and cook without boiling until very thick. Leave to cool.

Rum Butter

Makes 225 g/8 oz

100 g/4 oz Soft brown sugar
100 g/4 oz Butter, cut into pieces
10 ml/2 tsp Rum

Beat the sugar and butter with a wooden spoon or in a food processor or blender until smooth. Beat in the rum until the mixture is soft and light. Store in small jars or tubs.

Brandy Butter

Makes 450 g/1 lb

100 g/4 oz Butter
350 g/12 oz Soft brown sugar
1 Egg yolk
Grated rind of 1 orange
120 ml/4 fl oz Brandy

Beat the butter and sugar with a wooden spoon or in a food processor or blender until smooth, then beat in the remaining ingredients until creamy. Store in the fridge for up to 3 weeks.

Mincemeat

Makes 2.25 kg/5 lb

350 g/12 oz Raisins, chopped
225 g/8 oz Sultanas, chopped
225 g/8 oz Currants
450 g/1 lb Apples, peeled, cored and chopped
225 g/8 oz Mixed peel
225 g/8 oz Shredded suet
350 g/12 oz Soft brown sugar
Grated rind of 1 lemon
Grated rind of 1 orange
Juice of ½ lemon
Juice of ½ orange
25 g/1 oz Mixed spice
2.5 ml/½ tsp Nutmeg
300 ml/½ pt Brandy or rum

Mix all the ingredients together well and pack in airtight jars. Store for a few weeks before use.

Breads and Teabreads

Whether you make bread in a food processor or prefer to knead it by hand, there is nothing like the smell of freshly baked bread filling the kitchen, and nothing like the taste of home-baked bread.

Use either fresh or dried yeast, whichever is more convenient. Both are simple to use; dried yeast can be kept in the cupboard for some time so you can always have some on hand. Easy-mix yeasts are blended into the dry ingredients and not set to work separately. If you use this type of yeast, adapt the recipes by following the instructions on the packet.

Always make sure you knead the dough sufficiently or you will not get good results. When the dough is ready, the texture changes to a soft, pliable, elastic dough.

When leaving dough to rise, cover it with a damp cloth or oiled clingfilm, or tie it loosely in an oiled plastic bag to prevent a skin forming.

Rising times will vary depending on the room temperature. Dough will take about 1 hour in a warm place, 2 hours at room temperature, 12 hours in a cool place or 24 hours in a refrigerator. You can use this to your advantage if you make up the dough and leave it to rise in a suitable place ready to be baked when you need it, but remember to allow the dough to return to room temperature before kneading it.

Most bread recipes can be used to make whichever shape of bread you prefer. Use a loaf tin for a standard-shaped loaf, or shape the dough and bake it on a greased baking sheet.

You can tell when a loaf is cooked as it will sound hollow when tapped on the bottom.

Wholemeal Bread

Makes 2 x 900 g/2 lb loaves

50 g/2 oz Fresh yeast OR
30 ml/2 tbsp Dried yeast

5 ml/1 tsp Sugar (if using dried
yeast)

900 ml/1½ pts Warm water

25 g/1 oz Lard

1.5 kg/3 lb Wholemeal flour

30ml/2 tbsp Salt

30 ml/2 tbsp Salt water

30 ml/2 tbsp Sesame or caraway
seeds

If using fresh yeast, blend it to a cream with a little water, then add the remaining water. If using dried yeast, dissolve the sugar in the water then stir in the yeast. Leave in a warm place for 10 to 15 minutes until frothy. Rub the lard into the flour and salt, then stir in the yeast. Work together to a firm dough which leaves the sides of the bowl cleanly. Knead on a lightly floured surface or in a processor until elastic and no longer sticky. Place the dough in an oiled bowl, cover and leave to rise until doubled in size and springy to the touch.

Knead the dough again until firm, divide in half and place in 2 greased loaf tins. Brush the tops with salt water, cover and leave to prove for about 1½ hours until the dough reaches the top of the tins. Sprinkle with the sesame or caraway seeds. Bake in a preheated oven at 230°C/450°F/gas mark 8 for about 40 minutes until golden brown.

Variations
You can shape this loaf how you like.

Omit the seeds if you wish, or substitute chopped nuts, cracked wheat or poppy seeds.

White Loaf

Makes 2 x 900 g/2 lb loaves

25 g/1 oz Fresh yeast OR
15 ml/1 tbsp Dried yeast

5 ml/1 tsp Sugar (if using dried
yeast)

900 ml/1½ pts Warm water

25 g/1 oz Lard

1.5 kg/3 lb Strong plain flour

30 ml/2 tbsp Salt

If using fresh yeast, blend it to a cream with a little water, then add the remaining water. If using dried yeast, dissolve the sugar in the water then stir in the yeast. Leave in a warm place for 10 to 15 minutes until frothy. Rub the lard into the flour and salt, then stir in the yeast. Work together to a firm dough which leaves the sides of the bowl cleanly. Knead on a lightly floured surface or in a processor until elastic and no longer sticky. Place the dough in an oiled bowl, cover and leave to rise until doubled in size and springy to the touch.

Knead the dough again until firm, divide in half and place in 2 greased loaf tins. Cover and leave to prove for about 1½ hours until the dough reaches the top of the tins. Bake in a preheated oven at 230°C/450°F/gas mark 8 for about 40 minutes until golden brown.

Variations
You can shape this loaf how you like: into rolls, 4 small loaves or other loaf shapes.

Buttered Rolls

Makes 12 rolls

450 g/1 lb White Bread dough
(page 309)
100 g/4 oz Butter or margarine, cut
into pieces

Make the bread dough and leave it to rise until doubled in size and springy to the touch.

Knead the dough again and work in the butter or margarine. Make into about 12 rolls and place them, well apart, on a greased baking tray. Cover and leave to prove before baking in a preheated oven at 230°C/450°F/gas mark 8 for about 20 minutes.

French Rolls

Makes 12 rolls

1 Egg, well beaten
15 g/½ oz Fresh yeast OR
10 ml/2 tsp Dried yeast
150 ml/¼ pt Warm milk
25 g/1 oz Butter or margarine
450 g/1 lb Strong plain flour

Mix together the egg, yeast and milk and leave in a warm place until frothy. Rub the butter or margarine into the flour, then beat in the yeast mixture. Do not knead. Cover and leave to rise until doubled in size and springy to the touch.

Shape into rolls and place them on a greased baking tray. Bake in a preheated oven at 230°C/450°F/gas mark 8 for about 20 minutes.

Excellent Rolls

Makes 8 rolls

25 g/1 oz Butter or margarine
300 ml/½ pt Milk
15 g/½ oz Fresh yeast OR
8 ml/½ tbsp Dried yeast
Pinch of salt
5 ml/1 tsp Sugar (if using dried
yeast)
900 g/2 lb Strong plain flour

Warm the butter and milk and add the yeast, salt and sugar, if using. Leave in a warm place for 10 minutes until frothy, then mix it into the flour and knead until the dough is pliable and no longer sticky. Cover and leave to rise until doubled in size and springy to the touch.

Knead again, shape into rolls and place them on a greased baking sheet. Cover and leave to prove for about 1 hour. Bake in a preheated oven at 230°C/450°F/gas mark 8 for about 20 minutes.

Milk Rolls

Makes 12 rolls

25 g/1 oz Fresh yeast OR
15 ml/1 tbsp Dried yeast
10 ml/2 tsp Sugar
1 Egg, beaten
300 ml/½ pt Warm milk
50 g/2 oz Butter or margarine
450 g/1 lb Strong plain flour
5 ml/1 tsp Salt

Mix the yeast, sugar, egg and milk and leave for 10 minutes until frothy.

Rub the butter or margarine into the flour and salt, then stir in the yeast mixture and mix to a firm dough. Knead until the dough is pliable and no longer sticky. Cover and leave to rise until doubled in size and springy to the touch.

Knead again, shape into rolls and place them on a greased baking sheet. Cover and leave to prove for 1 hour. Brush the tops with milk and bake in a preheated oven at 230°C/450°F/gas mark 8 for about 15 minutes.

Brentford Rolls

Makes 12 rolls

15 g/½ oz Fresh yeast OR 10 ml/2 tsp Dried yeast
2 Eggs
600 ml/1 pt Warm milk
50 g/2 oz Sugar
100 g/4 oz Butter or margarine
900 g/2 lb Strong plain flour
Pinch of salt

Mix the yeast, eggs, milk and sugar and leave in a warm place until frothy. Rub the butter or margarine into the flour and salt, then mix in the yeast mixture. Knead until the dough is pliable and no longer sticky. Cover and leave to rise until doubled in size and springy to the touch.

Knead the dough again, shape into rolls and place them on a greased baking sheet. Cover and leave to prove for about 1 hour. Bake in a preheated oven at 230°C/450°F/gas mark 8 for about 30 minutes.

Brioche

Makes 4 x 400 g/14 oz loaves

40 g/1½ oz Yeast
75 ml/5 tbsp Milk
75 ml/5 tbsp Water
225 g/8 oz 81% extraction flour
750 g/1½ lb Wholemeal flour
40 g/1½ oz Honey
8 Eggs, beaten
2.5 ml/½ tsp Salt
400 g/14 oz Butter or margarine, melted

Mix the yeast with the milk and water and stir into the 81% flour to make a dough. Cover and leave for 30 minutes to ferment. Add the wholemeal flour, honey, eggs and salt and knead well until the dough is pliable. Pour on the butter or margarine and continue kneading until the dough is clear. Cover and leave to rise until the dough is doubled in size and springy to the touch.

Knead lightly and divide the dough into 4. Place in greased brioche tins, cover and leave to prove in a warm place for 40 minutes. Bake in a preheated oven at 220°C/425°F/gas mark 7 for 30 minutes.

Brown Milk Bread

Makes 1 x 675 g/1½ lb loaf

450 g/1 lb Wholemeal flour
100 g/4 oz Strong plain flour
100 g/4 oz Butter or margarine
Pinch of salt
10 ml/2 tsp Baking powder
300 ml/½ pt Milk

Mix together the flours and rub in the butter or margarine. Add the salt and baking powder and mix to a dough with the milk. Place in a loaf tin and bake in a preheated oven at 220°C/425°F/gas mark 7 for about 20 minutes until well risen and golden brown.

Currant Loaf

Makes 1 x 900 g/2 lb loaf

150 g/5 oz Butter or margarine
450 g/1 lb Wholemeal flour
15 ml/1 tbsp Baking powder
Pinch of salt
175 g/6 oz Sugar
175 g/6 oz Currants
50 g/2 oz Mixed peel
2 Eggs
15 ml/1 tbsp Milk

Rub the butter or margarine into the flour, baking powder and salt. Add the sugar, currants and mixed peel. Beat the eggs and milk together and mix them well into the other ingredients. Add a little more milk if the mixture is too dry. Place in a greased loaf tin and bake in a preheated oven at 180°C/350°F/gas mark 4 for 30 to 40 minutes.

Coffee Time Rolls

Makes 12

600 ml/1 pt Milk
225 g/8 oz Butter or margarine
175 g/6 oz Sugar
225 g/8 oz Strong plain flour
20 ml/1½ tbsp Rose water
9 Eggs, separated

Boil the milk, butter and sugar and mix the flour and rose water into the boiling liquid. Stir in the well-beaten egg yolks and 7 of the whites. Place the dough in little heaps in a greased baking tin, brush with egg white and sprinkle with a little sugar. Bake in a preheated oven at 180°/350°F/gas mark 4 for about 20 minutes.

Currant Bread

Makes 2 x 450 g/1 lb loaves

900 g/2 lb White Bread dough (page 309)
15 g/½ oz Butter or margarine
225 g/8 oz Currants
15 ml/1 tbsp Black treacle
15 ml/1 tbsp Water

Make the dough and leave it to rise, until doubled in size and springy to the touch.

Knead the dough again, mix in the butter and currants and place in 2 greased loaf tins. Cover and leave to prove for about 1 hour. Bake in a preheated oven at 230°C/450°F/gas mark 8 for about 20 minutes. Mix the treacle and water and brush over the cooked loaves. Switch off the oven, and return the loaves to the oven to dry.

Raisin Loaf

Makes 2 x 450 g/1 lb loaves

15 g/½ oz Fresh yeast OR
15 ml/1 tbsp Dried yeast
5 ml/1 tsp Sugar (if using dried yeast)
450 ml/¾ pt Warm water
50 g/2 oz Butter or margarine
900 g/2 lb Strong plain flour
450 g/1 lb Raisins
10 ml/2 tsp Mixed spice

Mix the yeast, sugar and water and leave in a warm place for 10 minutes until frothy. Rub the butter into the flour, mix in the raisins and spice, then stir in the yeast mixture. Knead until the dough is pliable and no longer sticky. Cover and leave to rise until doubled in size and springy to the touch.

Knead again, and place in 2 greased loaf tins. Cover and leave to prove for 1 hour. Bake in a preheated oven at 230°C/450°F/gas mark 8 for about 20 minutes.

Chelsea Buns

Makes 9 buns

225 g/8 oz Strong plain flour
15 g/½ oz Fresh yeast OR
10 ml/2 tsp Dried yeast
100 ml/4 fl oz Warm milk
15 g/½ oz Butter or margarine
2.5 ml/½ tsp Salt
1 Egg, beaten
15 ml/1 tbsp Melted butter
75 g/3 oz Dried mixed fruit
15 g/½ oz Mixed peel
50 g/2 oz Soft brown sugar
15 ml/1 tbsp Honey

Mix 50 g/2 oz flour with the yeast and milk and leave in a warm place until frothy. Rub the butter or margarine into the remaining flour and the salt, add the egg, then add the yeast mixture. Knead until the dough is pliable and no longer sticky. Cover and leave to rise until doubled in size and springy to the touch.

Knead the dough again, roll into a rectangle 33 x 23 cm/13 x 9 in and brush with melted butter. Mix the dried fruit, peel and sugar and spread it over the dough. Roll up from one long side like a Swiss roll and seal the edge. Cut into 9 slices. Place them, well apart, on a greased baking sheet, cover and leave to prove for about 1 hour. Bake in a preheated oven at 190°C/375°F/gas mark 5 for about 20 minutes. Brush the warm buns with honey.

Spiced Buns

Makes 12 buns

25 g/1 oz Fresh yeast OR
15 ml/1 tbsp Dried yeast
25 g/1 oz Sugar
150 ml/¼ pt Warm milk
175 g/6 oz Butter or margarine
450 g/1 lb Strong plain flour
350 g/12 oz Currants
15 ml/1 tbsp Caraway seeds
15 ml/1 tbsp Honey

Mix the yeast, sugar and milk and leave in a warm place for 10 minutes until frothy. Rub the butter or margarine into the flour and mix in the currants and caraway seeds. Knead until the dough is pliable and no longer sticky. Cover and leave to rise until doubled in size and springy to the touch.

Knead gently, shape into rolls and place them on a greased baking sheet. Cover and leave to prove for 1 hour. Bake in a preheated oven at 230°C/450°F/gas mark 8 for about 15 minutes. Brush the warm buns with honey.

Sally Lunn

Makes 2 x 15 cm/6 in cakes

20 g/¾ oz Fresh yeast OR
20 ml/1½ tsp Dried yeast
150 ml/¼ pt Warm milk
225 g/8 oz Strong plain flour
Pinch of salt
50 g/2 oz Butter, melted
1 Egg, beaten
15 ml/1 tbsp Sugar
15 ml/1 tbsp Water

Mix the yeast and milk and leave in a warm place for 10 minutes until frothy. Stir the yeast mixture into the flour and salt and leave in a warm place for 15 minutes to let the mixture sponge slightly. Add the butter and egg, making a loose dough. Beat well, cover and leave to rise for 1 hour.

Knead lightly, then place in greased cake tins and bake in a preheated oven at 220°C/425°F/gas mark 7 for 20 minutes until golden brown.

While baking, boil the sugar and water for 2 minutes, then brush it over the warm cakes. To serve, slice the cake into 3 layers and toast lightly. Spread with clotted cream, reshape the cake and serve cut into wedges.

Hot Cross Buns

Makes 18 buns

25 g/1 oz Fresh yeast OR
15 ml/1 tbsp Dried yeast
300 ml/½ pt Warm milk
100 g/4 oz Caster sugar
75 g/3 oz Butter or margarine
450 g/1 lb Strong plain flour
50 g/2 oz Mixed peel
175 g/6 oz Currants
5 ml/1 tsp Mixed spice
15 ml/1 tbsp Honey

Mix the yeast, milk and sugar and leave in a warm place for 10 minutes until frothy. Rub the butter or margarine into the flour and mix in the peel, currants and spice. Stir in the yeast mixture and knead until the dough is pliable and no longer sticky.

Cover and leave to rise until doubled in size and springy to the touch.

Knead the dough again, then shape it into buns and place them on a greased baking tray. Cover and leave to prove for 1 hour. Cut a cross on each bun with a sharp knife. Bake in a preheated oven at 200°C/400°F/ gas mark 6 for about 20 minutes. Brush the warm buns with honey.

Tea Cakes

Makes 12 cakes

15 g/½ oz Fresh yeast OR
15 ml/1 tbsp Dried yeast

50 g/2 oz Sugar

300 ml/½ pt Warm milk

25 g/1 oz Butter or margarine

450 g/1 lb Strong plain flour

5 ml/1 tsp Salt

50 g/2 oz Sultanas

Milk for brushing

Mix the yeast, half the sugar and the milk and leave in a warm place for 10 minutes until frothy. Rub the butter or margarine into the flour, remaining sugar and salt, then add the yeast mixture and the sultanas. Knead until the dough is pliable and no longer sticky. Cover and leave to rise until doubled in size and springy to the touch.

Knead again, shape into rounds and place on a greased baking tray. Brush the tops with milk, cover and leave to prove for 1 hour. Bake in a preheated oven at 200°C/400°F/gas mark 6 for 20 minutes. When cool, serve toasted and buttered.

Old Joe's Malt Bread

Makes 4 x 450 g/1 lb loaves

900 g/2 lb Wholemeal flour

10 ml/2 tsp Salt

15 g/½ oz Butter or margarine

25 g/1 oz Fresh yeast

600 ml/1 pt Cool water

60 ml/4 tbsp Honey

30 ml/2 tbsp Black treacle

60 ml/4 tbsp Liquid malt extract

350 g/12 oz Sultanas

100 g/4 oz Dates, stoned and
chopped

15 ml/1 tbsp Golden syrup

Mix the flour and salt and rub in the butter or margarine. Dissolve the yeast in the water and add 45 ml/ 3 tbsp honey, the treacle and the malt extract. Pour this into the dry ingredients and knead until the dough is smooth and clear. Mix in the dried fruits. Cover and leave to rise until doubled in size and springy to the touch.

Knead again, then shape into loaves and place in greased tins. Cover and leave to prove in a warm place for 45 minutes. Bake in a preheated oven at 180°C/350°F/gas mark 4 for 35 minutes, making sure the loaves do not get too dark. Mix the remaining honey and the syrup and use it to glaze the baked loaves.

Wholemeal Scones

Makes 16

450 g/1 lb Wholemeal flour
20 g/¾ oz Baking powder
75 g/3 oz Soft brown sugar
5 ml/1 tsp Salt
90 ml/6 tbsp Oil
300 ml/½ pt Milk
1 Egg, beaten

Mix the flour, baking powder, sugar and salt, then stir in the oil. Gradually add the milk until the mixture forms a soft dough. Roll out to about 2.5 cm/ 1 in thick, cut into rounds and place them on a greased baking sheet. Brush with egg and leave to rest for 20 minutes before baking. Bake in a preheated oven at 230°C/450°F/gas mark 8 for 15 minutes.

West Country Scones

Makes 12

100 g/4 oz Butter or margarine
450 g/1 lb Self-raising flour
Pinch of salt
10 ml/2 tsp Baking powder
300 ml/½ pt Milk

Rub the butter or margarine into the flour, salt and baking powder. Mix together with the milk to a soft dough. Roll out, cut into rounds and place on a greased baking sheet. bake in a preheated oven at 220°C/ 425°F/gas mark 7 for 10 minutes. Serve with jam and clotted cream.

Autumn Mist Crown

Makes 2 x 750 g/1½ lb loaves

500 g/1¼ lb Wholemeal flour
20 g/¾ oz Baking powder
150 g/5 oz Soft brown sugar
5 ml/1 tsp Salt
2.5 ml/½ tsp Mace
75 g/3 oz Vegetable fat
3 Egg whites
300 ml/½ pt Milk
175 g/6 oz Wholemeal cake crumbs
50 g/2 oz Hazelnuts, ground
100 g/4 oz Marron glacé, chopped
75 g/3 oz Stem ginger, chopped
30 ml/2 tbsp Rum or brandy
1 Egg, beaten
30 ml/2 tbsp Honey

Mix the flour, baking powder, 75 g/ 3 oz sugar, salt and mace and rub in the fat. Mix in the egg whites and milk and knead until the dough is soft and pliable. Roll out into 2 rectangles 30 x 20 cm/12 x 8 in. Mix the cake crumbs, hazelnuts, marron glacé, ginger, rum or brandy and the remaining sugar. Mix with enough egg to give a spreading consistency. Brush the dough with the remaining egg and spread with the filling, leaving 2.5 cm/ 1 in free at the edge. Make into a roll and join the ends together into circles. Place the rounds on greased baking sheets, snip the tops with scissors for decoration and brush with the remaining egg. Cover and leave to rest for 10 minutes, then bake in a preheated oven at 230°C/ 450°F/gas mark 8 for 30 minutes. Glaze the baked loaves with honey, leave to cool and serve sliced.

Franz's Almond Stollen

Makes 3 x 400 g/14 oz loaves

500 g/1¼ lb 81% extraction flour
25 g/1 oz Rye flour
50 g/2 oz Soft brown sugar
75 g/3 oz Butter or margarine
25 g/1 oz Fresh yeast
300 ml/½ pt Warm water
2 Eggs, beaten
150 g/5 oz Currants
150 g/5 oz Sultanas
2.5 ml/½ tsp Cinnamon
50 g/2 oz Grated lemon rind
Grated rind and juice of 1 orange
100 g/4 oz Almond Paste (page 306)
15 ml/1 tbsp Honey
30 ml/2 tbsp Flaked almonds, toasted

Mix the flours and sugar and rub in the butter or margarine. Dissolve the yeast in warm water and add it to the mixture with 1 egg. Knead until the dough is pliable and elastic. Mix the fruit, spice and lemon and orange rind and juice into the dough. Cover and leave to rise until doubled in size.

Knead again, divide into 3 and roll out into ovals. Brush the edges with egg. Roll out the almond paste into 3 and place one piece in the centre of each piece of dough. Fold the dough over like a turnover but allowing 2.5 cm/1 in in overlap. Seal the edges. Cover and leave to prove in a warm place for 40 minutes. bake in a pre-heated oven at 220°C/425°F/gas mark 7 for 30 minutes. Mix the honey and melted butter or margarine and use it to glaze the baked loaves. Sprinkle with the almonds and leave to cool.

Malted Banana Loaf

Makes 4 x 450 g/1 lb loaves

275 g/10 oz Dark brown sugar
350 g/12 oz Butter or margarine
60 ml/4 tbsp Liquid malt extract
5 Eggs, beaten
450 g/1 lb Wholemeal flour
30 ml/2 tbsp Baking powder
2.5 ml/½ tsp Cinnamon
4 Bananas, mashed
100 g/4 oz Dried apricots, chopped
100 g/4 oz Hazelnuts, chopped
5 ml/1 tsp Rum

Cream the sugar and butter or margarine until light. Dissolve the malt extract in the eggs and add to the creamed mixture a little at a time, beating well. Mix in the flour, baking powder and cinnamon until clear. Reserve a few hazelnuts, then mix in the bananas, apricots, hazelnuts and rum. Divide into 4, place in greased baking tins and sprinkle with the reserved hazelnuts. Bake in a pre-heated oven at 180°C/350°F/gas mark 4 for 35 minutes.

Bavarian Rye Bread

Makes 3 x 450 g/1 lb loaves

400 g/14 oz Rye flour
50 g/2 oz Fresh yeast
1.2 litres/2 pts Warm water
1.75 kg/2½ lb Wheatmeal
25 g/1 oz Salt
15 g/½ oz Caraway seeds
15 g/½ oz Plain flour
30 ml/2 tbsp Water

To make a sour dough, mix 300 g/ 11 oz rye flour, 10 g/¼ oz yeast and 300 ml/½ pt warm water until clear. Cover and leave in a warm place overnight.

Mix the remaining rye flour with the wheatmeal and salt and add the sour dough. Dissolve the remainig yeast in the remaining warm water and mix into the dry ingredients until clear and smooth. Add the caraway seeds and mix for 1 minute. Cover and leave in a warm place for 20 minutes, then knead again, cover and leave to prove for a further 20 minutes.

Shape into round or long loaves, place in greased tins or on greased baking sheets and glaze with a flour and water mixture. Sprinkle some extra caraway seeds on top, if liked. Cover and leave to prove in a warm place for 40 minutes, then bake in a preheated oven at 230°C/450°F/gas mark 8 for 30 minutes.

Cottage Tea Bread

Makes 3 x 450 g/1 lb loaves

900 g/2 lb Wholemeal flour
25 g/1 oz Milk powder
5 ml/1 tsp Salt
25 g/1 oz Soft brown sugar
40 g/1½ oz Fresh yeast
600 ml/1 pt Warm water
1 Egg, beaten
25 g/1 oz Butter or margarine
275 g/10 oz Currants
225 g/8 oz Sultanas
175 g/6 oz Raisins
100 g/4 oz Mixed peel
5 ml/1 tsp Mixed spice
15 ml/1 tbsp Water
15 ml/1 tbsp Lemon juice
Pinch of mixed spice

Mix together the flour, milk powder, salt and sugar. Dissolve the yeast in the water and mix into the dry ingredients. Mix in the egg and butter or margarine and knead until the dough is smooth and elastic. Mix in the fruit and spice, cover and leave to rise until doubled in size and springy to the touch.

Knead again, leave to rest for 15 minutes then place in greased tins, cover and leave to prove in a warm place for 45 minutes. Bake in a preheated oven at 220°C/425°F/gas mark 7 for 25 minutes. Mix the water, lemon juice and spice and use to glaze the top of the baked loaves.

Figaro Rolls

Makes 12 rolls

100 g/4 oz Figs, chopped
15 ml/1 tbsp Light malt extract
90 ml/6 tbsp Honey
Grated rind of ½ lemon or orange
300 ml/½ pt Warm water
450 g/1 lb Wholemeal flour
20 g/¾ oz Milk powder
5 ml/1 tsp Salt
40 g/1½ oz Butter or margarine
25 g/1 oz Yeast
2.5 ml/½ tsp Nutmeg
1 Egg, beaten
15 ml/1 tbsp Sesame seeds

Soak the figs, malt extract, 75 ml/ 5 tbsp honey and lemon or orange rind in half the warm water for 1 hour.

Sieve the flour, milk powder and salt and rub in the butter or margarine. Dissolve the yeast in the remaining warm water and honey and mix into the dry ingredients with the fig mixture. Knead until the dough is smooth and cover and leave to rise until doubled in size.

Knead again, leave to rest for 15 minutes, knead, then leave to rest for a further 15 minutes. Shape into rolls and place them on a greased baking sheet. Brush with beaten egg and sprinkle with sesame seeds. Cover and leave to prove in a warm place for 30 minutes. Bake in a pre-heated oven at 230°C/450°F/gas mark 8 for 15 minutes.

Harvest Cheese Plait

Makes 3 x 450 g/1 lb loaves

750 g/1¾ lb 81% extraction flour
10 ml/2 tsp Salt
25 g/1 oz Milk powder
20 g/¾ oz Fresh yeast
2.5 ml/½ tsp Ascorbic acid
600 ml/1 pt Warm water
225 g/8 oz Cheddar cheese, grated
5 ml/1 tsp Mustard powder
2.5 ml/½ tsp Cayenne pepper
15 ml/1 tbsp Oats

Sieve the flour, salt and milk powder into a bowl. Dissolve the yeast and ascorbic acid in the warm water and mix into the dry ingredients. Knead until the dough is smooth and clear, cover and leave to rise until doubled in size and springy to the touch.

Reserve 30 ml/1 tbsp cheese, then knead the remaining cheese, the mustard and cayenne into the dough and leave it to rest for 15 minutes. Shape the dough into 9 long sausages, join the ends in threes and plait them together. Place in greased tins, sprinkle with oats and leave in a warm place for 15 minutes. Bake at 230°C/450°F/gas mark 8 for 30 minutes, then remove from the oven and sprinkle with the reserved cheese. Return to the oven for 5 minutes until golden brown.

Forest Rounds

Makes 3 x 175 g/12 oz loaves

450 g/1 lb Wholemeal flour
25 g/1 oz Baking powder
40 g/1½ oz Carob powder
5 ml/1 tsp Salt
50 g/2 oz Hazelnuts, ground
50 g/2 oz Mixed nuts, chopped
75 g/3 oz Vegetable fat
90 ml/6 tbsp Honey
300 ml/½ pt Milk
2.5 ml/½ tsp Vanilla essence
1 Egg, beaten

Mix the flour, baking powder, carob and salt. Reserve a few nuts for topping and mix in the remainder. Rub in the fat. Mix the honey, milk and vanilla essence, add to the dry ingredients and knead until the dough is soft and pliable. Divide into 3 flat rounds, place on a greased baking sheet and mark into 6. Brush with egg and sprinkle with the reserved nuts. Bake in a preheated oven at 230°C/450°F/gas mark 8 for 15 minutes.

Herb Bread

Makes 3 x 175 g/12 oz loaves

900 g/2 lb Wholemeal flour
5 ml/1 tsp Salt
50 g/2 oz Vegetable fat
40 g/1½ oz Yeast
40 g/1½ oz Soft brown sugar
600 ml/1 pt Warm water
2.5 ml/½ tsp Thyme
2.5 ml/½ tsp Parsley
2.5 ml/½ tsp Basil
2. 5ml/½ tsp Oregano
2.5 ml/½ tsp Marjoram
5 ml/1 tsp Poppy seeds

Combine the flour and salt and rub in the fat. Mix in the yeast, sugar and water, then work in the herbs and knead until the dough is pliable and no longer sticky. Cover and leave to rise until doubled in size and springy to the touch.

Knead again and place in greased tins or shape and place on baking sheets. Cover and leave to prove in a warm place for 45 minutes. Sprinkle with poppy seeds and bake in a preheated oven at 230°C/450°F/gas mark 8 for 30 minutes.

Mango Curls

Makes 3 x 400 g/14 oz loaves

1 Mango, peeled, cored and chopped
10 ml/2 tsp Ground ginger
350 g/12 oz Raisins
450 g/1 lb Wholemeal flour
5 ml/1 tsp Salt
25 g/1 oz Milk powder
40 g/1½ oz Butter or margarine
20 g/¾ oz Fresh yeast
60 ml/4 tbsp Honey
300 ml/½ pt Warm water
1 Egg, beaten

Mix the mango, 8 ml/1½ tsp ginger and the raisins. Mix the flour, salt and milk powder and rub in the butter or margarine. Dissolve the yeast and half the honey in the warm water and add to the dry ingredients. Knead until the dough is smooth and elastic, then cover and leave to rise until doubled in size.

Knead again and mix in the mango mixture. Cover and leave to rest for 15 minutes. Divide into 3 long loaves, place on greased baking trays and brush with egg. Cover and leave to prove in a warm place for 40 minutes. Bake in a preheated oven at 220°C/425°F/gas mark 7 for 20 minutes until golden brown. Mix the reserved honey and ginger and use it to glaze the baked loaves.

Freda's Nut Bread

Makes 3 x 450 g/1 lb loaves

500 g/1¼ lb Wholemeal flour
100 g/4 oz Oats
5 ml/1 tsp Salt
10 ml/2 tsp Soy flour
40 g/1½ oz Soft brown sugar
40 g/1½ oz Fresh yeast
15 g/½ oz Light malt extract
600 ml/1 pt Warm water
225 g/8 oz Nuts, chopped (almonds, peanuts, cashews or hazelnuts)
175 g/6 oz Currants
100 g/4 oz Dates, chopped
100 g/4 oz Raisins
5 ml/1 tsp Cinnamon
20 g/¾ oz Vegetable fat
1 Egg, beaten
15 ml/1 tbsp Honey
15 ml/1 tbsp Golden syrup

Mix the flour, oats, salt, soy flour and sugar. Dissolve the yeast and malt extract in the warm water and mix into the dry ingredients. Knead until the dough is smooth and clear. Reserve a few nuts, then mix in the remaining nuts, the fruit, spice and fat into the dough. Cover and leave to rise until doubled in size and springy to the touch.

Knead again, shape the dough into flat rounds and mark them into 8. Place them on greased baking sheets, brush the tops with beaten egg and sprinkle with the reserved nuts. Cover and leave to prove in a warm place for 40 minutes. Bake in a preheated oven at 230°C/450°F/gas mark 8 for 30 minutes. Mix the honey and syrup and use to glaze the baked loaves.

Samos Bread

Makes 3 x 450 g/1 lb loaves

900 g/2 lb Wholemeal flour
10 ml/2 tsp Salt
25 g/1 oz Milk powder
25 g/1 oz Vegetable fat
20 g/ ¾ oz Fresh yeast
30 ml/2 tbsp Honey
30 ml/2 tbsp Malt extract
600 ml/1 pt Warm water
25 g/1 oz Sunflower seeds, toasted
50 g/2 oz Sesame seeds, roasted

Mix all the dry ingredients except the seeds and rub in the fat. Dissolve the yeast, honey and malt extract in the warm water and mix into the dry ingredients. Knead until the dough is smooth then add the seeds and knead for a further 5 minutes. Divide the dough into greased loaf tins, cover and leave to prove in a warm place for 40 minutes. Bake in a preheated oven at 230°C/450°F/gas mark 8 for 30 minutes until golden brown.

Kentucky Sweet Corn Bread

Makes 3 x 450 g/1 lb loaves

450 g/1 lb Fine cornmeal
225 g/8 oz Wholemeal flour
15 ml/1 tbsp Baking powder
2.5 ml/½ tsp Salt
10 ml/2 tsp Honey
2 Eggs
60 ml/4 tbsp Oil
450 ml/¾ pt Milk
225 g/8 oz Sweetcorn
50 g/2 oz Millet flakes

Mix the cornmeal, flour, baking powder and salt. Mix the honey, 1 egg, oil and milk and mix it into the dry ingredients. Knead until the dough is soft and pliable, then mix in the sweetcorn. Divided into 3, shape into long batons and place on a greased baking sheet. Brush with egg and sprinkle with millet flakes. Cover and leave to rest for 15 minutes, then bake in a preheated oven at 220°C/425°F/gas mark 7 for 30 minutes.

Morning Glory Bread

Makes 1 x 900 g/2 lb loaf

25 g/1 oz Liquid malt extract
100 g/4 oz Whole wheat grains
450 ml/¾ pt Warm water
750 g/1½ lb Wholemeal flour
25 g/1 oz Milk powder
5 ml/1 tsp Salt
25 g/1 oz Vegetable fat
30 ml/2 tbsp Honey
25 g/1 oz Fresh yeast

Mix the malt extract, wheat grains and warm water and leave to soak overnight.

Sieve the dry ingredients and add the malt mixture, fat and honey. Dissolve the yeast in a little warm water, add to the mixture and mix thoroughly for 5 to 10 minutes until smooth and elastic. Cover and leave to rise until doubled in size.

Knead again and place in a greased 900 g/2 lb loaf tin, cover and leave to prove until doubled in size. Bake in a preheated oven at 220°C/425°F/gas mark 7 for 30 minutes.

Panastan Bread

Makes 3 x 450 g/1 lb loaves

15 g/½ oz Sunflower seeds
15 g/½ oz Sesame seeds
15 g/½ oz Wheatgerm
450 g/1 lb Wholemeal flour
5 ml/1 tsp Salt
25 g/1 oz Butter or margarine
5 ml/1 tsp Light malt extract
60 ml/4 tbsp Honey
25 g/1 oz Yeast
1 Egg
150 ml/¼ pt Warm water
175 g/6 oz Sultanas
15 g/½ oz Mixed peel
30 ml/2 tbsp Flaked wheat

Toast the seeds and wheatgerm until golden brown. Mix them with the flour and salt and rub in the butter or margarine. Mix the malt extract, honey, yeast and egg in the warm water until clear and smooth then mix into the dry ingredients. Mix the fruit with the seeds and wheatgerm and add to the dough. Knead the dough until smooth, cover and leave to rise until doubled in size.

Knead again, shape into long loaves and place in greased tins, cover and leave to prove in a warm place for 40 minutes. Sprinkle with flaked wheat and bake in a preheated oven at 230°C/450°F/gas mark 8 for 30 minutes.

Seville Bread

Makes 4 x 450 g/1 lb loaves

500 g/1¼ lb 81% extraction flour
65 g/2½ oz Soft brown sugar
2.5 ml/½ tsp Salt
15 ml/1 tbsp Milk powder
65 g/2½ oz Vegetable fat
25 g/1 oz Fresh yeast
350 ml/12 fl oz Warm water
Grated rind and juice of 1 orange
Grated rind and juice of 1 lemon
Grated rind and juice of 1 lime
450 g/1 lb Sultanas
30 ml/2 tbsp Honey

Mix the flour, 15 g/½ oz sugar, salt and milk powder and rub in 15 g/½ oz fat. Dissolve the yeast in the warm water and mix it into the dry ingredients. Knead until the dough is smooth and elastic. Cover and leave to rise until doubled in size.

Mix the rind and juice of the fruits with the sultanas and add it to the dough. Cream the remaining sugar and fat and add this to the dough, kneading well. Divide the dough into 4 and roll each piece into 3 long sausages. Plait the strands together, place on a greased baking sheets, cover and leave to prove in a warm place for 40 minutes.

Bake in a preheated oven at 220°C/425°F/gas mark 7 for 35 minutes. Glaze the baked loaves with honey.

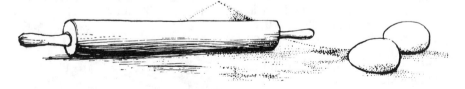

Toledo Bread

Makes 2 x 450 g/1 lb loaves

50 g/2 oz Adzuki beans	
450 g/1 lb Wholemeal flour	
5 ml/1 tsp Salt	
5 ml/1 tsp Soy flour	
20 g/¾ oz Butter or margarine	
300 ml/½ pt Warm water	
25 g/1 oz Fresh yeast	
50 g/2 oz Canned tomatoes, chopped	
30 ml/2 tbsp Tomato purée	
25 mg Ascorbic acid tablet	
5 ml/1 tsp Chilli powder	
2.5 ml/½ tsp Oregano	
25 g/1 oz Onion, chopped	
1 Garlic clove, chopped	
50 g/2 oz Cheese, grated	

Soak the adzuki beans overnight in cold water, then drain and place in fresh water, bring to the boil and simmer for 40 minutes. Drain well.

Mix the flour, salt, soy flour and rub in the butter or margarine. Mix the water and yeast and mix it into the dry ingredients. Add the tomatoes, tomato purée, ascorbic acid, chilli powder and oregano and knead until the dough is smooth. Cover and leave to rest for 10 minutes.

Mix in the onion, garlic and beans, cover and leave to rest for 10 minutes. Divide between greased loaf tins, cover and leave to prove in a warm place for 40 minutes. Bake in a preheated oven at 230°C/450°F/gas mark 8 for 15 minutes, then sprinkle with the cheese and return to the oven for a further 5 minutes until browned.

Tropicana Bread

Makes 3 x 400 g/14 oz loaves

350 g/12 oz 81% extraction flour	
50 g/2 oz Rolled oats	
2.5 ml/½ tsp Salt	
5 ml/1 tsp Soy flour	
25 g/1 oz Soft brown sugar	
25 g/1 oz Butter or margarine	
25 g/1 oz Fresh yeast	
5 ml/1 tsp Black treacle	
300 ml/½ pt Warm water	
50 g/2 oz Mixed nuts, chopped	
Pinch of mixed spice	
75 g/3 oz Pineapple, chopped	
25 g/1 oz Coconut flakes	
Pinch of ground ginger	
50 g/2 oz Desiccated coconut	
1 Egg, beaten	

Mix the flour, oats, salt, soy flour and sugar and rub in the butter or margarine. Dissolve the yeast and treacle in the warm water and add to the dry ingredients. Knead until the dough is smooth, then cover and leave to rise until doubled in size.

Knead again and mix in the nuts, spice, pineapple, coconut flakes, ginger and 40 g/1½ oz desiccated coconut. Cover and leave to prove in a warm place for 20 minutes. Divide into 3 and place on a greased baking sheet. Brush with egg and sprinkle with the reserved desiccated coconut. Bake in a preheated oven at 230°C/450°F/gas mark 8 for 30 minutes.

Wong Bread

Makes 4 x 450 g/1 lb loaves

450 g/1 lb Wholemeal flour
275 g/10 oz Rye flour
15 g/½ oz Soy flour
10 ml/2 tsp Salt
15 g/½ oz Butter or margarine
25 g/1 oz Fresh yeast
600 ml/½ pt Warm water
175 g/3 oz Parmesan cheese, grated
30 ml/2 tbsp Oil
1 Onion, chopped
1 Garlic clove, chopped
225 g/8 oz Beansprouts
2 Celery stalks, chopped
15 g/1 oz Root ginger, finely chopped

Mix the flours and salt and rub in the butter or margarine. Dissolve the yeast in the warm water, add to the dry ingredients and mix to a smooth dough, then add half the cheese. Cover and leave to rise until doubled in size.

Heat the oil and stir-fry the vegetables, then mix them into the dough and leave it to rest for 15 minutes. Divide the dough into 4 rounds, mark them into 8 and place on a greased baking tray. Cover and leave to prove in a warm place for 40 minutes. Bake in a preheated oven at 230°C/450°F/gas mark 8 for 30 minutes.

Pitta Breads

Makes 4 pitta breads

2.5 ml/½ tsp Honey
300 ml/½ pt Warm water
25 g/1 oz Fresh yeast
450 g/1 lb Strong plain flour
10 ml/2 tsp Salt
30 ml/2 tbsp Olive oil

Dissolve the honey in half the water. Blend in the yeast and leave until a soft curd forms on the water. Mix the flour and and salt, pour the yeast into the centre and add the remaining water and oil. Mix to a soft dough, then knead for about 8 minutes. Shape the dough into an oval, rub with oil, cover with a cloth and leave until doubled in size.

Punch down the dough and knead out any creases. Divide into 4, roll into balls and leave to rise, uncovered, for 30 minutes. Roll out the balls into ovals 3 mm/⅛ in thick, lay on greased and floured baking sheets and leave for a further 30 minutes. Bake in a preheated oven at 240°C/475°F/gas mark 9 for 10 minutes. Wrap in a cloth immediately to soften the bread and cool on a wire rack.

Soda Bread

Makes 3 x 450 g/1 lb loaves

750 g/1¾ lb Wholemeal flour
5 ml/1 tsp Salt
5 ml/1 tsp Bicarbonate of soda
40 g/1½ oz Butter or margarine
600 ml/1 pt Buttermilk

Mix the flour, salt and bicarbonate of soda then rub in the butter or margarine. Mix in the buttermilk to make a soft dough. Roll out into 3 rounds and place on a greased baking sheet. Mark into quarters, brush with egg, cover and leave to rest for 30 minutes before baking. Bake in a preheated oven at 230°C/450°F/gas mark 8 for 25 minutes or until the base sounds hollow when tapped.

Rusks

Makes 24 rusks

5 Eggs, beaten
300 ml/½ pt Warm milk
100 g/4 oz Butter or margarine
100 g/4 oz Fresh yeast OR
50 g/2 oz Dried yeast
75 g/3 oz Sugar
100 g/4 oz Strong plain flour

Mix together the eggs, milk and butter. Add the yeast and sugar and leave in a warm place until frothy. Gradually mix in enough flour to make a very light batter, cover and leave it to rise in a warm place for 30 minutes.

Add a little more flour to stiffen the mixture, knead well, place in greased loaf tins and flatten a little. Bake in a preheated oven at 230°C/450°F/gas mark 8 for about 20 minutes. When cool, cut into slices. Serve warmed and buttered.

Cakes

Whatever type of cake you prefer — rich fruit cake or light sponge — there are plenty of choices here for you to try, ideal for family teas, offering to special guests or just enjoying with a cup of tea.

Honey and Almond Cake

Makes 1 x 20 cm/8 in square cake

225 g/8 oz Carrots, grated
75 g/3 oz Almonds, chopped
2 Eggs, beaten
100 ml/4 fl oz Honey
60 ml/4 tbsp Oil
150 ml/¼ pt Milk
150 g/5 oz Wholemeal flour
10 ml/2 tsp Salt
10 ml/2 tsp Bicarbonate of soda
15 ml/1 tbsp Cinnamon
Lemon Glacé Icing (page 303) (optional)

Mix the carrots and nuts. Beat the eggs with the honey, oil and milk, then mix it into the carrot mixture. Mix together the flour, salt, bicarbonate of soda and cinnamon and stir into the carrot mixture. Spread the batter evenly in a greased 20 cm/8 in square tin and bake in a preheated oven at 150°C/300°F/gas mark 2 for 1¼ hours. Cool in the tin for 10 minutes then finish cooling on a wire rack. Ice when cool, if liked.

Apple Cake

Makes 1 x 20 cm/8 in cake

175 g/6 oz Self-raising flour
5 ml/1 tsp Baking powder
Pinch of salt
125 g/5 oz Caster sugar
125 g/5 oz Butter or margarine
1 Egg, beaten
175 ml/6 fl oz Milk
3 Eating apples, peeled, cored and sliced
2.5 ml/½ tsp Cinnamon
15 ml/1 tbsp Honey

Mix the flour, baking powder and salt, then stir in the caster sugar. Rub in the butter or margarine until the mixture resembles fine breadcrumbs. Mix in the egg and milk and pour the mixture into a greased 20 cm/8 in cake tin. Press the apple slices into the top, sprinkle with the cinnamon and brush with the honey. Bake in a preheated oven at 200°C/400°F/gas mark 6 for 45 minutes.

Dutch Fried Apple Cake

Makes 1 x 20 cm/8 in cake

| 100 g/4 oz Unsalted butter |
| 175 g/6 oz Digestive biscuits, crushed |
| 2 Dessert apples, peeled, cored and sliced |
| 100 g/4 oz Sultanas |
| 225 g/8 oz Gouda cheese, finely grated |
| 25 g/1 oz Plain flour |
| 75 ml/5 tbsp Single cream |
| 2.5 ml/½ tsp Mixed spice |
| Grated rind and juice of 1 lemon |
| 3 Eggs, separated |
| 100 g/4 oz Caster sugar |
| 2 Red-skinned apples, sliced |
| 30 ml/2 tbsp Apricot jam, sieved |

Melt half the butter in a saucepan and stir in the biscuit crumbs. Press the mixture into the base of a loose-bottomed 20 cm/8 in cake tin. Fry the dessert apples in the remaining butter until soft and golden. Drain off any excess fat, allow to cool slightly, then spread over the biscuit base and sprinkle with the sultanas. Mix the cheese, flour, cream, spice and lemon rind and juice. Mix the egg yolks and sugar together and stir into the cheese mixture until well blended. Whisk the egg whites until stiff and fold them in. Turn the cheese mixture gently into the tin and bake in a preheated oven at 180°C/350°F/gas mark 4 for 40 minutes. Cool in the tin on a wire rack.

When cold, arrange the red-skinned apples in rings around the top of the cake. Warm the apricot jam until liquid and brush it over them.

St Clement's Cheesecake

Makes 1 x 20 cm/8 in cake

| 50 g/2 oz Butter or margarine |
| 100 g/4 oz Digestive biscuits, crushed |
| 2 Eggs, separated |
| Pinch of salt |
| 100 g/4 oz Caster sugar |
| 45 ml/3 tbsp Orange juice |
| 45 ml/3 tbsp Lemon juice |
| 15 g/½ oz Gelatine |
| 30 ml/2 tbsp Cold water |
| 350 g/12 oz Cottage cheese, sieved |
| 150 ml/¼ pt Double cream, whipped |
| 1 Orange, peeled and sliced |

Rub a 20 cm/8 in loose-bottomed cake tin with the butter and sprinkle with the biscuits crumbs. Beat the egg yolks with the salt and half the sugar until thick and creamy. Put into a bowl with the orange and lemon juices and stir over a pan of hot water until the mixture begins to thicken and will coat the back of a spoon. Dissolve the gelatine in the cold water and heat gently until syrupy. Stir into the fruit juice mixture, then leave to cool. Stir in the cottage cheese and cream. Whisk the egg whites until stiff and fold in the remaining sugar. Fold into the cheesecake mixture and pour it into the cake tin. Chill until firm. Turn out to serve and sprinkle with any loose crumbs. Serve garnished with orange slices.

Raspberry Cheesecake

Makes 1 x 15 cm/6 in cake

75 g/3 oz Butter or margarine, melted
175 g/6 oz Digestive biscuits, crushed
3 Eggs, separated
300 ml/½ pt Milk
25 g/1 oz Caster sugar
15 g/½ oz Gelatine
30 ml/2 tbsp Cold water
225 g/8 oz Cream cheese
Grated rind and juice of ½ lemon
450 g/1 lb Fresh raspberries, hulled

Mix the butter and biscuits and press the mixture into the base of a loose-bottomed 15 cm/6 in cake tin. Chill while making the filling. Whisk the egg yolks, then pour into a saucepan with the milk and heat gently, stirring continuously, until the custard thickens. Remove from the heat and stir in the sugar. Whisk the egg whites until stiff. Soften the gelatine in the water, then dissolve over a pan of hot water. Beat the cheese until soft, then whisk in the gelatine, custard and lemon rind and juice, and continue whisking until the mixture thickens. Fold in the whisked egg whites and spoon the mixture over the base. Leave in a cool place to set. Just before serving, remove the cheesecake from the tin and cover with the raspberries.

Apricot Cheesecake

Makes 1 x 18 cm/7 in cake

75 g/3 oz Butter or margarine
100 g/4 oz Plain flour
100 g/4 oz Caster sugar
25 g/1 oz Hazelnuts, ground
30-45 ml/2-3 tbsp Cold water
100 g/4 oz Dried apricots, soaked and chopped
Grated rind and juice of 1 lemon
100 g/4 oz Curd cheese
100 g/4 oz Cream cheese
25 g/1 oz Cornflour
2 Eggs, separated
15 ml/1 tbsp Icing sugar

Rub the butter or margarine into the flour until the mixture resembles fine breadcrumbs. Stir in half the sugar and the hazelnuts, then add sufficient cold water to make a firm pastry. Roll out and use to line an 18 cm/7 in loose-bottomed flan ring and spread the apricots over the base. Purée the lemon rind and juice and cheeses in a food processor or blender. Blend in the remaining sugar, the cornflour and egg yolks until smooth and creamy. Whisk the egg whites until stiff then fold them into the mixture and spread it over the flan. Bake in a preheated oven at 180°C/350°F/gas mark 5 for 30 minutes until well risen and golden brown. Allow to cool slightly then sieve the icing sugar over the top and serve warm or cold.

Ginger and Lemon Cheesecake

Makes 1 x 20 cm/8 in cake

50 g/2 oz Butter or margarine
175 g/6 oz Gingernut biscuits, crushed
15 g/½ oz Gelatine
30 ml/2 tbsp Water
2 Lemons
100 g/4 oz Cottage cheese
100 g/4 oz Cream cheese
50 g/2 oz Caster sugar
150 ml/¼ pt Natural yoghurt
150 ml/¼ pt Double cream

Melt the butter or margarine and stir in the biscuit crumbs. Press into the base of a 20 cm/8 in flan ring. Mix the gelatine and water and dissolve over a pan of hot water. Pare 3 strips of lemon rind from one lemon. Grate the remaining rind of both lemons. Quarter the lemons, remove the pips and skin and purée the flesh in a food processor or blender. Add the cheeses and process to mix. Then add the sugar, yoghurt and cream, process again. Pour in the gelatine mixture and process. Pour into the biscuit flan base and leave in the fridge to set for 1 hour. Decorate with the strips of lemon rind and extra cream, if liked.

Carrot and Almond Cake

Makes 1 x 18 cm/7 in cake

5 Eggs, separated
200 g/7 oz Soft brown sugar
15 ml/1 tbsp Lemon juice
275 g/10 oz Young carrots, grated
225 g/8 oz Ground almonds
25 g/1 oz 81% extraction flour
5 ml/1 tsp Cinnamon
25 g/1 oz Butter or margarine, melted
65 g/2½ oz Soft brown sugar
20 ml/1½ tbsp Single cream
75 g/3 oz Chopped mixed nuts

Beat the egg yolks until frothy. Beat in the sugar until smooth and creamy, then beat in the lemon juice. Beat in one-third of the carrots, then one-third of the almonds, and continue in this way until they are all included. Stir in the flour and cinnamon. Whisk the egg whites until stiff, then fold them into the mixture. Turn the mixture into a greased and lined deep 18 cm/7 in cake tin and bake in a preheated oven at 180°C/350°F/gas mark 4 for 1 hour. Cover the cake loosely with greaseproof paper and reduce the heat to 160°C/325°F/gas mark 3 for a further 15 minutes or until the cake shrinks slightly from the sides of the tin and the centre is still moist. Cool the cake in the tin until just warm then turn out on to a wire rack to finish cooling. Combine the melted butter, sugar, cream and nuts, cover the cake and heat under the grill until golden brown.

Banana Cake

Makes 1 x 18 x 7.5 cm/8 x 3 in cake

450 g/1 lb Ripe bananas, mashed
50 g/2 oz Mixed nuts, chopped
120 ml/4 fl oz Sunflower oil
100 g/4 oz Raisins
75 g/3 oz Rolled oats
125 g/5 oz Wholemeal flour
2.5 ml/½ tsp Almond essence
Pinch of salt

Mix all the ingredients together to a soft, moist mixture. Spoon into a greased 450 g/1 lb loaf tin and bake in a preheated oven at 190°C/375°F/gas mark 5 for 1 hour. Cool in the tin for 10 minutes before turning out.

Moist Chocolate Cake

Makes 1 x 20 cm/8 in cake

200 g/7 oz Plain flour
30 ml/2 tbsp Cocoa
5 ml/1 tsp Bicarbonate of soda
5 ml/1 tsp Baking powder
125 g/5 oz Caster sugar
30 ml/2 tbsp Golden syrup
2 Eggs, beaten
150 ml/¼ pt Oil
150 ml/¼ pt Milk
150 ml/¼ pt Double or whipping cream, whipped

Beat all the ingredients except the cream together to a batter. Pour into 2 greased and lined 20 cm/8 in cake tins and bake in a preheated oven at 160°C/325°F/gas mark 3 for 35 minutes. Sandwich together with whipped cream when cool.

Christmas Cake

Makes 1 x 23 cm/9 in cake

350 g/12 oz Butter or margarine, softened
350 g/12 oz Soft brown sugar
6 Eggs
450 g/1 lb Plain flour
Pinch of salt
5 ml/1 tsp Mixed spice
225 g/8 oz Raisins
450 g/1 lb Sultanas
225 g/8 oz Currants
175 g/6 oz Mixed peel
50 g/2 oz Glacé cherries, chopped
100 g/4 oz Blanched almonds, chopped
30 ml/2 tbsp Black treacle or molasses
45 ml/3 tbsp Brandy

Cream the butter or margarine and sugar until soft, then beat in the eggs, one at a time. Fold in the flour, salt and spice, then mix in the remaining ingredients. Spoon into a greased and lined 23 cm/9 in cake tin and bake at 140°C/275°F/gas mark 1 for 6½ hours. Leave to cool completely, then wrap in foil and store in an airtight container for at least 3 weeks before covering with Almond Paste (page 306) and decorating with Royal Icing (page 304), if liked.

Chocolate Biscuit Cake

Makes 1 x 450 g/1 lb cake

2 Eggs, beaten

25 g/1 oz Caster sugar

225 g/8 oz Butter or margarine, melted

15 ml/1 tbsp Rum or brandy

225 g/8 oz Plain chocolate, melted

225 g/8 oz Rich Tea biscuits, broken into small pieces

Beat the eggs and caster sugar together, then stir in the butter or margarine, brandy and chocolate. Stir in the biscuits and fold together so they are all covered with chocolate mix. Pour into a 450 g/1 lb loaf tin lined with overlapping foil and shake gently to help mixture to settle. Leave in the fridge overnight, then turn out and serve in thin slices.

Toffee-Top Cherry Cake

Makes 1 x 20 cm/8 in square cake

100 g/4 oz Almonds

225 g/8 oz Glacé cherries, halved

225 g/8 oz Butter or margarine

225 g/8 oz Caster sugar

3 Eggs, beaten

100 g/4 oz Self-raising flour

50 g/2 oz Ground almonds

5 ml/1 tsp Baking powder

5 ml/1 tsp Almond essence

Grease and line a 20 cm/8 in square cake tin and sprinkle the almonds and cherries over the base. Melt 50 g/2 oz butter or margarine and 50 g/2 oz sugar, then pour it over the cherry mixture. Beat the remaining butter and sugar until light and fluffy, then beat in the eggs and mix in the flour, ground almonds, baking powder and almond essence. Spoon the mixture into the tin and level the top. Bake in a preheated oven at 160°C/325°F/gas mark 3 for 1 hour. Cool for a few minutes in the tin, then turn out carefully to finish cooling on a wire rack.

Cherry Cobblestone Cake

Makes 1 x 22 x 12 cm/8½ x 4½ in cake

175 g/6 oz Soft margarine

175 g/6 oz Caster sugar

3 Eggs, beaten

225 g/8 oz Plain flour

2.5 ml/½ tsp Baking powder

100 g/4 oz Sultanas

125 g/5 oz Glacé cherries, quartered

225 g/8 oz Fresh cherries, halved

30 ml/2 tbsp Apricot jam

Beat the margarine until soft, then beat in the caster sugar. Mix in the eggs, then the flour, baking powder, sultanas and glacé cherries. Spoon into a greased 900 g/2 lb loaf tin and bake in a preheated oven at 160°C/325°F/gas mark 3 for 2½ hours. Leave in the tin for 5 minutes, then turn out on to a wire rack.

Arrange the fresh cherries in a row on top of the cake. Boil the apricot jam, then sieve it and brush it over the top of the cake to glaze it.

Coconut and Carrot Cake

Makes 1 x 20 cm/8 in cake

350 g/12 oz Wholemeal flour
5 ml/1 tsp Baking powder
225 g/8 oz Soft brown sugar
5 ml/1 tsp Cinnamon
2.5 ml/½ tsp Nutmeg
350 g/12 oz Carrots, grated
50 g/2 oz Desiccated coconut
3 Eggs, beaten
75 ml/5 tbsp Milk
200 ml/7 fl oz Oil
15 ml/1 tbsp Icing sugar

Mix the flour, baking powder, sugar, cinnamon and nutmeg. Stir in the carrot and coconut, then the eggs, milk and oil. Spoon into a greased and lined 20 cm/8 in loose-bottomed cake tin and bake in a preheated oven at 180°C/350°F/gas mark 4 for 1½ hours until firm. Leave to cool in the tin, then turn out and sprinkle with icing sugar.

Cumberland Cake

Makes 1 x 20 cm/8 in cake

225 g/8 oz Lard
225 g/8 oz Caster sugar
225 g/8 oz Golden syrup
5 ml/1 tsp Bicarbonate of soda
15 ml/1 tbsp Milk
450 g/1 lb Plain flour
2.5 ml/½ tsp Cinnamon
5 ml/1 tsp Ground ginger
225 g/8 oz Currants
50 g/2 oz Grated lemon rind
1 Egg, beaten

Melt the lard, sugar and syrup in a saucepan. Dissolve the bicarbonate of soda in the milk and stir into the syrup. Beat in the dry ingredients, then the egg and a little more milk if necessary to give a soft consistency. Turn the mixture into a greased 20 cm/8 in cake tin and bake in a preheated oven at 180°C/350°F/gas mark 4 for 2 hours.

Sugar-Free Fruit Cake

Makes 1 x 18 cm/7 in cake

175 g/6 oz Plain flour
175 g/6 oz Wholemeal flour
10 ml/2 tsp Baking powder
5 ml/1 tsp Mixed spice
100 g/4 oz Butter or margarine
75 g/3 oz Currants
75 g/3 oz Raisins
75 g/3 oz Dates, stoned and chopped
1 Ripe banana, mashed
2 Eggs, beaten
60 ml/4 tbsp Orange juice

Mix the flours, baking powder and spice and rub in the butter or margarine. Stir in the fruit and eggs and add enough orange juice to make a soft dropping consistency. Spoon into a greased 18 cm/7 in cake tin and bake in a preheated oven at 180°C/350°F/gas mark 4 for 1¼ hours until the centre springs back when pressed lightly.

Dundee Cake

Makes 1 x 20 cm/8 in cake

225 g/8 oz Butter or margarine
225 g/8 oz Caster sugar
4 Eggs, beaten
225 g/8 oz Plain flour
Pinch of salt
350 g/12 oz Sultanas
350 g/12 oz Currants
175 g/6 oz Mixed peel
100 g/4 oz Glacé cherries, chopped
Grated rind of ½ lemon
75 g/3 oz Whole almonds, blanched

Cream the butter or margarine and sugar until light and fluffy. Beat in the eggs, one at a time, then fold in the mixed flour and salt. Mix in the sultanas, currants, peel, glacé cherries and lemon rind. Chop 25 g/1 oz almonds and mix them into the cake. Split the remaining almonds. Spoon the mixture into a greased and lined 20 cm/8 in cake tin and arrange the almonds, rounded side up, over the cake. Tie a band of brown paper round the tin extending 5 cm/2 in above the top and bake in a preheated oven at 150°C/300°F/gas mark 3 for 3½ hours. Reduce the heat to 140°C/275°F/gas mark 1 and cover the cake with a sheet of greaseproof paper for the last hour if it begins to brown too quickly. Cool in the tin for 30 minutes, then turn out and cool on a wire rack. The cake is best kept in an airtight container for 2 weeks before eating.

Hazelnut Torte

Makes 1 x 15 cm/6 in cake

2 Eggs
125 g/5 oz Caster sugar
100 g/4 oz Hazelnuts, ground
300ml/½ pt Double cream, whipped
50 g/2 oz Butter or margarine
60 ml/4 tbsp Milk
50 g/2 oz Cocoa powder
5 ml/1 tsp Vanilla essence
225 g/8 oz Icing sugar
12 Whole hazelnuts

Whisk the eggs and caster sugar until light and fluffy. Fold in the ground hazelnuts. Spoon the mixture into 2 greased 15 cm/6 in tins and bake in a preheated oven at 200°C/400°F/gas mark 6 for 15 minutes until golden brown. Leave to cool in the tins.

Sandwich the layers together with most of the whipped cream. Place the butter or margarine and milk in a saucepan and heat until boiling. Stir in the cocoa and simmer for 30 seconds. Remove from the heat and stir in the vanilla essence, then beat in the icing sugar. Spread the icing on top of the cake. Decorate with the remaining whipped cream and the hazelnuts.

Sticky Gingerbread

Makes 1 x 25 cm/10 in square cake

100 g/4 oz Butter or margarine
175 g/6 oz Golden syrup
175 g/6 oz Black treacle or molasses
100 g/4 oz Soft brown sugar
275 g/10 oz Plain flour
10 ml/2 tsp Cinnamon
5 ml/1 tsp Bicarbonate of soda
2 Eggs, beaten
150 ml/¼ pt Hot water

Melt the butter or margarine, syrup, treacle and sugar, then mix them into the flour, cinnamon and bicarbonate of soda. Beat in the eggs and hot water. Pour the mixture into a greased and lined 25 cm/10 in square tin and bake in a preheated oven at 180°C/350°F/gas mark 4 for 45 minutes.

Orange Sandwich Cake

Makes 1 x 18 cm/7 in cake

100 g/4 oz Butter or margarine
100 g/4 oz Caster sugar
2 Eggs, beaten
100 g/4 oz Plain flour
Grated rind of 1 orange
Pinch of salt
2.5 ml/½ tsp Baking powder
175 g/6 oz Orange Butter Icing (page 302)

Cream the butter or margarine and sugar until light and fluffy. Beat in the eggs, adding a spoonful of the flour if the mixture begins to curdle. Mix in the orange rind. Sift together the flour, salt and baking powder and mix lightly into the mixture. Divide the mixture between 2 greased and lined 18 cm/7 in sandwich tins and bake at 180°C/350°F/gas mark 4 for 25 minutes until lightly browned. Leave to cool. Sandwich together with orange butter icing.

Honeyed-Rhubarb Cake

Makes 2 x 20 x 7.5 cm/8 x 3 in cakes

100 ml/4 fl oz Oil
225 g/8 oz Honey
1 Egg
15 ml/1 tbsp Bicarbonate of soda
150 ml/¼ pt Natural yoghurt
350 g/12 oz Wholemeal flour
10 ml/2 tsp Salt
350 g/12 oz Rhubarb, finely chopped
5 ml/1 tsp Vanilla essence
50 g/2 oz Mixed nuts, chopped
75 g/3 oz Muscovado sugar
5 ml/1 tsp Cinnamon
25 g/1 oz Butter or margarine

Mix the oil and honey, add the egg and beat well. Dissolve the bicarbonate of soda in the yoghurt, then add it to the honey mixture alternately with the mixed flour and salt. Stir in the rhubarb, vanilla essence and nuts. Spoon into 2 greased 450 g/1 lb loaf tins. Mix the sugar, cinnamon and butter or margarine and spread over the cake mixture. Bake in a preheated oven at 160°C/325°F/gas mark 3 for 1 hour.

Pineapple Cheesecake

Makes 1 x 20 cm/8 in cake

175 g/6 oz Digestive biscuits, crushed
75 g/3 oz Butter or margarine, melted
3 Eggs, separated
75 g/3 oz Caster sugar
425 g/15 oz Canned pineapple, drained and chopped
150 ml/¼ pt Pineapple juice
225 g/8 oz Cheddar cheese, finely grated
150 ml/¼ pt Milk
150 ml/¼ pt Single cream
150 ml/¼ pt Double cream
15 ml/1 tbsp Gelatine
150 ml/¼ pt Whipping cream, whipped

Stir the biscuits into the melted butter and press the mixture into a greased and lined 20 cm/8 in loose-bottomed cake tin. Chill until firm. Reserve some pineapple for decoration and spread the rest over the base.

Whisk the egg yolks, sugar and half the pineapple juice in a bowl over a pan of hot water until thick. Mix together the cheese and milk. Whisk the single and double creams until thick. Add to the cheese, then stir into the egg mixture. Dissolve the gelatine in the remaining juice over a pan of hot water, cool slightly, then stir into the mixture and chill until almost setting. Whisk the egg whites until stiff and fold into the mixture. Pour into the tin and refrigerate until set. Turn out and decorate with whipped cream and the reserved pineapple.

Coffee-Iced Walnut Cake

Makes 1 x 20 cm/8 in cake

4 Eggs
100 g/4 oz Caster sugar
100 g/4 oz Self-raising flour
100 g/4 oz Walnuts, ground
50 g/2 oz Icing sugar
1 Egg white
100 g/4 oz Unsalted butter, cut into pieces
5 ml/1 tsp Instant coffee
5 ml/1 tsp Boiling water

Place the eggs and caster sugar in a large bowl over a pan of hot water, making sure the bowl does not touch the water. Whisk until light and frothy and thick enough to leave a trail from the whisk. Remove from the heat and lightly fold in the flour and nuts using a metal spoon. Pour into a greased loose-bottomed 20 cm/ 8 in cake tin and bake in a preheated oven at 190°C/375°F/gas mark 5 for 20 minutes until brown. Leave to cool.

To make the icing, place the icing sugar and egg white in a bowl over a pan of hot water and whisk for about 10 minutes until thick and glossy. Remove from the heat and beat in the butter. Mix the coffee and water and stir this into the icing. Chill for 30 minutes then spread over the top and sides of the cake.

Madeira Cake

Makes 1 x 20 cm/8 in round cake

175 g/6 oz Butter or margarine
175 g/6 oz Caster sugar
3 Eggs, beaten
225 g/8 oz Plain flour
7.5 ml/1½ tsp Baking powder
30 ml/2 tbsp Milk
Grated rind of 1 lemon
10 ml/2 tsp Vanilla essence

Cream the butter until soft, then beat in the sugar. Mix in the eggs, one at a time, then stir in the remaining ingredients until well blended. Spoon into a greased and lined 20 cm/8 in cake tin and bake in a preheated oven at 160°C/325°F/gas mark 3 for 1½ hours until a wooden cocktail stick inserted into the centre comes out clean. Cool in the tin for 5 minutes, then turn out on to a wire rack.

Sweetheart Cake

Makes 2 x 20 cm/8 in square cakes

450 g/1 lb Puff Pastry (page 146)
450 g/1 lb Currants
Juice of 1 lemon
50 g/2 oz Soft brown sugar
50 g/2 oz Butter, grated
Water
30 ml/2 tbsp Caster sugar

Divide the pastry into 4, roll out and use 2 pieces to line 2 greased 20 cm/8 in square tins. Cover with currants. Mix the lemon juice with the sugar and sprinkle over the currants. Cover with butter then top with the remaining pastry. Brush the pastry lids with cold water, sprinkle generously with sugar and bake in a preheated oven at 220°C/425°F/gas mark 7 for 30 minutes until the tops are faintly brown.

Victoria Sandwich Cake

Makes 1 x 18 cm/7 in cake

100 g/4 oz Butter or margarine
100 g/4 oz Caster sugar
2 Eggs, beaten
100 g/4 oz Plain flour
Pinch of salt
2.5 ml/½ tsp Baking powder
60 ml/4 tbsp Jam
300 ml/½ pt Double cream
30 ml/2 tbsp Icing sugar

Cream the butter or margarine and sugar until light. Beat in the eggs and lightly stir in the flour, salt and baking powder. Spoon into 2 greased and lined 18 cm/7 in sandwich tins and bake in a preheated oven at 180°C/350°F/gas mark 4 for 25 minutes until lightly browned and springy to the touch. Cool on a wire rack. Sandwich together with the jam and cream when cold and sprinkle with the sieved icing sugar.

Almond Macaroons

Makes 20

100 g/4 oz Ground almonds
175 g/6 oz Caster sugar
2 Egg whites
Few drops of vanilla essence
10 Whole almonds, split

Mix together the ground almonds and sugar. Whisk the egg whites until stiff then fold in the sugar and almonds and the vanilla essence. Form into small balls and place on a greased baking tray lined with rice paper. Flatten each ball slightly and place a split almond on top. Bake in a preheated oven at 180°C/350°F/gas mark 4 for 20 minutes until golden brown round the edges and slightly moist in the centre.

Apple and Blackcurrant Crumble Bars

Makes 20

175 g/6 oz Plain flour
5 ml/1 tsp Baking powder
2.5 ml/½ tsp Salt
175 g/6 oz Butter or margarine
225 g/8 oz Soft brown sugar
100 g/4 oz Rolled oats
225 g/8 oz Blackcurrants
500 g/1¼ lb Cooking apples, peeled, cored and chopped
30 ml/2 tbsp Cornflour
10 ml/2 tsp Cinnamon
2.5 ml/½ tsp Nutmeg
2.5 ml/½ tsp Allspice

Mix the flour, baking powder and salt and rub in the butter or margarine. Mix in the sugar and rolled oats and press half the mixture into a greased 33 x 23 cm/13 x 9 in baking tin. Top with blackcurrants. Mix the apples, cornflour and spices and spread over the blackcurrants. Top with the remaining mixture and bake in a preheated oven at 180°C/350°F/gas mark 4 for 35 minutes. Leave to cool and cut into bars.

Date Slices

Makes 16 rolls

225 g/8 oz Dates, stoned and chopped
30 ml/2 tbsp Honey
30 ml/2 tbsp Lemon juice
225 g/8 oz Wholemeal flour
225 g/8 oz Rolled oats
225 g/8 oz Butter or margarine
75 g/3 oz Soft brown sugar

Put the dates, honey and lemon juice in a saucepan and simmer gently until the dates are soft. Allow to cool slightly. Mix the flour and oats, rub in the butter or margarine and mix in the sugar. Press half this mixture into a shallow greased and lined 20 cm/8 in square tin, spread the date mixture on top then cover with the remaining flour mixture and press down firmly. Bake in a preheated oven at 190°C/375°F/gas mark 5 for 35 minutes. Cut into slices while still warm then leave to cool in the tin.

Bakewell Fingers

Makes 16

175 g/6 oz Butter or margarine
25 g/1 oz Lard
175 g/6 oz Plain flour
30-45 ml/2-3 tbsp Water
30 ml/2 tbsp Raspberry jam
100 g/4 oz Caster sugar
2 Eggs, beaten
50 g/2 oz Ground almonds
100 g/4 oz Self-raising flour
25 g/1 oz Icing sugar

Rub 50 g/2 oz butter or margarine and the lard into the flour until the mixture resembles fine breadcrumbs. Mix in just enough water to make a firm pastry, roll it out and use it to line a greased swiss roll tin. Save the pastry trimmings for decoration. Spread the jam over the pastry. Beat the remaining butter or margarine until soft, then beat in the sugar, followed by the eggs, ground almonds and self-raising flour. Spoon the mixture into the tin, covering the jam and pastry completely. Roll out the pastry trimmings and cut into long strips. Twist these and lay them over the top of the sponge mixture. Bake in a preheated oven at 190°C/375°F/gas mark 5 for 25 minutes. Leave to cool slightly, then cut into fingers and leave to cool in the tin.

Mix the icing sugar with enough water to make a smooth paste and pipe icing lines over the fingers or trickle the icing from a teaspoon.

Chocolate Éclairs

Makes 12

50 g/2 oz Butter or margarine
75 ml/5 tbsp Milk
75 ml/5 tbsp Water
60 g/2½ oz Plain flour
Pinch of salt
2 Eggs, beaten
300 ml/½ pt Double cream
225 g/8 oz Chocolate Glacé Icing (page 303)

Melt the butter with the milk and water over a low heat then turn up the heat and bring to the boil. Remove from the heat and stir in the flour and salt, then beat just until the pastry comes away from the sides of the pan. Cool slightly, then beat in the eggs a little at a time. Spoon the mixture into a piping bag with 1 cm/½ in plain nozzle and pipe lengths on to a greased baking tray. Bake in a preheated oven at 220°C/425°F/gas mark 7 for 20 minutes. Remove from the oven and slit the eclairs lengthways to allow the steam to escape, then leave to cool. When cool, fill with the whipped cream and top with glacé icing.

Cider Squares

Makes 16

225 g/8 oz Sultanas
150 ml/¼ pt Dry cider
100 g/4 oz Butter or margarine
100 g/4 oz Soft brown sugar
2 Eggs, beaten
225 g/8 oz Plain flour
5 ml/1 tsp Bicarbonate of soda

Soak the sultanas in the cider overnight.

Cream the butter or margarine and sugar until pale and fluffy, then beat in the eggs and half the flour and bicarbonate of soda. Mix in the sultanas and cider, then fold in the remaining flour and pour into a greased 18 cm/7 in square cake tin and bake in a preheated oven at 180°C/350°F/gas mark 4 for 1 hour until well risen and firm. Leave to cool in the tin for 30 minutes, then turn out on to a wire rack. Cut into squares when cool.

Chocolate Chip Muffins

Makes 12

175 g/6 oz Plain flour
40 g/1½ oz Cocoa powder
100 g/4 oz Caster sugar
10 ml/2 tsp Baking powder
2.5 ml/½ tsp Salt
100 g/4 oz Chocolate chips
1 Egg
250 ml/8 fl oz Milk
120 ml/4 fl oz Oil
2.5 ml/½ tsp Vanilla essence

Mix the flour, cocoa, sugar, baking powder, salt and chocolate chips. Beat the egg, milk, oil and vanilla essence. Make a well in the centre of the dry ingredients, pour in the egg mixture and stir together until well mixed but still lumpy. Spoon into greased muffin tins and bake in a preheated oven at 200°C/400°F/gas mark 6 for 20 minutes until well risen and springy to the touch.

Chocolate Fingers

Makes 20

100 g/4 oz Soft margarine
100 g/4 oz Caster sugar
100 g/4 oz Self-raising flour
2 Eggs, beaten
50 g/2 oz Cooking chocolate
15 ml/1 tbsp Golden syrup
50 g/2 oz Icing sugar
15-30 ml/1-2 tbsp Hot water

Beat the margarine until soft, then beat in the sugar, flour and finally the eggs. Turn the mixture into a greased and floured swiss roll tin and bake in a preheated oven at 180°C/350°F/gas mark 4 for 20 minutes.

Melt the chocolate in a small bowl over a saucepan of hot water. Stir in the syrup and icing sugar and mix well. Add enough hot water to make the mixture smooth and thick. Spread the warm icing on the cake and mark with a fork to make a pattern. Cut the cake into fingers with a bread knife dipped in hot water.

Fudge-Topped Chocolate Brownies

Makes 16

225 g/8 oz Granulated sugar

3 Eggs

75 ml/5 tbsp Oil

5 ml/1 tsp Vanilla essence

100 g/4 oz Plain flour

Pinch of baking powder

Salt

50 g/2 oz Cocoa powder

100 g/4 oz Walnuts, chopped

225 g/8 oz Soft brown sugar

75 ml/5 tbsp Double cream

25 g/1 oz Butter or margarine

Beat the granulated sugar, eggs, oil and vanilla essence. Sieve the flour, baking powder, a pinch of salt and the cocoa into the mixture, add the walnuts and beat all together for 1 minute. Pour the mixture into a greased and lined 20 cm/8 in square tin and bake in a preheated oven at 180°C/350°F/gas mark 4 for 30 minutes until just firm. Leave to cool in the tin.

Put the sugar, cream, butter or margarine and a pinch of salt in a saucepan and dissolve over a low heat, stirring, then bring to the boil. Remove from the heat, stir in a few drops of vanilla essence and beat well until thick. Spread over the brownies, leave to set, then cut into squares.

Quick Chocolate Crispies

Makes 20

3 Mars bars, cut into pieces

75 g/3 oz Butter or margarine

75 g/3 oz Rice Krispies

Melt the Mars bars and butter and stir in the Rice Krispies. Place spoonfuls into cake cases, or press the mixture into a 20 cm/8 in square tin, allow to cool and cut into squares.

Variation
If you make the square cake, cover it with melted chocolate and allow to set before cutting into squares.

Crunchy Flapjacks

Makes 16

75 g/3 oz Butter or margarine

50 g/2 oz Golden syrup

100 g/4 oz Soft brown sugar

175 g/6 oz Rolled oats

Melt the butter or margarine with the syrup, then mix into the sugar and oats. Press into a greased 20 cm/8 in shallow square tin and bake in a preheated oven at 180°C/350°F/gas mark 4 for 20 minutes. Cut into fingers while still warm.

Coffee Cakes

Makes 24

450 g/1 lb Wholemeal flour
25 g/1 oz Baking powder
5 ml/1 tsp Salt
225 g/8 oz Butter or margarine
225 g/8 oz Soft brown sugar
1 Egg, beaten
100 g/4 oz Currants
5 ml/1 tsp Decaffeinated instant coffee
5 ml/1 tsp Hot water
60 ml/4 tbsp Honey

Mix the flour, baking powder and salt, rub in the butter or margarine and blend in the sugar. Add the egg and mix until the dough is smooth and no longer sticky. Add the currants. Mix the coffee and water and add it to the dough. Divide into balls, flatten slightly and place, well apart, on greased baking trays. Press a thumb into the centre of each cake and spoon in a little honey. Bake in a preheated oven at 220°C/425°F/gas mark 7 for 15 minutes until golden and light.

Special Frangipan Tartlets

Makes 24

150 g/5 oz Butter or margarine
200 g/7 oz Plain flour
10 ml/2 tsp Grated orange rind
30 ml/2 tbsp Orange juice
50 g/2 oz Caster sugar
1 Egg
25 g/1 oz Ground almonds
100 g/4 oz Icing sugar
15 ml/1 tbsp Water
Glacé cherries, halved

Rub 75 g/3 oz butter or margarine into 175 g/6 oz flour until the mixture resembles fine breadcrumbs. Mix in the orange rind, then bind with the juice until the mixture forms a pastry. Roll out, cut into rounds and line 24 greased bun tins. Cream the remaining butter or margarine with the caster sugar, mix in the egg, then the remaining flour and the ground almonds. Divide the mixture between the pastry cases and bake in a preheated oven at 200°C/400°F/gas mark 6 for 15 minutes. Leave to cool.

Sieve the icing sugar, then gradually mix in the water until smooth. Spread over the cakes and top each one with half a cherry.

Fig Surprises

Makes 12

275 g/10 oz Plain flour
Pinch of salt
100 g/4 oz Butter or margarine
75 g/3 oz Lard, diced
50 g/2 oz Caster sugar
175 ml/6 fl oz Water
225 g/8 oz Dried figs, chopped
75 g/3 oz Walnuts, chopped
50 g/2 oz Currants
50 g/2 oz Raisins
15 ml/1 tbsp Milk

Mix the flour and salt, then rub in the butter or margarine and lard until the mixture resembles fine breadcrumbs. Stir in the sugar and bind with 30-45 ml/2-3 tbsp water to make a pastry. Put in the fridge to chill.

Place the remaining water in a saucepan with the figs, walnuts, currants and raisins, bring to the boil and simmer, stirring, until the water has evaporated and the fruit is soft. Leave to cool.

Divide the dough in half, roll out and use one piece to line a greased 28 x 18 cm/11 x 7 in tin. Spread the fruit mixture over the pastry, then cover with the remaining pastry, sealing the edges well. Mark into 12 squares and brush the top with milk. Bake in a preheated oven at 190°C/375°F/gas mark 5 for 40 minutes until golden brown. Cut into squares when cool.

Biscuits and Cookies

There are so many types of biscuits in the shops, many people don't think it is worth baking your own, but it is very quick and easy and the taste is worth any trouble. Biscuits can be frozen in a hard container, separated by sheets of greaseproof, or you can freeze the mixture ready to bake.

Peppermint Fingers

Makes 18

50 g/2 oz Butter or margarine
50 g/2 oz Caster sugar
100 g/4 oz Plain flour
175 g/6 oz Icing sugar
15-30 ml/1-2 tbsp Hot water
2.5 ml/½ tsp Peppermint essence
175 g/6 oz Plain chocolate

Whisk the butter and sugar together until pale and fluffy then stir in the flour and knead to a smooth dough. Press into a small swiss roll tin, prick with a fork and bake in a preheated oven at 180°C/350°F/gas mark 4 for 10 minutes until golden brown. Leave to cool.

Mix the icing sugar with the water and essence and spread on top of the biscuit base. Leave to cool. Melt the chocolate in a bowl over a pan of hot water and spread over the icing. Cut into fingers when cold.

Lady Abbess's Puffs

Makes 24

75 g/3 oz Ground almonds
50 g/2 oz Caster sugar
15 ml/1 tbsp Butter or margarine
2 Egg whites
30 ml/2 tbsp Milk
75 g/3 oz Jam
150 ml/¼ pt Double or whipping cream, whipped

Mix the almonds, sugar and butter or margarine. Whisk the egg whites until stiff, then fold them into the mixture. Add enough milk to make a thick paste. Place spoonfuls on a greased baking sheet and hollow out the centres. Bake in a preheated oven at 150°C/300°F/gas mark 2 for 15 minutes. When cold, put a spoonful of jam on each puff and cover with whipped cream.

Oatcakes

Makes 8

175 g/6 oz Fine oatmeal
50 g/2 oz 81% extraction flour
Salt
Pinch of bicarbonate of soda
25 g/1 oz Butter or margarine
75-120 ml/3-4 fl oz Hot water
Oatmeal for dusting

Mix the oatmeal, flour, salt and bicarbonate of soda. Melt the butter or margarine and add to the dry ingredients with enough hot water to make a stiff dough. Turn on to a surface dusted with oatmeal and knead until smooth. Divide in half and roll out into large rounds as thinly as possible. Cut each round into quarters and place on an un-greased baking sheet dusted with oatmeal. Bake in a preheated oven at 180°C/350°F/gas mark 4 for 20 minutes until the edges begin to brown. Cool on the sheets and store in an airtight container.

American Biscuits

Makes 36

75 g/3 oz Butter or margarine
450 g/1 lb Plain flour
150 ml/¼ pt Milk

Rub the butter or margarine into the flour and mix well with the milk. Place spoonfuls of the mixture on to a greased baking tray and bake in a preheated oven at 180°C/350°F/gas mark 4 for 10 minutes.

Lemon Puffs

Makes 16

225 g/8 oz Caster Sugar
Grated rind of 1 lemon
2 Egg whites

Mix the sugar and lemon rind. Whisk the egg whites until stiff, then beat them into the sugar and lemon mixture. Place spoonfuls on greased baking parchment on baking sheets and bake in a preheated oven at 160°C/325°F/gas mark 3 for 15 minutes. Do not remove the paper until the puffs are cold.

Iced Chocolate Biscuits

Makes 24

225 g/8 oz Caster sugar
175 g/6 oz Ground almonds
75 g/3 oz Chocolate, grated
2 Egg whites
100 g/4 oz Icing sugar
15 ml/1 tbsp Cocoa powder
15 ml/1 tbsp Hot water

Mix the sugar, almonds and choco-late. Whisk the egg whites until stiff and fold them into the mixture. Place spoonfuls of the mixture on to a greased baking tray and bake in a preheated oven at 180°C/350°F/gas mark 4 for 10 minutes.

When the biscuits are cool, sift the icing sugar and 'cocoa, and mix to a glacé icing with the hot water. Spread over the biscuits.

Almond Biscuits

Makes 24

100 g/4 oz Ground almonds
100 g/4 oz Caster sugar
Grated rind of 1 lemon
3 Eggs, separated

Mix the almonds, sugar and lemon rind. Beat the egg yolks thoroughly and add to the mixture. Whisk the egg whites until stiff and fold them into the mixture. Put a spoonful into paper cases and bake in a preheated oven at 180°C/350°F/gas mark 4 for about 10 minutes until crisp.

Cracknels

Makes 24

225 g/8 oz Plain flour
5 ml/1 tsp Nutmeg
1 Egg yolk, beaten
15 ml/1 tbsp Rose water
Cold water (optional)
50 g/2 oz Butter or margarine, softened

Mix the flour, nutmeg, egg yolks and rose water to a stiff paste, adding a little cold water if necessary. Make into small balls and roll in the butter or margarine. Bring a saucepan of water to the boil, drop in the cracknels and boil until they float to the surface, then remove them, rinse in cold water, drain and place them on a greased baking sheet. Bake in a preheated oven at 180°C/350°F/gas mark 4 for 10 minutes.

Crack Nuts

Makes 24

225 g/8 oz Plain flour
225 g/8 oz Caster sugar
100 g/4 oz Butter or margarine
3 Eggs, beaten
30 ml/2 tbsp Caraway seeds
Egg white to glaze
Caster sugar for sprinkling

Mix the flour, sugar and butter, then add the eggs and caraway seeds. Roll out as thin as possible, then cut into rounds and place them on a greased baking sheet. Brush with egg white and sprinkle with caster sugar. Bake in a preheated oven at 160°C/325°F/gas mark 3 for 10 minutes.

Ginger Nuts

Makes 24

175 g/6 oz Plain flour
100 g/4 oz Fine oatmeal
75 g/3 oz Sugar
5 ml/1 tsp Ground ginger
5 ml/1 tsp Mixed spice
5 ml/1 tsp Bicarbonate of soda
50 g/2 oz Lard
175 g/6 oz Black treacle
A little milk

Mix the dry ingredients. Rub in the lard, then mix to a pliable dough with the treacle. Roll out to 1 cm/½ in thick, cut into rounds and place them on a greased baking sheet. Brush with milk and bake in a preheated oven at 180°C/350°F/gas mark 4 for 15 minutes.

Ginger Biscuits

Makes 16

3 Eggs, separated
175 g/6 oz Caster sugar
75 g/3 oz Plain flour
5 ml/1 tsp Ground ginger

Beat the egg yolks with the caster sugar until thick. Whisk the egg whites until stiff, then fold them into the mixture. Stir in the flour and ginger. Place spoonfuls on a greased baking sheet and bake in a preheated oven at 150°C/300°F/gas mark 2 for 15 minutes.

Old Leigh Cookies

Makes 24

225 g/8 oz Butter or margarine
400 g/14 oz Soft brown sugar
1 Egg, beaten
Few drops of vanilla essence
450 g/1 lb Wholemeal flour
75 g/3 oz Desiccated coconut
50 g/2 oz Glacé cherries, chopped

Cream the butter or margarine and sugar together until light. Beat in the egg and vanilla essence, then fold in the flour, coconut and cherries. Roll out into a long sausage shape and refrigerate until hard. Cut into round biscuits and place on greased baking trays. Bake in a preheated oven at 190°C/375°F/gas mark 5 until golden brown.

Buttery Treacle Nuts

Makes 24

225 g/8 oz Black treacle
375 g/12 oz Butter or margarine
225 g/8 oz Soft brown sugar
20 ml/1½ tbsp Ground ginger
15 ml/1 tbsp Mixed peel, finely chopped
5 ml/1 tsp Caraway seeds
1 Egg
50 g/2 oz Plain flour

Mix the treacle, butter, sugar, ginger, mixed peel and caraway seeds. Add the egg, and stir in enough flour to make a stiff paste. Place spoonfuls on a greased baking sheet and bake in a preheated oven at 150°C/300°F/gas mark 2 for 20 minutes.

Jumbles

Makes 24

75 g/3 oz Caster sugar
225 g/8 oz Plain flour
10 ml/2 tsp Ground ginger
75 g/3 oz Butter or margarine
175 g/6 oz Black treacle

Mix the sugar, flour and ginger. Bring the butter or margarine and treacle to the boil, then pour it into the dry ingredients. Mix well until smooth, then roll out thinly straight on to a greased baking sheet. Mark into squares with the back of a knife, then bake in a preheated oven at 150°C/300°F/gas mark 2 for about 10 minutes until crisp. Divide into portions as marked while still warm.

Treacle and Ginger Buttons

Makes 24

225 g/8 oz Black treacle
75 g/3 oz Caster sugar
5 ml/1 tsp Ground ginger
10 ml/2 tsp Caraway seeds
50 g/2 oz Butter or margarine
175 g/6 oz Plain flour

Mix all the ingredients together well. Drop spoonfuls on to a greased baking sheet and bake in a preheated oven at 150°C/300°F/gas mark 2 for 10 minutes.

Hard Biscuits

Makes 16

25 g/1 oz Butter or margarine
150 ml/¼ pt Skimmed milk
225 g/8 oz Plain flour

Warm the butter in the milk and mix in the flour to a very stiff paste. Beat it well until very smooth. Roll out thinly and cut into rounds. Place them on a greased baking sheet, prick all over with a fork and bake in a preheated oven at 160°C/325°F/gas mark 3 for 6 minutes.

Kringles

Makes 16

3 Eggs, separated
50 g/2 oz Butter or margarine, softened
225 g/8 oz Plain flour
50 g/2 oz Caster sugar

Beat 3 egg yolks with 2 egg whites, then mix in the butter. Stir into the flour and sugar to form a paste. Roll out to 1 cm/½ in thick, cut into rounds and place on a greased baking sheet. Prick all over with a fork then bake in a preheated oven at 160°C/325°F/gas mark 3 for 15 minutes.

Muesli Biscuits

Makes 30

100 g/4 oz Butter or margarine
100 g/4 oz Honey
75 g/3 oz Muscovado sugar
100 g/4 oz Wholemeal flour
100 g/4 oz Rolled oats
50 g/2 oz Raisins
50 g/2 oz Sultanas
50 g/2 oz Dates, chopped
50 g/2 oz Dried apricots, chopped
25 g/1 oz Walnuts, chopped
25 g/1 oz Hazelnuts, chopped

Melt the butter or margarine, honey and sugar, then stir in the remaining ingredients. Roll out on a floured surface, cut into rounds and bake in a preheated oven at 180°C/350°F/gas mark 4 for 20 minutes.

Orange and Chocolate Chip Biscuits

Makes 30

50 g/2 oz Butter or margarine
75 g/3 oz Lard
175 g/6 oz Soft brown sugar
200 g/7 oz Wholemeal flour
75 g/3 oz Ground almonds or hazelnuts
10 ml/2 tsp Baking powder
75 g/3 oz Chocolate drops
Grated rind of 2 oranges
15 ml/1 tbsp Orange juice
1 Egg, beaten
30 ml/2 tbsp Demerara sugar

Beat the butter or margarine with the sugar until soft, then add all the remaining ingredients except the demerara sugar and mix well. Roll out on a floured surface, cut into rounds and sprinkle with the demerara sugar. Bake in a preheated oven at 180°C/350°F/gas mark 4 for 20 minutes.

Plain Biscuits

Makes 24

450 g/1 lb Plain flour
1 Egg yolk
300 ml/½ pt Milk

Mix the ingredients together, gradually adding the milk until it makes a stiff paste. Knead until smooth, roll out very thinly and cut into rounds. Place them on a greased baking sheet and bake in a preheated oven at 150°C/300°F/gas mark 2 for 20 minutes until dry and crisp.

Sizzy's Shortbread

Serves 4-6

100 g/4 oz Soft brown sugar
100 g/4 oz Honey
225 g/8 oz Butter or margarine
225 g/8 oz Vegetable fat
750 g/1½ lb Wholemeal flour
30 ml/2 tbsp Demerara sugar

Beat the sugar, honey and fats to a paste then blend in the flour until smooth. Roll out to a rectangle about 5 mm/¼ in thick, place on a greased baking tray and prick all over with a fork. Mark into fingers, but do not cut all the way through. Bake in a preheated oven at 200°C/400°F/gas mark 6 for 15 minutes until golden brown. Sprinkle with demerara sugar.

Newton Biscuits

Makes 24

175 g/6 oz Butter or margarine
450 g/1 lb Plain flour
2.5 ml/½ tsp Baking powder
Few drops of almond essence
30 ml/2 tbsp Golden syrup
50 g/2 oz Flaked almonds

Rub the butter or margarine into the flour, add the baking powder and almond essence and make into a stiff paste with the golden syrup. Roll out, sprinkle with almonds and roll these in, then cut into rounds and place them on greased baking sheets. Bake in a preheated oven at 160°C/325°F/gas mark 3 for 20 minutes until golden brown.

Viennese Whirls

Makes 12

25 g/1 oz Butter or margarine
100 g/4 oz Soft brown sugar
225 g/8 oz Wholemeal flour
50 g/2 oz Ground almonds
100 g/4 oz Raspberry jam

Cream the butter or margarine and sugar together until light and fluffy. Blend in the flour and almonds and cream until light and clear. Pipe the mixture into biscuits, well apart, through a star nozzle on a greased baking sheet. Bake in a preheated oven at 200°C/400°F/gas mark 6 for 15 minutes until brown. Cool, then sandwich together with jam.

Tonbridge Biscuits

Makes 24

75 g/3 oz Butter or margarine, cut into pieces
225 g/8 oz Plain flour
75 g/3 oz Caster sugar
1 Egg, beaten
1 Egg white, whisked
30 ml/2 tbsp Caraway seeds

Rub the butter or margarine into the flour until the mixture resembles fine breadcrumbs, then mix in the sugar. Add the egg and mix to a stiff paste. Roll out on a floured surface, cut into rounds and place on a greased baking sheet. Prick the biscuits with a fork, brush with egg white and sprinkle with caraway seeds. Bake in a preheated oven at 180°C/350°F/gas mark 4 for 10 minutes.

Nut Biscuits

Makes 24

50 g/2 oz Butter or margarine
225 g/8 oz Plain flour
5 ml/1 tsp Baking powder
Pinch of salt
50 g/2 oz Chopped mixed nuts
150 ml/¼ pt Warm milk

Rub the butter or margarine into the flour, baking powder and salt. Add the nuts and mix to a firm paste with just enough milk. Roll out and cut into rounds. Place on a greased baking sheet and bake in a preheated oven at 180°C/350°F/gas mark 4 for 15 minutes.

Oatmeal Biscuits

Makes 16

125 g/5 oz Wholemeal flour
2.5 ml/½ tsp Bicarbonate of soda
Pinch of salt
100 g/4 oz Butter or margarine
50 g/2 oz Oatmeal
50 g/2 oz Soft brown sugar
1 Egg, beaten
15 ml/1 tbsp Water

Mix the flour, bicarbonate of soda and salt, then rub in the butter or margarine. Mix in the oatmeal and sugar. Beat the egg with water and add it to the mixture to form a stiff paste, adding a little more water if necessary. Roll out, cut into rounds and place on a greased and floured baking sheet. Bake in a preheated oven at 180°C/350°F/gas mark 4 for 20 minutes.

Picnic Biscuits

Makes 16

25 g/1 oz Butter or margarine
225 g/8 oz Plain flour
2.5 ml/½ tsp Bicarbonate of soda
25 g/1 oz Caster sugar
45 ml/3 tbsp Milk

Work the butter into the flour and add the bicarbonate of soda and the sugar. Mix to a paste with the milk, adding a little more or less as necessary. Knead until very smooth, roll out to 5 mm/¼ in thick and cut into small rounds. Place them on a greased baking sheet, prick with a fork and bake in a preheated oven at 150°C/300°F/gas mark 2 for 15 minutes.

Rice Biscuits

Makes 24

75 g/3 oz Caster sugar
2 Eggs
50 g/2 oz Butter or margarine
225 g/8 oz Rice flour
25 g/1 oz Currants

Beat together the sugar, eggs and butter or margarine. Mix the flour and currants and add to the mixture, beating well. Roll out and cut into rounds. Place them on a greased and floured baking tray and bake in a preheated oven at 150°C/300°F/gas mark 2 for 20 minutes.

Savoy Biscuits

Makes 24

3 Eggs, separated
225 g/8 oz Plain flour
225 g/8 oz Caster sugar

Beat the egg yolks well and gradually add the flour. Whisk 2 egg whites with the sugar until stiff, then add to the flour mixture and beat well. Place spoonfuls on a greased baking sheet and bake in a preheated oven at 160°C/325°F/gas mark 3 for 12 minutes.

Spiced Biscuits

Makes 12–15

100 g/4 oz Soft margarine
100 g/4 oz Caster sugar
1 Egg, separated
225 g/8 oz Plain flour
5 ml/1 tsp Mixed spice
75 g/3 oz Currants
15–30 ml/1–2 tbsp Milk
Caster sugar for sprinkling

Cream together the margarine and sugar. Add the egg yolk. Add the flour, spice, currants and enough milk to make a soft dough. Knead the dough lightly, then roll out to 5 mm/¼ in thick and cut into 5 cm/2 in rounds. Place on a greased baking tray and bake in a preheated oven at 200°C/400°F/gas mark 6 for 10 minutes. Remove from the oven, brush with egg white and sprinkle with caster sugar. Return to the oven for a further 5–10 minutes until golden. Cool on a wire rack.

Brandy Snaps

Makes 12

50 g/2 oz Butter or margarine
50 g/2 oz Caster sugar
50 g/2 oz Golden syrup
50 g/2 oz Plain flour
2.5 ml/½ tsp Ground ginger

Put the butter, sugar and syrup in saucepan and beat slowly over a low heat until melted. Remove from the heat and mix in the flour and ginger. Place spoonfuls of the mixture on greased baking trays, allowing plenty of space for the mixture to spread. Bake in a preheated oven at 180°C/350°F/gas mark 4 for 10 minutes until golden brown. Leave to firm for a minute, then remove with a palette knife and roll round the greased handle of a wooden spoon . Slip off the spoon and leave to cool on a wire rack. If the mixture becomes too hard to shape, return to the oven for 1 to 2 minutes to soften.

Shortbread Biscuits

Makes 24

100 g/4 oz Butter or margarine
50 g/2 oz Caster sugar
225 g/8 oz Plain flour

Cream the butter or margarine and sugar, then gradually add the flour and mix well. Roll out and cut into rounds. Place them on a greased baking sheet and prick with a fork. Bake in a preheated oven at 160°C/325°F/gas mark 3 for 20 minutes.

Wine Biscuits

Makes 24

50 g/2 oz Butter or margarine
225 g/8 oz Plain flour
50 g/2 oz Caster sugar
1 Egg
15 ml/1 tbsp Cream
5 ml/1 tsp Caraway seeds

Rub the butter or margarine into the flour. Add the sugar and mix to a paste with the egg and cream. Stir in the caraway seeds. Place spoonfuls on a greased baking sheet and bake in a preheated oven at 220°C/425°F/gas mark 7 for 10 minutes.

Butterscotch Crisps

Makes 48

100 g/4 oz Butter or margarine
100 g/4 oz Muscovado sugar
1 Egg, beaten
Few drops of vanilla essence
225 g/8 oz Plain flour
8 ml/1½ tsp Baking powder
Pinch of salt

Cream the butter or margarine and sugar until light. Beat in the egg and vanilla essence. Sift together the flour, baking powder and salt and mix into the creamed mixture. Shape the dough into 3 rolls about 5 cm/2 in in diameter, wrap in greaseproof paper and chill overnight.

Cut into slices 3 mm/⅛ in thick, place on ungreased baking sheets and bake in a preheated oven at 190°C/375°F/gas mark 5 for 10 minutes until lightly browned.

Digestive Biscuits

Makes 24

175 g/6 oz Wholemeal plain flour
50 g/2 oz Plain flour
50 g/2 oz Medium oatmeal
2.5 ml/½ tsp Salt
5 ml/1 tsp Baking powder
100 g/4 oz Butter or margarine
30 ml/2 tbsp Soft brown sugar
60 ml/4 tbsp Milk

Mix the flours, oatmeal, salt and baking powder. Rub in the fat, then mix in the sugar. Mix to a dough with the milk and knead well. Roll out on a floured surface and cut into rounds. Place on a greased baking sheet and bake in a preheated oven at 180°C/350°F/gas mark 4 for 15 minutes.

Yarmouth Biscuits

Makes 24

100 g/4 oz Plain flour
225 g/8 oz Caster sugar
100 g/4 oz Butter or margarine
175 g/6 oz Currants
1 Egg, beaten

Mix the flour and sugar and rub in the butter or margarine. Mix in the currants, then gradually work in enough egg to make a stiff dough. Roll out and cut into rounds. Place on greased baking parchment on a baking sheet and bake in a preheated oven at 220°C/425°F/gas mark 7 for 10 minutes.

True Lovers' Knot

Makes 12

225 g/8 oz Puff Pastry
(page 146)
75 g/3 oz Jam

Roll out the puff pastry to a thin sheet and cut into 9 cm/3½ in squares. Fold each corner into the centre and press in the sides to form a knot shape. Place on a baking sheet and bake in a preheated oven at 200°C/400°F/gas mark 6 for 10 minutes. When cool, place a spoonful of jam in the centre of each knot.

Cherry Biscuits

Makes 16

175 g/6 oz Plain flour
25 g/1 oz Cornflour
100 g/4 oz Caster sugar
100 g/4 oz Soft margarine
50 g/2 oz Glacé cherries, chopped

Mix the flours and 75 g/3 oz sugar, then rub in the margarine until the mixture resembles fine breadcrumbs. Stir in the glacé cherries and mix well. Press the mixture into a greased swiss roll tin and bake in a preheated oven at 160°C/325°F/gas mark 3 for 20 minutes. Sprinkle with the reserved caster sugar while hot and mark into fingers. Leave to cool in the tin.

Orange and Walnut Biscuits

Makes 16

100 g/4 oz Butter or margarine
75 g/3 oz Caster sugar
Grated rind of ½ orange
150 g/5 oz Self-raising flour
50 g/2 oz Walnuts, ground

Beat the butter or margarine, 50 g/ 2 oz sugar and the orange rind until smooth and creamy. Add the flour and nuts and beat again until the mixture begins to hold together. Form into balls and flatten on to a greased baking tray. Bake in a pre-heated oven at 190°C/375°F/gas mark 5 for 10 minutes until brown round the edges. Sprinkle with the reserved sugar and leave to cool slightly before removing from the tray.

Yorkshire Parkin

Makes 24

10 ml/2 tsp Ground ginger
225 g/8 oz Plain flour
225 g/8 oz Fine oatmeal
100 g/4 oz Lard
2.5 ml/½ tsp Bicarbonate of soda
15 ml/1 tbsp Milk
450 g/1 lb Black treacle or
  molasses, warmed

Mix the ginger, flour and oatmeal, then rub in the lard. Dissolve the bicarbonate of soda in the milk and stir it into the dry ingredients with the treacle or molasses. The mixture should be quite soft. Pour into a baking tin and bake in a preheated oven at 160°C/325°F/gas mark 3 for 1 hour.

Jams, Jellies and Marmalades

You can make jams and marmalades with almost any fruit, and it is an excellent way of using up excess fruit, if you grow your own, or making the best of cheap fruits in the shops. Make sure that you use good quality fruit, though, to get the best results.

It is the pectin in the fruits which makes jams set, and different fruits have different levels of pectin. Cooking apples, currants, plums and gooseberries all have a high pectin content and therefore set well, so are often mixed with cherries or strawberries, for example, which have less pectin and do not set as well.

Preserving sugar is ideal, but you can use cube or granulated sugar just as well. Brown sugar, honey and syrup all give distinctive flavours, but do not set as well, so if you want to try these, it is better to substitute them for one-quarter of the sugar in the recipe, then use ordinary sugar for the remainder. Sugar quantities vary according to the amount of sugar in the fruit itself. Warm the sugar in the oven before you use it to speed up the cooking process.

Soft-skinned fruits can be soaked with sugar before cooking to harden the skins and help keep the fruits whole. Start by cooking the fruit slowly to release the pectin, soften the skins and preserve the colour. Once the sugar has dissolved, jams need to be boiled rapidly without stirring. A large preserving pan is the best utensil because it allows plenty of room for a rolling boil.

It will take between 5 and 35 minutes to boil jams to setting point. If you use a thermometer, setting point is 104C/220F. If you do not have a thermometer, simply place a saucer in the fridge to chill while the jam is boiling. When you think the jam is ready, place a spoonful on the chilled saucer. When it cools, press it with your finger. If it wrinkles, the jam has reached setting point. If not, boil for another 5 minutes and test again.

Always warm jars before you pour in hot jam, place a disc of waxed paper on the top and screw down the cap when the jam has cooled.

Orchard Jam

Makes 2.25 kg/5 lb

1.2 1/2 pts Water
750 g/1½ lb Sugar
Grated rind and juice of 1 orange
450 g/1 lb Raisins
1.5 kg/3 lb Apples, peeled, cored and diced
2.5 ml/½ tsp Ground cloves
2.5 ml/½ tsp Cinnamon

Boil the water and sugar, then add the orange rind and juice and the raisins and simmer for 15 minutes. Add the apples and spices and boil for a further 15 minutes then pour into warmed jars.

Apple and Ginger Jam

Makes 1.5 kg/3 lb

900 g/2 lb Apples, peeled, cored and sliced
675 g/1½ lb Sugar
40 g/1½ oz Crystallised ginger, finely chopped
450 ml/¾ pt Water
Grated rind and juice of 1 lemon

Place layers of apple, sugar and ginger in a bowl and pour over the water. Leave overnight. Place in a pan, bring to the boil and simmer for 30 minutes. Add the lemon rind and juice, bring back to the boil and simmer for a further 30 minutes until the fruit and syrup are transparent. Stir well and pour into warmed jars.

Apple and Blackberry Jam

Makes 1.5 kg/3 lb

450 g/1 lb Cooking apples, peeled, cored and sliced
300 ml/½ pt Water
450 g/1 lb Blackberries
900 g/2 lb Sugar, warmed

Place the apples and water in a pan and simmer gently until soft. Add the blackberries, bring to the boil, and simmer until the blackberries are soft. Stir in the warm sugar until dissolved, then boil for about 10 minutes to setting point. Stir well and pour into warmed jars.

Crofton Apricot Jam

Makes 1.75 kg/4lb

225 g/8 oz Dried apricots
1.2 litres/2 pts Water
900 g/2 lb Cooking apples, peeled, cored and chopped
Finely grated rind and juice of 2 lemons
1.5 kg/3 lb Sugar, warmed
25 g/1 oz Flaked almonds, cut into strips

Soak the apricots in 900 ml/1½ pts water for 24 hours. Simmer the apples in the remaining water until soft, then add the apricots and their soaking liquid with the lemon rind and juice and boil for 10 minutes. Stir in the warmed sugar until dissolved, then boil for about 15 minutes to setting point. Stir in the almonds and pour into warmed jars.

Fresh Apricot Jam

Makes 1.5 kg/3 lb

675 g/1½ lb Apricots, halved and stoned
300 ml/½ pt Water
15 g/½ oz Butter
900 g/2 lb Sugar, warmed

Put the apricots and water in a pan and simmer for 10 minutes. Stir in the butter and warmed sugar until dissolved, then boil for about 20 minutes to setting point. Stir well and pour into warmed jars.

Dried Apricot Jam

Makes 2.25 kg/5 lb

450 g/1 lb Dried apricots
1.2 litres/2 pts Water
Juice of 1 lemon
1.5 kg/3 lb Sugar, warmed

Put the apricots, water and lemon juice in a pan, bring to the boil and simmer until the fruit is soft. Stir in the warmed sugar until dissolved, then boil for about 15 minutes to setting point. Stir well and pour into warmed jars.

Banana Jam

Makes 900 g/2 lb

450 g/1 lb Bananas, sliced
900 ml/1½ pts Orange or apple juice
Juice of 1 lemon
350 g/12 oz Soft brown sugar

Stir all the ingredients over a low heat until the sugar has dissolved. Bring to the boil, then simmer gently, stirring occasionally, for about 10 minutes until the mixture thickens. Stir well and pour into warmed jars.

Blackberry Jam

Makes 1.5 kg/3 lb

900 g/2 lb Blackberries
15 g/½ oz Butter
900 g/2 lb Sugar, warmed

Bring the blackberries slowly to the boil over a low heat, adding a little water if there is very little juice. Add the butter and simmer until the fruit is soft. Stir in the warmed sugar until dissolved, then boil for about 10 minutes to setting point. Stir well and pour into warmed jars.

Blackcurrant Jam

Makes 1.5 kg/3 lb

675 g/1½ lb Blackcurrants
600 ml/1 pt Water
1.5 kg/3 lb Sugar, warmed

Put the blackcurrants and water in a pan and simmer for 10 minutes. Stir in the warmed sugar until dissolved, then boil for about 5 minutes to setting point. Stir well and pour into warmed jars.

Blackcurrant and Rhubarb Jam

Makes 2.25 kg/5 lb

900 g/2 lb Blackcurrants
350 g/12 oz Rhubarb, cut into 2.5 cm/ 1 in pieces
1.2 litres/2 pts Water
25 g/1 oz Butter or margarine
1.75 kg/4 lb Sugar, warmed

Put the blackcurrants, rhubarb and water in a pan and simmer for 45 minutes. Stir in the butter and boil for 10 minutes. Stir in the warmed sugar until dissolved, then boil for about 5 minutes to setting point. Stir well and pour into warmed jars.

Cherry Jam

Makes 1.75 kg/4 lb

1.5 kg/3 lb Morello cherries
Juice of 2 lemons
900 g/2 lb Sugar, warmed

Put the cherries and lemon juice in a pan and simmer until the fruit is soft. Stir in the warmed sugar until dissolved, then boil for about 15 minutes to setting point. Stir well and pour into warmed jars.

Date Jam

Makes 1.75 kg/4 lb

450 g/1 lb Dates, stoned and chopped
300 ml/½ pt Water
225 g/8 oz Sugar, warmed
Grated rind and juice of 1 lemon

Simmer the dates in the water for 30 minutes. Stir in the warmed sugar, lemon rind and juice until dissolved, then boil until thick, stirring occasionally. Stir well and pour into warm jars.

Gooseberry Jam

Makes 2.25 kg/5 lb

900 g/2 lb Gooseberries, topped and
    tailed
500 ml/18 fl oz Water
1.5 kg/3 lb Sugar, warmed

Put the fruit and water in a saucepan
and simmer until the fruit is soft. Stir
in the warmed sugar until dissolved,
then boil for about 15 minutes to
setting point. Skim and pour into
warmed jars.

Greengage Jam

Makes 2.25 kg/5 lb

1.5 kg/3 lb Greengages, halved
150 ml/¼ pt Water
1.5 kg/3 lb Sugar, warmed

Put the fruit and water in a pan and
simmer gently until tender. Firmer
varieties of greengage may need a
little extra water and cooking times
will vary. Stir in the warmed sugar
until dissolved, then boil for about
20 minutes to setting point, removing
the stones as they come to the
surface. Skim and pour into warmed
jars.

Marrow Jam

Makes 2.25 kg/5 lb

1.75 kg/4 lb Marrow, peeled and
    diced
1.5 kg/3 lb Sugar
Grated rind and juice of 2 lemons
100 g/4 oz Stem ginger, chopped

Layer the marrow and sugar in a bowl
and leave in a cool place for 24 hours.
Put in a preserving pan with the lemon
rind and juice and stem ginger. Stir
over a low heat until the sugar has
dissolved, then boil for 45 minutes
until the marrow is clear and tender.
Pour into warmed jars.

Rhubarb Jam

Makes 2.25 kg/5 lb

1.5 kg/3 lb Rhubarb, cut into 5 cm/
    2 in pieces
1.5 kg/3 lb Preserving sugar, warmed
Rind and juice of 1 lemon
25 g/1 oz Root ginger, bruised
25 g/1 oz Butter

Layer the rhubarb and sugar in a
bowl and leave to stand in a cool
place for 24 hours.
    Pour into a pan with the lemon
juice. Tie the ginger and lemon rind in
a piece of muslin and add it to the
pan. Bring to the boil, stirring carefully to avoid breaking up the fruit,
then boil rapidly for about 15 minutes
to setting point. Stir in the butter,
then leave the jam in the pan until
fairly cool, when a thin skin begins to
form on top. Stir gently, then spoon
into warmed jars.

Plum Jam

Makes 2.25 kg/5 lb

1.5 kg/3 lb Plums, halved and
    stoned

300 ml/½ pt Water

1.5 kg/3 lb Sugar, warmed

Put the fruit and water in a pan and simmer until tender. Stir in the warmed sugar until dissolved, then boil for about 15 minutes to setting point. Skim and pour into warmed jars.

Raspberry Jam

Makes 2.25 kg/5 lb

1.5 kg/3 lb Hulled raspberries

1.5 kg/3 lb Sugar, warmed

Place the fruit in a saucepan and simmer gently until the juice begins fo flow. Stir in the warmed sugar until dissolved, then boil for about 10 minutes to setting point. Stir well and pour into warmed jars.

Strawberry and Raspberry Jam

Makes 2.25 kg/5 lb

900 g/2 lb Hulled strawberries

450 g/1 lb Raspberries

1.5 kg/3 lb Sugar, warmed

Put the fruit in a pan, bring to the boil and crush lightly with a wooden spoon so that the juices run. Stir in the warmed sugar until dissolved, then boil for 5 minutes to setting point. Stir well and pour into warmed jars.

Strawberry Jam

Makes 2.25 kg/5 lb

1.75 kg/4 lb Hulled strawberries

1.6 kg/3½ lb Sugar, warmed

Juice of 1 lemon

25 g/1 oz Butter

Layer the strawberries and sugar in a bowl and leave to stand in a cool place for 24 hours.

Pour into a pan with the lemon juice, bring to the boil, stirring carefully to avoid breaking up the fruit, then boil rapidly for about 10 minutes to setting point. Stir in the butter, then leave the jam in the pan until fairly cool, when a thin skin begins to form on top. Stir gently, then spoon into warmed jars.

Blackberry Jelly

Makes 1.5 kg/3 lb

1.75 kg/4 lb Blackberries

Juice of 2 lemons

300 ml/½ pt Water

Pinch of cinnamon

Sugar, warmed

Put the blackberries in a pan with the lemon juice, water and cinnamon and simmer for 30 minutes until the fruit is very soft. Strain through a jelly bag, measure the juice and return it to the pan. Stir in 450 g/1 lb warmed sugar to each 600 ml/1 pt juice until dissolved, then boil for 15 minutes to setting point. Pour into warmed jars.

Crab Apple Jelly

Makes 1.5 kg/3 lb

1.75 kg/4 lb Crab apples, roughly chopped
2.25 litres/4 pts Water
Sugar, warmed

Put the fruit and water in a pan and boil until the apples are soft. Strain through a jelly bag, measure the juice and return it to the pan. Stir in 450 g/1 lb warmed sugar to each 600 ml/1 pt juice until dissolved, then boil for about 10 minutes to setting point. Pour into warmed jars.

Mint Jelly

Makes 1.75 kg/4 lb

2.75 kg/6 lb Apples, roughly chopped
1.2 litres/2 pts Water
Bunch of mint
15 ml/1 tbsp Lemon juice
Sugar, warmed

Put the apples and water in a pan and boil until soft. Strain through a jelly bag, measure the juice and return it to the pan. Stir in 450 g/1 lb warmed sugar to each 600 ml/1 pt juice until dissolved, then add half the mint and boil for about 10 minutes to setting point. Remove the sprigs of mint, chop the remainder and stir it into the jelly. Pour into warmed jars.

Redcurrant Jelly

Makes 900 g/2 lb

1.5 kg/3 lb Redcurrants
1.25 litres/2¼ pts Water
Sugar, warmed

Put the fruit and water in a pan, bring to the boil and simmer for 20 minutes until the fruit is pulpy. Strain the juice through a jelly bag. Measure the juice, return it to the pan and add 450 g/1 lb sugar for each 600 ml/1 pt juice. Stir over a low heat until the sugar has dissolved, then boil for 10 minutes to setting point, skim and pour into warmed jars.

Cottage Marmalade

Makes 900 g/2 lb

450 g/1 lb Rhubarb, chopped
3 Oranges
Water
450 g/1 lb Sugar, warmed

Put the rhubarb in a pan. Grate the orange rind and add it to the rhubarb. Remove the pith from the oranges and take out the pips. Tie them in a piece of muslin and add it to the pan. Slice the oranges across and cut each slice in quarters. Add to the pan and just cover with water. Bring to the boil, then simmer for 20 minutes until the fruit is soft, then remove the bag of pips. Stir in the warmed sugar, then boil for about 15 minutes to setting point. Leave to cool slightly, stir well and pour into warmed jars.

Grapefruit Marmalade

Makes 3 kg/6 lb

1 kg/2¼ lb Grapefruit
3 Lemons
3 litres/5 pts Water
3 kg/6 lb Sugar, warmed

Cut the fruit in half then squeeze out and reserve the juice. Chop the peel and tie the pips in a muslin bag. Soak the peel in 1.5 litres/3 pts cold water overnight.

Put the water, peel, pips and remaining water into a preserving pan and simmer for 1½ hours until the peel is soft. Discard the pips. Stir in the warmed sugar until dissolved, then boil for about 20 minutes to setting point. Skim, leave to cool slightly, stir well and pour into warmed jars.

Orange Marmalade

Makes 3 kg/6 lb

1.5 kg/3 lb Seville oranges
2 Lemons
4 litres/7 pts Water
2.75 kg/6 lb Sugar, warmed

Cut the fruit in half then squeeze out and reserve the juice. Chop the peel and tie the pips in a muslin bag. Soak the peel in 1.5 litres/3 pts cold water overnight.

Put the water, peel, pips and remaining water into a preserving pan and simmer for 1½ hours until the peel is soft. Discard the pips. Stir in the warmed sugar until dissolved, then boil for about 20 minutes to setting point. Skim, leave to cool slightly, stir well and pour into warmed jars.

Lemon Curd

Makes 450 g/1 lb

75 g/3 oz Butter or margarine
225 g/8 oz Sugar
Grated rind and juice of 2 lemons
2 Eggs, beaten

Place the butter or margarine, sugar, lemon rind and juice in a bowl over a pan of boiling water and stir until the sugar has dissolved. Stir in the eggs, and continue stirring until the mixture is thick enough to coat the back of a spoon. Pour into warmed jars and store in the fridge.

Orange Jelly Marmalade

Makes 1.7 kg/4 lb

900 g/2 lb Seville oranges
2 Lemons
3 litres/5 pts Water
1.5 kg/3 lb Sugar, warmed

Wash and scald the fruit in boiling water. Squeeze the juice from the lemons and reserve. Peel the oranges. Shred the orange peel finely and place in a pan with 900 ml/1½ pts water, cover and cook gently for 1½ hours. Coarsely chop the rest of the fruit and place in another pan with the pith, lemon juice and remaining water. Simmer gently for 2 hours.

Drain the liquid from the peel and add to the other pan. Strain the pulp through a scaled jelly bag, then return the juice to the pan with the sugar and stir until dissolved. Add the peel shreds. Bring to the boil and boil for about 20 minutes to setting point. Skim, leave to cool slightly, then pour into warmed jars.

Three Fruit Marmalade

Makes 1.5 kg/4 lb

2 Grapefruit
2 Oranges
1.2 litres/2 pts Water
Juice of 2 lemons
900 g/2 lb Sugar, warmed

Quarter the grapefruit and remove the skin, pith and pips. Chop the flesh and place in a pan. Quarter the oranges and remove the pips. Remove the flesh from half the segments, chop finely and add to the pan. Slice the remaining segments and add to the pan. Tie all the pips in a muslin bag and place in the pan. Add the water and lemon juice, bring to the boil and simmer for about 2 hours until the rind is soft. Remove the muslin bag.

Stir in the sugar until dissolved, then boil for about 10 minutes to setting point. Skim, leave to cool slightly, then stir well and pour into warmed jars.

Pickles and Chutneys

You can make pickles and chutneys to take advantage of gluts of fruits, such as tomatoes, and to make up your own combinations to go with your favourite foods. Boiling vinegar does smell rather strongly, so an extractor fan or an open window is a good idea, as is keeping the kitchen door closed to stop the aroma spreading over the house. The taste makes it all worthwhile, though.

Always warm jars before pouring in hot chutney and do not cover with a circle of paper, as you would with jam. Use plastic lids, never metal, as metal will react with the vinegar in the pickle and spoil the preserve.

Pickled Onions

Makes 2.25 kg/5 lb

2.25 kg/5 lb Small onions or shallots
225 g/8 oz Salt
2.25 1/4 pts Water
1.2 litres/2 pts Vinegar
25 g/1 oz Pickling spice tied in muslin
10 ml/2 tsp Sugar

Pour boiling water over the onions or shallots. Lift them out carefully with a slotted spoon and peel them. Boil the salt and water, leave to cool, then pour over the onions and leave them to stand for 48 hours.

Drain the onions and pack them into jars. Boil the vinegar and spice for 5 minutes, then remove the spice.

Pour over the onions or shallots and add 5 ml/1 tsp sugar to each jar. Cover and leave for 1 month before eating.

Pickled Red Cabbage

Makes 1.5 kg/3 lb

1 Red cabbage
Salt
600 ml/1 pt Vinegar
25 g/1 oz Pickling spice tied in muslin
5 ml/1 tsp Mustard powder

Quarter the cabbage and cut out the centre stalk. Shred the cabbage finely, put on a large flat dish and sprinkle with salt. Leave to stand in a cool place for 24 hours.

Drain the cabbage thoroughly, then pack it into jars. Boil the vinegar, spice and mustard for 5 minutes then leave until cold and remove the spices. Pour over the cabbage and cover.

Pickled Green Walnuts

Makes 1.75 kg/4 lb

1.75 kg/4 lb Green walnuts
1.2 litres/2 pts Water
225 g/8 oz Salt
1.2 litres/2 pts Vinegar
25 g/1 oz Pickling spice tied in muslin
15 ml/1 tbsp Mustard powder

Use the walnuts in June or early July while the kernels are still soft and the outer casings are bright green and firm. Prick the green casing of the walnuts all over with a fork. Boil the water and salt together and pour over the walnuts. Leave to soak for 5 days.

Drain the walnuts and put them on wooden trays in a sunny place to turn black, turning them frequently. Boil the vinegar, spice and mustard for 10 minutes, then remove the spices. Pack the walnuts into jars and pour over the vinegar. Cover and keep for at least 2 weeks before using.

Apple Chutney

Makes 1.5 kg/3 lb

900 g/2 lb Cooking apples, peeled, cored and chopped
225 g/8 oz Sultanas, chopped
1 Onion, finely chopped
Grated rind and juice of 1 lemon
5 ml/1 tsp Ground ginger
450 ml/¾ pt Vinegar
5 ml/1 tsp Caraway seeds
450 g/1 lb Soft brown sugar

Put the apples, sultanas, onion, lemon rind and juice, ginger and half the vinegar in a pan, bring to the boil and simmer for 20 minutes until the mixture is soft. Add the caraway seeds. Mix together the sugar and remaining vinegar, add it to the pan and simmer until the chutney thickens. Pour into warmed jars.

Autumn Chutney

Makes 2.25 kg/5 lb

600 ml/1 pt Vinegar

25 g/1 oz Pickling spice tied in muslin

15 ml/1 tbsp Salt

15 g/½ tsp Ground ginger

450 g/1 lb Golden syrup

450 g/1 lb Pears, peeled, cored and chopped

450 g/1 lb Apples, peeled, cored and chopped

225 g/8 oz Onions, chopped

225 g/8 oz Dates, stoned and chopped

Put the vinegar, spice, salt, mustard, ginger and syrup in a pan, bring to the boil and boil for 5 minutes. Add the pears, apples, onions and dates and simmer until thick and brown. Spoon into warmed jars.

Banana Chutney

Makes 2.25 kg/5 lb

16 Bananas, sliced

900 g/2 lb Onions, finely chopped

450 g/1 lb Dates, stoned and minced

225 g/8 oz Crystallised ginger, chopped

15 ml/1 tbsp Salt

25 g/1 oz Pickling spice tied in muslin

1.2 litres/2 pts Vinegar

450 g/1 lb Sugar

Put the bananas, onions, dates, ginger, salt, spice and vinegar into a pan, bring to the boil and boil for

5 minutes. Remove the spices, stir in the sugar and simmer over a low heat until rich and brown. Spoon into warmed jars.

No-Cook Date Chutney

Makes 1.75 kg/4 lb

25 g/1 oz Pickling spice tied in muslin

600 ml/1 pt Vinegar

900 g/2 lb Dates, stoned and minced

450 g/1 lb Crystallised ginger, minced

10 ml/2 tsp Mustard powder

90 ml/6 tbsp Golden syrup

Put the spice and vinegar in a pan, bring to the boil and simmer for 7 minutes. Stir in the remaining ingredients thoroughly, leave to stand until cool and stir again before spooning into jars.

Lanchester Chutney

Makes 2.25 kg/5 lb

1.5 kg/3 lb Cooking apples, peeled, cored and finely chopped

3 Onions, chopped

4 Tomatoes, skinned and chopped

350 g/12 oz Sultanas

15 ml/1 tbsp Soy sauce

30 ml/2 tbsp Oil

15 ml/1 tbsp Salt

5 ml/1 tsp Ground ginger

5 ml/1 tsp Anchovy essence

2.5 ml/½ tsp Pepper

300 ml/½ pt Vinegar

Put all the ingredients in a pan, bring to the boil and simmer gently until thick and brown. Spoon into warmed jars.

Old-Fashioned Chutney

Makes 2.25 kg/5 lb

450 g/1 lb Pears, peeled, cored and chopped
450 g/1 lb Apples, peeled, cored and chopped
225 g/8 oz Onions, chopped
600 ml/1 pt Vinegar
225 g/8 oz Dates, chopped
15 ml/1 tbsp Salt
450 g/1 lb Golden syrup
Pinch of ground ginger
15 ml/1 tbsp Mustard powder

Put the pears, apples, onions and vinegar in a pan, bring to the boil and simmer until tender. Stir in the remaining ingredients and boil until thick and golden. Stir well and pour into warmed jars.

Marrow Chutney

Makes 2.25 kg/5 lb

1 Large marrow, peeled and diced
50 g/2 oz Salt
1.2 litres/2 pts Vinegar
15 ml/1 tbsp Mustard powder
15 g/½ oz Turmeric
25 g/1 oz Ground ginger
100 g/4 oz Sugar
2 Large onions, chopped

Weigh the marrow flesh; there should be about 1.5 kg/3 lb. Sprinkle with the salt and leave to stand for 24 hours.

Drain off the liquid and put the marrow in a pan with the remaining ingredients, bring to the boil, then simmer until thick and brown. Spoon into warmed jars.

Peggy's Pear Chutney

Makes 2.25 kg/5 lb

900 g/2 lb Pears, peeled, cored and chopped
225 g/8 oz Onions, chopped
15 ml/1 tbsp Salt
350 g/12 oz Sugar
15 g/½ oz Ground ginger
225 g/8 oz Dates, stoned and chopped
100 g/4 oz Sultanas
10 ml/2 tsp Mustard powder
600 ml/1 pt Vinegar

Put all the ingredients in a pan, bring to the boil, then simmer until thick and brown. Pour into warmed jars.

Spiced Orange Chutney

Makes 2.25 kg/5 lb

750 g/1½ lb Cooking apples, peeled, cored and chopped

100 g/4 oz Peeled oranges, chopped

350 g/12 oz Dates, stoned and minced

350 g/12 oz Red tomatoes, sliced

750 g/1½ lb Sugar

1.5 litres/3 pts Vinegar

25 g/1 oz Chilli peppers, chopped

10 ml/2 tsp Salt

Put all the ingredients in a pan, bring to the boil and simmer until thick and brown. Spoon into warmed jars.

Note
If you prefer a milder chutney, substitute 5 ml/1 tsp ground ginger for the chilli peppers.

Stanhope Rhubarb Chutney

Makes 2.25 kg/5 lb

900 g/2 lb Rhubarb, chopped

450 g/1 lb Sultanas

900 g/2 lb Soft brown sugar

1 Large onion, chopped

25 g/1 oz Salt

25 g/1 oz Ground ginger

2.5 ml/½ tsp Pepper

2 Lemons, peeled, depipped and chopped

600 ml/1 pt Vinegar

Put all the ingredients in a pan, bring to the boil, then simmer until thick and brown. Pour into warmed jars.

Spicy Red Tomato Chutney

Makes 2.25 kg/5 lb

450 g/1 lb Ripe tomatoes, skinned and chopped

450 g/1 lb Cooking apples, peeled, cored and chopped

225 g/8 oz Onions, chopped

225 g/8 oz Sultanas

225 g/8 oz Crystallised ginger

5 ml/1 tsp Salt

6 Chilli peppers, chopped

225 g/8 oz Sugar

600 ml/1 pt Vinegar

Put all the ingredients in a pan, bring to the boil, then simmer until thick and brown. Spoon into warmed jars.

Note
This is a hot chutney, but you can omit the chilli peppers if you prefer a milder chutney.

Green Tomato Chutney

Makes 24

1.5 kg/3 lb Green tomatoes, skinned and finely chopped

225 g/8 oz Onions, finely chopped

225 g/8 oz Apples, peeled, cored and finely chopped

25 g/1 oz Pickling spice tied in muslin

600 ml/1 pt Vinegar

225 g/8 oz Soft brown sugar

10 ml/2 tsp Salt

Put all the ingredients in a pan and boil gently until soft and thick. Remove the spice and pour the chutney into warmed jars.

Wolviston Piccalilli

Makes 2.25 kg/5 lb

450 g/1 lb Onions, diced

450 g/1 lb Marrow, peeled and
    diced

450 g/1 lb Cauliflower florets

Salt

450 ml/¾ pt Vinegar

25 g/1 oz Pickling spice tied in
    muslin

15 g/½ oz Turmeric

50 g/2 oz Mustard powder

10 ml/2 tsp Plain flour

Mix the vegetables in a bowl, sprinkle with salt and leave to stand in a cool place for 48 hours.

Shake off any remaining salt, put in a pan with the vinegar and pickling spice, bring to the boil and simmer until the vegetables are soft. Remove the bag of spices and add the turmeric. Mix the mustard and flour to a paste with a little cold vinegar, then stir it into the pan and boil for a few more minutes. Stir well and pour into warmed jars.

Stanhope Mustard Pickle

Makes 2.25 kg/5 lb

1.5 kg/3 lb Onions, chopped

1.5 kg/3 lb Cauliflower florets

Salt

50 g/2 oz Plain flour

225 g/8 oz Sugar

10 ml/2 tsp Mustard powder

15 ml/1 tbsp Turmeric

900 ml/1½ pts Vinegar

Mix the onions and cauliflower, sprinkle with salt and leave in a cool place for 48 hours.

Mix the flour, sugar, mustard and turmeric to a paste with a little vinegar. Bring the remaining vinegar to the boil and pour into the paste, stirring continuously. Return to the pan and stir over a low heat until the sauce thickens. Shake the surplus salt off the vegetables, add them to the pan and simmer gently for 5 minutes. Stir well and pour into warmed jars.

Tomato Ketchup

Makes 2.75 kg/6 lb

2.75 kg/6 lb Ripe tomatoes, quartered	
225 g/8 oz Granulated sugar	
300 ml/½ pt Vinegar	
25 g/1 oz Pickling spice tied in muslin	
5 ml/1 tsp Paprika	
10 ml/2 tsp Salt	
Pinch of cayenne pepper	

Put the tomatoes in a pan and cook over a gentle heat until the juices run, then bring to the boil and boil until reduced to a pulp. Rub them through a sieve and return the purée to a clean pan. Stir in the remaining ingredients, bring to the boil and simmer until the mixture has a sauce consistency. Remove the spice, pour into warmed jars and screw down the tops, then unscrew by a quarter turn. Stand the jars on a trivet in a deep pan. Fill the pan with water to within 5 cm/1 in of the top of the bottle. Bring the water to simmering point and simmer for 20 minutes. Seal carefully and leave to cool.

Bramble Ketchup

Makes 2.25 kg/5 lb

1.75 kg/4 lb Blackberries	
900 g/2 lb Sugar	
600 ml/1 pt Vinegar	
10 ml/2 tsp Ground cloves	
10 ml/2 tsp Cinnamon	
5 ml/1 tsp Allspice	

Put all the ingredients into a pan, bring to the boil, then simmer until thick. Push through a sieve, then bring back to the boil and pour into warmed jars. Screw down the tops then unscrew by a quarter turn. Stand the jars on a trivet in a deep pan. Fill the pan with water to within 2.5 cm/1 in of the top of the bottles. Bring the water to simmering point and simmer for 20 minutes. Seal carefully and leave to cool.

Drinks and Syrups

Here are some new ideas for drinks for children, to quench your thirst on a hot summer day, and to serve at parties for those who are driving and those who are not. The fruit syrups are easily made and can be used with ice creams and desserts or diluted as really fruity cordials.

Lemon Squash

Makes 1.75 litres/3 pts

Grated rind and juice of 8 lemons
1.75 kg/4 lb Sugar
1.5 litres/3 pts Boiling water

Place the lemon rind, sugar and water in a large saucepan and boil for 10 minutes. Leave to cool, add the lemon juice, then strain and dilute to taste. Serve with ice garnished with a slice of lemon.

Variations

You can use the same recipe to make squash with other citrus fruits, such as oranges. Adjust the amount of sugar as necessary since orange squash will obviously need less than lemon squash.

Apple and Fig Cordial

Makes 900 ml/2 pts

450 g/1 lb Cooking apples, peeled
  and chopped
100 g/4 oz Figs, soaked and
  chopped
1.2 litres/2 pts Boiling water
75 g/3 oz Sugar
Grated rind of ½ lemon

Place the fruit and water in a large saucepan and boil for 15 minutes. Strain the liquor back into a saucepan, add the sugar and lemon juice and boil for a further 10 minutes, carefully tasting and adding more sugar if necessary. Allow to cool and serve with ice and garnished with a sprig of mint.

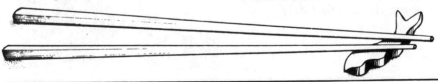

Honey and Lemon Squash

Makes 600 ml/1 pt

600 ml/1 pt Honey Syrup
  (page 376)
60 ml/4 tbsp Lemon Squash
  (page 371)
600 ml/1 pt Soda water

Mix all the ingredients together and serve with ice.

Variation
If you replace the soda water with boiling water, you can make a soothing drink for sore throats.

Spiced Tomato Juice

Makes 1 litres/1¾ pts

4 Whole cloves
3 Celery tops with leaves
750 ml/1¼ pts Tomato juice
250 ml/8 fl oz Water
15 ml/1 tbsp Golden granulated
  sugar
5 ml/1 tsp Worcestershire sauce
Pinch of cayenne pepper
2.5 ml/½ tsp Salt
10 ml/ 2 tsp Lemon juice

Tie the cloves and celery tops in a piece of cloth. Put all the ingredients in a saucepan, bring to the boil and simmer for 20 minutes, uncovered. Strain into a jug, cool and chill. The juice can be stored in the fridge in a screw-top jar for 3 to 4 days.

Instant Orangeade

Makes 1.75 litres/3 pts

Rind and juice of 4 oranges
100 g/4 oz Caster sugar
300 ml/½ pt Boiling water
1 bottle Soda water (optional)

Place the orange rind and juice, sugar and water in a jug and stir until the sugar has dissolved, then strain and mix with soda water to taste. serve with ice and garnished with a slice of orange.

Pineapple Crush

Makes 4 glasses

Juice of 1 grapefruit
1 Orange
1 Lemon
1 Celery stalk, chopped
300 g/11 oz Canned pineapple in
  natural juice
120 ml/4 fl oz Water
Fruit slices to garnish

Place the grapefruit juice in a food processor or blender. Peel the orange and lemon, remove the pith and add the flesh to the processor with the celery, pineapple and juice and water. Process until frothy then pour into tall glasses and add crushed ice. Garnish with sliced fruits of your choice.

Hawaiian Iced Coffee

Makes 2 glasses

300 g/11 oz Canned pineapple in natural juice	
300 ml/½ pt Milk	
10 ml/2 tsp Instant coffee	
10 ml/2 tsp Hot water	
1 scoop Vanilla ice cream	
5 ml/1 tsp Sugar	

Place the pineapple pieces and juice in a food processor or blender and process for 10 seconds. Add the milk and process again. Mix the coffee and hot water and add to the processor with the ice cream and process until frothy. Taste and sprinkle in a little sugar if necessary.

Brazilian Banana Milkshake

Serves 2

600 ml/1 pt Cold milk
150 ml/¼ pt Banana yoghurt
1 Banana, mashed
25 g/1 oz Walnuts, chopped

Blend together the milk, yoghurt and banana in a food processor or blender or whisk until smooth. Serve sprinkled with walnuts.

Yoghurt Smoothie

Serves 4

600 ml/1 pt Cold milk
300 ml/½ pt Fruit yoghurt

Blend the ingredients together in a food processor or blender or whisk until smooth.

Snow Foam

Serves 2

600 ml/1 pt Milk
6 Marshmallows, chopped
5 ml/1 tsp Cinnamon

Heat the milk, stir in the chopped marshmallows and heat until they begin to melt. Pour into cups and serve sprinkled with cinnamon.

Banana Whip

Makes 600 ml/1 pt

450 ml/¾ pt Milk
1 Ripe banana, chopped
1 scoop Ice cream

Process the milk, banana and ice cream in a food processor or blender until frothy. Pour into tall glasses and add ice cubes.

373

Lemonade Surprise

Makes 4 glasses

Juice of 1 lemon

15 ml/1 tbsp Orange Syrup
(page 376)

150 ml/¼ pt Sherry

Chopped ice

5 ml/1 tsp Strawberry Syrup
(page 376)

15 ml/1 tbsp Port

900 ml/1½ pts Soda water

Place the lemon juice, orange syrup
and sherry in a cocktail shaker and
fill with chopped ice. Mix together,
then divide between tall glasses. Add
the strawberry syrup and port, then
fill with soda water.

Cider-Brandy Cup

Makes 1.75 litres/3 pts

1.2 litres/2 pts Dry cider

2 Oranges, sliced

150 ml/¼ pt Brandy

Juice of 1 lemon

1 Bottle soda water

Place the cider, 1 orange, brandy and
lemon juice in a jug and stand the jug
in a bowl of ice for an hour or so, or
until needed, then strain into a
serving jug and add soda water to
taste. Serve with ice and garnish with
slices of orange.

Mulled Cider

Serves 4

1.2 litres/2 pts Medium dry cider

40 g/1½ oz Muscovado sugar

Pinch of salt

4 Whole cloves

Piece of cinnamon stick 5 cm/2 in
long

4 Whole allspice

Strip of orange peel

Put the cider, sugar and salt in a
saucepan. Tie the spices loosely in a
piece of cloth and add it to the pan.
Bring gently to the boil, cover and
simmer for 15 minutes. Serve hot in
mugs.

Wine Refresher

Makes 1.75 litres/3 pts

600 ml/1 pt Claret

225 g/8 oz Caster sugar

1 Lemon, finely sliced

¼ Cucumber, sliced

600 ml/1 pt Soda water

600 ml/1 pt Lemonade

Place the wine, sugar, lemon and
cucumber slices in a jug and stir until
the sugar has dissolved. Stand the
jug in a bowl of ice and leave for an
hour or so or until needed, then
strain and add the soda water and
lemonade. Serve with ice.

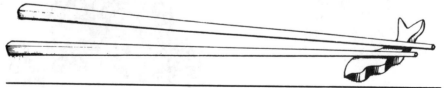

Port-of-Call Party Punch

Serves 6-8

1.2 litres/2 pts Burgundy wine
100 ml/4 fl oz Port wine
60 ml/4 tbsp Cherry brandy
Juice of 1½ lemons
Juice of 3 oranges
75 g/3 oz Caster sugar
1.2 litres/2 pts Soda water
Fresh fruit, sliced

Mix all the ingredients except the sugar, soda water and fruit. Add the sugar to taste and stir until it dissolves. Pour the mixture over a large block of ice in a punch bowl. Add the soda water just before serving and float some fruit on top.

Claret Cup

Makes 1.75 litres/3 pts

750 ml/1¼ pts Claret
50 g/2 oz Caster sugar
2 Oranges, thinly sliced
1 Lemon, thinly sliced
¼ Cucumber, sliced
150 ml/¼ pt Brandy
1 bottle Soda water

Reserve a few orange slices for garnish, then place the claret, sugar, oranges and lemon in a jug and stir until the sugar has dissolved. Add the cucumber and brandy. Stand the jug in a bowl of ice for an hour or so, or until needed, then strain and add soda water to taste. Serve with ice in tall glasses garnished with the reserved orange slices.

Maraschino-Splashed Cider Cup

Makes 1.75 litres/3 pts

1.2 litres/2 pts Cider
100 g/4 oz Sugar
Grated rind of 1 lemon
½ Cucumber, sliced
150 ml/¼ pt Maraschino
1 bottle Soda water

Reserve a few slices of cucumber for garnish, then place the cider, sugar, lemon rind and cucumber in a jug and stir until the sugar has dissolved. Stand the jug in a bowl of ice for an hour or so, or until needed, then strain into a serving jug and add the maraschino and soda water to taste. Serve with ice and garnished with a slice of cucumber.

Egg and Coconut Nogg

Makes 2 glasses

2 Eggs
150 ml/¼ pt Milk
10 ml/2 tsp Caster sugar
30 ml/2 tbsp Sherry
25 g/1 oz Creamed coconut, diced
Pinch of nutmeg

Place one whole egg, including the shell, in a food processor or blender. Add the other egg without its shell and the milk and sugar and process until frothy and smooth. Add the sherry and coconut and blend again. Serve sprinkled with grated nutmeg.

Sugar Syrup

Makes 600 ml/1 pt

450 g/1 lb Caster sugar
600 ml/1 pt Water

Boil together the sugar and water for 10 minutes, skim the froth from the top. Leave to cool, then bottle in screw-top jars.

Honey Syrup

Makes 600 ml/1 pt

450 g/1 lb Honey
Juice of 3 lemons
450 ml/¾ pt Water

Mix the honey and lemon juice, then add enough water to make a syrupy consistency. Store in screw-top jars.

Lemon Syrup

Makes 600 ml/1 pt

350 g/12 oz Caster sugar
600 ml/1 pt Boiling water
Finely pared rind and juice of 2 lemons
25 g/1 oz Citric acid

Warm the sugar and water until the sugar has dissolved, then simmer for 15 minutes. Add the lemon rind and juice and the citric acid. Stir well and strain into screw-top jars.

Orange Syrup

Makes 600 ml/1 pt

Finely pared rind and juice of 6 oranges
450 g/1 lb Caster sugar

Place the orange rind and juice and caster sugar in a heavy-based saucepan and stir over a low heat until the sugar has dissolved. Simmer gently for 15 minutes, skim and leave to cool. Store in screw-top jars.

Strawberry Syrup

Makes 600 ml/1 pt

450 g/1 lb Strawberries
1.2 litres/2 pts Boiling water
450 g/1 lb Caster sugar

Crush the strawberries and pour over the boiling water. Stir well and leave to stand for 24 hours, then strain through a fine sieve or cloth into a saucepan. Stir in the sugar and boil until syrupy, then store in screw-top jars.

Variation
You can make Cherry Syrup, Elderberry Syrup, Redcurrant Syrup or Raspberry Syrup in the same way.

Index